BAITED
The Ambush of Mission 1890

Deadliest Helicopter Rescue Mission of the Korean War

BY
Captain Tracy D. Connors

Author of
Truckbusters From Dogpatch,
The Combat Diary of the 18th Fighter-
Bomber Wing in the Korean War,
1950-1953

Published by BelleAire Pres, LLC, Gainesville, Florida

Copyright © 2007-2008 by BelleAire Press. Jacket illustration copyright 2007 by BelleAire Press. All rights reserved. No part of this book may be reproduced or transmitted in any form or by any means, electronic or mechanical, including photocopying, recording, or by any information storage and retrieval system, without the prior written permission of the publisher, except where permitted by law.

Visit us on the web: www.belleairepress.com

Library of Congress Cataloging-in-Publication Data

Connors, Tracy Daniel

Ambushed Air Rescue/Tracy Daniel Connors

Summary:

Baited Trap is the story of Mission 1890, one of the most heroic—and costly—air rescues of the Korean War. This heroic helicopter rescue mission is explained in compelling detail, creating a detailed personal account of what five incredibly brave and determined Air Force and Navy airmen achieved on June 25, 1952 in the infamous "Iron Triangle."

On the second anniversary of the start of the Korean War, four U.S. airmen team up to grab a downed Navy pilot off the side of a mountain that was heavily defended by Chinese Communist troops. Under withering ground fire, Captain Wayne Lear made three hovering approaches in the lumbering H-5 "Dragonfly" rescue helicopter to the spot where Ensign Ron Eaton had flashed them with his survival mirror. Each time the helicopter took hits. Both Lear and his medical technician, SSgt. Bobby Holloway, were wounded.

Overhead, Captain Elliot Ayer, How Flight Leader, his wingman, 1st Lt. Archie Connors, and other Mustang pilots from the 18th Fighter-Bomber Wing provided covering fire, repeatedly attacking the ground batteries.

Finally, after the third attempt under heavy fire, with Eaton on board, Lear nursed the badly damaged helicopter down the valley towards the safety of UN lines that were almost within sight. Seconds later, a lucky hit in the rotor changed the rescue into one of the most deadly missions of the Korean War.

The families of the missing airmen entered the surreal, wrenching, bureaucratic world of the Missing In Action. A final section relates the poignant stories of what the families of Mission 1890 went through after it was quiet on the mountain. How they coped with their losses will inspire others.

ISBN 0-9640138-3-5 ISBN13 978-0-9640138-3-4

The text of this book is set in 12 point Times New Roman.

Printed in the United States of America

2007

For

First Lieutenant Archie Connors, USAF

Captain Wayne Lear, USAF

Ensign Ron Eaton, USN

who gave their lives in defense of Freedom on Wednesday afternoon, June 25, 1952, during the Korean War's most daring—and costly— helicopter rescue mission.

Whether their "supreme sacrifice will long be remembered by a grateful nation"

...depends on you!

TABLE OF CONTENTS

Chapter One   Pages 1-11
Beating to Quarters

Just before daybreak at sea off the Korean coast, June 25, 1952, the second anniversary of the beginning of the Korean War, Navy fighter pilot Ensign Ron Eaton, is jolted out of a sound sleep by the claxon of the General Alarm aboard his aircraft carrier. The USS Bon Homme Richard (CV 31) is about to begin another day of combat air operations against targets in North Korea. Today will be Eaton's third combat mission. It will also be his last.

Ensign Ron Eaton

Chapter Two   Pages 12-22
Truckbusters At Dogpatch

Three hours later, one hundred miles away from the Bon Homme Richard, at K-46, a dusty air base carved out between two mountains, the airmen of the 67th Squadron, 18th Fighter-Bomber Wing are also preparing for combat operations as day breaks. How Flight of the 67th Squadron has been designated as the Rescue Combat Air Patrol (RESCAP) flight for the Fifth Air Force. If any UN pilot goes down that day, How Flight will be called to use its old, but still lethal F-51 Mustangs to keep enemy ground troops at bay and protect the slow, vulnerable helicopter as it attempts a pilot pickup. How Flight includes 1st Lt. Archie Connors, just returning to combat flying after a tragic period of emergency leave to be with his wife as she fought for her life after a serious car accident. Today he will fly "Number Two," position next to Number One position of the Flight Leader, the position he should be flying in himself had he not been called home on emergency leave. Today will be his 33rd combat mission. It will also be his last.

1st Lt. Archie Connors

Chapter Three   Pages 23-37
That Others May Live

Later that same morning, at a dusty advanced operating area (until recently a rice paddy), Captain Wayne Lear and Medical Technician Bobby Holloway arrive in their H-5 helicopter from a nearby Mobile Army Surgical Hospital. They wait near their helicopter for a call from the Joint Operations Center in Seoul that would send them off into enemy territory to attempt a pilot pickup. Their unit, the

Capt. Wayne Lear

Third Air Rescue Squadron, Detachment One, like the 18th Wing, had been in Korea since shortly after the war had begun two years earlier. Aviation history is being made by 3ARS as its Korean War operations prove. Lear and Holloway are standing by at an advanced air strip as the Corsairs of VF-74 launch from the carrier to hit enemy targets. It will be Lear's last combat mission and Holloway will begin a harrowing ordeal as a prisoner of war that will last for over a year.

Chapter Four   Pages 38-44
Crippled Corsair

At noon, VF 74 attacks trucks and supply dumps south of Wonsan, North Korea. On the way back to his carrier, Eaton is forced to bail out of his Corsair after he reports he is losing power. The day's tragic events are speeding up.

Chapter Five   Pages 44-73
Ron Eaton, "Hard Luck Kid"

Now shortly after noon, Ens. Ron Eaton hides in the underbrush of a nameless mountain valley in North Korea. Other Corsairs of his flight, under heavy fire themselves, strafe enemy troops to keep him from being captured. Ron's childhood in Wilmington, Massachusetts and college years at Acadia University tell the story of a fine young man who was determined to overcome a chronic shortage of money to complete his education and to earn his Navy Wings of Gold. VF-74, "the Be-Devilers," Ron's attack squadron, prepares for deployment and operations from the aircraft carrier USS Bon Homme Richard (CV 31). As the rescue effort begins to take shape, the youngest pilot in VF-74, hides in the brush, waiting and hoping for rescue. In fact, he is being used as the bait in an enormous trap.

Chapter Six   Pages 74-78
Elliot Ayer, Flight Leader Mission 1890

Captain Elliot Ayer has recently been restored to his WWII Air Force Captaincy and returned to flying status. He had reverted to Master Sergeant for seven years following the down-sizing of the Air Force after WWII. He will be the Mission 1890 Flight Leader, the Rescue Combat Air Patrol that will attempt to pick up Ron Eaton.

Chapter Seven   Pages 79-157
Archie and Frankie Connors

Mission 1890's Number Two pilot, 1st Lt. Archie Connors, is out to complete as many missions as possible and to prove to himself that he is as good a fighter pilot as his friends who have already begun rotating home as they completed their 100 missions. Archie comes from a Florida pioneer family, and he has shown himself to be a leader while in high school and college.  After Air Force pilot training, he marries Frankie Simpson and is posted to Korea and the 67th Fighter-Bomber Squadron, 18th F-B Wing, whose combat record ranks it among America's most distinguished miliary units. Archie waits at K-46 to see if Mission 1890 will be activated.

Chapter Eight   Pages 158-171
Rescue Helicopters in Combat

As Wayne Lear and Bobby Holloway wait for a possible mission at an advanced air base, they are helping write the emerging history and doctrine of rescue helicopter operations, a new capability that began to show promise with the arrival of the first helicopters to perform  this mission at the end of World War Two. The operations of the Third Air Rescue Squadron that flies both helicopters and fixed wing aircraft illustrate the promise and the short-comings of rescue helicopter operations.

Chapter Nine   Pages 172-191
Wayne and Della Lear

Rescue helicopter pilot Wayne Lear has come a long way from the cockpit of the B-29 he had originally flown eight years before at the end of World War Two. Wayne married his beautiful wife, Della Marie, in 1945. Their courtship and married life together took them to post-war Japan, helicopter pilot training, a tour at Air Rescue Headquarters in Washington, and the transition into the H-19, a much more capable aircraft that the H-5.  After being posted to the Third Air Rescue Squadron in Korea, Wayne begins flying medical evacuation missions. His letters to Della reflect his empathy with the suffering he saw every day. When many of his badly wounded patients die, Wayne grieves for them and wonders about his ability to deal with the emotions of seeing and being a part of such tragedy.

Chapter Ten   Pages 192-199
Bobby Dale Holloway, Medical Technician

Waiting with Wayne Lear was Airman Bobby Holloway, a trained Medical Technician. Bobby's youth in Ruston, Louisiana, and early Air Force service taught him self-reliance and important skills he will need to survive before Wednesday, June 25th is over. Holloway relates his experiences as a medical technician in earlier missions. If Mission 1890 were called for on this Wednesday, it would be Holloway's 22nd mission. He would not complete the mission for 14 months.

Chapter Eleven   Pages 197-218
Mission 1890 and the Baited Trap

As the lumbering H-5 rescue helicopter approaches the area, Ayer, Connors and other How Flight Mustangs pound enemy positions near where Eaton lies hiding in the brush. The hillsides on either side of the valley erupt with ground fire—from side arms to heavy anti-aircraft weapons. Clearly, it is a trap—baited with the downed pilot. Lear can abort the mission at any time. However, over the

next twenty minutes, he makes three hovering approaches under heavy fire to reach the spot where Eaton had signalled to them with his survival mirror. On each harrowing approach, the helicopter takes hits. Both Lear and Holloway are wounded. Overhead, Ayer directs his Mustangs in repeated strafing and bombing runs against the deadly defenders. Connors joins Ayer in the attacks and makes sure as "Number Two man," he covers the leader's butt as best he can as they dive, jink and circle in the narrow valley where enemy soldiers fire everything they have at the protecting aircraft. Finally, after the third attempt under withering fire, Lear and Holloway have Eaton on board. The wounded Lear nurses the damaged helicopter back down the valley with his precious cargo for over five dogged miles as the blistering anti-aircraft fire pours down from the nearby hills. Seconds later, with friendly lines almost in sight, a lucky hit in the rotor changes a harrowing, but successful rescue, into the deadliest helicopter rescue mission of the Korean War.

Chapter Twelve   Pages 219-317
After the Mission—Captivity and Bureaucracy

As far as the Air Force is concerned, Mission 1890 is over. However, it is far from over for Bobby Holloway and the families affected by the losses. As Holloway tries to survive a brutal imprisonment in North Korea, the families have to face the dispair of not knowing what happened, or when or if their loved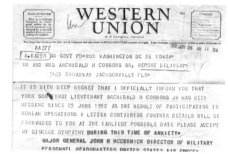
ones are alive or dead. Although the Department of Defense attempts to help them in some ways, the bureaucracy is often frustrating to the families, particularly in providing information to them about what happened. After the Armistice is signed in July 1953, a prisoner of war repatriation process is begun that eventually brings Holloway home to his family, and also to face Della Lear for the first time. Over the following months, their relationship becomes a courtship and they marry in December 1953. Archie's remains are identified from among those returned during Operation Glory and the devastated Connors' family prepares for his funeral.

Epilogue   Pages 318-332

Mission 1890 and its losses would affect all of the families involved to this day. The "rest of the story" proves the strength of the human spirit and its ability to rebuild both hope and the lives on which it is founded.

Notes   Pages 334-344
Glossary   Pages 345-378
Index   Pages 379-386

Baited Trap
The Ambush of Mission 1890
Deadliest helicopter rescue mission of the Korean War

For the Third Air Rescue Squadron (3ARS), the 18th Fighter-Bomber Wing and the U.S. Air Force, Mission 1890 was over about 1630 on 25 June 1952. For the families, however, it will never be over. The "story" of Mission 1890 continues to this day. Long after the shooting had ended on that North Korean plateau, the families were caught up in the agonies and bleaknesses of the "missing in action, presumed alive" world—an empty life of hanging on to any shred of information, parsing every word of every sentence of every turgid letter from the "Bureau of Personnel," and writing letters of hope to other family members and trying to sound up beat and positive, even when all reasonable hope was a distant glimmer at the end of a bleak tunnel of dread.

USS Bon Homme Richard (CV 31) *turns into the wind to launch aircraft, followed by its plane guard destroyer. (NARA)*

Hangar Deck. *F9F "Panther" jets and F4U-4 Corsair fighter-bombers crowd the Bonny Dick's hangar deck.*

Chapter One

Beating To Quarters

Wednesday, June 25, 1952
Second Anniversary of the Korean War

Sea of Japan Off East Coast of North Korea
Operating Area "Sugar"

Ensign Ronald "Ron" Dow Eaton was jolted awake at 0426 by the bugle call for "General Quarters." There was no sleeping through that piercing series of four-note intervals played by a member of the ship's band over the general announcing system—called the "1 MC." A few seconds later, as Dow and everyone else on the USS Bon Homme Richard (CV 31)—known affectionately to her crew as "The Bonny Dick"—were rolling out of their racks, the Boatswain's Mate of the Watch on the bridge keyed his microphone and barked "General Quarters, General Quarters for dawn alert." [1]

Most of the ship's company headed to their GQ stations just in case the ship's silhouette was a target for a possible enemy submarine as the relative safety of darkness vanished when the sun came up from the direction of Japan. After a few minutes the ship secured from General Quarters and set the normal steaming watches.

The ship was not under attack, but was stirring itself to life as it prepared for another long day of launching and recovering aircraft during combat operations off the coast of North Korea.

Easing out of his bunk, Eaton winced slightly as he momentarily forgot his ankle injury and put too much weight on his foot. He grabbed the bunk rail to steady himself.

Several weeks earlier his plane—an F4U Corsair fighter-bomber—had been accidentally pushed off the flight deck at night while the flight deck crew was respotting the deck. After falling nearly fifty feet from the flight deck into the sea, with remarkable presence of mind, Eaton had managed to free himself from the rapidly sinking aircraft and despite his seriously injured ankle, swim to the surface, pop the CO2 cartridges of his Mae West life preserver and hope for rescue. After an anxious hour of floating and swimming in the shark-infested waters off Hawaii, a rescue destroyer had found and recovered the grateful young pilot.

In the weeks since then, the ankle had healed—almost. However, it was still very tender. Eaton had finally convinced the flight surgeon that he was ready to be returned to "flying status." He had completed his first two combat missions on Monday and Tuesday—working over North Korean power plants. He was anxious to add to his mission total. Today would be the third combat mission for the eager young pilot from Wilmington, Massachusetts.

The ship had reached the combat zone on Sunday. Early on Monday morning, June 23rd, Eaton and his fellow pilots from VF-74 had flown their first combat missions over North Korea.

"We were to take part in the joint Air Force-Navy strike against the as yet untouched North Korea hydro-electric plants," CDR Charles D. Fonvielle, Jr., the "Be-Deviler" Commander later reported. Although the

Junior Officer's Bunkroom aboard USS Bon Homme Richard (CV 31). Ensign Ron Eaton would have lived with several other "JO's" in a room like this. Most of his time would have been spent in the Ready Room, the squadron office seeing to his many collateral duties, or in the ship's Wardroom where the officers ate and enjoyed a lounge area to read or to play cards or Acey Duecy—when they weren't on duty or had unfinished work. (NARA)

operations on Monday were delayed until the afternoon, the Navy aircraft were able to get in one good, effective strike that afternoon that "practically destroyed all the targets assigned." Task Force 77 had planned carefully and had four aircraft carriers operating in the area, including: USS Princeton, USS Boxer and USS Philippine Sea, in addition to the USS Bon Homme Richard. It was the first time since World War II that four aircraft carriers had conducted joint combat operations. The operation "went off efficiently and without mishap," Fonvielle noted.

Eaton's flight conducted both flak suppression and dive bombing attacks on the major targets. The sixteen aircraft of VF-74 struck Kyosen station Two and Fusen Station Two on Monday afternoon. On Tuesday afternoon, they went back for "finishing off" strikes against Kyosen Station Four. Another late afternoon mission on Tuesday was called by Fifth Air Force against troop and supply concentrations near the front lines.

In the pre-dawn hours of Wednesday morning, June 25, 1952, the Bon Homme Richard was steaming as a unit of Task Force 77 in operating area "Sugar" in the Sea of Japan off the Korean coast. It had joined TF 77 off the eastern coast of Korea, near the 38th Parallel, on Monday after departing Yokosuka, Japan. The task force was under orders to conduct "offensive air operations and strikes with United Nations Forces against North Korean and Chinese Communist Forces," the ship's log noted. It marked the return of the carrier to the Korean Theater of Operations after an absence of nearly seven months.

The SOPA—Senior Officer Present Afloat—was VADM J. J. "Jocko" Clark,[2] Commander of the Seventh Fleet, who was embarked in the USS Philippine Sea (CV 47), steaming in the formation. The Officer in Tactical Command was RADM [Apollo] Soucek, Commander, Carrier Division Three, embarked in USS Boxer (CV 21). Other ships in the task force included USS Juneau (CLAA 119), USS Princeton (CV 37), USS Helena (CA 75), and 13 destroyers surrounding the capital ships with an ASW (anti-submarine warfare) screen. The task force was taking no chances. Although no enemy surface ships or submarines were expected, the ships were in readiness condition three, the ships were darkened and the formation was steering a zigzag course.

Flight quarters would sound at 0700 according to the Richard's Plan of the Day. On the bridge, the "Mid Watch" Officer of the Deck (0001-0400), LT D. F. Mueller, just before turning the watch over to his relief, had ordered Main Control to light off an additional four boilers. It normally took several hours to bring a boiler "on line" and ready to deliver full steam pressure to the engines that drove the ship's four large screws. His relief on the "Morning Watch" (0400-0800), ENS D. K. Mosher, would be ordering speeds in excess of 25 knots and would require all eight boilers on line for the higher speeds needed to conduct air operations in the light wind conditions that were predicted for morning air operations—4-8 knots.

Just two days before, Typhoon Dinah had been over Ishigaki Shima on a north to northeast course that had caused some concern regarding the ship's ability to carry out operations during the operating period, Richard's Captain Paul W. Watson reported. On Monday, the typhoon was off the southern coast of Kyushu, but then veered to a northeast course and moved up the south coast of Japan. The new course not only missed TF 77, but drew in "polar air" that formed a high over the operating area. "As a result, the weather remained operational through the period except for short periods due to fog and low stratus along the northeast coast of Korea. It offered three days of good flying conditions and TF 77 aircraft made the best of them," the ship's log noted.

Eaton and his several other roommates in one of the "Bonny Dick's" JO (Junior Officer) Bunkrooms, slipped into their bath robes and flip-flops for a trip to the nearest Officer's Head. Time for a quick shower and shave before heading up to the Wardroom for breakfast. Lucky for them the sea water temperature was about 70 degrees, making it relatively easy for the ship's evaporators to distill enough sea water for cooling, cooking—and hot showers. When the "evaps" could not keep up with the demand, "water hours" would be declared and showers would be severely limited.

As he pulled on his robe, Eaton glanced over at the picture on his cramped little desk. A very pretty face gazed out at him.

Dorothy Sharp—"Dolly" to him and her friends—gazed back at him. He smiled as he passed by her picture, then picked up his shaving kit, and headed down the passageway to the head. He knew she had a similar picture of him on her dresser. They had decided to get married when he returned from his first deployment. As he was leaving Boston for the last time before deploying, they had arranged for portraits to be taken of each other. He carried hers. She kept his.

Eaton hurried through his shower. All hands were encouraged to take a "Navy shower." Wet down quickly. Soap up with the water turned off. Then, rinse the soap off—quickly. It

Dorothy "Dolly" Sharp. *Dolly anxiously awaited Ron Eaton's return so they could be married.*

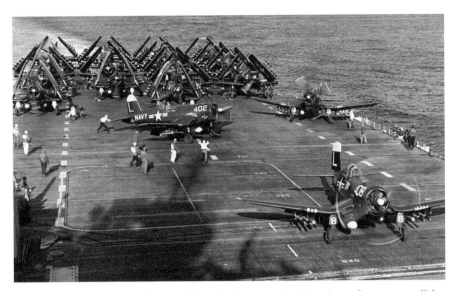

saved water and moved men through the crowded heads as fast as possible. Shaving could be done in the head if there was a free basin. Or, each officer's stateroom had a wash basin that could be used for shaving.

Soon, Eaton was clean and shaved and in his flight suit heading aft to the wardroom and breakfast. He was scheduled for another mission today, his third in as many days.

Off to the Target. *A Corsair from VF-74 taxis forward prior to launch on a combat mission over North Korea.*

At 0700 flight quarters was sounded and Ensign Mosher ordered the Foxtrot flag flown "at the dip"—about half way up the signal halyard—alerting the other ships in the task force that the Bonny Dick was preparing to commence flight operations.

Eaton and his fellow pilots had reported to the squadron's ready room for their mission briefing.

The Richard's Air Group, Commanded by CDR G. B. Brown, included nine squadrons flying 40 aircraft—F9F Panther jets (VF-71 and VF-72), F4U-4 Corsairs (VF-74 and VC-4), AD Skyraiders (VA-75, VC-12, VC-33, VC-61) and helicopters (HU-1).

Shortly before 0800 Captain Watson was called on the intercom by the Air Boss in PriFli (Primary Flight Control), who asked permission to commence air operations according to the schedule that had been approved and routed throughout the ship. On the bridge, ENS Mosher carefully transcribed the flight operations schedule onto the inside of the bridge window in grease pencil. As each event was completed, a quick swipe with the handy rag removed the information and left the next event—time of launch, number and type of aircraft—on the top of the list.

Mosher confirmed to the Captain that the ship was ready to commence flight operations—on course and with speed sufficient to provide enough wind down the deck for launch.

Reaching for a switch to his left, Watson lit up the green light indicating a "green deck," permission to launch. Simultaneously, Mosher ordered the Signal Bridge to "Close up Foxtrot"—two block the white flag with the red diamond in the center to the top of the yardarm. Air operations were underway.

An F4U-4 Corsair launches with a full load of ordnance.

At 0758 the Richard launched its first aircraft. Eight minutes later the launch was complete. LT C. C. Payne, the on-coming underway OOD for the Morning Watch (0800-1200), then reduced speed to fifteen knots along with the rest of the formation.

At 0933, Lt. Payne brought the carrier into the wind again on a southerly course of 179 degrees and increased speed to 28 knots. The wind was light, about 6-8 knots and generally from the south to southwest. Conducting flight operations in these "light air" conditions meant that the ship would have to be at nearly maximum speed—All Ahead Flank—to get the needed "wind down the deck" for launch and recovery. [3]

AT 0957 LT Payne maneuvered the ship into the wind to recover aircraft launched several hours before. Now it was important not only to have the wind down the deck at about 30-35 knots, but also about 5 degrees to port to ensure that the stack gases were being blown slightly to the starboard side of the descent course being used by the pilots as they lined up on the flight deck and its arresting gear. The "light brown haze" of the smoke from the eight boilers on line could obscure the pilots vision.

From time to time, LT Payne would pop his head out of the bridge to personally check the density of the stack gases. Even more of a risk than the haze to the landing pilots "in the groove," were the "burbles" of hot air and gas coming from the stack and the wind flowing around the island structure that threatened the precise control needed during the final seconds of an approach—unless the relative wind was slightly to port of the ship's bow. The pilots needed clear, undisturbed air in which to maneuver the aircraft for a landing, particularly the pilots of the F4U Corsairs.

Keeping the relative wind slightly to port gave the pilots an unobstructed view of the flight deck and undisturbed air as they completed the always tricky maneuvers to line the plane up properly prior to landing—actually more of a controlled crash.

At 1054, LT Payne changed course to 170 and the ship's speed to 21 knots—the winds were picking up somewhat as the morning advanced and not quite enough speed was needed—and began the 1100 launch. In five minutes, the aircraft were in the air and heading towards their targets in North Korea. One of the pilots en route to his target after that launch was Ensign Ron Eaton, starting out with other Corsairs of VA-74 on his third combat mission.

F4U Corsair Fighter Bomber

The F4U Corsairs that Ensign Ron Eaton and other pilots of Fighter Squadron 74 were flying had been designed in the late 1930s and manufactured in time to become one of the most famous fighters of World War Two.

The Corsair acquired many nicknames: "Hose Nose," "Bent Wing Bird," "Hog" and "Ensign Eliminator," the latter due to unforgiving stall and landing characteristics. When wind conditions were right, the air intakes on the wings produced a distinctive whistling sound. Japanese ground troops called it "Whistling Death."

The double Wasp radial engine delivered 1,850 hp for take-off, giving it a top speed of 405 mph.

Six Colt-Browning .50-cal. machine guns were mounted in the wings outside the propeller arc, thus eliminating the need for synchronization.

It weighed a maximum of 10,074 pounds and had an effective range of slightly over 1,000 miles.

The F4U-4 ("dash Four" version) was one of the more important variants of the Corsair. It had evolved into a fighter-bomber, although the Navy never officially recognized it as such. It carried six Colt-Browning .50-cal. wing mounted machine guns, plus it could carry two 1,000-lb bombs or eight 5-inch rockets.

The "bent wing" design allowed the massive prop to clear the deck and kept the distance between the deck and the wing short enough to allow a short, stout landing gear assembly.

One of the biggest problems for the pilots was the long nose that stuck out 14 feet in front of the cockpit. When the Corsair was sitting in take-off position, the nose blocked forward vision up to 12 degrees above the horizon. During carrier landings, once the plane was lined up with the flight deck on final approach, the pilot could not actually see the LSO or Landing Signal Officer (called "Paddles" because he used colorful or lighted hand-held signaling paddles and body language to direct the pilot during the landing).

Carrier pilots jockeyed their planes, whatever the type of aircraft, to have the plane reach stall speed just as the tail hook was snagging the arresting gear. This was a major problem for Corsair pilots. As the F4U dropped into stall speed, the left wing tended to drop quickly. Hitting the deck at such an attitude could cause the landing gear to collapse. Even on a "normal" approach in a Corsair, the plane landed so heavily that the shock absorbers "bottomed out" as the plane slammed onto the wooden deck. The resulting recoil would often cause the plane to bounce high into the air. If the tailhook failed to engage an arresting cable—failed to "trap"—the aircraft could plow into the "pack"—the planes spotted forward on the flight deck. The result was a catastrophic loss of planes and a major fire.

Finally, the British devised a method of landing the Corsair on their aircraft carriers that overcame the visibility problems created by the long nose. Instead of pilots using the downwind-port turn to crosswind-port turn to line up on final approach method, British Corsair pilots learned to turn downwind, then break into a slow, continuous port turn that aligned the heavy fighter with the deck at the very last second before the aircraft touched down for a trap. The pilot was able to keep the LSO in sight right up to the final moments when the plane was crossing the "round down" over the fantail. At that point, the LSO would give the "cut" sign across the throat with a paddle or a "wave off" directing another attempt.

Chapter Two

Truckbusters At Dogpatch

Wednesday, June 25, 1952
0600
18th Fighter-Bomber Wing
K-46 Hoengsong, South Korea

The Operations Complex for the 18th Fighter-Bomber Group at K-46. The large building in center foreground is Group Operations. Other buildings (l-r) include: 39th Fighter-Interceptor Squadron Operations, 12th Fighter-Bomber Squadron Operations, 67th Fighter-Bomber Squadron Operations, 2 Squadron SAAF Operations. The sand bagged building is the briefing/debriefing room. The single runway is at left alongside which the Wing's F-51 Mustang fighter-bombers were parked, maintained, refueled and rearmed for combat missions that often started before dawn and continued after dark, even though the Mustang was not equipped for night combat missions. The tents at extreme right were quarters—summer and winter—for the airmen and officers of the 18th Wing. (Peterburs)

Flight line at K-46 in Spring 1952.

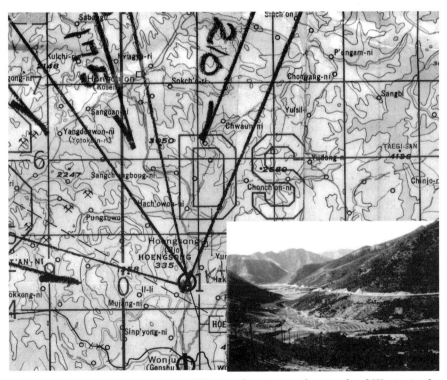

K-46 Air Base *near Hoengsong, SK was about ten miles north of Wonju in the central highlands of South Korea. (Above) Pilots flying from K-46 annotated their lap maps with lines of bearing to and from the base drawn with grease pencil. (Stapley) K-46 was ringed with mountains ranging from 2,000-3,000 feet. Pilots called the valley approach to the K-46 strip "Deadman's Gulch." (Peterburs)*

The 67th Squadron How Flight "Hilton" at K-46 in Spring 1952. (Urquhart)

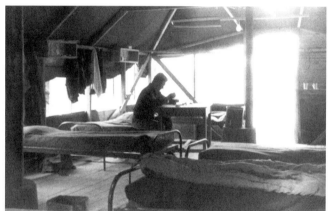

Interior of How Flight "Hilton" at K-46 during warmer Spring weather. 1st Lt. Tim Urquhart works at a table building model cars. A diesel oil heater and flue can be seen at right center of photograph. (Urquhart)

Over a hundred miles from the Bon Homme Richard's off-shore position, at an air strip about fifty miles east of Seoul that had been carved out between mountains, the pilots and ground crews of the 18th Fighter-Bomber Wing also were preparing for another day of combat operations. The Richard had participated in one other period of combat operations during the previous year. For the 18th Wing however, it was just another dangerous, mission-filled day of close air support and armed interdiction in what would soon be two solid years of Korean combat operations. [1]

No bugle call awakened 1st Lt. Archie Connors that Wednesday morning as he slept on a cot in the ten-man "army" tent that was the hard scrabble home of "H" Flight (pronounced "How" based on the phonetic alphabet used in the military at the time) of the 67th Fighter-Bomber Squadron. Instead, since he had a mission scheduled that day, a messenger from the Operations Office shook his shoulder.

Home Sweet Tent. *Airman First Class Robert Cranston, a Crew Chief for the 67th Squadron from January 1952 until November 1952, recalled the flimsy tents as "COLD, WET & HOT—to the extreme." (Cranston)*

"Lt. Connors, wake up, you've got a mission today." The airman then moved around the tent to wake up Captain Elliot D. Ayer, How Flight leader, and Lieutenants John Hill and Bill McShane, who would also fly the RESCAP (Rescue Combat Air Patrol) mission with Ayer and Connors.

That Wednesday, How Flight was the designated RESCAP for the Fifth Air Force (FAF).

In June, 1952, the 67th Fighter-Bomber Squadron, as one of four air squadrons that made up the 18th Fighter-Bomber Group, was operating from K-46, a forward operations air base "approximately seven miles North North East of Wonju," the Commanding Officer of the 67th, Major Stanley A. Long, explained in his monthly report. K-46 was just a rough air field between mountain ranges, approximately five miles southwest of Hoensong, South Korea. The primary mission of the squadron during this period was the "tactical interdiction of the enemy's transportation system."

"Main Street" for the 18th Fighter-Bomber Wing at K-46. *From right to left is the Communications Center and the Operations Offices for the Two Squadron South African Air Force (SAAF), the 67th Fighter-Bomber Squadron and the 12th Fighter-Bomber Squadron. (Urquhart)*

Quarters *at K-46 were large tents with wooden floors. The tents were "conveniently" located on either side of the latrine—the large building in the center. "The smell knocks you out," Lt. Archie Connors mentioned in a letter to his mother, Eva, as he described the primitive conditions that existed at K-46. (Urquhart)*

It also fulfilled other missions for the Fifth Air Force, including Rescue Combat Air Patrol. [2]

At the beginning of June, 1952, the 67th Squadron had 44 officers and 175 enlisted personnel assigned.

1st Lt. Archie Connors had been assigned to the 67th early in January 1952. After three months of combat missions, he had been called back to Jacksonville, Florida for what became 45 days of emergency leave. During a trip to Jacksonville from St. Louis in their brand new "Henry J," Archie's wife, Lutye "Frankie" Connors, had skidded off an icy road in North Georgia and had nearly been killed. *[Note: Frankie hated the name "Lutye," and never used it except on legal documents. Throughout the text she will be called Frankie, as she would have wished.]* Frankie was eight months pregnant with their daughter who had been stillborn just three weeks before

Mustangs of the 67th Squadron at K-46 *loaded with auxillary fuel tanks (drop tanks) and ready for a high endurance Rescue Combat Air Patrol (RESCAP) mission "usually for a pilot that was down behind enemy lines," noted Robert Cranston. "During post flight we would perform any needed maintance, refuel, load ammo, rockets and two 500-lb. bombs or napalm. If the upcoming mission was to fly CAP for a downed pilot, we would change the bombs for extra fuel tanks. This would add about four hours flying time. We usually flew two flights per day—if you could keep your plane together." (Cranston)*

her birth as a result of the accident. They named the infant Sharon Lee. A trip taken to ensure that Sharon Lee was born in Jacksonville, resulted in her being buried there, instead. The accident would have life long effects on Frankie and the entire Connors family.

Following a brief refresher period at the squadron's gunnery range to hone his combat flying skills after a month and a half out of the cockpit, Connors was again flying combat missions—sometimes two a day. He was determined to get his 100 missions over with and go home—the sooner the better. Most of his friends that had seen him through flight school and had

1st Lt. Archie Connors and his wife, Frankie *at Jacksonville Beach, Florida in 1950, shortly before he entered Air Force flight training. They both wrote each other letters on Wednesday, June 25, 1952. She was still recuperating from nearly fatal injuries she had suffered in a car accident in April 1952 that had taken him home on emergency leave for 45 days.*

(Left) ***How Flight*** *clowns for an unknown cameraman in early July 1952. 1st Lt. William E. McShane, Capt. Elliot D. Ayer (Flight Leader), 1st Lt. John E. Hill, 2nd Lt. W. Timmons ("Tim") Urquhart, Capt. Charles T. Hudson and Capt. E. W. Aubuchon (seated). They stand with their Korean "House Boy." Capt. Ayer had recently succeeded 1st Lt. Wilfred "Budd" Stapley as Flight Leader. Ayer chose Connors, McShane and Hill to accompany him on Mission 1890. (Urquhart)*
(Right) **Captain Elliot D. Ayer**

reported with him to the 18th in January, had already finished their missions and been rotated back to the "Z.I."—Zone of the Interior, home, the United States. Far too many of them, like Mel Sousa and George Patton, had already been killed in action or were missing. He had little time for writing letters and he certainly did not want Frankie, still recuperating from her injuries and the death of their daughter in the car accident, to know the extraordinary dangers he was facing as a fighter bomber pilot in combat.

Connors, Ayer, Hill and McShane rolled off their hard, canvas cots, grabbed their shaving kits and headed next door to the latrine tent. While they didn't have far to walk, the stench from the latrine was almost unbearable when the wind was in the wrong direction—as it always was for someone living in the tents clustered nearby that housed the 1,700 officers and airmen living in "Dogpatch."

After what they called taking care of "SSS"—shit, shower, and shave—the four headed up the hill to the Wing's mess hall for a meal of dehydrated eggs and milk and other "food." Even two years into the Korean War the Air Force had not solved its logistical challenges in supplying its units with supplies and equipment. There were constant shortages reported monthly by the units that ranged from food to rescue gear, Scotch tape to

```
SECRET:  SEND IN THE CLEAR BY AUTH OF COL MEYERS DEPUTY FOR OPERATION
FROM:  COMAF FIVE KOREA                          EMERGENCY
                                                 Secret
TO:    COMFTRBMRWG 18 KOREA K-10    FOR SPECIAL HANDLING
       COMFTRBMRWG 18 KOREA K-13
OPC  3680                           DTG  281000

THIS IS FRAG ORDER OF FIFTH AIR FORCE OPS ORD  ONE ONE NINE DASH FIVE ONE
FOR  TWO NINE APRIL FIVE ONE        PD
```

H. 18th Ftr-Bmr Wg will:

(1) Dispatch 28 sorties effort to atk previously recommended tunnels on MSR fr Kaesong to Sariwon and perform armed recon in area indicated below. Acft w/b loaded at Gp CO's discr w/max ord and/or fuel to most effectively accomplish asgd mission. Acft w/ck in and out w/Mellow. All eny aflds w/i asgd areas w/b recon and personnel w/b atkd. Act rept req. JOC w/b notified of Mission no and TTRS.

Mission No	Area
Start w/1801	Area bounded by line fr YC-4080 to CT-1080, S to bb line, W along bb line and coast to YC-4010, N to YC-4080.

(2) Commit 2, 4 ship flts at K-13 for JOC alert fr 0530 until 30 min before sunset. Acft w/b loaded max nap, 5 in HVAR, and 50 cal ammo. Mission No to start w/1870. Acft w/ck in and out w/Greenhorn.

(3) Dispatch acft to Mellow to perform close spt w/TACPs as indicated below. Acft w/b loaded max nap, 5 in HVARs 50 cal ammo.

Mission No	No Acft	Aprx TTR	TOT	TACP
1850	4	1210	1250	Rakeoff CS-1767
1851	4	1450	1530	Rakeoff CS-1767
1852	4	1610	1650	Rakeoff CS-1767
1853	4	1635	1715	Shovel DT-2306
1854	4	1650	1730	Rakeoff CS-1767

PAR THREE XRAY PAREN ONE THREE SEE EXTRACT FOR ANY PERTINENT INFOR-
MATION PD ACT ADDRESSEE UPON RECEIVING THIS MSG ACK RECEIPT TO ABLE
DASH THREE DUTY OFFICER JOC IMMN PD

OPC/STS/ /   GILBERT I MEYERS, COLONEL, USAF
                              DEPUTY FOR OPERATIONS

                              PAGE   OF   PAGES

Frag Order. *This is a copy of an actual Frag Order ["frag"-ment of the daily Operations Order] for 29 April 1951. It originated daily from Fifth Air Force Headquarters in Seoul and outlined missions for each Wing. Such messages were classified SECRET "Special Handling." It was a message like this that alerted the 18th Fighter-Bomber Wing to assign a RESCAP Mission to one of its squadrons. The 67th Fighter-Bomber Squadron was ordered to schedule the mission. (NARA)* grease pencils. The food was usually awful and even now there were occasional shortages.

After the breakfast, of sorts, the foursome headed back down to their tent to pick up their flying kit before meeting at the 67th Squadron's Operations Office for a briefing on how the mission would be flown, if at all. There was always the chance that no pilot would be shot down that day and the mission would remain just an unused number on the Frag.

On the way out of the mess tent, they tried not to look at the "puking wall." Many pilots were so nervous before a mission that after chow they would no sooner get outside the tent than nausea would overtake them. It was nauseating just to look at the wall. Others said it wasn't the nervousness, but the almost inedible food that caused the vomiting. Whatever the reason, they tried not to look as they headed back to their tent and then the Operations Office.

When they arrived at the Operations Office about 0730, they reviewed the Frag Order for June 25th along with safety notices and other postings on the "Fighting Cocks" bulletin board. They also reported in with the Commander of the 67th Squadron.

Major Stanley A. Long, Commander of the squadron was at his desk in the Operations Office. Long had been Commander since April, when he had succeeded Lt. Col. Julian Crow.

Like the rest of the 67th Squadron, Long was bone tired. Three weeks before, he had moved his squadron's administrative offices from K-10, near Chinhae in the southeastern corner of South Korea, up to K-46. Then, for

Pilots congregate outside the 67th Squadron Operations Office (right) at K-46 *to compare notes on recent missions. (Urquhart)*

almost a week he had been involved almost around the clock in planning and carrying out attacks on major hydroelectric facilities in North Korea.

Born in August 1918, during WWII Long flew with the 11th Air Force in the Aleutian Theater as Commander of the 54th Fighter Squadron flying the P-38 Lightning aircraft. During 100 missions in the Lightning, he scored three kills on Japanese aircraft. Between WWII and the Korean War, he was the owner and operator of "Long's Air Activities" and taught flying courses to civilian pilots.

Today, Wednesday, 25 June 1952, promised to be just another day at the office for Long, albeit the "office" was a tin roofed shack on an advanced operating base just a few minutes flying time below the "bomb line" that ran roughly east and west across the 38th Parallel.

Long and his Operations Officer had reviewed the Frag Order, the daily combat operations directive sent from Headquarters, Fifth Air Force in Seoul,

Major Stanley A. Long, Commander, 67th Fighter-Bomber Squadron, 18th Fighter-Bomber Group, 18th Fighter-Bomber Wing, K-46 Korea.

when it had arrived by teletype the previous afternoon. The message was addressed to COMFTRBMRWG 18 KOREA K-46 and arrived via a teletype at the 18th Wing Headquarters Communication Office just down the dirt street at K-46. There, the appropriate sections were stapled together and distributed to the various squadrons of the 18th Fighter-Bomber Group, including the 67th "Fighting Cocks" Squadron, the 12th "Foxy Few" Squadron, and the 2 Squadron SAAF, the "Flying Cheetahs."

Among other missions, the 67th had been designated by the 18th Group to provide a flight—four fighter-bombers—to be on standby all day in the event they were needed for RESCAP duties.

Long had decided to assign the rescue duty to How Flight, now led by Captain Elliot Dean Ayer. Long was very impressed with Captain Ayer, an exceptional pilot and leader.

After they had familiarized themselves with the latest safety notes and the Frag Order, How Flight drew their flying gear and headed down to the nearby flight line to pre-flight their aircraft—the venerable F-51D Mustang. ³

After letting their engines warm up, How Flight shut them down and climbed out of the cockpits leaving much of their gear in place. If Mission 1890 was actually called, they had to be ready to get into the air within five minutes or so of the alert. Meanwhile, they would hang out in the Operations Office, reading magazines, writing letters and shooting the breeze with fellow pilots.

Inside the 67th "Red Scarfer's" Squadron Operations Office, 1st Lt. C. J. Gossett (left) and 2nd W. T. Urquhart, two other members of How Flight stand the duty. On the morning of June 25, 1952, How Flight's RESCAP Mission 1890 would be waiting here if the mission was laid on by the Joint Operations Center at Fifth Air Force in Seoul. (Urquhart)

Chapter Three

That Others May Live

Wednesday, June 25, 1952
0700
Third Air Rescue Squadron, Detachment One
8055th MASH behind Front Lines

Early that Wednesday morning, June 25, 1952, rescue helicopter pilot Captain Wayne Lear from Santa Ana, California and Medical Technician Bobby Holloway from Ruston, Louisiana, of the Third Air Rescue Squadron, Detachment One, had begun a ten-day tour of duty with the 8055th MASH (Mobile Army Surgical Hospital). The MASH was located not far from the front lines northeast of the squadron's headquarters at K-16, the Seoul Municipal Airport.

Members of the 3rd Air Rescue Squadron watch as their comrades warm up two H-5 helicopters in preparation for a mission to the front lines in March 1952. The Emergency Hospital is in the background. (NARA)

23

(Left) Captain Leslie Wayne Lear and (right) Staff Sergeant Bobby Dale Holloway. Lear had arrived in Korea in May and had been assigned to the Third Air Rescue Squadron as its training officer. Ironically, after receiving extensive training in the newer, much more capable H-19, Lear was assigned to fly the older, more vulnerable H-5 on frequent missions because the detachment commander, Major Emerson E. Heller, did not "trust" the H-19. SSgt. Bobby Holloway flew with Lear as the Medical Technician. An avid hunter before joining the Air Force, Holloway would need to know how to use a carbine before the day was over.

They were to spend the next ten days transporting wounded soldiers or downed pilots to the hospital from an advanced "strip" just behind the bomb line—in reality a collection of tents and supplies grouped in a dry rice paddy just behind the front lines. After being on call all day for whatever rescue mission might be needed, at dusk, they would fly back to the MASH, where they slept in a ten-man tent and ate with the hospital staff. The food was very good, Holloway later recalled.

They had left the relative comforts of the MASH early that morning in an H-5 "Dragonfly" helicopter, number 49-2000. At the "base" just a few miles behind the lines, they landed near some tents that served as an Operations Office, shut down the engine, topped off the fuel, and waited for any rescue missions that might be assigned to them by the JOC in Seoul.

This was only the second time that medic Holloway had been on call for pilot rescue duty—"pilot pickup" they called it. On standby, they waited near their aircraft.

First Air Force Unit in Korean War

On this same date two years before, in 1950, the Third Air Rescue Squadron had first deployed detachments to Korea to perform search and rescue. "It was perhaps the first Air Force Unit to participate in the Korean action since on that memorable day one of its B-17's was turned back on its flight from the Tokyo International Airport (Haneda Air Base) to the Kimpo Airdrome at Seoul," noted Col. Klair E. Back, 3rd ARS Commanding Officer in the squadron's unit history "Scramble," published in 1952. "On board the Rescue aircraft was Mr. Muccio, United States Ambassador to Korea, returning from high level talks in Tokyo with General Douglas MacArthur and his Staff." [1]

Col. Klair Back

At the outset of hostilities, the squadron's primary mission involved intercepting and escorting endangered aircraft over the land areas of Japan and adjacent seas. Heightened combat operations and a worsening tactical situation soon required that the mission be expanded to include the rescue of stranded personnel behind enemy lines and aero-medical helicopter evacuation.

UN soldier being evacuated *to a rear line hospital where complete medical attention will be received, the Air Force caption explained. Blood plasma has been flowing into his veins since the Communist bullet found its mark and will continue to flow even in flight through a special device created by Capt. Benjamin Johnson of Jacksonville, Fla. The entire evacuation took 25 minutes. The 3rd Air Rescue Squadron, Korea, carried out these evacuations throughout the Korean War and is credited with rescuing thousands of servicemen. (NARA)*

A significant innovation in the use of the helicopter that was adopted during the Korean War was medical evacuation. For critically wounded soldiers at frontline aid stations, helicopter medical evacuations changed a tortuous, possibly fatal ten- to fourteen-hour road trip into a one-hour flight to a rear MASH unit.

Rotary wing aviation itself was less than a decade old and helicopters had seen very limited use in WWII until U.S. pilots and crew flew them in combat missions in Korea. It was immediately apparent that the helicopter was the most expedient way to reach the wounded and to transport them from or near the front lines back to aid stations—Mobile Army Surgical Hospitals—or even hospital ships for rapid treatment.

Trail Blazing Rescue Operations

The first element of the 3rd Air Rescue Squadron to arrive in Korea with helicopters set up operations at Taegu Air Base on July 22, 1950, then moved to Pusan Air Base as North Korean forces surged down the peninsula and began tightening what soon became known as the "Pusan Perimeter." By August 30th the helicopter element was separated from Flight D and assigned its own name, Detachment H (later changed to Detachment F). Sub-components of the detachment, called "Elements" were also co-located with various Mobile Army Surgical Hospital (M.A.S.H.) units to provide prompt transport of emergency medical cases. By early September the overworked crews and pilots of Detachment H were creating the first air doctrine and operational procedures for helicopter rescue operations. [2]

From June 1950 to the end of hostilities in July 1953, ARS 3 rescued almost 10,000 UN personnel, nearly 1,000 from behind enemy lines, and over 200 from the water. For numerous commendable and heroic rescues, the 3rd ARS/ARG earned three Distinguished Unit Citations. [3]

"The outstanding service of the 3rd Air Rescue Squadron has contributed in great measure to the combat efficiency and high morale of the Far East Command's tactical air arm and to the United Nations Command's fight against Communist aggression," wrote General Mark W. Clark, Commanding General, Far East Command. "Day and night you stand ready to reach far behind enemy lines to rescue a downed airman, and missions of mercy in times of civil disaster are accomplished with the same selflessness and courage that characterize your performance of tactical missions."

"Throughout the United States Air Force today there are countless airmen who are living proof of a job well done by the Third Rescue Squadron," Lt. Gen. Glenn O. Barcus, Commanding General Fifth Air Force noted. "In the finest traditions of the United States Air Force, our rescue teams have returned downed airmen to safety and to duty." [3]

H-5's awaiting missions at an advanced base in Korea. *(NARA)*

The work and accomplishments of the Third Air Rescue Squadron were perhaps best summed up by Brigadier General Delmar T. Spivey, Commanding General, Japan Air Defense Force who noted, "for many it is a personal story. It is a life and death saga, the tale of miraculous escape from an obvious deathtrap for many an airman stranded behind enemy lines or downed at sea. To such men, the hovering helicopter or the rescue boat parachuting down from its mother B-29 holds an unforgettable significance.[4] It has meant new hope and a chance to fight again; it has meant life often where death seemed certain. For the rest of us—for the many who will never know a personal indebtedness for the first work of the Third—this record is a source of stirring inspiration. It is a privilege to salute you men of the Third. Yours is a record of high courage and valor, a story of sacrifice and service in the interest of your fellowmen."

"The Air Rescue Service," Col. Klair Back explained in the January 1952 unit history, "is the USAF organization which provides world-wide air rescue service for all U.S. military activities, and renders air rescue service upon request to civil aviation of the U.S. and to civil and military aviation of other countries in accordance with International Civil Aviation organization procedures and policies of the Department of Defense."

Back had assumed command of the 3rd ARS in August 1950 and continued as Commander until June 1953, when he was reassigned to command an airbase in the Z.I.—Zone of the Interior, Air Force slang for the continental United States. During his tenure the squadron grew from 537 personnel in September 1950, to a wartime high of 1,015 in January 1952.

The subject of air rescue naturally separates into three parts, Back explained: the search for, aid to, and evacuation of survivors of aircraft accidents. "Another important function is to assure survival in remote areas. Rescue operations require close understanding and cooperation and operating procedures among separate commands and agencies. An efficient rescue requires the use of all available facilities, prompt delivery of information, competent evaluations, and positive, immediate action. There is quite a variation in operating conditions between ZI and overseas installations. In the ZI such agencies as Coast Guard, sheriff's aero squadrons, highway patrols, civil air patrol's, Army, Navy and National Guard are often called to assist you the search. Rescue squadrons in this country naturally do not have this many agencies to call on for assistance."

"Rescue operational plans and facilities must be consistent with their relative importance to normal or tactical rations. Efficient coordination of such facilities depends upon well conceived air rescue plans for each area, which clearly define the responsibility of the Army and other participants and provide a clear communications and operations procedure for all parties to the plan," Back noted. [5]

Third Air Rescue Squadron

At the beginning of 1952, 3rd ARS was headquartered in Tokyo, Japan. Its component commands included Flight A (Johnson AB, Japan), Flight B (Komaki AB, Japan), Flight C (Misawa AB, Japan) and Flight D (Ashiya AB, Japan). In addition, Detachment One was based in Seoul at K-16, the municipal airport. Detachment One was further subdivided into several "elements" that operated aircraft from other locations, including Cho-do Island and the 8055th MASH.

The 3rd ARS was regularly augmented with personnel from the 2nd ARS (later redesignated 2nd Air Rescue Group) based in the Philippines.

H-5 and SA-16. *Two means of survival which played important roles in the successful rescue and evacuation of hundreds of United States Air Force and UN ground force personnel are represented here as an H-5 helicopter lowers gently for a landing near an SA-I6 "Albatross" amphibian. Both types were assigned to the veteran U.S. Air Force 3rd Air Rescue Squadron, and often teamed their capabilities to perform spectacular rescues and evacuations. On many occasions, the tiny "wind-mills" rescued troops from rough terrain near the fighting lines, and speedily evacuated them to airstrips from which the longer-range SA-46s can take off to complete the journey to rear area hospitals. (NARA)*

Captain Wayne Lear *(left) listens to a briefing on the H-5 "Dragonfly" helicopter similar to the one he would fly on June 25, 1952. (NARA)*

Aircraft limitations at the start of the Korean War forced the 3rd ARS to confine air rescue flights to short range rescue.

The Third Air Rescue Squadron flew a variety of aircraft to fulfill its mission requirements, including the:

L-5, a highly maneuverable liaison aircraft (similar to a civilian Piper Cub) used in helicopter escort, supply drops, and medical evacuation from small airfields;

H-5 ("Dragonfly") Sikorsky helicopters capable of operating in mountainous and rice paddy terrain;

SB-17, an obsolescent search and rescue version of the B-17 Flying Fortress bomber; and,

SC-47 transport, which assisted in searches and hauled critically needed supplies to outlying units.

The squadron soon phased out the SB-17, and added the SB-29 and the amphibious SA-16 ("Albatross").

H-5 Helicopter

At the beginning of the Korean War and for many months thereafter, the only USAF helicopter being used in Korea was the H-5. [6]

During its service life, the H-5 was used for rescue and humanitarian missions throughout the world. It gained its greatest fame, however, during the Korean War when it was called upon almost daily to rescue United Nations' pilots shot down behind enemy lines and to evacuate wounded personnel from frontline areas to hospital ships off shore or to mobile Army surgical hospitals behind the frontlines.

Cruising speed for the H-5 was about sixty knots and it could not take off above 4,000 feet. More critically, its maximum range was about 150 miles. The H-5 had limited instrument flight capabilities meaning it could not be operated safely in rain, hail, wind or darkness. It had no armor—too much weight—and no weapons other than a carbine carried by the crewman. Protection from anti-aircraft and small arms fire was provided during missions by a Combat Air Patrol (CAP).

As a rescue helicopter flying in combat the Dragonfly had major drawbacks and shortcomings. However, it was the only aircraft that was capable of performing rescue missions where conventional aircraft could not operate.

Early Rescue Operations

During the first weeks of the Korean War the H-5's of Detachment H were used primarily for search and rescue (SAR) missions to support the Fifth Air Force. On 16 September, Major General Earle E. Partridge, FAF Commander established pilot pickups as the primary mission for the helicopter detachment. Front line evacuations were the second priority and helicopters were not to be used for any purpose other than these without permission from FAF.

Following the landings at Inchon and the collapse of the Pusan Perimeter, UN forces advanced rapidly up the Korean peninsula. Air Force units followed the advancing front lines as fast as possible, relocating as needed to stay as close to the front lines as possible to cut down on mission flight time. During October, November and December, elements of the 3rd ARS were moved to Sariwon, Sinmak, Pyongyang, Anju, Kunuri and Sinanju in North Korea, as they followed the UN advance and then its retreat following the intervention by the Chinese Communists in late November 1950.

During the UN airborne assault on Pyongyang in October 1950, 3 ARS evacuated forty-seven injured paratroopers from drop zones at Sunchon and Sukchon. In March 1951, the squadron tested the new model H-19 helicopter, which proved invaluable in multiple evacuations and greatly extended the operational range for rotary-wing rescues.

In December 1951, H-5s participated in a highly successful experiment by flying wounded soldiers directly from frontline aid stations to a hospital ship off the Korean coast.

Second Korean Winter

At the beginning of 1952, Colonel Back noted in his report that the squadron's strength was slightly above that authorized, 175 officers on board with 158 authorized. The squadron had 832 Airmen on board with 740 authorized. On paper, it appeared to be over authorized strength. However, because its units were widely scattered, there was no way the squadron could centralize more than basic command functions.

Among the staff officers promoted that month was Captain Emerson E. Heller to Major with a "spot" or temporary promotion. In April, Heller became Commander of ARS 3, Detachment One operating from K-16, near Seoul.

The Air Rescue Service was a component of MATS—Military Air Transportation Service. Therefore when Major General Joseph T. Smith, MATS Commanding General, arrived in the Far East Theater on 24 January, Col. Back was delighted to provide for him a briefing on rescue activities in the theater. The next day, General Smith flew to Korea to visit the Rescue Coordination Center in the Joint Operations Center at Fifth Air Force Headquarters in Seoul. While Smith was on hand, a "pilot pickup" mission was performed by the helicopter detachment—Detachment One—or simply known as "Det One." General Smith "received a first-hand insight of a coordinated rescue mission," Back noted in his report. [7]

During that period the squadron proposed that a "suitable vessel for landing helicopters on be stationed in Northern Korean waters to improve our winter pilot pickup operations. Fifth Air Force has proposed the same type of operation to FEAF for use the remainder of this winter. At the present time, ice and cold water operations have restricted the operation of SA-16's. Consequently, the bulk of the pilot pickups have fallen to the H-5's. From our present northernmost Korean base, it is still an extremely distant flight to the Sinanju area where the majority of pilot pickups are being accomplished. At times, headwinds are so strong that an H-5 can not get into the pilot pickup area. If a ship could be made available for usage as a mobile landing platform and quarters for the H-5 crew, it could be stationed in the most strategic positions. The proposed operation has great possibilities." [8]

The proposed operation did have great possibilities, but they did not become a reality until a new type of U. S. Navy ship was designed from the keel up as a platform from which to operate helicopters—with many different missions, including rescue.

During January, the squadron conducted five medical evacuations, one intercept and two search missions. All missions were successful.

Both Land and Para-Rescue activities, if they were to be successful, required "intelligent cooperation from other agencies," the squadron noted as the reason for a demonstration of those capabilities for "VIP's of the Army and Air Force" on January 22nd. "The show was very successful even though certain modifications were introduced due to very high wind conditions."

The experience level of newly assigned personnel in the H-5 was so low that it "presented an operation and training problem." Col. Back wrote to Headquarters, Air Rescue Service requesting that a minimum of 75 helicopter flying hours be established for H-5 pilots slated for assignment to 3rd ARS.

ARS 3, Detachment One

At the beginning of 1952, Detachment One of the 3rd ARS was commanded by newly promoted Lt. Col. Ferdinand L. Svore. It had 24 officers authorized, and 29 actually assigned to the unit. It was authorized 104 Airmen, but had 125 on board.

During January, the weather over the entire Korean peninsula was generally fair. As a result, air combat missions were up and so were rescue missions. In order to provide "fully adequate rescue facilities for the increased air activity over North Korea, Detachment One found it necessary to station an additional two helicopters, thereby increasing the total complement to four aircraft, on the island of Paengnyong-do, the location of Element C, Detachment 1, 3rd ARS. The Officer in Charge was Major Emerson Heller. Each day, weather permitting, two helicopters were dispatched from Paengnyong-do to Cho-do Island to standby for a possible

H-5 helicopters of the 3rd Air Rescue Squadron parked at an advance air base near Suwon, Korea in March 1952. The increased use of helicopters on rescue missions during the Korean War became a significant factor in saving lives. From 1950-1953, men of the 3rd ARS Squadron (later designated a group) earned more than 1,000 personal citations and commendations. By the war's end, ARS crews were credited with the rescue of 9,898 United Nation's personnel. Nine hundred ninety six of those represented combat saves. (NARA)

Factory Direct. On February 20, 1952, four dissassembled H-19's were flown in two C-124's from Westover Field, Massachusetts to Korea. It was the first time that an aircraft was delivered directly from the factory to the gaining command. Note the "Secret" classification. (USAFHRA)

pilot pickup. After several occasions when weather forced the helicopter crews to RON (Remain Overnight) on Cho-do, Detachment One arranged for a storage area for POL (petroleum and logistics) supplies, a rice paddy for landing purposes and a "native hut" to house RON-ing crews.

During January, Detachment One flew a total of 524 sorties. One hundred twenty one patients were flown to and from front line stations and hospitals; eight United Nations flying personnel were rescued by Det One helicopters and L-5's.

In January, in addition to eight successful helicopter rescues, two missions were aborted "due to intense enemy fire in the immediate pick-up area." These unit history entries confirm that a pilot could and sometimes did abort a rescue mission if intense ground fire was encountered.

On February 20, 1952, two C-124's took off from Westover Field, Massachusetts en route to Korea with four dissembled H-19's. It would be the first time that an aircraft was delivered directly from the factory to the gaining command. The tail cone, main rotor blades and landing gear were the only major portions of the helicopter removed from the fuselage. "These aircraft were urgently needed to support the mission of Detachment One in Korea."

The two new H-19's arrived at the Detachment One's K-16 (Seoul) location on 29 February "causing some excitement among Detachment personnel. The new aircraft will be placed on operational flight status as soon as an acceptance inspection can be completed."

Detachment One prepared a "survey of all the Pilot Pickup attempts from behind enemy lines" that covered the period 1 August 1951 through

18 February 1952. During that nearly seven month period, the Detachment had attempted forty pilot pickups, of which 18 were successful. "Helicopters were fired on, by varying types of fire, on 22 of those missions, with two helicopters lost due to enemy fire and two being damaged." In other words, less than half of the pilot pickup missions attempted had been successful and enemy fire was deadly to the slow moving, unarmored and unarmed helicopters.

During February, Detachment One performed 33 front line evacuations with 48 UN soldiers being transported to the 8055th Mobile Army Surgical Hospital. Also during that month, 48 sorties were flown transporting 74 patients to the 121st Air Evacuation Hospital.

On 11 March, Lt. Gen. George E. Stratemeyer, sent his "most heartfelt congratulations" to all personnel of the 3rd Air Rescue Squadron "for the outstanding performance of duty during the past two years of fighting in Korea," and awarded the squadron a Presidential Citation.

In March, Detachment One received new aircraft, new pilots and strengthened facilities at the Cho-do island location. The month "also showed a decrease in pilot pickup missions along the battle lines, a slight increase in front line evacuations and an increase in over water activity.

In addition to several other pilot pickups that month, Major Emerson Heller, accompanied by aero-medical specialist Pfc James H. Garns, rescued a downed F4U pilot.

"While CAP aircraft stilled enemy anti-aircraft fire, Major Heller hovered the helicopter while Pfc Garns secured the hoist sling around the downed pilot; takeoff was accomplished with the pilot dangling and Pfc Garns hoisted him into the helicopter without difficulty."

Later, Heller was awarded a Distinguished Flying Cross for "extraordinary achievement while participating in aerial flight on 5 March 1952. As a pilot of an intricate and highly vulnerable helicopter, Major Heller flew over dangerous icy waters to the mouth of an enemy river and in spite of enemy artillery fire rescued and brought to safety a United Nations' pilot who had parachuted into the enemy water. Fully aware that rescue for himself and his crewman would have been impossible in case of emergency, Major Heller located the pilot afloat on an ice floe and after directing the fighter cover to help quiet enemy fire, found it necessary because of restricted visibility to rely entirely upon the verbal instructions of his Aero-Medical Specialist to position and hover the capricious machine over the downed pilot. In spite of the delicacy of the operation and enemy fire, Major Heller demonstrated his exceptional airmanship rescued [sic] the pilot and returned him to friendly territory."

On March 30th, Heller, Garns and two others "departed for Johnson AFB to take part in the Squadron [golf] tournament," the unit report noted.

During March the Detachment completed 36 sorties for front line evacuation, 32 sorties for hospital evacuations, 2 sorties for behind the lines evacuations and 6 sorties for pilot pickups. Also in March, the Detachment received four additional H-19A's. "Considerable trouble is being experienced in obtaining parts for these aircraft although it is expected that parts should begin arriving soon."

In April, Major Heller relieved Lt. Col. Svore as Commander of 3rd ARS Detachment One.

"The month of April showed a sharp increase in Front Line evacuations," Heller noted in his first unit report (77 in April, versus 36 in March). "There was also an increase in Hospital evacuations and Pilot Pick Ups (41 hospital evacuations, versus 32 in March, and 14 pilot pick-up sorties in April, versus 6 in March). The increase in medical evacuations can be attributed partially to the increase of hemorrhagic fever cases."

"Statistically speaking," May was the high month of the year for Detachment One, Heller noted, prematurely as it turned out. One hundred thirteen sorties carried 138 patients from Front Line positions to MASH hospitals and 87 sorties were flown to rear-area hospitals transporting 122 patients. Thirty pilot pick up alerts and attempts were flown with 15 UN pilots being picked up. At the Peace Camp, 190 sorties were flown to Panmunjom carrying 385 delegates."

Heller spoke too soon because in June Detachment One flew 246 Front Line Evacuations, 144 Hospital evacuations, and 7 pilot pickup attempts, with 5 pilots actually retrieved.

An Inspector General Inspection Team from ARS completed an inspection of the squadron on 8 May 1952. "The team seemed impressed by the overall condition of this unit as they gave us a rating of excellent."

In May, the Detachment One history records that personnel gains included "Captain Leslie W. Lear" and "Airman 1C Bobby D. Holloway."

In June, Heller reported the operation of Detachment One was "still being hindered by the non-availability of H-19 parts in this theater. Items that were particularly scarce were gear boxes and rotor heads."

Effective 9 June operational control of 3rd ARS was assigned by FEAF to the Japan Air Defense Force.

On 10 June Col. Richard Kight, Commander of the Air Rescue Service headquartered in Washington, D.C., arrived at Johnson AB to visit 3rd ARS. The next day he flew to Korea to visit the Commanding General 5th Air Force and the Joint Operations Center at FAF Headquarters, in addition to Detachment One. On 12 June, he returned to K-16 from a visit to Fifth Air Force Headquarters in Seoul. After "dinner at Detachment One Mess," his plan departed for Johnson AB in Japan. He had traveled half way around the world from Washington, D.C to spend a total of one day actually in Korea and just several hours with Detachment One, his one unit stationed on the front lines conducting rescues and medical evacuations, often under fire.

Mission 1890

On 26 June, Detachment One reported that it "lost one H-5 aircraft and crew involved in a pilot pick-up mission. The aircraft and crew plus the retrieved pilot were shot down behind enemy lines. All personnel are listed as missing in action. On the same day, one more H-5 received damage on take-off. The crew of the damaged aircraft was uninjured. This aircraft and crew was supporting the lost crew behind enemy lines at the time of the accident."

Later, the report Engineering section of the unit history report notes that "H-5H #49-2000 was lost be [sic] enemy action on a rescue mission behind enemy lines in Korea."

Even later in the history, a "reconstructed account" was offered "of a pilot pick up mission on which two of our air crew members are missing in action."

"Captain Lear and A/1C Holloway in H5H #2000, made pickup of a downed pilot at CT 8274. When nearing the area Captain Lear requested the CAP to make a pass and check for ground fire, CAP received negative fire. The helicopter went in and received machine gun fire on the first pass, then pulled up and requested the CAP to go in and strafe the area. CAP aircraft beat up the area and the helicopter went in again, made the pick up and started out, receiving heavy machine gun fire. As the helicopter reached about 1200 feet and about six miles south of the pick up point, the CAP reported pieces falling off and helicopter went into a diving spiral. Three men were seen to bail out the right side, the first one got out at approximately 800 feet, his chute opened and he landed all right. He was immediately surrounded by enemy troops and presumed to be captured. The 2nd and 3rd men got out at approximately 500' and 300'. Their chutes did not open."

This highly abbreviated and frequently inaccurate account of Mission 1890 is all that Major Heller entered into the unit's official record for June 1952. Its inaccuracy and incompleteness became a metaphor for Mission 1890 itself—the deadliest helicopter rescue mission of the Korean War—and for what the families endured for years after the mission itself was officially over.

The backup helicopter initially sent to try and rescue the airmen on Mission 1890, itself crashed while heading to the location. Piloted by Captain Jennings, the H-5 crashed during a take-off after it landed to leave the medic behind "in as much as there were three people to be picked up from the downed helicopter," Jennings noted in his report. *[A previous explanation regarding the limitations of the under-powered H-5 is pertinent here.]* A gust of wind drifted the helicopter into barbed wire entanglements throwing the H-5 over on its side "causing major damage to the helicopter."

There is no mention of why an H-19 was not sent instead. The choice of an H-5 to rescue a rescue mission was terribly flawed by the inability of the obsolescent aircraft to perform the mission.

Z Day

In June, the unit history report mentions "Z Day" for the first time, "the day 3rd ARS will be reorganized into Group-Squadron formation." A tentative date of 1 July "cannot be met." The reorganization orders finally went into effect on 14 November 1952—General Order 157, Headquarters Military Air Transport Service. It authorized the redesignation of the 3rd Air Rescue Squadron to the 3rd Air Rescue Group. The subordinate units that were formerly designated Flights "A" through "D" and Detachment One were redesignated as well. Flights "A" through "D" became 36th through 39th Air Rescue Squadrons, respectively. Detachment One was now assigned to the 3rd ARG vice ARS.

Major Emerson E. Heller was relieved as Commander of Detachment One in July by Lt. Colonel Gerald J. Crosson, who flew both helicopters and fixed wing aircraft. Heller had command of the Detachment/squadron for less than three months, an unusually short time before transfer. His early departure left significant fact finding and paperwork unfinished pertaining to those involved in Mission 1890.

By July the squadron was reporting that the "H-19A proved its worth many times over during the month of July. Early in the month the H-19 was committed to front line evacuations from the 8055th MASH to ease the work load of the H-5's. The H-19 proved far superior for this type of operation; greater pay load, higher safety factor, faster evacuations, and easy access to the patients, enabling the medics to administer first aid in flight."

In July Detachment One completed 168 Front Line Evacuations, 153 Hospital Evacuations, 8 Blood Runs, 6 Pilot Pickup Attempts (with 7 pilots picked up), 4 food drops, and the rescue of 710 flood victims.

Had an H-19 been used as the rescue helicopter for Mission 1890, the outcome might well have been much different.

Chapter Four

Crippled Corsair

Wednesday, June 25, 1952
1200
South of Wonsan, North Korea

By noon June 25th, Ensign Ron Eaton was attacking trucks and supply dumps "on the east coast of Korea" with pilots of VA-74—the Bedevilers—and other units. His flight had been assigned a target south of Wonsan, North Korea, an area heavily defended by Communist forces, a

Fires and explosions along dug-in enemy positions *blocking the advance of United Nations ground forces pinpoint the impact of rockets and bombs from Air Force and Navy fighter-bombers during a close air support mission. Enemy positions were spotted by T-6 "Mosquito" observation planes of the 6147th Tactical Control Group. The spotter planes marked the target site using smoke grenades. Fifth Air Force and Navy tactical aircraft then supplied "the knockout blow," the Air Force reported. (NARA)*

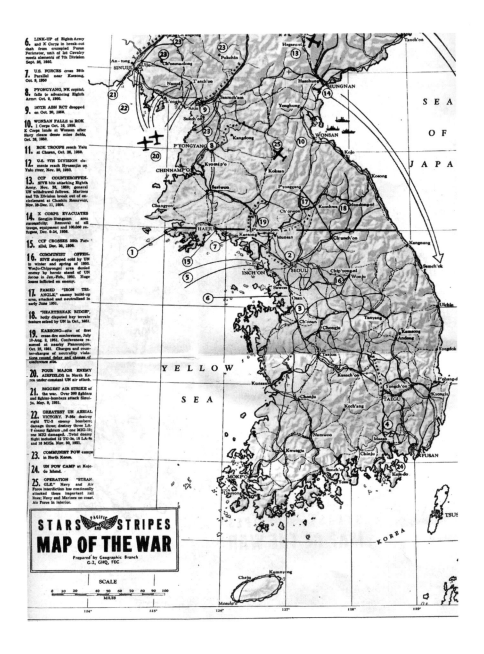

In this "Map of the War" published by Stars and Stripes, the Number 10 indicates the Wonsan area of operations; Number "17" rests over the "Iron Triangle" area; and, Number 18 is the general area where Captain Wayne Lear and SSgt Bob Holloway waited near their rescue helicopter. The so-called "Iron Triangle" of the Korean War—Chorwon-Kumhwa-Pyonggang—was a heavily defended triangularly shaped area of relatively flat terrain about 30 miles north of the 38^{tth}Parallel in the mountains of east-central North Korea. (Holloway)

Napalm bombing attack on a Communist occupied Korean village. (NARA)

strike "on rail lines and on troop and supply concentrations near the front lines," [1] the ship's log noted.

Photo analysis had revealed "the greatest troop and supply accumulations of the war" behind Communist lines, and "intelligence indicated

HVAR In Flight. This photo shows the path of a high-velocity aerial rocket from the point of its release to within a few feet of its target. An F-9F "Pantherjet" of the 1st Marine Air Wing was summoned to the area by a T-6 "Mosquito" observation craft of the 6147th Tactical Control Group working with "Mellow" Control. The target was effectively neutralized. (NARA)

the imminence of a general offensive." ² There were even rumors that the enemy was thinking of kidnapping the U.N. armistice delegation on June 25th. U.S. Marines were prepared to protect the truce team if the talks broke down. The atmosphere at the Panmunjom truce talks was poisonous.

Naval forces had kept the North Korean port of Wonsan under naval siege since shortly after the Inchon landing in September 1950. The blockade was established to provide support for the U.S. Eight Army on the east coast, and to take advantage of the gunnery ships stationed in the area. By June 1952, the siege was "routine" and institutionalized. So much so that the OTC—Officer in Tactical Command—afloat was given the tongue-in-cheek honorific title of "Mayor of Wonsan." A large gilt key was also passed along as the "key to the city."

Communist forces had responded to the siege by installing shore batteries and antiaircraft emplacements. As many as 80,000 troops were stationed in the area, troops that would otherwise have been facing U.N. forces elsewhere on the lines. The siege of Wonsan also required a sizable,

Mosquito Mellow. *Flying high over Korean front lines in an unarmed Fifth Air Force C-47, the crew of "Mosquito Mellow" from the 6147th Tactical Control Group carries on its work as though it were securely located in an office on the ground, the Air Force caption noted. Mosquito Mellow would have responded to the urgent "downed pilot" message from Eaton's flight leader. The message was relayed by Mosquito Mellow to Fifth Air Force Joint Operations Center in Seoul who then directed the 18th Fighter-Bomber Wing to launch Mission 1890. (NARA)*

primarily U.S. Navy—force off shore to maintain offensive operations, defend nearby islands, and to keep the harbor free from mines. Minesweeps, tenders, tugs and destroyers were maintained permanently on station requiring a considerable investment in units, manpower and resources. Some critics maintained that the siege should never have been put in place to begin with. Others, credited it with doing considerable damage to enemy forces and maintaining a drain on his resources. In any event, it had been in place so long that it would be difficult to abandon without appearing to be a victory for Communist forces.

Captured records indicated that nearby North Korean division commanders were pre-occupied with the possibility of an amphibious landing at Wonsan, followed by an Eighth Army thrust north through the so-called "Iron Triangle." Such a concept was considered by UN commanders, but was not attempted. Meanwhile, the enemy kept three infantry divisions in the neighborhood, plus Chinese forces further inland in order to launch a planned all-out counterattack four days after any such amphibious landing. This concentration of troops and military units was dug in all around Wonsan and put up fierce anti-aircraft fire during regular air attacks in the area. The numerous ground forces would also make the extraction of a downed pilot difficult to impossible.

U.S. Naval forces moved ahead with plans and preparations to improve Wonsan area positions by strengthening island fortifications, preparing clear mission statements for ships operating in the area and constructing an emergency airstrip on the island of Yo Do. For six months Army and Air Force construction units had not moved ahead with the plans to build the airstrip. In May 1952, the Navy received permission for one of its amphibious construction battalions—SeaBees—to build the strip. While under fire from nearby enemy positions, the SeeBees completed the 2,400-foot runway in sixteen days instead of the 45 days that had been projected for the project. By July, eight Corsairs, damaged or low on fuel, had used the emergency strip.

Eaton's flight path took him through the heavy defenses in and around Wonsan. He and his flight had hit their targets near the front lines—"a truck pool and supply concentration southwest of Wonsan"—shortly after noon. Soon, they were headed back to the Bon Homme Richard at an altitude of about 10,000 feet, not a height at which anti-aircraft fire was usually effective. However, Communist gunners were well dug in, ranged and often directed by radar. Either a well aimed round or a "lucky hit" struck Eaton's Corsair.

He radioed that he had been hit and advised his flight leader that the oil pressure was dropping rapidly. He was ordered to return to the carrier. Two of his wingmen were assigned to escort him back and to provide cover, if needed.

Meanwhile, he attempted to head the crippled Corsair towards the coastline and the relative safety of water where rescue would be much easier. The mountainous terrain would make a belly landing much more risky that bailing out, if that was necessary.

The damage to the aircraft's engine was extensive, however, and in a few short minutes, Eaton radioed that he was abandoning his aircraft. Eaton parachuted to the ground—not realizing that he was landing in the middle of a major concentration of enemy troops and emplacements.

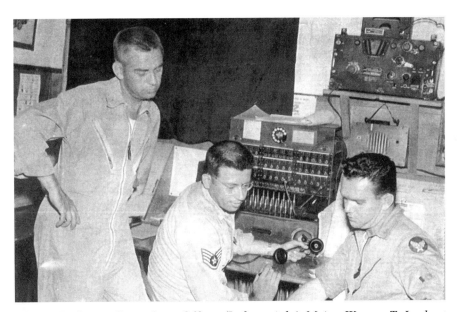

18th F-B Group Operations Office. (Left to right) Major Warren T. Lenhart (standing), S/Sgt. George Falder and Capt. Ernest Woodrick. An on-duty team such as that led above by Major Lenhart received the JOC message from Seoul and alerted the 67th Squadron RESCAP for take-off. (Photo courtesy Ione R. Lenhart)

Chapter Five

Ron Eaton

"The Hardluck Kid"

Ronald Eaton's father, Bernard, had been born in Nova Scotia on April 3, 1898 and moved to the United States in 1917. Six years later, he married Elsie Anderson of Lynn, Massachusetts.

Young Ron grew up on Park Street West in North Reading, Massachusetts. When he was about 7 or 8, the Eaton family moved several miles away to Wilmington, Massachusetts, a beautiful little village on Silver Lake about 25 miles northwest of Boston.

Ronald Eaton *was born in this Park Street West house in North Redding, Massachusetts.*

In 1938, the Eaton Family portrait *included: Everard Eaton, father Bernard Eaton, and Forrest Eaton in the back row. The center row included Bernie, Eva, mother Elsie, and Ron "Ronnie." The front row included: "the twins" Verlie and Verna, and Joyce.*

Silver Lake *creates a focal point near the center of Wilmington, Massachusetts. When Ron Eaton was a teenager there, he worked at the nearby ice house washing off the straw used to insulate the precious necessity.*

In 1945, the Eaton family moved again.

For some time, Bernard and Elsie had had their eye on a graceful, three-storied Victorian home located at the apex of a major intersection in Wilmington at 80 Main Street. It stood on a large, grassy lot that extended from Silver Lake down to Lubbers Brook. The triangular shaped lot was located at the junction of Glen Road and Main Street. Glen Road was once the "main" road into the center of town and dated back to at least 1741. The easterly bounds of the lot included an old ditch that dated to 1720 or earlier, that connected Silver Lake with the brook and served to keep the millpond of the Harnden Mill at the required operating level for the spillway.

After they moved into the 80 Main Street home, Ron was active in the Boy Scouts and with his church group, the South Tewksbury Methodist Church, just a short distance from their new home. [1]

In those days, Silver Lake was known as Sandy Pond. It was a quiet and beautiful place. There were still ice houses across the pond owned by the Union Ice Company of Boston. The superintendent of the Ice Company, John Wilde, lived nearby. Each winter ice was harvested and stored, and in the summer it was sent to Boston by freight car, to be sold. It was a thriving business.

Growing Up In Wilmington

In high school, Ron played on the Wilmington High School football team for three years. "Number 15" played hard. Several years later, his Navy records noted that he had sustained a broken arm when he was 15 playing football.

Eaton had blue eyes and wavy brown hair. He packed 152 muscular pounds on a wiry 5'8" frame. He was strong, agile and had fast reflexes—all good qualities for high school athletics and later, for service as a Navy fighter pilot.

"Ron worked every job he could get as a teenager—from shoveling snow off the railroad tracks to cutting ice from local ponds or washing off the hay and sawdust they used to insulate the precious ice from the summer heat," remembered his sister, Joyce. Ron called her "Joy." When he wasn't working at some job to earn spending money, he was with his many friends. The high school dances down at the grange hall were very popular.

Eaton graduated from Wilmington High School in 1947, very popular with his friends and a hard worker with plans for the future. His friends remember him to this day as a "good guy...a great friend."

The Wilmington High School "Blue Book, Class of 1947," in the "Can You Imagine" Section lists Eaton, R. "A woman-hater." Ron Eaton, most assuredly, was not a woman hater. Elsewhere in the yearbook, in the "How We Recognize Them" section, Ron Eaton was described "as a little chap with big ideas."

The Blue Book noted that Ron Eaton was in the college preparatory program throughout his high school years, played football during his Sophomore, Junior and Senior years, and sang in the Glee Club throughout

By 1948, the Eaton Family *included: mother Elsie in front row holding Wayne, Joyce and Bernard. The center row included Verna, Forrest, and Ronald. The back row included: Bernie, Everard, Eva and Verlie.*

high school—both the mixed chorus and the boys chorus. His hobby was "sports." His pet peeve was "wise guys." His ambition was to become an "electrical engineer." Ron was on call to run the movie projector—Bell & Howell or an AmPro—and was selected as a "hall monitor."

In the Class of 1947 "Will," the members of the "Class of 1947 do make and declare this to be our last will and testament"…to Ron Eaton, "a small black notebook so that he may keep a list of all his women."

On 27 February 1947, even before he graduated from high school, Ron Eaton enlisted in the Naval Reserve. In some respects, his choice of military service was pre-ordained—all his brothers had chosen the Navy, as well. One of his brothers, Wayne, later explained with tongue in cheek that he had chosen the Navy because if he ever had to die, at least he would die clean.

Acadia University

If he was going to become an electrical engineer, Ron's plans for the future included a college education.

He decided to attend Acadia University in Wolfville, Nova Scotia, Canada. The small, but prestigious school was located near his father's

Aerial view of Acadia University in Wolfville, Nova Scotia. Eaton attended Acadia for two years as an Engineering student. (Acadia University)

boyhood home. In fact, his grandmother, Florence May and Aunt Alba, still lived not far away.

Horton Academy in Nova Scotia at Horton (now Wolfville) was founded by Baptists in 1828. Ten years later, an attempt to name the institution "Queen's College" after Queen Victoria was denied and Acadia College (University in 1891) was adopted.

From the start, Acadia established a curriculum that included "instruction in the usual branches of English Literature, and of scientific, classical, and other studies, which usually comprise the course of education at an Academy and College. The new institution was to be open to "children and persons of any religious denomination" and it was suggested that the diet and dress of the Scholars should be of the plainest kind."

Over the years, the small school grew steadily and acquired the faculty, buildings and funding needed to offer a quality education for its students. By the time Ron Eaton attended in the late 1940's, Acadia was in the midst of an enrollment "boom" of veterans returning after the war to obtain or continue their educations. Eaton was also a student there when Dr. Watson Kirkconnel was installed as the new President, replacing Dr. Frederic William Patterson, who had served since 1923. A new building program was soon underway.

During his two year program at Acadia, Eaton attended many of his classes in Carnegie Hall, the Engineering Building. He lived at the Westwood Residence during his Freshman year, and moved to War Memorial House for his second year.

Eaton was a diligent student who was constantly challenged to find enough money to pay for his education.

Carnegie Hall at Acadia University, *the Engineering Building where Ron Eaton attended classes. (Gerald Wood, Wolfville, NS)*

Acadia University Engineering Class of 1948 poses for its yearbook photograph. Eaton stands in the third row slightly right of the photograph's center. (Acadia University)

On September 11, 1948, he wrote to his father: "I have been at surveying camp for the last week and a half. Things are going along just fine at camp, I know the instructors personally, and if I need any help they are glad to oblige. I went over to see Grandma last Sunday and she told me that Uncle Clem was going to let me borrow $200.00 to help me finish off the year. I have $200 for waiting on tables and Mom has $90. I have $24 for books and $20 or maybe less from last years waiting, towel return and breakage deposit totaling $534 (it might be a little less)." He asked that his Mom send the money "so I can make my first down payment of $150.00." He also asked that she "see what she can do about getting me a couple of overcoats. My old [Navy] peacoat will do to bang around in. Hope things are going along okay at home. If you need my help at home Dad, write to me and tell me so, and I will come home. Tell Forrest (if I stay this year), that I am sorry I can't make his wedding as much as I would like to. But things just work that way. He missed Everard's. I miss his."

Six weeks later, on November 1, 1948, Eaton recorded the various expenses he was trying to cover by waiting tables. Tuition and board for Eaton at Acadia University was $290.00 per semester. Chemistry and physics laboratory fees added $10, plus "universal fees" and laundry services, brought the semester total to $333.50. By waiting tables, Eaton was able to reduce the total by $44.70 per semester.

As he neared the end of his third semester at Acadia, on January 30, 1949, Eaton happily reported that exams were over. His grades included:

Chemistry (B), Math (B), Physics (D-), Drawing 2 (B), Surveying (A-) and Engineering 4 (B). Classes resumed the following day and it was "back to the old grind….Brr-rrr it's cold in this room," he wrote from Memorial Residence Hall. As in most of his letters home while in college, Eaton outlined what he was doing to earn or borrow enough money to keep himself in school.

Two weeks later, on February 13, 1949, Eaton had not heard from his parents "in close to a month, what has happened?" He was concerned that a "statement" he needed from them regarding financial aid from the University had not yet arrived. "If we expect to get any help from the University I better have it in by this coming Saturday."

He was taking Engineering, English, Drawing, and Physics.

"Out of 36 hours of class a week" Eaton had just "9 hours off from class in a week to do my homework…you can easily see that that is not enough time. So I have to spend practically all my evening working and boy, do I get tired come the end of a week. We are told to spend 5 hours of study on each subject a week and I have 8 subjects. Pretty rugged!! Don't forget to drop me a line."

"Dad, do you remember the shoes you tapped [repaired] for me while I was home? Well, your knife slipped and it cut the side of my shoe. There is a hole in the boot of my shoe (upper part_ ½ [inch] long in the crease that bends when I walk, the soles are worn out now, and on that side there is a piece 1-inch long taken out that you nailed to, so the cobbler can't put another sole on them. On the whole they are pretty well beat. Considering how much wear they have given me I can't complain. I got them a year ago next month, and have worn them practically every day since. So, if you find a pair of shoes around somewhere, please forward them—size 10 to 10 ½. I will be alright for a while, but do the best you can. How are things at home? Is Dad back to work? (I hope!)."

On February 20, 1949, Eaton happily reported, "We needn't worry any longer about the money. I went over to see Mr. Mosher yesterday and gave him my statement telling him what I thought I could give him by the end of this semester. Counting my waiting, income tax return and the $8 I'll get on the few books I turn back in, I figured that I will have roughly

Ron Eaton's Acadia University yearbook photograph. (Acadia University)

$190.000. My bill is going to be approximately $320 so that means I will have to borrow about $130 from the University. Mr. Mosher looked up my marks, conduct, activities, etc. to find out what kind of a student I am and if it was worth the loan. He asked me how old I was and I told him 19, so he asked me if there was anyone to sign for the loan, such as, Dad or Mom. I told him Dad would sign, so he told me to go over to see him April First, and he would give me a paper to send to Dad to have signed. So, you will get a letter with the paper in it about April 4th or 5th."

"Dad, do you want to keep your eyes and ears open for a job for me when I get back. Something in my line. Because come May all of the students will be out looking for work, and if I have a few places in mind to try it will help a lot."

"Received your letter Thursday. Thanks a lot for the $2 it sure will come in handy. Also thank the kids for the Valentines. They are very cute. Sorry to hear that Joy and Wayne are sick. Hope that they are both better by now."

"I got tired of being waiter's waiter, so I switched over to waiting on students. I like it alright, it is change. There is more work to waiting on students but it is alright."

Navy Flight Training

In 1949 Ron Eaton earned his two-year degree from Acadia University. Almost immediately, the Navy ordered him to active duty at NAS Pensacola, Florida.

On March 25, 1950, Ron Eaton was appointed a Student Officer with the rank of Lt. (j.g.). As Commander of the Second Platoon in Company B, he wore "two gold bars" on his collar instead of those small anchors. Becoming a student officer entitled Eaton "to overnights on Saturday night" and gave him Liberty on Wednesday night. He commanded 35 Naval Air Cadets—for two weeks. He was soon assigned to Whiting Field—to start flying.

"Keep your eyes open for the Navy Air Cadets in the news reel," he alerted his parents, "as the Warner Bros. Pathe news took some news reels of us this morning. You may see me on the outside rank of the group marching by. These news reels were taken at the Graduation of Class 24-49. We graduate in two weeks—too bad they couldn't have waited two weeks and you could have seen me get my diploma from Pre-Flight. I understand that they take individual pictures of each Cadet that graduates from Pre-Flight and send them directly to the local newspaper of the Cadet. So, keep a look out in the Sun in about two weeks time."

Completing Pre-Flight

"I finally made it through Pre-Flight," Eaton wrote to his parents on 8 April 1950, just an hour after graduating. "All of the officers," he said, considered it "the most Military and most excellently executed Graduation they have seen," Eaton wrote.

Eaton earned the highest mark in his class in Navigation. In the final class standing he ranked in the middle of the class.

His check out physical revealed that he had gained 14 pounds since joining the Navy and he had put on 1 ½ inches around the chest. However, he had "stayed the same height and kept the same waist."

His next assignment was at Whiting Field. Soon, he would actually be flying.

"If we don't get our leave in June, I am going to pick up a little buggy down here for a couple or three hundred. This Whiting Airfield I have been telling you about is 45 miles from Pensacola and there are no other large cities around. So, when Liberty comes around we need some means of transportation."

Ron only owed Uncle Clem $70 at this point. "We had to buy some clothes" for graduation, Eaton explained "so that we could have a full [sea] bag for our inspection. Also our class party is tonight and that is going to take money. However, I'll have Uncle Clem paid off by the middle of May and I have until June to have it all back. Of course, then comes Grandma and Aunt Alba."

He wished them a happy Easter and explained that "we are going to have a sunrise service over on the football field at 10:00 a.m. And, being a choir member I am supposed to attend, so I guess I might as well stay up all night after our party tonight. Ha Ha."

"Boy, did I ever pick up a sunburn last Sunday down at the beach! It has mostly turned to tan now though. I'll be right black before I get back home next."

"You never tell me how Brother Wayne is making out in school nor the other kids. How about a little 'info' in the next letter, huh?"

Whiting Field

Eaton had been assigned to Whiting Field "for almost two weeks now," by April 20, 1950. "I got the first mail I have received from anyone yesterday." He hadn't received "any letters from home in a long while. 'Wot happened?' Is everybody so busy getting Eva ready for her wedding that there is no time to write?"

Eaton was up at 0530, get the room squared away, then to chow at 0630 and "time for morning formation." At 0700 "we have to be down to the hanger at the squadron and have to hang around and watch the blackboards 8x10 feet and see at what time our flights start. We have flights going on every hour on the half hour starting at 0730. I haven't got an instructor yet so I have to hang around all morning waiting for an instructor. I should get one tomorrow, though. At the beginning our class will have an hours flying time every morning between 0730-1200. There is not any way to tell what time it is coming up until they post it on these blackboards."

The afternoons were devoted to Ground School from 1300-1700, followed by athletics from 1700-1800. Then evening chow, an hour to rest and then start on homework. "Pretty busy day, what do you say?"

Also on 20 April, Naval Aviation Cadet Ronald Eaton put tongue firmly in cheek and composed a letter to "Mr. and Mrs. Eaton," in response to a wedding invitation he had received inviting him to his sister, Eva's wedding. "This is to inform you that I will be unable to attend the wedding of your daughter, Evangeline, because the U.S. Navy will not grant permission for a leave of absence at this time. I would like very much to be present, but as you can see, it is utterly impossible. I wish to send my best wishes to your daughter and also to Mr. Brown. I hope they will be very happy. Very truly yours, Ronald D. Eaton"

"I got your cookies Mom," Eaton wrote on May 27, 1950, "and they were wonderful, as usual. They all got here in one piece…the boys have all asked me to thank you for them as they really hit the spot Tuesday night when we were working at Navigation."

Eaton was nearly through with Ground School, just two more weeks to go. He had accumulated 13 hops, including one with a "check pilot" who let Eaton take the controls. The check pilot gave Eaton an "up" and told him he "flew an above average hop." Three cadets received "downs" that went into their records and were, "of course, given more attention."

Ready To Solo

He was scheduled to solo in about a week. "What a thrill that is going to be, up in the air all alone with no instructor to tell me what to do," he noted.

"Got a look at my jacket [personnel record]," he wrote, "and it looks pretty good, if I do say so myself. Yesterday, I did so well in my recovery from stalls and spins, that the instructor took over and we climbed to 8,000 feet. We did some acrobatics, we flew upside down, did some barrel rolls and split "S's" and a couple of wing overs. Boy, what fun that is!! After that, he took me down to a small field and we shot precision landings. Precision landing is the art of setting a plane down between two yellow lines that are twenty feet apart."

Eaton inquired about his brothers and sisters. "Is Wayne going to get promoted this year? He better get busy on his Arithmetic if he wants to get anywhere, tell him. How about the girls? Are they getting along alright? Is Bernie working now?"

Besides, I love flying

"The Navy gave us NavCad's a foul blow a week ago," Eaton reported. "They came out with the news that us NavCads will not all be able to serve with the Fleet after we get our wings. Only one out of three will be selected for active duty. On account of this a lot of fellows have been quitting. You remember my buddy from Vermont, well he is one of the many that are quitting. But I figure this way if enough of them quit the better chance I have. Besides, I love flying, and I don't know where I would go to work if I did leave or get washed out. You could keep your eyes open in case I don't make it. I am due to get my wings about one year from June. So, if I don't get my two years with the Fleet I will try to go back to school and fly for the Reserve on the weekends. I will be able to pick up $60-$100 flying just a few hours on the weekends. Another thing I was thinking about was checking to see if the R.C.A.F. is looking for pilots and what the deal is on it."

There would be no leave at the end of June in 1950 as there had been in previous years. When the Navy began to run out of money at the end of the fiscal year (June 30), in previous years it would cut back on purchases of aviation gasoline, and give its NavCad students more leave. But not this year," he noted.

"So, I won't get home again until next Christmas," Eaton told them. "I am a little disappointed too, as I bought a nice set of whites for the leave. Those white uniforms sure look nice. I will have a couple of snaps [photographs] taken and send them to you if you like."

Ground School Completed

"I received your letter earlier this week," he wrote on June 9, 1950, "but I have had no time to answer it because I have been going into Pensacola every night to choir practice. Pensacola is having a Fiesta. They call it the Fiesta of Five Flags because Pensacola has been ruled by five different countries or governments. The Navy has contributed a choir of fifty voices. They have provided the transportation every night and furnished us with special liberty much to the envy of a lot of other Navcads."

Eaton reported that he "didn't get to solo this week as the weather has been too bad. We have had a stationary front hovering over the vicinity since last Sunday, so I only got one hop in this week. And don't tell anyone, but it was the worst hop I have ever flown and ever hope to fly. My instructor even got a little impatient with me but he apologized later saying that I was doing so well on my last five hops that he couldn't imagine what had gotten into me. I blame it on not having flown in so long. One hop every four days for two weeks gets a guy a little rusty especially if he is just learning. My marks in Ground School are up with the best. I got the highest mark in the class on the Navigation final. It gave me a final average of 54 out of a possible 60. I should be checking out of Ground School a week from today and become an all day flying student."

He received a letter from "Grandma the same day I got a letter from you. She said that Aunt Alba has been [ill with] the Flu." Eaton noted that he owed Grandma and Aunt Alba $150.00 and went on to discuss how he was planning to pay them back.

"I guess the story of Gas Leave has been fired into a cocked hat, as they said definitely that there will be no Gas Leave as there is plenty of gasoline."

During that period the Navy would also grant "basket leave" to students under instruction over the Christmas Holiday period. Leave "chits" would be prepared and submitted. Following the student's safe return from Christmas leave, the chits would be destroyed, thus not counting against the 30 days per year of "Annual Leave" allotted to each serviceman or woman.

Eaton had received Elsie's cookies and reported "they were wonderful. And all the other boys send their thanks."

"They are giving us a course on the Atomic Bomb and its effects and how to counteract the deadly radioactive ray it releases. The course is very interesting and they have a movie with every lecture."

"Well, I have to get my room squared away as liberty starts immediately and I have to get cleaned up before I go to the Fiesta tonight. The Fiesta has been going on all this week and will wind up with a bang Saturday night."

Gunnery Runs In A Hellcat

"Golly, I haven't written to you in a long while have I," Eaton began a letter to his mother on March 11, 1951. "Time is just slipping between my fingers. You see I am flying two hops a day two hours apiece. I am making gunnery runs in my "Hellcat" now and started flying instruments last Thursday. I have an instrument hop tomorrow morning at six o'clock."

Eaton thanked Elsie for "the cookies and my handkerchiefs."

"Also, the fudge was very good and my roommates and I all appreciated it very much."

"My buddy Johnny Hansford and I were in town last weekend and we were looking over the used cars. After looking over many autos not caring about buying anything anyway, we came across a 1940 Plymouth for $50.00 as it was. They charged us $2.05 for transfer papers. So, for $26.02 ½ apiece, John and I got transportation to and from town, a radio, heater, spotlight, overdrive and everything works. I can't understand why they were selling it so low, but the only things that are a little fouled up are the electrical wiring under the instrument panel. I've got so many loose wires I don't know what they go to. The tires are fairly good. We have three good recaps and one smooth tire on the car. We have two spare tires both smooth. The cars uses very little gas—19 miles/gal. And it uses no oil at all."

Eaton sent Elsie "some money as I only got $50.00 last payday."

Eaton inquired about his father and asked Elsie "how things are going with Dad. Your last letter sounded very promising. Do you think that there will be any chance of Dad and I taking that trip to Florida. And maybe Bernie and you if you would like to."

On 23 April 1951, at NAS Pensacola, Florida, he completed the demanding physical required before his appointment as a Naval Air Cadet. Ron Eaton—229 25 61—was well on his way to earning his Navy "Wings of Gold."

Wearing Civilian Clothes Again

"It sure feels good to wear civilian clothes after so long," Eaton wrote on June 10, 1951. He was then stationed at NAS Corpus Christi, Texas assigned to the Naval School of All-Weather Flight.

Eaton made particular note of his "individual room…running hot and cold water in each room with a medicine cabinet with a mirror over each sink. Our beds are inner spring mattresses and our beds themselves have springs six inches high. I have a huge closet for hanging all my uniforms. An overhead light, a floor lamp (adjustable to any degree of brightness), a light over my medicine cabinet. Also, I have a straight back chair and a writing desk, an over stuffed lounge chair, a small magazine table, and a dresser with a large mirror on it. My dresser has six drawers in it. Oh yes, I forgot something, they also gave me a waste paper basket, the floors are tile and the walls are well painted. The shower is situated right across the hall from my room. Also, there are Venetian blinds on the windows. Do you remember I told you that they were not taking enough out of my pay, Mom? Well, they finally decided that they would make up for that by taking all of what they didn't take out, all out at once, so you will get a check for $183.00. Use as much of it as you need, Mom for bills that are bothering you, etc. You should start getting $124.00 a month in your allotment, Mom. Also, I was thinking of claiming Wayne or one of the girls too,. That might give you more money."

Eaton also suggested that now the Navy had given him an insurance policy, his parents could explore using any existing policy on him for its cash value.

Eaton announced he would try to get home in late July on leave.

His next duty station was Norfolk, Virginia. However, he didn't "expect to be there any longer than time enough to get my orders to a permanent squadron. I have been lucky to date and have got everything I have ever put in for in the Navy. The only thing I have left that I want is to be stationed at Quonset Point, Rhode Island or Squantum, Massachusetts. This is probably the only thing that I won't get. They will likely say we want you to go to Jacksonville, Florida."

"Well, this has been quite a long letter, so I think I will finish it off.

Could Parents Be "Dependents"?

"I guess this letter will have to be mostly about business," Eaton warned his parents in his next letter of June 20, 1951. "About that allotment Mom, the only way they can approve it is by my sending you more than half of your income each month." Apparently, Eaton was exploring how to get his parents counted as his "dependents." If that could be done, they would receive an allotment from the government and they would have other benefits, including access to the base exchange and commissary.

At that point, Eaton was sending his parents $183.00 per month of his salary.

New Naval aviator Ensign Ron Eaton poses in "choker whites" with proud sisters Verlie and Joyce to his right and Verna to his left. A friend, Shirley Russell, stands at far right.

Proud Mom, Elsie Eaton *poses with her new Ensign beside the parlor window of their home in Wilmington, Massachusetts soon after Ron earned his Navy "Wings of Gold." (Eaton family)*

Eaton was worried about his father wanting to be claimed as a dependent. He was concerned that "it would really foul me up if they ever found out. So I am going to have to go down to disbursing tomorrow and stop the allotment. However, Mom if you need some money don't hesitate to write as I will be able to scrape some up," Eaton wrote.

Eaton was now flying the SNB (Beechcraft) trainer. "It is a two engine passenger plane. It will carry a pilot, co-pilot and five passengers. I made my first five landings in it yesterday." *[Navy slang for the SNB was "bug smasher."]*

"Boy are we treated with respect around here now that we have got our Wings and Commission," Eaton noted. "Everybody saying 'Yes, sir!' and 'No, sir!'"

As a newly commissioned Ensign, Eaton was now required to have his personal calling cards. "Tell Forrest he is not the only one that has cards. I have my own private ones," Eaton explained. "They are compulsory, as we have to have them when we report aboard a new station and pay our social call to the Captain or Commanding Officer. Also, when the Captain puts on a party we leave them in a platter especially provided. Also, tell that brother of mine he owes me two letters."

Dolly and Ron

Ron's sister, Joyce, graduated from Wilmington High School in 1951. One of her school friends was a classmate, Dorothy Sharp. Her friends called her "Dolly."

Dorothy "Dolly" Sharp and Ensign Ronald Dow Eaton had these matching portraits made just prior to his departure for a deployment with VF-74 aboard the USS Bon Homme Richard to the Korean War theatre of operations. They had agreed to marry upon his return. (Dorothy Sharp Clements)

Dolly Sharp was born in Cambridge, Massachusetts on 23 August 1933, the third of five children—three boys and two girls. The Sharp family moved to Wilmington in 1935, when Dolly was two.

Dolly attended Wilmington schools and graduated in 1951, receiving her diploma at the same time as her friend, Joyce Eaton. Dolly did not know Joyce's older brother, Ron, who was away at Acadia College and then on active duty with the Navy. Besides, the Eatons lived near the Tewksbury town line and the Sharps lived near the Andover-North Reading area. There were no bus lines to connect the miles between them. The young people socialized at school. During the summer the families in Dolly's neighborhood "chummed with the kids in North Reading."

After graduation, Dolly worked as a Secretary at New England Life Insurance Company in Boston. In the evenings, she attended classes at Burdett College.

Not long after she graduated from high school, Dolly met Ron on a blind date soon after he had completed Navy flight training. Through mutual friends, Audrey and Tupper Riddle, Dolly and Ron "went out to a movie and got a bite to eat." For the both of them, "it was love at first sight." Soon, Dolly and Ron were making plans for the future.

Nineteen year old Dolly and the 23-year old Ensign dated for over a year.

Even though Ron was heavily involved with his squadron and in getting ready for a deployment on an aircraft carrier heading to the western Pacific, he redoubled his efforts to get leave whenever he could to get home. After he returned from a "REFTRA" (refresher training exercise) in Guantanamo Bay, Cuba, they "spent a lot of time together." Before long they "were making plans to marry when he returned from Korea," Dolly explained. They talked over his plans to return to Acadia University and to complete his Bachelor's Degree.

On some of the occasions when young Eaton would get back home, he would fly himself in his F4U-4 "Corsair," fighter-bomber aircraft. "Whenever he flew over the house he would always dip his wings," Dolly remembered, "there was no mistaking his plane with the bent wings. My family always enjoyed that and we waved to him," she recalled.

Ron took her down to NAS South Weymouth to a dance. In his high collar dress white uniform—"choker whites" he called them—he was very dashing and handsome.

He took Dolly down to the flight line to show her the airplane that he was flying, the F4U-4 Corsair. It was a powerful fighter aircraft with the distinctive "gull" wing. But to Dolly it didn't look very big at all. "You're going to fight a war—in this?" she asked him.

He was wonderful to his family. Ron would take Dolly with him shopping at the local stores where he would fill many baskets with food and supplies that went back to 80 Main Street.

He thought of other people before he thought of himself, she remembered.

Dolly Sharp's younger brother, Don, was very impressed with his sister's boyfriend, Ron Eaton. Once, when Ron had visited their home, he had brought with him some of the equipment he carried with him in the air-

Ensign Ron Eaton flew into various Naval facilities near Boston any time he could during the months preceeding his deployment with VF-74 in Spring 1952. Here he poses with his Hellcat at NAS South Weymouth. (Eaton Family)

plane—equipment that he was counting on to help get him to safety when it was needed.

On that occasion, Ron sat down in the middle of the Sharp's living room and spread his "gear" out all around him and explained to his rapt audience all the things that were necessary for him to do if his plane were ever forced down. For the rest of their lives, Dolly and Don would remember Ron Eaton sitting there surrounded

Pampered Plymouth. Ron Eaton was very particular about his car, its appearance and maintenance. (Eaton family)

by his Mae West, flares, inflatable raft and other equipment, explaining patiently the function of each. He was emphatic that if he had to "ditch" his aircraft, he had to "make sure to remove all identifying marks from his person," Dolly recalled.

Ron Eaton was "a very warm and caring person." It was obvious to Dolly and her family that "in all ways he truly loved his family, whether it was a trip to the grocery story to make sure his Mom had the items she needed before his next trip home, teasing his sisters, or helping his youngest brother, Wayne, with his homework," Dolly remembered.

Eaton was always "loving and thoughtful to me," Sharp remembered. She could only recall one disagreement with Ron, and "that had something to do with Ron giving my Dad's car a push—very carefully—to the nearest garage—with his car." Eaton "loved that car and didn't want any dents in it!" Sharp recalled.

Dolly and Ron loved "musicals, whether it was on stage or at the movies." Eaton's favorite song was *"You'll Never Walk Alone."* Before he left on what was to be his last deployment, Dolly bought him a small, 45 rpm record player and some records to take with him. Ensigns shared a small stateroom on the carrier, but she knew he would fit that record player in somewhere—and he did.

As their relationship deepened, Ron and Dolly began to make plans for the future. He was a Baptist; Dolly was Catholic. They both "had a great love of God" however, and often discussed the Bible and their faiths. Dolly went to church with him on several occasions, but he did not get to go to church with her before he left to report to the Bon Homme Richard.

Both Ron and Dolly had come from families that included members of different religious faiths, yet they all loved each other and respected the differing views. Dolly's father was Methodist and she "loved him dearly." She "fully accepted the fact that Ron was Baptist and I didn't want to change him. He came to the realization that I couldn't become a Baptist and so we agreed to get married in the Catholic Church. We agree that if my Mom and Dad had a wonderful mixed marriage, it was possible for us."

Ron obtained leave in February and went home to see his girl and his family. "I had my wedding gown," Ron's sister Joyce recalled. "I was getting married September 14th. I showed him my gown. He told me how many missions he had to complete and told me he was going to do all he could to finish them so he could get home again."

The Be-Devilers VF-74

Soon after he was designated a Naval aviator, Ensign Ron Eaton began training in the F4U-4 Corsair, and was then ordered to join VF-74, the "Bedevilers," a component squadron of Carrier Air Group 7.

The squadron he was joining was originally established in 1944 as VBF-20, flying Corsair's from NAS Wildwood, New Jersey. By November 1946, the squadron was redesignated as VF-10A and assigned to CAG-9 onboard USS Philippine Sea (CVA 47). The squadron was then based at NAS Charleston, Rhode Island. After four years as VF-10A, the squadron was renamed VF-92 in 1948. On 15 January 1950, the Bedevilers were designated VF-74 and would retain that number for the next forty four years.

Shortly after becoming VF-74, the BeDevilers reverted to the F4U-4 Corsair and deployed to the Mediterranean aboard USS Franklin D. Roosevelt (CVA 42).

In May 1952, CAG-7 was transferred to the Pacific Fleet and deployed to Korean waters onboard the USS Bon Homme Richard (CVA 31). From May 1952 through January 1953, the squadron flew more than 1,500 combat sorties, primarily ground attack missions against North Korean targets.

Toward the end of the deployment the Squadron began the transition from prop-driven Corsairs to the F2H Banshee, the first jet aircraft for the squadron.

VF-74 Prepares for WestPac Deployment

From 1 January 1952 until 16 May 1952, VF 74 was attached for operational control to Air Group Seven. The squadron administrative command was located at NAS Quonset Point, Rhode Island. However, the squadron conducted various operations during that period that took it to NAS Atlantic City, New Jersey, NAAS Oceana, Virginia (near Virginia Beach), and aboard USS Leyte (CV 32) operating off Quonset Point, Rhode Island.

While it was based at Quonset Point, the squadron was "engaged in the usual program of squadron training interspersed with various operational tasks assigned by Commander Air Force, Atlantic Fleet." For one week in January and for two weeks in February, the squadron worked with OPDEV 4 at Atlantic City, New Jersey. "In these operations, our planes conducted operations as directed by OpDev 4 in the evaluation of a special and highly classified project," the squadron reported. 1

During the first week in February, "our planes and pilots operated from NAAS Oceana participating in Air Dex (Air Defense Exercise) "George." These operations were conducted for the most part for the benefit of the ships operating off the coast. However, our pilots got good experience in conducting aerial strikes in various sized strike groups against a task force at sea."

When the squadron received its order to deploy with Air Group Seven to the west coast, it was "confronted with three major tasks"—screening of pilots and enlisted personnel to determine those who were due for release from duty during the projected cruise and who would therefore require replacements, exchange of aircraft in order to obtain a complement of planes whose service tours would expire after completion of the project cruise, and incorporation of changes and modifications to the aircraft necessary for combat operations." There was also the challenge of "intensive operational training to bring the proficiency of the pilots up to the optimum."

The Squadron averaged 24 pilots and 150 enlisted personnel during this period. However, in screening the personnel "who were eligible for early release and who did not desire to extend their enlistments or active duty contracts, it was found that 7 pilots were requesting early release to inactive duty and some 82 men were either scheduled for early discharge or rotation to shore duties." One pilot, LTJG Thomas M. Kastner, was still hospitalized as a result of nighttime flying accident and was not medically fit for flight duties. Commander Air Force Atlantic Fleet "soon provided 8 volunteer pilots with experience in the F4U 'Corsair' and the necessary enlisted rates so that upon deployment the squadron was at its complement of 25 pilots and 107 enlisted men."

The squadron's Maintenance Department was soon busy transferring "old aircraft and accepting new planes and installing armor plate." Other planes were sent to NAS Norfolk, Virginia where FASRON 3 installed new IFF (Interrogative Friend or Foe) equipment. All of the planes were also sent to the Overhaul and Repair activity at NAS Quonset Point, Rhode Island to have AERO 14 rocket launchers installed on the aircraft.

Training for the pilots was increased to include intensive rocket and bombing flights, plus close air support training exercises at "Joe English Pond north of Boston with TACRON 4, receiving indoctrination that was later to prove very worthwhile."

In April, carrier landing training—daylight and night time—was stepped up and "occupied most of the flight schedule." On 25 April the Squadron began operating with USS Leyte (CV 32) "for carrier qualifications and refresher qualification both day and night for all of the pilots. The squadron left the Leyte on 6 May 1952, allowing just four days "to assemble itself for the forthcoming deployment to the West Coast. Commander Charles D. Fonvielle, Jr., Squadron Commander, departed NAS Quonset Point on 9 May 1952 with the sixteen squadron planes, and proceeded to NAS San Diego, California via Dallas, Texas. The sixteen pilots and planes spent two days in Dallas visiting the Chance Vought factory there, where most of the pilots were interested to learn that the Corsair was still rolling off the assembly lines."

USS Bon Homme Richard (CV 31), a 27,100-ton Essex *class aircraft carrier, was built at the New York Navy Yard, Brooklyn, New York. She was commissioned in late 1944, just in time to join other new, fast carriers in the Pacific combat zone in March 1945 that took part in the final raids on Japan. With the end of hostilities in mid-August,* Bon Homme Richard *continued operations off Japan until September, when she returned to the United States. "Magic Carpet" personnel transportation duties occupied her into 1946. She was thereafter generally inactive until decommissioning at Seattle, Washington, in January 1947. Bon Homme Richard was recommissioned in January 1951 for Korean War service and deployed to the Western Pacific that May, sending her planes against enemy targets in Korea until the deployment ended late in the year. A second combat tour followed from May-December 1952, during which she was redesignated CVA ("A"-Attack) 31.*

From 10 May to 15 May the squadron moved from Quonset Point to NAS San Diego, California, where its planes and personnel were loaded aboard Bon Homme Richard.

The carrier transited to Pearl Harbor during the week of 20-27 May and enjoyed two weeks of operations—and liberty—in and around the Hawaiian Islands. "The ship with Air Group 7 aboard remained in the Hawaiian area for two weeks, operating under COMFAIRHAWAII [Commander, Fleet Air Forces, Hawaii]. While there, VF-74 participated in closed air support exercises with the First Air and Naval Gun Fire Liaison Company at Makua Valley dropping live ammunition."

An unnamed Lieutenant is parodied in the Bon Homme Richard's Cruise Book, perhaps as a result of an overindulgence in Hawaiian pleasures. (Eaton Family)

On 3 June the Air Group "received an Operational Readiness Inspection (ORI) conducted by ComFairHawaii. On this inspection the Air Group received a mark of 'outstanding' in five subjects, 'excellent' in four and 'good' in two with an overall mark of 'Excellent.'" [2]

"Plane in the water. This is not a drill!"

On Wednesday, May 28, 1952, the Bon Homme Richard got underway from Berth F-12 on Ford Island, Oahu, Hawaii, heading for the open sea to conduct training operations. By 1335 she was at 20 knots and heading south with Ensign G. A. Reed as the Officer of the Deck (underway), the watch officer in charge of the ship's daily routine and maneuvering—the "deck and the conn." [2]

At 1411, the destroyer USS Epperson (DD 719) rendezvoused and was placed in "plane guard" station 1,000 yards astern of the carrier, following in the larger ship's wake. Twenty minutes later both ships conducted anti-aircraft firing exercises. At 1726, the new OOD, Lt. R.H. Brown increased speed to 27 knots to get the relative wind at 5 degrees to port (left) of the bow and at least 30 knots "down the deck" to best launch or recover aircraft.

At 1840, another destroyer, USS Philip (DD 498) joined the formation and was placed ahead of the carrier to provide ASW protection, a standard precaution even though no enemy submarines were expected. At 1857, Lt. D. F. Mueller, the OOD on the second "dogged watch," maneuvered the ship to recover the aircraft launched an hour earlier. [3]

Soon after beginning the recovery, an aircraft failed to catch an arresting wire and crashed into the Number One barrier. Although the crash damaged the barrier, damage to the aircraft was negligible. Recovery of aircraft was completed by 1945 as Lt. Mueller was being relieved by Ensign D. K. Mosher for the evening watch—2000-2400. By 2130 Ensign Mosher had completed launching aircraft into the wing on a course of 085 and a speed of 17 knots. By 2140 the carrier was on a course of 130 and was changing course to 140. At 2146 an F4U aircraft "went into the water off the starboard bow." The aircraft, with its pilot, Ensign Ron Eaton "was being spotted forward when the right wheel went over the deck edge combing on the starboard side forward."

[4]Ensign Mosher immediately sounded the alarm throughout the ship "Plane in the water. This is no drill." He used the Primary Tactical and Maneuvering radiotelephone on the bridge (PriTac) to notify the plane guard destroyers of the emergency. Meanwhile, he reversed course to 320, then reduced speed and finally stopped all engines. For over ten minutes the Richard remained at "All Stop," as it and its destroyers tried to locate the missing pilot. At 2218, Ensign Mosher changed course to 140 and ordered "All head slow," to regain steerageway for the carrier. [5]

Finally, at 2222, "PriTac" crackled out the good news, Ensign Ronald Eaton had been recovered by USS Philip. The tension on the bridge immediately relaxed as Mosher maneuvered the ship into place to recover

The second USS Philip (DD 498) *was commissioned 21 November 1942. From 1943 until the end of World War II she was heavily engaged in combat operations in the western Pacific. At the end of the war, after service in the Atlantic Fleet she was placed out of commission, in reserve in 1947. Recommissioned at Charleston, S.C. 30 June 1950, and homeported in Pearl Harbor, Philip participated in advanced hunter-killer exercises. During the autumn of 1950 Philip acted as plane guard for the aircraft bearing President Harry S Truman to his mid-ocean conference with General Douglas MacArthur on Wake Island. She then served with Task Force 77 in the Sea of Japan screening the fast carrier task force as it conducted air operations against enemy forces in North Korea.*

the aircraft that had been circling the ship in a holding pattern, conserving fuel until the lost pilot could be found and flight operations resumed. The last aircraft was recovered at 2335. The carrier stood down from flight quarters as watch standers around the ship converged on the galley for "Mid Rats"—midnight rations.

On the night of 26 May 1952, in the Hawaiian operating area Ensign Ronald D. Eaton, 543824/1315, U.S. Naval Reserve, "had an opportunity to become acquainted with the Destroyer Navy," the squadron history laconically reported. "Taxiing forward at night ENS Eaton's Corsair was parked on the starboard side of the ship forward, with the out-board wheel of his plane resting on the flight deck coaming. Before ENS Eaton could get out of the plane, it fell over the side. He managed to clear the plane immediately after impact with the water and had approximately an hour and fifteen minutes wait in his 'Mae West' before he was picked up in the dark night by the destroyer plane guard, the USS Philip."

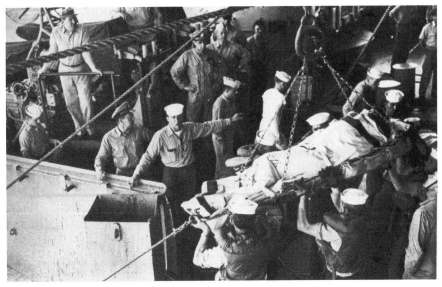

"We Get Ronnie Back," the ship's Cruise Book later noted. Strapped securely to a litter, Ensign Ron Eaton is high lined back aboard the USS Bon Homme Richard after his Corsair fighter was accidentally pushed off the flight deck. He narrowly escaped going down with the plane, but survived with only an injured foot. VF-74 Commanding Officer, CDR Charles D. Fonvielle, Jr. (center, with hands on hips), oversees Eaton's safe return after the unusual ordeal.

Ransomed For Ice Cream

After his plane in the water ordeal, Eaton tried to explain the mishap in a light vein. He knew his family was worried. He sat down at his portable typewriter and composed some verse in which he tells what happened from his perspective.

Pilots were needed for this night, Just for taxi; not for flight,
The plane I manned was number seven, the plane ahead was number eleven.
'Start the props' soon was heard, with the signal, I concurred.
From man to man I was passed; at my final spot I was at last.
'Cut your engine.' 'Hold your brake.' This was done with rapid rate,
I was told, 'She wasn't chocked.' So I kept my brakes locked.
Very soon the man returned, he looked at me, much concerned,
The night was dark, but who would think my plane would roll into the drink.
Without delay the plane did sink, and soon the carrier ship was indistinct.
In my mind there came in sight, my girl's face, like a shining light.
Up swam I, from the mess. Then pulled the toggles of my 'Mae West.'
This was done with much success, and CO^2 went in my vest.
'Man overboard!' the ship's horn blast. Not long before had the ship's crew posted,
A plane high above, circled round. This kept my hopes, I'd be found.
I tried at once, to use a flare. The first one gave me slight despair,
Boy! Lucky me! I had a pair. The second attempt lit quite fair.
The waves above were rising steep and the sea below was plenty deep.
With huge lights the ship did seek. One would hit me and then retreat.
Planes still searched from the sky, I held my vest light way up high,
As the tin can came nearby, to myself, I heaved a sigh.
With all my might I did shout, having every hope, They would pull me out.
A yellow light, and then a boat, I thanked God. I was still afloat.

Injured—a foot was badly wrenched—and tired, Eaton was fished out.

The next morning the destroyer and carrier rendezvoused to effect a Stokes stretcher highline personnel transfer for Eaton, who had sustained an

Dear Joy,

Just a few lines before I turn in for the night.

Your letters came a couple of days ago and it was nice hearing from you. I'm glad to hear that things are going so well at home.

Tell the folks I start flying next week as my bruises are getting much better and the pain from them is all about gone. They may play my account as to what happened over WHDH if the Navy will release it for publication.

Hawaii is very beautiful and the climate here is just wonderful. The beaches are just covered with all kinds of people. If you get more money than you know what to do with come on out here to Hawaii and have a nice vacation.

This is our last weekend on the beach and then we shove off for Japan. By the time we get well underway you will have this letter. Boy will I have sea stories to tell you when I get home. They are going to put the light out here in the Ready Room as the night flyers have to get their eyes ready for night flying.

Give my love to everyone,

Your brother,
Ron

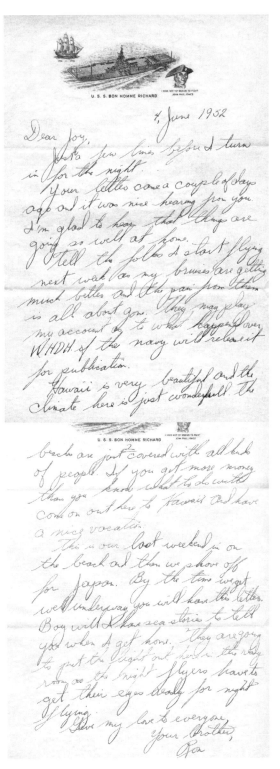

ankle injury during the fall. Soon, Eaton was back aboard the carrier after it had paid a heavy price for his return. The destroyer had "demanded" a ransom for the handsome young pilot and was given many gallons of ice cream for its successful rescue.

It was a close call for Ensign Ronald Dow Eaton.

The "Bonny Dick" Rejoins the War

Weighing anchor from Pearl Harbor on 9 June, the carrier transited to Yokosuka, Japan and arrived on 21 June. On 16 June, the "Bonny Dick" changed operational control— "chopped"—to the OPCON of Commander, Naval Forces Far East.

The Bon Homme Richard arrived in Yokosuka on 18 June and spent the next three days "mainly with intelligence and operational briefings. The USS Valley Forge, being relieved by the USS Bon Homme Richard, was in Yokosuka at this time. The pilots of VF-74 were able to pick up valuable information about their operational procedures and mistakes." The carrier got underway from Yokosuka, Japan on Saturday morning, 21 June 1952 *en route* to its assigned operating area. The next day it joined Task Force 77 "in the Korean Combat Zone" off the eastern coast of Korea near the 38th Parallel. TF 77 was a powerful armada of four U.S. aircraft carriers, including in addition to the Bon Homme Richard, the USS Boxer (CV 21), USS

Pilots in the Bon Homme Richard ready room complete mission briefing and check their personal equipment prior to a mission in 1952. *(NARA)*

Philippine Sea (CV 47) and USS Princeton (CV 37), supported by various heavy support and screening ships. "The four-carrier operations, the first since World War II, went off efficiently and without mishap." [6]

Lights Out Across North Korea

At 0528 on Monday morning, 23 June, the USS Bon Homme Richard rendezvoused with TF 77. Its Officer of the Deck checked in with the OTC (Officer in Tactical Command), using PRITAC, the Primary Tactical and Maneuvering Circuit, and after receiving a "Roger," responded with "Alpha Juliett"—reporting for duty. It marked the return of the "Bonny Dick" to the Korean theater of operations after an absence of nearly seven months.

Seven hours later it sent its "Foxtrot" flag—white with a red diamond in the middle—up the flag hoist—at the dip—fluttering slightly below the "closed up" or "two blocked" position on the flag hoist. This announced it was "preparing to commence flight operations." A few minutes later, at 1415 India, "Foxtrot," was closed up as the carrier picked up speed and headed into the wind to launch 13 AD's, 13 F4U4's and 19 F9F'2's to strike power plants and electrical installations in previously restricted areas in North Korea. [7]

The strikes, coordinated through the Joint Operations Center, were "a spectacular success," the Richard's action report noted, "resulting in total

The F4U Corsair's gull shaped wing was among its most distinctive features. Bombs are winched into place prior to a mission from the USS Bon Homme Richard (CV 31) in 1952. (NARA)

destruction of the transformer and power house of Fusen #2 Hydro-Electric Plant; 80% destruction to the transformer yard and turbine building of Kyosen #2 Hydro-Electric Plant, rendering both plants, exclusive targets of BHR planes, permanently non-operational." [8]

"Early on the morning of the 23rd our pilots manned the ready rooms for their first flight over Korea. We were to take part in the joint Air Force-Navy strike against the as yet untouched North Korea hydro-electric plants. The operations were delayed until the afternoon, but the Navy was still able to put out one good effective strike on the afternoon of the 23rd that practically destroyed all the targets assigned."

On 23 June and 24 June 1952, VF-74 "participated in the first strike against the North Korean hydro-electric complexes, attacking Kyosen Stations 2 and 4 and Fusen 2," the Squadron history noted. In the strikes on the hydro-electric stations, the planes of VF-74 "were engaged in both flak suppression and attacks on the major targets. Our planes participated in the strike on Kyosen Station 2 and Fusen Station 2 on the afternoon of the 23rd and on the 24th in the 'finishing off' strikes were assigned Kyosen Station 4 as a target."

On Tuesday, June 24th, the Bon Homme Richard launched 42 offensive sorties against Kyosen #4 Hydro-Electric Power plant, "a target that had been attacked by planes of another carrier the preceding day, but which photographic interpretation indicated was not severely damaged and might be operable." BHR aircraft reported destroying the powerhouse, a fuel storage tank and transformer yard. [9]

Later in the day of the 24th and on the 25th VF-74 was engaged in strikes on rail lines and on troop and supply concentrations near the front lines."

On Wednesday morning, June 25th, the Bonny Dick was still steaming in company with and as a unit of Task Force 77 in operating area "Sugar"

The Bon Homme Richard's Cruise Book captioned this launch photograph, "Off Again!"

in the Sea of Japan off the Korean coast.

After launching from his carrier at 1054, Ensign Ron Eaton had bombed enemy positions near the front lines with his flight of VCorsairs. At about noon, as he returned from the mission, he was hit by antiaircraft fire and had bailed out south of Wonson, North Korea. Before he was on the ground, his flight leader was contacting Mellow Control, the Fifth Air Force's airborne command center to advise them of Eaton's situation and to get help started his way.

Mission 1890 would be needed after all.

"Go Get'em Fellas," was the caption on this photograph published in the Bon Homme Richard's cruisebook.

Chapter Six

Elliot Dean Ayer

Mission 1890 Flight Leader

Captain Elliot Dean Ayer, How Flight Leader for Mission 1890, was born in Greenfield, Massachusetts on April 30, 1921, the son of Dean Willard and Bertha Ayer of Manchester, Connecticut.

Ayer was almost too big to be a fighter pilot. At 6 feet, 1 ½ inches tall and weighing 200 pounds, he filled the Mustang's small cockpit. [1]

He was married to Marguerite Savage Ayer, who lived in Tallahassee, Florida. They had two small boys, Fred and Boyd.

Ayer was a WW II veteran. At the time (then) Corporal Elliot Ayer applied for appointment as an Aviation Cadet on 24 July 1942, he was an anti-aircraft gunner assigned to the 19th Infantry and a Pearl Harbor Veteran. Aged 16 years and 7 months, he had enlisted in the Regular Army for a three-year tour and entered active service on 1 December 1939.

The Army Air Corps sent him for preflight training at Santa Ana, California [also the hometown of Captain Wayne Lear], primary flight school at Oxnard, California, basic flight school at Dolaris, California and advanced flight school at Luke Field, Arizona. After successfully completing flight training, he was commissioned a Second Lieutenant on 3 November 1943. Just nine months later he was promoted to First Lieutenant.

He was promoted to Captain on 7 August 1946. After the war ended, then Captain Ayer was stationed at Shaw Field, SC and was separated on 17 September 1946. The records noted under "battles and campaigns," European African Middle Eastern Campaign Medal, Northern Apennines, Italian Campaign, Southern France, Po Valley, Rome-Arno." He had served with the Army Air Forces in both the Continental United States and in the European Theatre of Operations.

His Summary of Military Occupation recorded that Ayer "Piloted single engine fighter aircraft to maintain air superiority over the enemy to enable other units to carry out their missions during the Rome Arno, Po Valley, Northern Apennines, Southern France and Italian Campaigns. Took off, operated, and landed aircraft under varying flying conditions and such hazards as adverse weather, enemy attack, and low altitude and night flying. Flew dive-bombing, escort, and strafing missions. Maintained flight records and reported observations made during mission." He had served as a fighter pilot and as a B-25 medium bomber pilot, in addition to duties as an Air Operations Officer.

By the end of World War Two, in addition to many service awards, Captain Ayer had been

(Above) Elliot Dean Ayer and Marguerite Savage Ayer at about the time they were married, shortly after World War II. (Ayer)

(Below) Elliot, Marguerite and her sister, Ruby Stanford (front, right), enjoy some off-duty time together just prior to his shipping out for Korean in 1952. (Ayer)

awarded the Distinguished Flying Cross and the Air Medal with three Oak Leaf clusters.

When demobilization policies were announced in 1946, the rapidly down-sizing Air Force gave Captain Ayer an extraordinarily difficult choice to make—he could leave the Air Force as a Captain or continue on active duty—as a Master Sergeant. He chose to stay in the Air Force as a Master Sergeant. From 1946 until 1951, Master Sergeant Ayer served as an Aircraft Approach Controller GCA. His Enlisted Record and Honorable Discharge on 1 October 1949 mentions only a Good Conduct Medal, American Defense Service Medal and a World War II Victory Medal. On 2 October 1949, Master Sergeant Ayer reenlisted in the U.S. Air Force for three more years at Eglin Air Force Base.

Ayer was "discharged" on 13 May 1951 to "accept active duty as a commissioned officer." On 14 May 1951, he was reappointed a Captain—AO 758 753. The extraordinarily dedicated WWII combat pilot and senior NCO was back in the cockpit.

By spring 1952, Ayer was in Korea and assigned to the 67th Fighter-Bomber Squadron, 18th Fighter-Bomber Wing based at K-46.

On March 6, 1952, Ayer wrote to his cousin Lloyd Savage in Tallahassee, Florida:

"Hi Lloyd,

How's everything in Tallahassee these days? Fine I hope.

There really isn't much to write about from here as every day is just like the day before. I'm flying '51's which is the same type aircraft I used to fly over to Tallahassee just before I left. I have 13 missions so far. The missions come rather slow as we have so many pilots and so few aircraft. We average about 10 missions a month. The type of missions we fly are close support which I like the best. On these missions we work right up on the front lines and we either have napalm or bombs and in addition we carry rockets and 6—.50-caliber guns. You can really work over a trench or bunker position with that equipment. We also cut railroads and bridges, strafe trucks—trains, etc. and fly armed reconnaissance. When we get 100 missions we can go home. At the same time we build up 3 points a month on the point system so even if we don't get 100 missions in one year we can go home on points.

By the way—we can buy Canadian Club and all the real good brands of whisky for $3.00 here and over in Japan for only $2.00. Rough, hey!

That's about all the news from here for now. Drop a line if you get a chance. Say hello to Harriet and the boys for me. Best wishes to all.

Best of luck, Lloyd, "Ed"

K-46 Aerial View. The Operations Office for the 67th Fighter-Bomber Squadron at K-46, near Hoengsong, SK, was the third small building from the left in the row at center. It was in this building that How Flight Leader Captain Elliot Ayer, 1st Lt. Archie Connors, 1st Lt. William McShane and 1st Lt. John Hill waited on stand-by for Mission 1890. The other buildings belonged to other squadrons attached to the 18th Fighter-Bomber Group, including the 12th "Foxy Few" Squadron, and 2 Squadron South African Air Force, the "Flying Cheetahs." Until several months before, the "Cobra in the Sky" 39th Fighter Interceptor Squadron had been a component of the 18th Wing, until most of its pilots had been reassigned to other squadrons being equipped with the F-86 Sabrejet. The 18th would not transition into the F-86 until February 1953. (Cranston)

Experienced Flight Commander

On 5 July 1952, Major Stanley Long, Commander of the 67th Fighter-Bomber Squadron completed an "Officer Effectiveness Report" on Captain Elliot D. Ayer covering the period 11 April 1952 through 30 June 1952. As a Flight Leader (1124E), Ayer "leads flights of single-engine fighter aircraft to obtain air superiority over the enemy. Receives instructions regarding mission, route, formation, altitude, weather conditions and other information; accomplishes mission by offensive action. Flies on strafing, interceptor, patrol, escort or protective missions." Long's overall evaluations of Ayer were consistently in the "excellent" column of the evaluation.

"Officer reported on," Long noted, "is a well experienced Flight Commander who has demonstrated qualities of good leadership throughout his tour under my supervision. He has an excellent flying safety record. I would recommend further assignment in positions of great responsibility for this officer. He exercises a high degree of judgment in the economical management of personnel and resources under his supervision, commensurate with his responsibilities."

Long had great confidence in Ayer's flying and leadership abilities. He wasn't quite as sure about one of Ayer's pilots, 1st Lt. Archie Connors, who had just returned from 45 days of emergency leave to attend his wife, badly injured in an auto accident that nearly killed her. Connors had over 30 missions, but he had just completed a refresher training program to resharpen his flying skills after nearly two months out of the cockpit. While he had participated in the heavy raids on Monday and Tuesday, Long decided to assign Connors as the Number Two member of the flight, flying as wingman for Ayer, the position normally reserved for the most junior or least experienced pilot in the four-plane flight—if the pilot rescue Mission 1890 was needed.

Another Mustang Mission. As the four pilots of How Flight waited to see if Mission 1890 would be needed on Wednesday, June 25th, other 67th Squadron Mustangs taxied past the rows of empty napalm tanks as they headed out on another mission from K-46. The bent prop on the plane at far left shows the result of a crash landing. (NARA)

Chapter Seven

Archie Connors
Mission 1890 Number Two Man

By the time Japan surrendered in August 1945, and World War Two was over, the Connors family of Jacksonville, Florida was counting its blessings. April had brought a grim national funeral narrated on the radio by a weeping Arthur Godfrey. The news soon after, that the Germans had surrendered—Victory in Europe—or "VE Day"—brought national rejoicing and helped dispel some of the gloom after FDR's sudden death.

Arch and Eva Connors pose with their family of seven in 1929. Front row, left to right, William Gerald, Mary Elizabeth, Florence, Lucille and Julia Cleo. Back row, left to right, Arch (holding Archie), Eva and Woodrow. This is the earliest family photograph in which Archie appears. As a toddler, his balance was so good that Arch would show him off by letting him stand up in one of his hands.

Melson and Broadway. *About 1921 Arch Connors moved his small, 3-room home to the corner of Melson and Broadway Avenues in west Jacksonville and expanded it considerably. The "new" house had three bedrooms, living room, dining room, large wrap around front porch--and indoor plumbing. Although much improved over their first cottage, the Connors new home could not be called a big house. However, it was filled with love and laughter--and some tears--for the seventy years that it was the family "headquarters." In this photograph taken in the late 1930's, granddaughter Kathryn Coles can be seen playing in the yard with her baby stroller.*

    The two oldest sons, Woodrow and Gerald ("Gerry") had not been drafted or called for duty, notwithstanding the fact that they had been in the Florida National Guard as teenagers. Their construction and woodworking skills were more important to the war effort at home building PT boats and government buildings at nearby Naval Air Station (NAS) Jacksonville. However, by the time Japan surrendered, Gerry had been drafted and was headed for basic training at Camp Blanding. The end of the war brought a quick military discharge.

    Daughters Julia and Mary were married and living in Jacksonville. Lucille and Florence were still at home finishing their schooling.

    Younger son, Archie, had joined the Navy immediately after graduating from Robert E. Lee High School in July 1945, but with the war now over, he should soon be home.

    Archibald Haddock Connors, Jr.—everyone called him "Archie"—was the youngest of the seven Connors children. He was a bright student, although he could have done much better in school if his attention had not been so focused on sports—at which he excelled. He played football on the Robert E. Lee High School team that had a winning season. He was a state champion wrestler and runner up in the pole vault. To his nephews and nieces, he looked ten feet tall, but in reality he was slightly taller than his father, Arch, who stood about 5' 7" tall. But the blond haired, brown-eyed

(Left) In this snapshot of Archie in about 1939 one sees the mischievous bravado that made him the center of attention--and also got him into trouble with parents and teachers on occasion. (Below) Archie pesters a girlfriend playfully.

Archie stands beneath the Camphor tree in the Connors front yard with niece Kathryn Coles and nephew Tracy Connors in this 1943 snapshot.

Archie was solid, wiry muscle. His nephew, Tracy, remembered watching in awe, as Archie would jump up to catch the horizontal bar, then do a series of <u>one-handed</u> pull-ups.

Even though the older Connors siblings were already married, with families of their own, on most Sundays those that were in town would pile themselves into their cars and head towards West Jacksonville's Woodstock Park neighborhood to be together. That was also true for extended family members. Although not large by today's standards, the Connors' home at the corner of Melson and Broadway Avenues was a very frequent destination for cousins from Nassau County to the north or from "down state."

That Sunday after V-J Day was typical for hundreds of Sundays for many decades at the Connors home. Shortly before one, after attending their respective churches, the family began to arrive.

Actually, the Sunday dinner had started on Saturday. Archie's mother, Eva May Haddock Connors, would spent a good portion of that day on her front porch, sitting on the old glider swing with a full hamper of speckled butter beans by her side. She would size unwary visitors up as potential shelling partners to help her prepare for Sunday lunch. As was her custom for decades, every Sunday after church, Eva would prepare "Sunday dinner," a huge spread of chicken, vegetables, salads, breads, and desserts. She never knew exactly how many children and grandchildren would show up, but somehow there was always enough. Spotting a likely relative or especially a grandchild flying by en route to play in the camphor tree outside, she would sing out: "Hi honey, come sit next to me and let's talk."

A Florida Pioneer Family

They did talk, of course, to pass the time while they shelled beans or peas, Eva telling the favored grandchild about her girlhood, growing up on the Haddock family farm near Kings Ferry, a small lumber-milling town on the St. Marys River that flows east towards Fernandina, and serves as a border between Florida and Georgia. The Haddock's were among Florida's pioneer families, including Braddocks, Carletons, Vanzants, Higgenbothams, and Libbys, that had moved from Georgia over into North Florida in about 1815 after securing Spanish land grants. Eva told her grandchildren lots of stories about what it was like "in the old days" to pass the time while they helped her shell beans—lots of beans and peas and corn for the hungry mouths of loved ones to whom she fed literally thousands of wonderful meals for many decades.

Her father, Rufus Goldwire Haddock, owned 500 acres of "piney woods" a few miles from Kings Ferry, Florida in Nassau County, from which he harvested lumber and resin. Rufus supplemented the family income by delivering the mail by horse and buggy. Originally, he had owned

Captain Goodbread stands at the bow of the packet steamer Hildegarde *while it loads stores and passengers at Kings Ferry for the trip to Fernandia. The boy at left is David Miller Haddock, one of Eva's younger brothers. The young girl sitting on the log in the foreground is Ruth Connors Biddy, Arch Connors' sister. The girl to her right is one of their cousins, Mabel Carleton. The Hildegarde made the trip up the St. Marys River twice weekly. Arch and Eva traveled on the Hildegarde during part of their honeymoon trip.*

a much larger parcel of land, but it was too far from town. He traded it for a homestead closer to King's Ferry so his children could attend the one-room school.

Being closer to town meant the Rufus and Mary Jane Haddock children—Zach, Bill, Mary, Eva, Ginny, Paul, Harley, and Miller—now had to walk only three miles through the woods and wade across a stream,

The Kings Ferry docks *as they looked about 1908. At right, between the Hilliard & Bailey docks and the Mizell mill is the T.W. Russell home. This once abandoned home is now restored.*

keeping a wary eye out for snakes, to the one-room school house where they completed the equivalent of the eighth grade. Eva's most memorable teacher was a one-armed man who was a hard disciplinarian. She remembers that he would sneak up behind any boys who were misbehaving and clobber them with his one good arm! Understandably, this teacher was not well liked and the parents quickly found another teacher. Sometimes when there was no teacher available, Eva taught the other children.

Every night before going to bed, the whole family gathered in the parlor for Bible reading, prayer, and hymn singing with the pump organ. On Sundays, whenever there was a preacher, the family dressed in their best clothes, climbed into the wagon and went to Ephesus Baptist Church (founded in 1845, the oldest Baptist Church in Florida). Everyone carried baskets of food that contained tasty fried chicken, baked hams, cakes and pies which they shared on tables under the large oak trees. They called it "dinner on the grounds."

Rufus Goldwire Haddock, Eva's father, was a Nassau County farmer who traded away good farming land to enable his children to go to school.

Eva was baptized in the St. Mary's River and no matter what heartaches or challenges life brought her, she remained an inspiring example of selfless Christian love to her family and friends, her granddaughter Kathryn Coles McCluskey recalled.

Eva's first ride in an automobile was memorable. It was an open-top motorcar, and before they had reached their destination, it started to rain. It filled up the bottom of the car, over the tops of her button-up shoes. When they finally arrived and she opened the car door, a torrent of water cascaded out, nearly knocking down a 10-year-old boy. Then her straw hat collapsed, giving her another faceful of water. To the end of her days, she remembered this event like it happened yesterday and would end the story laughing uncontrollably at the memories it brought back.

The saddest day of Eva's early life was her fifteenth birthday. On that day she was called solemnly into her parents' bedroom to say good-bye to her dying mother. Mary Jane Vanzant Haddock had been seriously ill with Bright's Disease for months, and her kidneys had finally failed. Just before her mother died, Eva wept at her bedside and as her mother had asked, promised "to take care of the boys." Eva was the oldest girl left at home—her sisters were all married and had families of their own to care for.

William Vanzant and his wife, *Ernie (Libby), and little Ernest (who died in 1978). This photograph was made just three weeks before* ***Mary Jane Vanzant Haddock*** *(right front) died on February 17, 1906, her daughter Eva's fifteenth birthday. Mary Jane had been taken into Jacksonville to see the doctor by her brother, "Willie," who was "always trying to help her," Eva (right) remembered. One doctor said "it was her kidneys. I don't know. She had a lot of trouble with headaches—so severe—she had a fall. She fell on some steps and hit the stair railing. It cut a big place on her forehead. After that healed she began to have headaches. Sister Zona used to say 'I believe mother must have had a tumor probably, to have had those headaches.' She would nearly go out of her mind those headaches would be so severe. The doctor said it was kidney trouble, but I don't know. In those days they didn't make tests and they didn't have anything like they have now." Just before she died, Mary Jane asked those nursing her to "tell the girls to come here," she wanted to talk to them. "She told us to be good," Eva told her grandson, Tracy. "I never thought about her dying, you know, then, we thought she was just sick." But after asking Eva to take good care of her younger brothers, Paul, Harley and Miller, Mary Jane died." She was almost 46.*

There were two little boys younger than Eva, and now she would cook and clean by herself for the whole family.

For the next seven years she willingly worked and scrubbed and lovingly cared for the motherless children, though she was only a slip of a girl herself. The youngest one was only three. Until the end of their lives, the younger brothers loved her and honored her as if she were their own mother.

Almost a century after her mother died, Eva said she missed her still.

Arch and Eva Connors on their wedding day in 1912.

Eva met Arch Connors at church as a child. He was five years older and as serious and hardworking as she was. They didn't become sweethearts until she was about nineteen, when he approached her father, Rufus Haddock, for her hand in marriage. Rufus referred him to Eva, but she said she wasn't ready to marry. She was a pretty blond with sparkling blue eyes, and lots of young men came to call on her. However, she didn't seem to care for any of them.

Three years later, after he had become an expert carpenter and developed good job prospects, Arch came back to Kings Ferry and asked her again. This time she felt her younger brothers were old enough to take care of themselves, and she said yes. They were married on May 5, 1912, and boarded the "Hildegarde" to travel downstream to Fernandina for their honeymoon.

One of Arch's favorite sayings in later years was that he had married Eva "not because she was the prettiest girl in town or the smartest—although she was—but because she was the sweetest."

Sunday Dinner

At about 12:30 on any typical Sunday during the mid-Forties, the first of the Connors-Haddock family began to arrive to gather around Eva's bountiful table—

Woodrow, Arch and Eva's oldest son, blond, blue eyed and very serious, arrived first, still driving a vintage Ford Model A. *[New cars were not yet coming off the assembly lines that had been converted in 1942 to wartime production of tanks, jeeps and trucks.]* Woodrow was working at Huckins Yacht Corporation, where he had been building PT and crash boats at the former yacht construction yard for several years. His woodworking skills were such that his was considered a "critical occupation" and made it unlikely that he would be subject to the draft.

Woodrow had married the "girl down the street," Miriam Morris, the daughter of a Seaboard Railroad telegrapher who had recently bought a cute bungalow a block further down Melson Avenue from the Connors home. Miriam and Woodrow had two sons, Tracy, born in 1939 and David, born in 1942. Archie was just 12 years older than his oldest nephew. In fact, he was closer in age to his nephew, Tracy, than he was to his older brothers and sister.

Julia Connors Coles, pretty and artistically talented, was newly married and a mother to Archie's first niece, Kathryn, who had been born in 1936.

Gerald ("Gerry") was the next oldest brother, married to Marjorie Cooper with whom he already had three children, Gerry, Jr., Bruce and Linda. Gerry was also a skilled wood worker, but the draft "list" had finally reached him, too. He was soon to be en route to Camp Blanding for induction and basic training. The war would end before he completed training.

Mary Elizabeth, who had married outdoors man Arthur Hagen when she was only 16, would arrive in her truck with her three young sons: Peter, Paul and Mark.

Florence, recently married, was expected to arrive any moment.

Lucille was still living at home while she decided which college to attend.

As each brother or sister arrived with their children, the noise level went up accordingly.

If the Sunday weather permitted, the grand kids would play outside in the large Camphor tree, in the yard, or on the big porch that wrapped around the house on two sides. In bad weather, they would be forced inside, where the passel, all under ten years of age, would be underfoot. Inevitably, "chases" around the living and dining room, became "fights" between the older grandchildren, all boys at the time.

The irrepressible Archie would often arrive after a "date." His entrance was noted by all. It was understood that he was the family's "best and brightest." His mischievous, I've-got-a-secret-you-don't-know smile lit up the room. Conversation ceased as all turned to smile at the family's fair-haired boy.

After a few moments saying hello to his brothers, Woodrow and Gerry, and to the other adults in the room, he would turn his attention to his adoring nephews (other than Kathryn, the nieces, at the time, were still in diapers). In seconds, all pretense of "adult" behavior was gone—a free-for-all was in progress—Archie against Tracy, David, Gerry, and Bruce. They didn't have a chance.

He would hold them down and give their heads a "nuggie," rubbing their hair hard with his knuckles. He was careful not to really hurt them—much. While he was anointing them with his presence, those not being administered to would be jumping on his back, only to be shaken off like pesky bugs. There was much laughing, squealing, and uproar.

Arch, from his "power position," a big overstuffed rocker in the corner of the living, would begin to send out warning grumbles.

Tiring of the game, Archie would shake them all off like puppies, and whisk into his room that adjoined the dining room, slam the door—seconds before several pairs of young sweaty hands lunged for the door knob, he would send the lock bolt home. Instantly, the house would resound as eight fists pounded on the door, and at least four feet would be kicking it.

A bellow would go up from the corner of the living room.
"ARCHIE!!!"

Arch's command was law in the house; even Archie knew not to cross him. Silence, then the door would open and Archie would emerge with a big smile. All was forgiven. Dinner was served. That "ritual" was repeated many times.

Good looking, personable and a natural leader, Archie was also frequently in trouble. He had a knack for mischief and fun that bordered on recklessness at time.

"We called Archie our 'desert' because he was last—and he was lots of fun," recalled his older sister, Lucy. "He had a lot of original ideas—for getting into trouble."

Every day when the Connors kids left for school, their mother, Eva would see them out the door and remind them to study hard and to behave themselves. If they didn't, Miss Annie R. Morgan, the strict, red-haired principal would telephone the news to Eva. Later, when Arch got home there would be hell to pay. If sparing the rod spoiled the children, the Connors' kids would be the best behaved in that part of Jacksonville.

In 1935, when Archie was in the third grade, he and his best buddy, Charlie Jackson, misbehaved in class and were kept after school—torture for an active kid like Archie. He thought the punishment was unfair, and when the teacher left the room

Archie Connors in a high school school yearbook photograph. He graduated from Jacksonville's Robert E. Lee Senior High School in 1945.

Arch and Eva Connors *pose formally in the early 1940s. (Right) At a family party Arch "cuts up" with Eva, trying to "force" a kiss on her. In reality, he kissed her every time he left or returned to their home.*

for a moment, he did too—around the corner into the cloakroom and out the ground level window. Seeing the teacher's car in the parking lot, he nonchalantly strolled over—and let the air out of a tire. He then went home. Long before he was in sight of Melson and Broadway, Miss Morgan was burning up the wires to Eva.

The next day found Archie staying after school again—and writing "I will never let the air out of my teacher's tire," five hundred times. Even worse, he then had to come straight home to chores and no "playing" privileges for two weeks. He begged his mother to whip him instead, but she could not be swayed even by the engaging smile and pathos of her youngest. The punishment had its desired effect—for a while.

Archie also had a well developed sense of humor. He was a master at the practical joke. His father, Arch, had been the designated neighborhood "air raid warden" during World War Two. That may sound quaint now, but was taken very seriously at the time. To perform his duties, should the need arise, he was issued a conically shaped canister-pump with a T-shaped handle. Vigorously pumped, the 3-foot rubber hose would send a finger-thick stream of water over 30 feet. Archie saw the potential for other uses.

As a high school senior, Archie would enlist a friend with a pickup truck, fill the pump to capacity, and call another friend to tell him to meet them on a designated corner. At the time and place, the vehicle would drive by slowly. When the "target" was within pump range, Archie would stand up from where he had been hiding in the truck bed, and with several vigorous strokes on the pump, thoroughly drench the unwitting friend. Inevitably, the sputtering victim would be ready to fight. However, Archie's charm and smile were enough to convince the victim to join in the game. Within minutes another friend had been called and convinced to go for a ride. This time, the first victim was manning the pump. The game went on until they ran out of friends, or the truck was full.

Arch Tries Pole Vaulting

Lucy remembered their childhood as being "short on playing equipment, so we invented games…we sometimes used Dad's bamboo fishing poles to pole vault over ditches. That was really exciting after a big rainstorm when the ditches were full."

On one occasion, the three boys were pole-vaulting in the back yard with a bamboo pole brought home by the youngest, Archie. Arriving home from work, Arch, then in his late Forties, watched the boys and decided he could do this, too. Without removing his cigar, he took the pole in hand and got a running start. His speed was good and the launch was flawless. However, in mid-vault, the bamboo pole snapped in two. Arch crashed to the ground—flat on his back.

Eva was in her "office"—the kitchen—in the critical stages of sweet potato pie-making and watching the proceedings through the double window over her sink. When she saw what Arch was about to attempt she was transfixed—with worry. She clapped her hand over her mouth in shock when she saw the pole break and Arch plummet to the ground. Her eyes were riveted on his still form as he lay there—without moving, staring at the sky. The boys ran into the house yelling for "MAMA!"

Finally, although it was in reality only a few seconds, she took her hand away from her mouth and started to breath again. Smiling, she turned to her frantic boys and said, "Don't worry! He's all right. See, he's still puffing on his cigar."

The pole-vaulting practice, for Archie at least, paid off years later. Always a fine athlete, he went on to become a state ranked pole-vaulter in high school and a member of the state champion relay team in college.

Destroyer Duty

Archie enlisted in the Navy on July 26, 1945, right after he graduated from Jacksonville's Robert E. Lee High School. Even though Archie was not yet 18, on August 1st his father, Arch, signed before a notary that as his parent, Archie had "no other legal guardian than me, and I do hereby consent to his enlistment in the U.S. Naval Reserve as [Seaman Second Class] subject to all the requirements and lawful commands of the Officers who may, from time to time, be placed over him..."

After Boot Camp in Maryland, he was sent home briefly after the shooting ended in August.

Most of the world was ecstatic over the news. Ginn Barnes, Woodrow and Miriam's closest neighbor in North Jacksonville's Pearl Court neighborhood, had come running across Vermillion Street shrieking that the Japanese had surrendered, she had heard it on WJAX—the war was over. The killing would stop. Never again, the radio announcers said, would America have to field a military force of any size. American could bring home all its boys-next-door-in-uniform.

In just a few months America demobilized, sending hundreds of now surplus Navy ships up the St. Johns River to rust and rot in huge nests of ships rafted together at Green Cove Springs—the Mothball Fleet. Over the years, one-by-one they would be cut loose and tugged away to be broken up for scrap.

The war might be over, but Archie remained on active duty for over a year, serving aboard the USS Conner (DD 582) and USS Charette (DD 581) in the Atlantic Fleet from January 23, 1946 to August 12, 1946—when he was honorably discharged. Although his service was brief, it made him eligible for the GI Bill, thus helping him go to college. Archie jokingly referred to himself as an "eighteen day veteran."

Reservists Stand Trick at Wheel

Seaman First Class Archie Connors (center) stands by to relieve Seaman Second Class Alson Wall at the helm of the Destroyer USS Tills. The Tills was on a 1946 training cruise in the Caribbean. Connors later served aboard the USS Conner (DD 582) and USS Charette (DD 581) in the Atlantic Fleet.

College Education—
Ticket To A Brighter Future

Jacksonville Junior College (now Jacksonville University) was chartered by the State of Florida as an institution of higher learning in 1934. For many years the small junior college struggled from one temporary location to another, never having more than 60 or 70 students enrolled at any one time. Classes met at night, Monday through Thursday, with lab work scheduled on Friday's. The downtown public library was the principal source of reference material. Courses offered in the early days of this

Student Council President. *In December, 1948 Archie Connors was elected President of the Jacksonville Junior College Student Council. The Florida Times Union ran this photograph of him installing the new officers of the sophomore class at JJC who "were inducted into office in an impressive ceremony at the Student Council meeting yesterday. Connors (left) inducts Philip Helow, Sophomore Class President, Rosemary McEachern, class secretary, and Shannon Poppell, sophomore vice president."*

now distinguished institution included: English, history, biology, chemistry, physics, math, accounting, advertising, psychology and Spanish.

Florida Relays 1948 *medals for the Sprint Medley Relay and the Mile Relay for Freshman and Junior College Class participatants. Archie Connors (first row, second from left) won these as a member of the Jacksonville Junior College Track Team.*

The fledgling college struggled along until 1943 when the Civitan Club raised the money to purchase a home for the college. Enlisting the help of other Jacksonville civic leaders, the club raised over $50,000 for the new home and for other facilities.

Following his discharge from the Navy in late 1946, Archie Connors enrolled at JJC. He would complete his two-year degree in Pre-Law in 1949.

Archie was elected Vice President of the JJC Student Council in 1948 and then President in 1949. He was still very active in sports and took home medals from the state competition in pole vaulting and relays that year. His sports reporting contributions to the school newspaper brought him a commendation from college president, Garth Akridge.

Archie loved sports, although he was not big enough physically to compete well in major contact sports. During 1948 he combined his love of sports and writing skills and served as Sports Editor for the Junior College *Fledging*.

On June 28, 1948 Garth Akridge, JJC President, sent Archie a letter explaining the "commendable service that you rendered the publication has been brought to my attention. You are to be commended for the unselfish service and fine teamwork that you have demonstrated and without which the newspaper would have been noticeably less successful. Your experiences in this connection should prove to be a continuous source of service and satisfaction to you. I feel confident that each member of the Board of Trustees, faculty, student body, and the other members of the Fledging staff would want to join me in expressing to you sincere appreciation for a good job well done."

On Friday evening of May 27, 1949 Archie and his parents were at the Jacksonville Woman's Club long before 8:00 p.m. It was the Fifteenth Annual Commencement Exercise for Jacksonville Junior College [now Jacksonville University]. Archie was one of 38 to graduate with the Class of 1949.

Swimming With Archie

In 1948 the Connors family did something it had never done before and would never do again—they had a "lake party." Eva's brother, David Miller Haddock's son, James had married Barbara Marie Binckley. The Binckley's had a water front vacation home on Lake Santa Fe, a drive of several hours from Jacksonville. The clan trooped down to Lake Sante Fe for a day of picnicking, swimming and just being together.

While the adults spread out all the delicious food in preparation for a memorable lunch, the younger kids and grand kids headed down to the lake.

Tracy was eight years old and had been swimming for about a year. His mother, Miriam would drive him from their North Shore neighborhood, down to Springfield Pool for his swimming lessons with the Red Cross. He had advanced from Beginner to Intermediate swimmer and was proud of his newly acquired ability.

A rare treat for the group was the fact that 21-year old Archie had decided to come along. After Navy duty at the end of World War II, he had used the GI Bill to start college. He had a heavy class load at Jacksonville Junior College and was increasingly absent from family functions.

Archie was an outstanding swimmer. He had kept himself in shape since his days at Robert E. Lee High School on the track, swimming and football teams. As a JJC Student he continued to run track and to coach swimming.

It was natural then for Archie to jump—not dive—off the dock (to test the water depth), and for him to strike out for deeper water with a strong crawl stroke. If Archie can do it, so can I, Tracy thought to himself, as he too, jumped into the deep water and struck out. Well, more like dog paddled out. Seeing his nephew's determination, Archie swam back to check on Tracy.

Connors Family 1948. By 1948, when Arch and Eva's family gathered in their front room for this photograph, their children and grandchildren were prospering. (Front row) Gerald Connors, Jr., John David Connors, Kathryn Coles, Tracy D. Connors, Peter Hagan, Paul Hagan. (Second row) Majorie Cooper Connors (holding W. Bruce Connors), Miriam Morris Connors, Arch and Eva Connors, Lucille Connors, Florence Connors Spink, Julia Connors Coles and Mary Elizabeth Connors Hagan (holding Mark Hagan). (Back row) William Gerald Connors, Sr., Woodrow Rufus Daniel Connors, Archibald Haddock Connors, Jr., and Claude Spink. Archie was attending Jacksonville Junior College.

"Are you sure you want to swim out further?" he asked him.

"Yes, I do!" Tracy answered, determined to keep up with the uncle he admired.

"Well, OK," Archie answered, treading water effortlessly and looking at him closely. "Put your arms around my neck and hold on," he instructed.

Tracy did so, and Archie began a slow but powerful breast stroke that moved them steadily out into the lake.

After they had gone about 100 yards out, Archie stopped and they treaded water there together. It was one of the few times that Tracy could remember actually being alone with Archie. Usually, when they were together, there were other family members around. Now, it was just the two of them—treading water together in the middle of the lake.

They talked about nothing much in particular, but it was very special to Tracy to be singled out for the first *mano a mano* time with Archie.

The special moments didn't last too long.

Their absence had been noted. Soon, Miller's wife, Blanche spotted them and yelled at Archie to "bring that boy back in here...right now!" Her tone was light hearted, but tinged with concern, as well.

Frankie Simpson. *Shortly after he graduated from Jacksonville Junior College, Archie went to a party and through a mutual friend, met a young woman named Frances Lutye Simpson, a visitor from St. Louis. "Frankie," was as beautiful as she was willful and headstrong. Archie soon told his mother, Eva that he had "met the girl I'm going to marry." His charming good looks and engaging personality, coupled with her beauty and spirited independence made them an extraordinarily handsome couple.*

Tracy knew the moment was over and paddled around behind Archie and put his arms around his neck. In a few moments, Archie was slowly breast stroking back towards the dock towing his nephew.

Tracy had never felt so safe or secure as when he was out in deep water—with Archie.

Into The Air Force

Following his graduation from JJC in 1949, Connors decided to join the Air Force, to use his two-year degree as the means to enter flight training. He had decided he wanted to be a fighter pilot. He "put in his papers" for appointment as an Aviation Cadet. It was also during this period that he went to a party and through a mutual friend, met a young woman named Frances "Frankie" Simpson, a visitor from St. Louis.

Frankie Simpson was a beautiful and poised graduate of finishing schools, who had just begun to acquire modeling jobs before she began visiting Jacksonville. "She had glossy chestnut hair falling almost to her waist," her future niece Kathryn Coles McCluskey recalled. "In an era when most women had bobbed hair, her glamorous, upswept hairdos turned heads."

Frankie was as beautiful as she was willful and headstrong. Her curvaceous figure and sassy independence immediately attracted the handsome, soon to be aviation cadet. Archie's sister, Lucille, remembered that Archie soon told his mother, Eva that he had "met the girl I'm going to marry." His charming good looks and engaging personality, coupled with her shapely form and beautiful features made them a striking couple.

"Make Archie behave!"

On Sunday, May 7, 1950 Frankie Simpson wrote Arch and Eva Connors from St. Louis, Missouri. She had recently returned from Jacksonville and a visit with Archie.

"Dear Folks, This is the first chance I've had to sit down and relax for

Archie and Frankie at Jacksonville Beach, Florida in 1950, shortly before he entered Air Force flight training.

a minute, so I knew I'd better write while I have time.

"I really miss you people and Florida, too. And would give anything to be there. But right now I know I have duties here so guess I'm stuck. My boss is so glad I'm back—wish I were half as happy. It's going to be rough going to work tomorrow, but I have to or starve to death and you know how I love to eat."

"Maybe you thought I was crazy Saturday night for calling Archie, but I was so blue and it did help me a lot. You have a wonderful son, but you know that. He's really treated me nice and his entire family has, too. I thank you all."

"How have you been getting along? Guess you are cooking every spare moment. Is Mr. Connors' eye any better—or won't he admit anything? He certainly hates to gripe."

"Everyone admires my tan and I'm really proud of it. All the other people up here look so white. I went swimming today and nearly froze to death. It's very different from Florida—darn it."

I've run out of things to say so had better close. You promised to answer, so please don't forget. Make Archie behave!" She closed with "Love, Frankie."

The Canasta Game

During that school year, Tracy spent a great deal of time over at his grandparents. From the time he could ride the bus by himself, he had been allowed to visit them frequently on weekends by taking the bus downtown, and changing to the one that stopped directly in front of their home in west Jacksonville.

In early 1950, his visits were particularly memorable—he was old enough to play Canasta.

Before television, remarkably enough, people actually read books in the evening, sometimes out loud to each other. Arch loved just about anything written about the West, particularly any novel by Zane Grey. Another popular pastime was playing cards. Canasta was Arch's favorite card game. Naturally, it was the game the family played after supper and Eva and Tracy had finished washing the dishes together. She washed, he dried.

The long dining room table would be cleared and the plastic table cloth (over the lace cloth) would be wiped clean. The cards were set out. The evening's entertainment had begun.

During the spring of 1950, some of those evenings were very special. Archie would join the gathering with his beautiful new fiancé, Frankie, visiting from St. Louis. Arch, puffing on his King Edward, sat at the head of the table. Eva sat to his right, as usual; it was the chair closest to the kitchen. Tracy sat beside her. Archie and Frankie would sit to Arch's left, across from Eva and Tracy.

Once the cards were dealt, the real fun began. Arch took Canasta, like most things in life, very seriously. He played to win, and he did win against almost all of his family—except Archie. The game would go on for hours with left-handed Frankie meticulously keeping score in neat rows. Most games were tight, nip and tuck battles between Arch and Archie. But Archie had a secret weapon—the hidden Canasta. Somehow, he would assemble the exact number and type of cards needed to "go out"—to conclude the hand. Those still holding cards were penalized their face value. In addition, the one with the hidden Canasta earned 600 points.

Arch Connors (wearing his "trademark" Panama hat) headed his own building construction company, A.H. Connors and Sons, later Connors Construction Company. His sons, Woodrow and Gerald, were his partners. In the years after WW II, the company built hundreds of new homes for Jacksonville residents, many of them returning veterans.

At the end of one exceptionally hard fought game, Arch was growing very nervous. He knew Archie's talent and suspected he was up to something. The heat in the room was beyond the ability of the fan sawing away in the attic. The tension mounted around the table as cards were drawn and discarded. Finally, those around the table saw a small flicker of a smile on the very corner of Arch's mouth. Just a flicker. Then it hit Tracy, Archie was working on his own hidden Canasta. His hand was so loaded with cards he could hardly hold them all.

It was then that Archie struck. With his shy, but devilish smile and a tilt of his head like "Oh well...," he fanned the cards down onto the plastic with an audible strumming sound. The card sharks around the table all knew what that meant—Archie had come up with yet another hidden Canasta and had "Gone Out," concluding that game with everyone being penalized by the number of points of the cards they held in their hand.

No one said a word. Only the laboring attic fan sucked away at the humid Florida air.

The ash fell off Arch's cigar onto the plastic tablecloth. Although he tried to control himself, he was incredulous, he couldn't help himself. "God dammit," he swore as he stood up quickly and threw his cards down onto the table. Then he walked rapidly to his bedroom and closed it behind him—hard.

Those left around the table looked at each other, eyes dancing with surprise and disbelief, then laughed until tears welled up—over their fingers—which were clamped firmly over their mouths.

Only Eva's delicious chocolate cake enticed Arch out of the room half an hour later, with no further mention of the incident or who won the game.

It was the family's last Canasta game with Archie. Soon after that, he entered Air Force flight training in Waco, Texas. He had decided to become a pilot. It seemed like a prudent thing to do. The country was at peace around the world. No wars or shooting conflicts in sight and the commercial aviation industry was growing rapidly. The $50,000 cost of training a new pilot was paid by the taxpayers. After serving their active duty military obligation for the training, military pilots could easily translate those skills into airline cockpits.

Pilot Training

On December 7, 1949, the Air Training Command at Scott Air Force Base, Illinois informed Archie that he had "been selected for assignment for aviation cadet training in Class 51-A.

The Agreement to Accept Aviation Cadet Appointment that Archie signed and returned, advised him that if he was married before or during the period of training that he would not be "extended privileges in addition to those afforded unmarried cadets." He would be required to live in barracks throughout the period of training and that no travel allowance or quarters would be available for his dependents during the period.

Archie Connors was going to get his chance to be an Air Force pilot—but first he had to get through cadet training. He reported for duty on May 29, 1950.

"In qualifying for this appointment, you have met the high standards necessarily required by the new United States Air Force. It is hoped that you will be successful in realizing an ambition to take your place in this organization as an officer and pilot," the Air Training Command letter said.

On May 26, 1950, Aviation Cadet A.H. Connors, Jr., enlisted in the USAF,

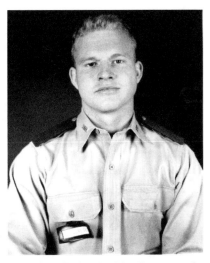

Aviation Cadet Archie Connors, the first official Air Force photograph made of the new cadet in June 1950.

and was assigned service number AF 14 353 100. On military active duty for the second time in his life, he had moved from Seaman First Class to Aviation Cadet, a rank he would hold for the next thirteen months.

A/C Connors was two months shy of his 23rd birthday when he joined the Air Force. His records from that time indicate that he carried a muscular 160 pounds on a 5' 7" frame. He had brown eyes, blond hair and a "ruddy" complexion. Under "sports" he noted that he excelled in track and football, and "participated" in swimming. He also noted coaching experience at both high school and college levels. [1]

By June 2nd, A/C Connors had arrived at Connally AFB, Texas, and had prepared an Application for National Service Life Insurance. The principal beneficiary was his mother, Eva May Haddock Connors. That life insurance policy would become a major issue several years later. Warrant Officer Hershell Winship, the Assistant Adjutant, certified "that applicant commenced regular and frequent aerial flights as an Aviation Cadet effective 1 June 1950 and is entitled to NSLI at Gov't expense under provisions of PL 658, 77 Congress."

The Korean War

In June 1950, nephew Tracy was a free and happy ten-year-old boy. Happy that he had just "graduated" from the fifth grade and free because it was now summer vacation. There were trees to climb, including the "big oak" across the street from his home on West 58th Street. As a rite of passage now that he was growing up rapidly—not a kid—any longer—he planned to conquer its massive trunk and limbs that summer.

There were boats to build in his father's garage, and float in the puddles formed in the as yet unpaved street—among the last to be paved in the Jacksonville, Florida neighborhood of North Shore.

In the summer of 1950 he was en route to the sixth grade of North Shore Elementary School.

Meanwhile, there were cookouts to be held in the back yard in preparation for joining the Boy Scouts in the fall, when he would be eleven years old and eligible. Miriam had designated her oldest frying pan for this purpose. Tracy and younger brother, David would slice potatoes up into big chunks, as they watched the fire carefully. Then, when the pan full of Crisco was hot enough, they would add the potatoes.

While they watched the potatoes cook, they toasted marshmallows. Just because they reversed the process didn't cause the potatoes to taste any less mouth-watering when they were finally done. Today, they would be called "home fries." Back then, they were just the best French fries in the world, especially with some salt and catsup.

Tracy's "world" that summer centered on a single square mile of territory in North Jacksonville, and included his neighborhood, his church, and his school. On June 25, 1950, his world and that of all Americans changed forever. On that day, North Korean armed forces invaded South Korea. Archie had worn his Air Force uniform for exactly three weeks.

A war had started in a country Americans knew little about. The Connors family didn't know it then, but it would involve them in tragedy and change their lives forever. Their family, like millions of other families of all nations, would soon learn that history books are simplistic. Historians and politicians assign dates to wars and conflicts—it began on this date and ended on that date. For the families involved, wars may start, but they never really end—for those families. For the Connors family, the Korean War began on a summer day in 1950, but the pain and loss it brought into their lives goes on to this day.

Two days later, on June 27th, the United Nations Security Council adopted a Resolution sponsored by the United States approving armed intervention on the side of the South Koreans. The report in the Jacksonville Journal noted that the Soviet delegation to the UN was absent from this session. President Truman had acted rapidly to push the Resolution through the UN. He remembered the critical mistakes made at Munich by British Prime Minister Neville Chamberlain in appeasing Hitler.

General Douglas MacArthur was given command of a 17-nation, U.N. force, half of which was United States forces, 43 percent South Korean, and about 9 percent other countries.

The papers and the radio were full of news about the Korean "police action," called that because war was never actually declared by Congress. And, throughout that summer, the reports made it clear the bad guys were kicking the bejesus out of the "police."

*(L-R) **RADM James H. Doyle, BGen E. K. Wright, General of the Army Douglas MacArthur and MGen Edward M. Almond** on the bridge of USS Mt. McKinley (AGC 7) during the Inchon Amphibious landing on 15 September 1950. (NARA) MacArthur was happy to take the credit for the "breakout." However Air Force Historian Robert Futrell credits effective close air support and interdiction in the weeks before the landing as the reason for the rapid turnaround and the collapse of the North Korean Army.*

On July 1st, the first U.S. ground forces landed in Korea. From the outset, they were on the defensive, being pushed steadily down the peninsula into a pocket—the "Pusan Perimeter"—around the port of Pusan.

The war in Korea WAS the news that summer, but it was far away in a country few had ever even heard of. It would soon move a lot closer.

On September 15, 1950, against the advice of his military planners, MacArthur led an amphibious landing at Inchon, taking the North Korean forces totally by surprise, and cutting them off near the middle of the peninsula. Meanwhile, the "trapped" forces at Pusan burst out of the defensive perimeter and blitzed up through South Korea. The risky landing had turned the tide of the war dramatically. The folks back home were jubilant. The worst was over. Speculation began that maybe "the boys" could be back home for Christmas.

During the social studies portion of his junior high school lessons, Tracy's fellow students would discuss the war. To them, born just before World War Two, American forces were supposed to be victorious. Yes, America had been caught off guard by those "dirty Commies," but once the country got into it, it was certain that America would win. After all, America had better equipment and better soldiers. Who could expect any outcome other than victory? General MacArthur reminded Americans that there is no substitute for victory.

Learning to Fly

From Texas on July 15, 1950 Archie wrote to his mother, Eva. "Dear Mom: Certainly enjoyed talking to you. Sure wish I was home now. We sure catch it. They have loosened up a lot though we can eat almost enough. I have to walk three hours this afternoon and next Saturday and the next after that."

"The flying is pretty good and our instructors are the best. Whenever we make a mistake they know it before we do it. Seems a little uncanny how they do it. I foul up all the time and he lets me know too. That's not too bad though for I know everyone is fouling up too."

"I am about average in my military standing, 24 demerits. My studies aren't quite up to par but that week in the hospital really fouled me up."

"We have a nice bunch of fellows here, nearly all of them have at least a year of college and come from good homes. That makes it nice because we have similar backgrounds."

"Frankie will be down in about a month or so and she will probably stay for a while with you and her other friend who lives out on Edgewood [Avenue, on Jacksonville's west side]. She should be pretty good company."

That's Sweat Kid. *Unidentified 2nd Classman "indoctrinating 4th Classman Air Cadet Archie Connors (left). "That's sweat kid," Archie wrote on the back of this photograph he sent Frankie. "But not anymore. I looked like h--- didn't I?"*

"I may be home before Christmas, that is, if I wash out. Quite a few fellows haven't got what it takes. They try hard and do their best but just can't seem to fly an airplane. Others don't look around enough; keep their head in the cockpit. That is called 'dangerous tendencies.'"

"Well Mom, I will write again tomorrow. Your Son, Archie. P.S. Tell Woody I will return the compliment as soon as I can."

Life As A Cadet

As a Fourth Classman, Aviation Cadet Connors lived in wooden barracks and wore a very basic uniform consisting of dungarees and a "fore and aft cap." When Reveille was sounded, they had to be ready to fall out in uniform literally within seconds of the "official" wake up alarm. Since shaving was impossible in the brief time allowed, they worked out a system of getting up before Reveille, then to quickly take turns shaving while classmates held a blanket over the window (to prevent any light from escaping from the officially still darkened barracks).

Meanwhile, Third Classmen, already up, shaved and dressed, were "patrolling" the areas outside the Fourth Classman barracks—looking for any lights. "If they spotted some light coming from your window, you had had it," Wilfred "Budd" Stapley remembered. [2]

They dared not get caught looking out of their room. Even a slight glance out of the window could earn the distracted Cadet another hour of military drill.

Just prior to Reveille, the shaved, uniformed Cadets would be poised by the door. At the sound of the wake up call, they would pour outside—

"elbows over @$$holes"—and into ranks, ready for inspection by Third Classmen ever ready to find flaws in uniforms or bearing. These meant Extra Military Instruction or EMI in the form of "tours" that were marched off—one hour of marching for each tour. Too many "tours" and a Cadet was washed out permanently.

The initial six weeks of pre-flight training was called "Ground school," and consisted of basic military subjects and introductions to subjects relating to aviation and aerodynamics. Pre-flight was pre-flight. The trainees were not even Cadets. "You are the lowest scum in the world," Stapley said.

Their days were spent mostly in school, with other periods devoted to tedious military drill instruction and to keeping the old barracks clean. The day lasted from about 0430 until 2030.

Following six weeks of ground school, the new "Cadet" was advanced to Fourth Classman—when the hazing started in earnest. Most of it conducted by those just a few weeks ahead of them in the training process. The Third Class was responsible for indoctrinating the fourth class into the cadet corps. Each class lasted about six weeks.

The "indoctrination" was intense and often mystifying to the Fourth Classmen.

The Aviation Cadets ate a "square meal"—perched on only the front three inches of their seats, backs ramrod straight, chests out, they kept their heads down as they brought food to their mouths from the plate, straight up to a point directly opposite their mouths, then in a straight line into their mouths.

This was the typical practice—until there was an "air raid." The cadet at the end of the mess table was the designated "tail gunner." Cadets sitting along the sides of the table were "side gunners."

At that time, milk was bottled in small half-pint glass containers capped with circular wax coated cardboard plugs that were removed or replaced by pull up tabs in the center of the

"This is known as a 'Brace,' something that a person should never get into," Archie wrote on the back of this snapshot sent to Frankie. *"The uniform that I am wearing is known as a 'raunchy' uniform."* Then he added, *"I love Frankie with all my heart!"* and drew a heart. *"Please note the wrinkles."*

plugs. Each time the cadet drank the milk, the plug was to be removed and then replaced—tightly.

During an "air raid," upper classmen would start the slow, upward wailing of an air raid "siren." The "tail gunners" would stand up and begin to fire their "weapons" loudly ...boom...boom...boom... following the imaginary "bogie" around the room.

Fourth Classmen had to quickly grab their milk container and that of a nearby Cadet to form a set of "binoculars," that were then brought up to the eyes in order to spot the "attacking aircraft." Of course, if the Cadet had

not replaced the plug tightly enough, the upended milk bottle immediately poured all remaining liquid all over the hapless Cadet. If a Cadet was caught "cheating"—sneaking his thumbs up and over the loose milk plugs—he was punished with a "tour," one hour of extra marching. The lesson being drilled into the Cadet by such "indoctrination," was attention to detail, and that in order to survive you had to depend on your buddy.

"Soloed TODAY!"

The big thrill for Fourth Classmen was "starting to fly." That was what it was all about...why they had joined the Air Force. "You could take an awful lot of 'stuff' if every day you were able to get into the cockpit of an airplane," Stapley remembered.

Most Cadet washouts came while they were Third Classmen. Beginning with the Third Classman period, Cadets began to get enough flight time for the Air Force to determine whether the student pilots did not yet have the training or experience to attempt to compensate or correct a landing in an aircraft bouncing from one wheel to another down the field.

On the big day, the proficient aviation cadet could announce, "I—Aviation Cadet Stapley, Wilfred C. of the supersonic second squadron...SOLOED TODAY!"

The entire mess hall would then cheer and clap.

As a Second or First Classman, Cadets were given more authority in their small worlds—Table Commandant—and were proud to wear some extra stripes on their Cadet shoulder boards. On October 26, 1950, Connors "old classification title Aviation Cadet" was "converted to Primary AFS Aviation Cadet." Perhaps because he could now foresee that he would make it through Air Force pilot training and get his commission, Archie and Frankie decided to get married.

The Mustang

On December 5, 1950, Airman Cadet A. H. Connors, Jr., was ordered to the 3615th Pilot Training Wing, Advanced Single Engine, at Craig AFB, Alabama. The Air Force had established an Advance Flying Training School at Craig Air Force Base near Selma, Alabama on May 3, 1941. Over the 37 years of its existence as an Air Force Base, Craig graduated over 30,000 student pilots after extensive training in fighter-type aircraft.

During six months of intensive training Archie had completed 135 flight hours in the T-6 aircraft, 57 of them solo hours. He had achieved an overall academic average of 77, with his best subjects being Aero Physics (92) and Flight Instruments (85). He earned a grade of only 69 in Principles of Flight early in the course of training, but his scores improved as the training progressed.

Soon his fledgling skills as an airman would be tested to the limit as he moved from the slow, stable Texan to the legendary F-51D [3] "Mustang." Halfway through Advanced Single Engine Aircraft training at Craig AFB, Archie, Budd and their classmates transitioned from T-6s trainers into true fighter aircraft.

"It was a big change," Stapley recalled. "The T-6 was a trainer aircraft, very stable. Very forgiving. If you made a sloppy slow roll—it would do that for you. If you made a sloppy slow roll in the F-51 you might just end up in a spin or a snap roll. I loved the '51, but it took a pilot to fly that bird," Stapley said.

The P-51 was truly a pilot's airplane. It operated effectively on the deck and all the way up to 40,000 ft. In maneuverability and load carrying capacity, it ranked with any other fighter in the world. For new pilots, mastering the P-51, and surviving to talk about it, would take plenty of hard work—it meant being not only a pilot, but a whole crew—pilot, navigator, gunner, bombardier and radio operator—all rolled into one. The markings on this aircraft indicate the photograph was taken over the Southwestern U.S. in the late Forties.

Magpie Flight of Class 51-D. *(L. to R.) 2nd Lt. Richard E. Chard of Rochester, Illinois, Flight Lieutenant Graham Hulse, RAF, 2nd Lt. Archie Connors, and 2nd Lt. William E. Gibson of The Dalles, Oregon. Flight Lieutenant Hulse was a qualified pilot at age 15 and flew a Spitfire in the Battle of Britain. In March 1953, then Squadron Leader Hulse was an exchange pilot assigned to the 336th Fighter Interceptor Squadron, with two MiG kills. On March 13, 1953 he was was shot down in North Korea when he flew right in front of his wingman's gun fire during a chaotic dogfight. Periodic communications with the downed pilot indicated that he evaded capture for over two weeks. However, he was never accounted for by the North Koreans, Chinese, or Soviets. This photograph commemorated Archie's solo flight in a Mustang.*

When the new pilots of Class 51-D began to study the pilot training manual for the F-51 Mustang, the first paragraph they read let them know that they were joining an elite group of war fighters.

A Pilot's Airplane

As Archie approached the F-51 he was to take on a solo flight for the first time, he remembered the background on the fighter that he had read in the pilot's manual.

"Like the Indian braves of the Old Southwest whose favorite in battle was the small speedy Mustang, young fighter pilots today, with their newly won wings, almost without exception want to fly the famous namesake of that sleek and powerful war horse." [4]

The P-515 is truly a pilot's airplane, the manual explained. "In mission after mission, it has proved that it can more than hold its own against any opposition. Its speed and range are tops. It operates effectively on the deck, and all the way up to 40,000 ft. In maneuverability and load carrying capacity, it ranks with any other fighter in the world."

The manual acknowledged that the original Mustangs were built for Britain's RAF. Flown by RAF pilots, Mustangs saw initial action in the summer of 1942. The British used the Mustang primarily for Reconnaissance and rhubarb missions—zooming in at low altitudes to strafe trains, troops, and enemy installations.

Second Lieutenant Wilfred C. "Budd" Stapley of Hammond, Indiana was Archie's roommate during their training at Craig AFB. Archie and Budd also trained at Luke AFB together.

The new P-51s were the first American built fighters to take the war back across the English Channel after Dunkirk. They were so successful that the United States AAF decided to adopt the Mustang as its own. Eventually, the Allison engine was replaced by the more powerful Rolls-Royce Merlin engine with a two-speed blower. Along with other improvements, the prop was increased from 3 to 4 blades. The new model would prove to be an unquestioned success and eventually would become the most successful fighter plane of World War Two. The Mustangs were feared by their adversaries at any altitude and mission from escorting bombers all the way to Poland to low altitude interdiction as they tree hopped back to their bases.

For new pilots, however, mastering the P-51, and surviving to talk about it, would take plenty of hard work. "For being a first rate fighter pilot means being not only a pilot, but a whole crew—pilot, navigator, gunner, bombardier and radio operator—all rolled into one." [5]

For Budd Stapley, his first time in the P-51 he found that he was very nervous, and his knees were shaking. Not because he was scared, but from anticipation. "This was what it was all about." As he headed down the runway on his first take off in the P-51, he thought to himself: "My God, I'm by myself…in a P-51." The "exaltation of flying that bird for the first time was something you never forget. I loved the '51," he remembered.

Archie and Frankie Get Married

Sometime during the winter of 1950, while he was still in flight training, Archie and Frankie decided to get married. Archie asked his brother,

Woodrow to attend the wedding and to be his best man. It was a long trip across Florida to Selma, Alabama in late January 1951—over ten hours—on two-lane roads in Woodrow's 1947 Dodge sedan. Woodrow drove. Miriam and Tracy sat up front. Arch, Eva and grandson, David were in the back seat. It was winter and very cold. The windows stayed up. Incredibly, Arch sat in the back smoking his cigars—in a closed car. He never asked permission, and no one spoke up to ask him not to. He could be what today would be called "insensitive." When he was smoking, the windows up front stayed cracked, regardless of the cold.

Wedding At Craig AFB. *Members of Archie's family drove non-stop from Jacksonville, Florida to Montgomery, Alabama to attend his wedding to Frances Simpson. Woodrow, Miriam, Tracy, David, Arch and Eva endured the close confines of Woodrow's 1947 Dodge sedan for the ride through bitterly cold weather in January 1951. After the ceremony, during which Woodrow served as best man and Miriam as matron of honor, they gathered on the steps of the chapel for one photograph by nephew, Tracy, with his trusty Brownie Hawkeye box camera. Nervous hands by the eleven-year old "photographer" nearly left the Chaplain out of the picture entirely.*

Later, Archie took Woodrow and Tracy out onto the "flight line" at Craig Air Force Base. He escorted them up and down rows of airplanes, many of them B-25s. Tracy remembered that General Doolittle had led a squadron of planes just like these in a daring raid over Japan not quite six months after Pearl Harbor.

Woodrow saw Tracy eyeing the bombers. He warned Tracy not to touch the planes, but the gravitational pull of the bombers was simply more than the eleven year-old could resist. What could a touch hurt, he asked himself? Archie and Woodrow walked slightly ahead of him. As he passed beneath the wing of this powerful, exotic bird he trailed his hand through the air and somehow, almost by some perverse "magic," his hand "accidentally" contacted the propeller.

The touch of the cold metal sent shivers up and down his back. Even as they trailed along the front surface of the blade, his fingers bonded to the atoms on the surface. For those few moments, he was a part of that plane which had and would again, roar down the runway and lift off into another world. For an instant the thought ran through his head what would happen to his hand if, at that precise moment, the engine would cough, catch, then rumble into full throttle.

(Upper right) **First official photograph** taken by the U.S. Air Force of Aviation Cadet Archie Connors. *(Below)* The same photograph was used in a news article announcing that he had completed pilot training.

Aviation Cadet Archibald H. Connors Jr., has been assigned to Craig Air Force Base, Selma, Ala., and will begin training in the F-51 Mustang fighter. He is the son of Mr. and Mrs. A. L. Connors Sr., 165 Broadway avenue.

Connors completed a seven-month period of basic flying training at Connally Air Force Base, Waco, Texas, logging more than 130 hours in the T-6 Texan. This training included dual and solo, night and instrument flying, cross country, aerobatic, navigation and related aerial academic subjects.

The cadet graduated from Lee high school and completed studies at Jacksonville Junior College where he lettered in track. He was vice president of the freshman class and president and vice chairman of the student council while attending junior college. He also was sports editor of the college publication.

From 1945 through 1947, Connors served in the Navy on destroyer duty.

Tracy's reverie took only seconds, but long enough for Woodrow to see his hand brush across the propeller. He glowered, chewed him out, and would have sent him back to the car where Miriam, Frankie and David were waiting. Tracy was devastated, head hung down, near tears.

Archie came to the rescue. Using all his charm, he implored Woodrow not to send Tracy back to the car. Finally, with a face that said it was against his better judgment but just for you, Archie, Woodrow nodded his head. Tracy could stay. He was ecstatic. Archie put his arm on Tracy's shoulder and led him down the flight line pointing out features of the various aircraft. With Archie's arm around his shoulder, Tracy remembered the swim in Lake Brooklyn with Archie and how safe he had felt.

The next day, Archie and Frankie were married in the base chapel. Miriam and Woodrow were the wedding party. The rest of the family sat in the Air Force Chapel pews. After the brief ceremony, the four of them plus the chaplain stood at the front entrance to the chapel. Proud of the fact that he could use his Brownie Hawkeye, Tracy lined them up in a row, asked them to smile, and took their picture. It was the only picture taken at their wedding. It was one of the last pictures Tracy would ever be able to take of Archie. And, not too many months later, Tracy was called on to make a photograph connected to Archie that haunted him the rest of his life.

Several days later, on February 1, 1951 AVC Connors started a monthly allotment to his new wife of $127.50. Three weeks later, on February 27, 1951, AVC Connors was assigned to the 3617th Training Squadron at Craig Air Force Base (Selma), Alabama. On that date he submitted a Certificate for Increased Allowances, noting that he had married Lutye F. Connors on January 27, 1951. Warrant Officer R. A. Fuller added to the form his certification that Connors "applied for Flying Training prior to 1 October 1949, and therefore was authorized to marry."

New Pilots

Archie was winding up his training to qualify for a commission and for designation as a Pilot.

On May 4, 1951 the Faculty Board for the Advanced Single Engine Pilot School at Craig AFB, Alabama went into session. "A quorum being present the board then proceeded to consider the physical, moral, educational, and professional qualifications of each trainee due to complete his training on or about June 22, 1951. The board finds that each trainee listed hereinafter is physically morally, educationally, and professionally qualified for the appointment as recommended and for the aeronautical rating has recommended." Aviation Cadet A. H. Connors Jr. was among those recommended for appointment as a Second Lieutenant in the United States Air

Force Reserve and granted the aeronautical rating of Pilot.

"To all the members of Class 51-D I extend my heartiest congratulations," Colonel John H. Bundy, USAF told the graduates as the Commanding Officer of Craig Air Force Base. "You are not only one of the best pilots in the world, but a fighter pilot in the world's best Air Force. In your new assignment we expect your utmost in the performance of your mission. Knowing that you have received the finest training in the world today, I am confident that this class will establish a record we will all be proud of," Bundy concluded. He was right about several things. Many of the 51-D Class would give their "utmost" in a mountainous land half way around the world and they certainly established a prideful record.

Truman Fires MacArthur

On April 14, 1951, President Harry Truman relieved General Douglas MacArthur as Commander of the Far East command and replaced him with General Matthew B. Ridgway. MacArthur had repeatedly requested authorization to bomb the bridges over the Yalu River to prevent Chinese troops and supplies from pouring into North Korea. MacArthur's firing created a firestorm of public indignation. Upon his arrival in the United States for

---

Instructor's Lament...
from the 51-D Classbook

The cadet is my pilot; Him I shall not want.
He makes me forced landings in rough pastures;
He leadeth me into trees and high-tension wires.
He destroys my confidence, he leads me into the paths of oncoming traffic.
Yea, though I ride through the air in the shadow of death, I fear all evil for he is with me;
His stick and rudder confuse me.
He prepares stalls and loops in the presence of
All planes in the air, my temper runneth over.
Surely goodness and mercy has followed me all
The days of my life and I shall be grateful if
You will spare my life and let this Yo Yo graduate.

the first time in eleven years, Gen. MacArthur received a hero's welcome and a ticker tape parade through Manhattan. He was invited to address a Joint Session of Congress. Interrupted by thirty ovations, he urged military action against Communist China. His warning that "In war, there is no substitute for victory," would haunt and bedevil America for years—many would say to this day. Soon, like the lyrics of the old song he quoted in his address, he would "fade away."

Meanwhile, Gen. Ridgway sent North Korea a proposal to negotiate a cease-fire agreement; however, further attempts to negotiate an armistice failed. In the ground war, UN forces captured "Heartbreak Ridge" north of Yangu.

Lt. Gen. James A. Van Fleet, USA, assumed command of the U.S. Eighth Army succeeding General Ridgway.

Three days later, President Truman signed an executive order extending U.S. military enlistments involuntarily by nine months, an indication of the manpower shortage facing the military services during the war.

The Air war in Korea was challenging—and deadly. Far East Air Forces (FEAF) was averaging over 1,000 combat sorties per day, of which nearly 350 were close air support—one of the highest daily totals prior to 1953. The 18th Fighter-Bomber Wing with four squadrons flying the

Visit To The Front. *Lt. Gen. Matthew Ridgway, MG Doyle Hickey and General Douglas MacArthur, CINC UN Forces in Korea in a jeep at a command post near Yang Yang, Korea on April 3, 1951. MacArthur had less than two weeks before he would be relieved of command and sent back to the United States. In mid-April, President Harry S Truman shocked the world by replacing General MacArthur, who had publicly criticized the administration's Korean War policies, with Lt. Gen. Matthew B. Ridgway, USA. (NARA)*

F-51D Mustang, was among the units most heavily relied upon for Close Air Support.

End of the Pipeline

As the war in Korea entered its second year, it had already killed over three million Koreans. American casualties then were over 15,000 dead and 75,000 wounded. The actual fighting would continue for another two years. Another 20,000 Americans would die in this "police action."

On June 18, 1951, A/C A. H. Connors, Jr. was honorably discharged by the Air Force to accept a commission as 2nd Lieutenant, USAFR. His new orders assigned him to Luke AFB, Arizona to begin 10 weeks of combat crew training in the F-51 fighter aircraft. From January 2, 1951 through June 22, 1951 he had accumulated over 64 hours in the T-6 trainer and 63 hours in the F-51 fighter-bomber aircraft.

On June 22, 1951, at Craig Air Force Base, Selma, Alabama, the Air Force Advanced Single Engine Pilot Training School graduated Aviation Cadet Class 51-D. One of the proud graduates at the base theater that Friday morning was Lieutenant A. H. Connors, Jr., USAF. "Having completed the required courses of instruction at the United States Air Force Advanced Single Engine Pilot School, Williams Air Force Base, Arizona," 2nd Lt. Connors was "rated PILOT effective 23 June 1951."

Frankie and Archie were happy indeed when he became 2nd Lt. Connors and graduated from the Advanced Single Engine Class 51-D. Classmate at right is not identified. (Below) Lt. Connors wears his wings and new gold bar at home during a well earned leave period shortly after completing the course of instruction at Craig AFB.

Archie had joined the Air Force to become a fighter pilot. Despite the warnings of family members and the pleas by Woodrow to be assigned to multi-engined aircraft, Archie chose to fly P-51 Mustangs. During World War II they were hot aircraft. Now jets were coming into their own and the Mustangs were already obsolescent. More ominously, the F-51's had been assigned the fighter-bomber role in Korea, the most dangerous combat flying of any assigned to any pilot, veteran or rookie, except for those who flew rescue helicopters.

Staying Alive
While Flying The P-51 "On the Deck"

The year before America entered WWII, President Franklin D. Roosevelt directed the military to produce 12,000 pilots annually, and Luke Field, Arizona was one of many new air bases built in response to his order. Located near Phoenix, Arizona, the site not only had year-round flying weather, it also enjoyed close proximity to vast stretches of desert ideal for bombing and gunnery practice.

Named for Lt. Frank Luke, Jr., a Phoenix native who was a WWI ace and the first aviator to receive the Medal of Honor, Luke field produced 17,321 fighter pilots for the United States and its allies. Of this number, only 280 Mustang pilots had graduated when the program was terminated and base closed. World War II was over.

Five years later, on February 1, 1951, Luke Air Force Base was reopened. The Korean War needed more fighter pilots than the Air Force could provide. The Mustang fighter-training program was one of the two programs conducted at the base. The other was the F-84 Thunderjet program.

By 1951, the "P" for pursuit designation that was common in WW II had been replaced by "F" for fighter and the P-51 became the F-51. The Mustang training program at Luke AFB began in 1951 and ended in 1953 after producing 624 graduates, including 2nd Lts. Archie Connors and Wilfred "Budd" Stapley.

On September 10, 1951, Connors and Stapley reported to Luke AFB, Arizona for intensive training in the F-51—Combat Crew Training. Their academic subjects included: armament, fighter attack, navigation, gun camera, recognition, climatology, geography, tactics, survival, flying safety, intelligence and physical conditioning.

The base was still in the process of being "reopened" in mid-1951—"there were still cement bags on the bar top in the Officers Club." A new "bird" colonel was arriving to take command at Luke.

As the new CO approached the Main Gate to the new base in his POV (privately owned vehicle), he noticed a movement almost at eye level directly ahead of him. Something was approaching his vehicle at an extraordinary rate of speed.

A moment later there was no mistaking the fact that an Mustang was streaking down the highway, virtually "on the deck," and then whooshed over his car and out of sight down the road.

The new Colonel restarted his car and entered the base for the first time. Soon after, he called an "all hands" meeting. All the officers were required to attend.

At the meeting he related to the group the story of how he had been "buzzed." He also told them that had the pilot made another pass at him, he would have had his number, and he would have been grounded.

2nd Lt. Wilfred "Budd" Stapley

Everyone there knew, including the new CO, at that particular time of day there were only three or four F-51s in the air. It would have been relatively easy to find out the identity of the pilot. However, it was not his intention to nail the pilot.

"I won't have a fighter pilot that won't 'buzz,'" he told the assembled officers. "But when you attempt a risky maneuver like that—use your head. That pilot was really pushing his luck," the Colonel pointed out.

Low level cross-country flying was in the "curriculum" for combat crew training. Connors, Stapley and their fellow pilots were now being told to fly their P-51s in ways that would have had them grounded or dismissed as pilots just a few months earlier. However, low level cross country was the kind of flying that would better prepare them for the harsh realities of combat in Korea—the kind of flying that left trails behind the speeding planes—of dust.

One Luke pilot brought back gun camera film that showed a truck—at twilight—directly ahead—with his lights flashing on and off at the F-51 heading right at him on the highway. "That is low!!!" Stapley remembered.

Some of the pilots training at Luke had flown in WWII. The older (more experienced) guys flew somewhat higher than the "younger guys." Back at the Luke O-Club, Budd and Archie were treated to a "tongue lashing" from one of the older pilots, who yelled out for all to hear at the bar:

"I saw you raise up to go over that cow." Of course, it was a compliment of sorts.

"Thank God," Stapley thought, "recognition." [4]

Update from Frankie

"Dearest Mom and Pop," Frankie wrote late on the morning of Friday, October 5th. "Received your letter yesterday and sure was glad to hear from you. We were so sorry to hear about Mr. Jackson [the husband of Eva's closest friend]. Hope he's a lot better by now."

"Archie doesn't think he'll get a leave before he goes to Stoneman [AFB]. And he may be in Stoneman any amount of time. The last class is still there and they've been there three weeks—if that means anything. I'm going to see him leave if I have to put up a pup tent in front of the General's quarters. I'll get a job of any kind so I can stay until he leaves [for Korea]. Archie is trying to talk me into staying with you but I'm so confused. I don't know what to do. I don't want him to worry about me while he's flying."

"He's pretty sure he'll be in Stoneman through the first week in November and I'll write you from California so you'll know more about it. I know you want to see him before he leaves and maybe you can get Pop to take off for a week or two. That's a long drive tho." *[From Jacksonville, Florida to California—before the Interstate highway system was built.]*

"I finished Archie's socks and he just loves them. He shows them off to everyone. I think he's trying to keep my morale up."

A sassy new pilot and Air Force 2nd Lieutenant teases his nephew, Tracy, as he and Frankie prepare to "bail out" of Jacksonville after a short leave period following his graduation from the Advance Single Engine School at Craig AFB, Alabama.

"He flew Wednesday night and is all finished with that. He still has an overnight flight to make and I dread that. They only have about 6 51's in commission now. They use live ammunition and they almost shoot each other down. So Archie only flies once or twice a day."

"We probably won't get to see Aunt Zona *[Arizona Haddock Walker, Eva's older sister who lived in Jacksonville Beach, FL]* because she gets here on a Monday and we leave the same week. But we're going to try and see Maxey *[Walker, Zona's son and Archie's cousin]* before we leave."

"I've told you all the news, which isn't much. Write us real soon and take care of yourselves. Tell everyone hello! Lots of love, Frankie and Archie."

A few days later, Archie wrote his mother, Eva a short, breezy note following a long distance telephone call. "Dear Mom, sure was glad to hear your voice. Hate to hear about Toro [their ill tempered cat]. Guess someone else will get all clawed up."

"Most of the fellows have been getting leaves after they finish, but they had leave coming to them while I owe the govt. about 10 days. So, it looks like I don't get to go. If we do get a week, Frankie and I will probably spend it in California."

"We have about two weeks left. The rough part is over. All that is left is air-to-air gunnery. Nice and cool at 15,000 ft., we don't have to pull G's any more either."

"Well, that's about all for now. We'll give you the poop as we hear it. Lots of love, Your Son."

On October 18, 1951, 2nd Lt. Connors was among a dozen pilots who successfully completed Class 51-21-FC (F-51 Fighter) and were confirmed to graduate on 20 October—released from the training squadron. From Luke AFB, Phoenix, Arizona it would be Camp Stoneman, California and on to Japan. The Korean War had ceased to be an abstract. From now on it would be an increasingly bitter reality for the Connors family.

"Let's just hope the next year flies by..."

On Monday, October 22, 1951, Frankie wrote: "Dearest Folks, Thought I'd better write you before we leave for California. We're leaving about Thursday and will try and find a place to live right away. From what we've heard, we may have to go to a hotel—it's so crowded. I'm going to try my best to stay until Archie leaves though."

"Yesterday I felt pretty good *[Frankie was in the early stages of her pregnancy]* so we went to see Maxey and Aunt Zona. We really enjoyed ourselves and didn't get back until late last night."

"Our cat had been gone for a week and I had been too sick to look for her. Just as we were going to bed we heard a faint 'meow' and there she was. Archie accused her of messing around but I think she's too young. She has a bad foot and is so skinny. Archie is taking her to the vet as soon as he gets in. She's really happy to be home. But now we have to take her with us, so tell Pop to be prepared. Tell him our cats aren't half as much trouble as our youngun's are going to be."

"Archie is so excited over a baby and I've been so sick that we're both a mess. Yesterday was the first day I could get up. I'll never know how you had 7!. The doc said the reason I was so sick and hurt so bad was I keep trying to lose it. He won't give me anything to make me feel better until he's sure it's going to stay. That's the reason he doesn't want me to travel but if I really get to feeling bad, I'll stop and check in at a hospital. So be prepared to put up with a problem—me and my cat."

"We're shipping everything except just what I'll have to have to Nashville so the car shouldn't be too loaded. Bring something warm for evenings and a pillow or two if you have room. It's going to be a long trip and we're all going to be so gloomy we can't stand each other. Let's just hope the next year flies by."

"Archie hopes to be back in 6 or 7 months, but that sounds too good to be true."

"We'll wire or write as soon as possible so have your bag packed and start pushing Pop 'outta' the door. Lots of Love, Frankie and Archie."

"P.S. Hide Pop's cigars."

From California to Korea

…Bag, B-4, brown
Bag, Barracks
Belt, blue web
Camera, Brownie Reflex
Cap, flight
Cap, garrison
Cap, Grey, Confederate
Drawers, cotton khaki
Shirt, blue, Oxford

Shirt, blue, poplin
Socks, white wool
Socks, wool OD
Sword, miniature w/case
Undershirt, wool; and a
Viewer, 35-mm…were among the items Archie carefully packed, with Frankie's help as he prepared to leave for Korea.

On November 5, 1951, Archie was given orders from Travis AFB—"destination Japan." A baggage allowance of 75 pounds was authorized for travel by air. An ounce or two of his 75 pounds included a small Confederate battle flag. This grandson of several Civil War veterans was taking the Confederate flag to war—again. His orders were strict in pointing out "dependents, friends, relatives or pets will not accompany or join officers at point of embarkation." A week later, orders were posted assigning him to the 35th Fighter Interceptor Wing.

Just two weeks later, he was in Japan and becoming part of the "Police Action." On arrival, he was briefed by Major Thomas F. Bailey, USAF, Commanding Officer of the 40th Fighter-Interceptor Squadron, "with regard to base policies and regulations concerning discipline, wearing of the uniform, conduct and personal finance."

Lt. Connors was properly trained, briefed and processed. He was ready to go to war—almost. The problem was that the 35th wasn't "in" the war. It was not flying combat sorties to Korea. Connors applied for a transfer to a combat squadron. He soon received orders to the 67th Fighter-Bomber Squadron, a component command of the 18th Fighter-Bomber Wing based at K-10, near Chinhae, South Korea, but flying most combat missions from an "advanced operating base" at K-46, 150 miles closer to the front lines near Wonju.

Dogpatch Christmas Card

As Archie was packing his bags and preparing to join the 67th Squadron with several of his friends from pilot training, the Wing was publishing its 1951 Christmas Card from "Dogpatch." In it the 18th Fighter-Bomber Wing took note of its twenty eight years of service and expressed pride in having established "a fine array of precedents and won for itself a proud position on the roster of great military outfits. In keeping with the tradition of American spirit and sacrifice during time of war, the Wing has contributed enormous quantities of human effort and achievement to every emergency which faced its homeland."

"While it is now the sleek and colorful jet which dominates the headlines and directs traffic in historical MIG Alley, the 18th, with its slow and obsolete fighters, is the hero of the front line soldier for whom it operates.

The once famed F-51 Mustang, strafing bunkers and implacements [sic] and playing havoc on battle-line supply lane, has become the Air Force's closest relation to the ground troop."

"The 18th fought side-by-side with the doughboy in the early, tragic days of the Korean War. It sent its fighters out with the Army and Marine patrols, when the seas were crowding the UN's bloody patch of territory. It followed the lines as they were slowly pushed up above the 38th, and was the first Air Force outfit to operate from a Base above that Parallel. No other Wing in Korea should feel justified in making any claims for glory without checking the records and pitting its feats with those of the 18th. Our proudest claim is out saddest memory, Major Lou Sebille, who died in a blaze of glory, and was awarded the Air Force's only Congressional Medal of Honor in Korea." *[Note: eventually there would be four such awards.]*

"Not even considering the competition with which it must vie for honors, the F-51s have given the Air Force its strongest contender for top place in the annals of military aviation, and the deeds of their pilots have won the profoundest admiration and respect of military men the world over."

As December 1951 turned into January 1952, Archie was transferred to the 67th Fighter-Bomber Squadron—"The Fighting Cocks"—and promptly ordered to complete two weeks of "Combat Flying Training." On January 16, 1952, when he revised his Flight Officer's Qualification Record, Archie noted that he had already completed 32 combat missions and 55 combat hours flying the F-51 over Korea.

Almost Mission Ready. *An armorer checks below the wings of this 12th Squadron F-51 that is being readied for a mission from K-46 in February 1952. Note 500-lb bombs on wheeled racks in the foreground. (Stapley)*

Combat Operations in January

In January 1952, the 18th Fighter-Bomber Group had been in combat for 18 consecutive months flying obsolescent F-51 Mustangs that had been configured as fighter-bombers. The 18th F-B Group included four combat squadrons—the 67th Squadron, 12th Squadron, 39th Fighter-Interceptor Squadron and 2 Squadron South African Air Force. *[The 39th FIS would be detached in May, 1952.]*

The primary mission of the 18th Fighter-Bomber Group continued to be the "tactical interdiction of the enemy's transportation system," noted Lt. Col. Julian Crow in his monthly report. [5] Crow was the Commanding Officer of the 67th Fighter-Bomber Squadron. After prior duties as the Executive Officer of the 12th Squadron, Crow had been reassigned in November 1951 as Commanding Officer of the 67th, succeeding Major Carl C. "Shorty" Colson.

Crow was directing most of his flights against railheads, communication lines and highways—all badly needed by the communists to move supplies and equipment to front-line positions. Sixty-seventh Squadron fighter-bombers flew nearly 500 sorties in January concentrating on rail and road-cutting missions and reported 99 rail cuts and three road cuts, along with the destruction of 13 pieces of enemy artillery, 48 buildings, 18 troop positions, 9 vehicles and 12 bunkers. Over 200 enemy troops were reported KIA by the 42 pilots flying combat sorties that month.

Archie and Budd Stapley were among the new pilots flying combat missions for the 67th Squadron in January—Connors (8) and Stapley (12).

Disposition of Forces

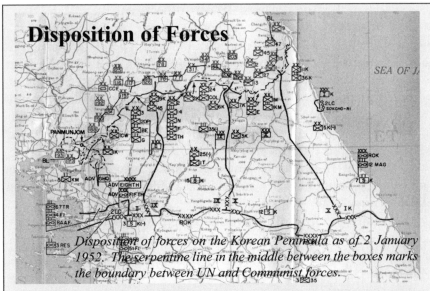

Disposition of forces on the Korean Peninsula as of 2 January 1952. The serpentine line in the middle between the boxes marks the boundary between UN and Communist forces.

Static, defensive-type ground warfare continued into January 1952. UNF air attacks were countered by active air opposition and increasingly heavy, often radar-directed anti-aircraft fire from Chinese Communist and North Korean Forces.

At Panmunjom, UN negotiators labored to bring about an armistice; however, "communist intransigence, evasiveness, and procrastination thwarted their efforts."

UN jet fighters inflicted costly losses on hostile MiG-15s. There was a strong perception among fighter-bomber pilots that they were frequently used as "bait" to entice MIGs into battle.

Although Far East Air Forces "lost only five jets in aerial combat, it saw enemy ground fire destroy forty-four other aircraft. These had been engaged in low-level bombing runs and strafing sweeps."

The official Air Force chronology makes frequent mention of actions in which jet fighter aircraft, heavy bomber aircraft or rescue helicopters were engaged, but rarely mentions actions by fighter-bomber squadrons flying the now outdated F-51 Mustang aircraft.

Fifth Air Force tactical strikes were directed primarily against railheads, communication lines, and highways over which the communists moved supplies and equipment to front-line positions. Fighter-bombers concentrated on rail-cutting missions but also provided vital close air support (CAS) for Eighth Army ground forces that included bombing, napalm, and rocket strikes.

(Adapted from U.S. Air Force Historical Research Agency. January 2002. The U.S. Air Force's First War: Korea 1950-1953 Significant Events. January 1952.)

The 67th Squadron gained 18 new officers and lost 17, leaving it with 52 officers assigned by the end of the month. Enlisted strength was 145 at the beginning of the month and 143 by February—"all sections of the organization, with the exception of pilot strength, continue to be below authorized strength." While replacements "arriving later in the month" appeared "better qualified than previous replacements and hold more rank," the volume of new men was "below the anticipated number in view of the many men from this organization who are to be rotated in February and March," Crow pointed out.

"Rotation remains the biggest single morale factor, with morale rising and falling as policy changes (and accompanying rumors and speculation) effect rotation," Crow reported.

"Complaints are still forth-coming from all quarters that publicity concerning the activities of this Wing should be much more widespread than at present," Crow concluded as he praised the hard work and sacrifices of his men. "It is felt that even while working with a severe shortage of qualified personnel this unit has met its combat commitments only because of the determination of the few qualified personnel still assigned and the eagerness of the new men to learn."

Behind "Dogpatch"

In the late 1920s, at the age of 19, Alfred Gerald Caplin ("Al Capp"), became the youngest syndicated cartoonist in America when he began drawing "Colonel Gilfeather," a daily panel for the Associated Press. In 1934, he took an idea for a new cartoon strip with a hillbilly theme to United Features Syndicate. At first "Li'l Abner" was carried by only eight newspapers. However, the hapless residents of Dogpatch struck a nerve in Depression-era America. In just three years it was reaching 253 newspapers with 15 million readers. Soon it was reaching hundreds of newspapers with a circulation of over 60 million readers.

Capp's colorful characters and zany life in Dogpatch were changing popular culture throughout America. For example, in 1937 he introduced the annual Sadie Hawkins Day race into the strip. Soon real life girl-asks-boy dances were being held across the country. In 1948, Capp's lovable Shmoo characters became a national sensation—and the largest mass merchandising phenomenon of its era.[1] When Capp married Li'l Abner and Daisy Mae in 1952, it was an event that made front-page news.

The heartless capitalist General Bullmoose, the human jinx Joe Bfstplk (followed by his own rain cloud), Evil Eye Fleegle (owner of the double whammy that could melt skyscrapers), Lonesome Polecat and Hairless Joe (who lived in a cave and concocted Kickapoo Joy Juice, the ultimate moonshine), Fearless Fosdick (the fumbling detective with a bullet-riddled

body), Moonbeam McSwine (gorgeous, but malodorous), and Mammy Yokum (a sweet old lady who could out box men).

Capp's Dogpatch was sadder and poorer than any stereotype of Appalachia. Its yokel residents were dumber than dumb, or else scoundrels and thieves. "Most of the men were too lazy to work, yet Dogpatch women were desperate enough to chase them. One preferred to live with hogs. Those who farmed

A copy of the original line art drawing provided by cartoonist Al Capp that created the 'Lil' Abner Truckbuster logo. "A Cappian patch," the Truckbuster unit newspaper reported, drawn by Al himself; is the pride of the Korean Dogpatchers. It features 'Lil' Abner piloting a P-51 with "Nancy O" riding on its tail. The patch was originated before Nancy O had a face. When Miss Kitty Panky, a Miami University student, became the girl with "the sweetest face in the world" and the face on Nancy O, she also became the sweetheart of the 18th's Dogpatchers in Korea." (Colton) their "tarnip" crop watched turnip termites descend every year, locust-like, to devour the crop. In the midst of the Great Depression, lowly Dogpatch allowed the most hard-up Americans to laugh at yokels worse off than they were. In Al Capp's own words Dogpatch was "an average stone-age community" nestled in a bleak valley, between two cheap and uninteresting hills, somewhere. To old friends, the denizens of Dogpatch will be old friends. To strangers, however, they will probably be strangers." *[Al Capp Enterprises. The Greatest Cartoonist of all time. http://www.lil-abner.com/index.html]*

In July 1950, "heat waves shimmered upward from rain pools alongside the airstrip" at K-9 near Pusan, South Korea. Eighteenth Fighter-Bomber Group Commander, Colonel Curtis Low, Captain George Bales, and S/Sgt Sandy Colton, a talented Journalist for the 18th, surveyed the "uninspiring Korean landscape" from their ankle-deep vantage point in the mud.

"Lower Slobovia or Dogpatch couldn't be worse than this" commented Low, while his two companions nodded agreement. So it was that "Dogpatch" began to eventually "seep through to the stateside press and become a familiar label of the 18th Fighter Bomber Wing.

Colton began datelining his news releases with the descriptive title and before long the 18th became identified as the "Dogpatchers of Korea." In fact, "the 18th became synonymous with Al Capp's comic strip village to such an extent that celebrities of the Bob Hope and Al Jolson stature were usually met with banners and signs proclaiming proudly that the 18th was truly an airborne version of the popular stateside cartoon strip."

No matter where the 18th Wing was based in Korea, that base was known as "Dogpatch, Korea," with every major facility on the base identified with cartoon characters based on Al Capp's denizens of Dogpatch.

How Flight

William "Tim" Urquhart, like Archie and Budd Stapley, was assigned to "H" (How) Flight, 67th Fighter Bomber Squadron, 18th Fighter Bomber Wing at K-10 and K-46 Korea. "Our combat operations were flown out of K-46, and our real headquarters and maintenance were at K-10 [Chinhae, SK]. Until we combat pilots wore out our welcome at K-10, we would stage out of K-46 for almost five days then catch a C-47 down to K-10 for two days of rest. I use the word 'rest' lightly, because we would do our level best to demolish the Officer's Club at K-10."

"A fighter squadron had 25 aircraft assigned to it and about 50 pilots (two per plane). They were divided into about six "flights" of about 8 pilots each, similar to an Army Company and Squads. We flew in a formation of four planes to a Flight. The Flight was further divided into two elements," Urquhart explained.

"Number One was the leader and the most experienced. Number Two was the most junior pilot and watched the leader's plane and did his darndest to keep up while in combat. Three and Four would operate together, with Number Three and Four hanging on, much like Two," Urquhart said. [6]

Precious Stationery. *2nd Lt. Archie Connors arrived in Korea in January 1952 to join the 67th Squadron after a brief assignment with the 35th Fighter Interceptor Squadron in Japan. The box he is carrying appears to be one usually containing stationery. In one of his letters he mentioned how scarce writing paper was at the time.*

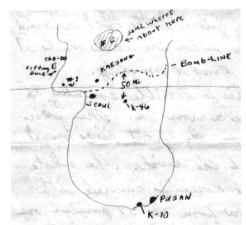

*"**Sitting Duck.**" Lt. Connors drew this rough map for his mother, Eva, of his first combat mission in Korea in early January 1952. "Here is what the situation looks like: #1 was my first mission," he explained. Note "sitting duck" reference near Cho-do Island.*

Living Conditions at K-46

"Our living conditions were rather primitive at K-46," Stapley recalled. "The TV show 'Mash' reproduces our accommodations rather well. What it doesn't depict is the oppressive heat in a tent in summer and the penetrating cold in winter. The tents were heated by diesel oil stoves with storage barrels outside connected by a copper line to the stove. Quite often, the oil would congeal in the line on cold nights and the fire would go out. The next morning, when the sun came out, the oil would flow into the stove and form a puddle in the bottom. We would light a newspapers, throw it into the stove, and stand back and enjoy the red glow coming from the stove and pipe. Sometimes the fire would get so hot that the stovepipe would fly out of the top of the tent like a rocket."

"A terrible country to have a war in..."

On January 23rd, Archie wrote his mother, Eva: "Well I guess it's about time. There is a bad shortage of stationery right now but it's getting better."

"We have it pretty good over here, gets a little cold now and then. When the snow melts it gets kind of muddy."

"This is a terrible country to have a war in. The jokers up on the front lines must catch the devil. The whole of North Korea is covered with snow from the 37th parallel on up. This country is just up and down. Very few level places."

"We had a little bit of excitement this morning. There were a lot of aborts and the crazy fools dropped their bombs all over the place. None of them went off, but the brass raised cain. Two bombs went off farther up the river and rattled the dishes. Never a dull moment."

"Got up at 5:30 to fly a plane back up here from down south. It sure was nice down there. No snow and sheets to sleep on, even running water in the commodes."

"Speaking of commodes, it is just a trough with a box over it and a hole in the box. Up here it's just a regular outdoor affair. If you have to go early in the morning the smell knocks you out."

"Here is what the situation looks like: #1 was my first mission."

"Thanks a lot for the fruit cake. Haven't tasted it yet but I will. Oh! Boy!"

"Tell Frankie to start a bank account and hope that my luck holds out. We'll have that cabin in the pines yet (complete with a few head of cattle)."

Ready for a mission in Linda Lee II. 1ˢᵗ Lt. Wilfred C. "Budd" Stapley (left) and 1ˢᵗ Lt. George V. Patton (right) sitting on the wing of "Linda Lee II" (Stapley's aircraft) prior to a mission. Patton, the namesake and nephew of General George Patton, was also an Army brat. His father, Stapley recalled, was a career army officer. The young Patton had flown a combat tour during WWII as a tail gunner on a B-17. (Stapley)

Luckiest guy!

On 27 January 1952, 1ˢᵗ Lt. George Patton, a Class 51-D graduate with Stapley and Connors, was on a close air support mission when he was hit by ground fire, Stapley recalled. Wrestling the badly damaged Mustang for control and trying to gain enough altitude to bail out, Patton also tried to get "disconnected" enough to bail out—but he was "hung up" on his equipment, straps, cables and harness. As he fought to keep the plane in the air and to get himself clear enough to bail out, the plane continued heading south—closer to the no-man's land between the UN and Communist forces.

Finally, when he was clear, he bailed out—and landed literally between the lines—in a minefield.

Friendly troops were trying to tell him he was in a minefield, but he didn't hear or understand the warnings. "Stay down. Stay down," they yelled, "we'll come out and get you."

Caught in the middle of a combat zone, Patton was in no frame of mind to sit there and wait to be rescued. All he had to do to be rescued was get over to those American voices…as fast as he could run. And run, he did, right through a mine field that he was later told was designed to ensure no person on foot could get through—alive.

"You are the luckiest guy…alive," they told him when he reached friendly troops south of the "bomb line."

To calm his nerves, they offered him a drink…and then another. By the time he had been picked up by a helicopter and returned to K-46, his "nerves" were much better. "George said after he found that out, it took about a pint of Kentucky's finest to settle his nerves," Stapley remembered. *[Note: Patton was KIA on 13 June 1952. "I was in Japan awaiting transportation home," Stapley recalled, "when I got word that George had been shot down on his last scheduled mission. It was during a mission to Ping Pong [Pyongyang, NK] and his wingman said a 90mm shell hit his aircraft in the cockpit. The aircraft fell in pieces."]*

"That's all for now. I won't wait so long for the next one [letter]. Your Son, Archie"

"P.S. This doesn't scare me half as bad as Mr. Lamb chasing me for stealing his sugar cane." Archie closed with what was probably false bravado.

Weather and Shortages Limit Sorties

In February the 18th Group was chronically short of available aircraft—combat sorties were among the lowest anyone could remember—the cause being a shortage of available aircraft and inclement weather. Also a factor that month was "the long missions the squadron had an abundance of this month. Many of the sorties, such as MSR caps and Cho-do Island caps, lasted three hours or longer." [7]

Tactics remained "essentially the same," although the 18th experimented with skip-bombing of railroads for a short time "with generally unsatisfactory results."

Fifth Air Force directed a change in rail cut bombing that "consisted of glide bombing specific rail embankments, rather than dive bombing a rail area." The change was accomplished over a ten-day period, but then was

"No missions this day for these planes" of the 67th Squadron, explained former Crew Chief Robert Cranston. *"One of the many days that we were snowed in at K-46"* during the winter of 1952. *"Life on the Flight Line,"* remembered Cranston, *"was seven days a week from 0500 preflight until post flight—weather permitting."* During winter months *"the planes had to be covered—wings, engine and canopy areas—due to the heavy snow."* Pre-flight in winter months included *"uncovering the plane, checking for leaks, visual check and run up."* Any liquid puddles under the plane *"could be fuel, oil, coolant—or melted snow."* To determine the exact source of the liquid—and potential problems—*"you would stick your finger in the puddle, then feel, smell or taste it. You could smell the fuel, feel the oil, and the coolant tasted sweet."* The *"taste the liquid"* problem solving routine also provided an opportunity for some good natured *"fun"* on the Flight Line. *"Sometimes, if you beat your 'neighbor' to preflight you could relieve yourself under his plane—then watch him check for coolant leaks."* Cranston admitted that he *"fell for it"* once himself—but only once. *(Cranston)*

Operation Strangle. *The twisted and battered skeletons of two Communist supply trains litter a switching center somewhere between Pyongyang and Sariwon. Note that the "through line" terminates abruptly at bomb crater in lower right of picture. Note also upended locomotives. This low level aerial photo is another excellent example of how "Operation Strangle" has disrupted Communist rail movement of supplies to their battle line forces in Korea, the Fifth Air Force claimed in January 1952. (NARA)*

apparently suspended. "After reverting back to our normal practice of dive bombing," Crow reported, "pilots were briefed to facilitate a relatively steep dive, thus creating a more pronounced crater effecting more damage."

Thanks for keeping 'em in the air. *Lt. Col. Julian Crow, Commanding Officer of the 67th Fighter-Bomber Squadron poses with senior NCOs of the 67th, including (L to R): Technical Sergeant Roy Pylant, 1st Sergeant Gleen, Master Sergeant Rose (line chief), and Sergeant Holt. (Pylant)*

As Operation Strangle continued, FAF was searching for new tactics to cut the railroads and to keep them out of commission. A new target area for rail cuts was assigned to 18th Group squadrons, "with the reconnaissance of MSR's [Main Supply Routes] more or less replacing the secondary targets formerly given flights returning from rail cuts. Interdiction missions against the enemy's transportation system, supply concentrations, troop billets, and artillery positions primarily remain our targets as in preceding months," the 12th Squadron reported in February.

Getting Jumped by 75 Migs

In February, 1952...up by the Yalu...How Flight was inbound on the target, when Stapley saw "golf balls" going by my cockpit. *[The "golf balls" were the tracer rounds from ground to air or air-to-air gunfire. From the ground it was called "flak."]* "I was used to them coming up at me, but these were going by from above and behind my plane," he remembered.

MIG Bait. *Mustang pilots were convinced that on occasion they were sent into "MIG Alley" as bait for FEAF F-86s. Sometimes the friendly jets were "late," and the Mustangs would be "jumped" by the MIGs and have to fight their way out of the trap. Most American F-51s in 1952 had their tail wheels locked in the down position due to mechanical problems. The extra drag took about 10 mph off cruising speed and burned more fuel. (Stapley)*

"Sleek U.S. Air Force F-86 "Sabre" jets of the 51st Fighter Interceptor Wing form this pattern of power as they patrol skylanes high over "MIG-Alley" in northwest Korea," an Air Force caption explained. Finally, in January 1953 the 18th Fighter-Bomber Wing would be ordered to transition into the Sabrejet—in combat and without standing down from fulfilling its missions—the only known Air Force unit to have even been required to do so, not once but twice during the Korean War.. The 18th Wing was the last American unit to fly the Mustang in combat. (NARA)

"What in @#@#$%," he exclaimed to himself, "and about that time the MIG goes diving past my aircraft. We had no idea that they were anywhere around. He had been shooting at me, but remember, I never flew my aircraft in a "straight and level" attitude once I passed the Bomb Line." [Pilots called the constant weaving and bobbing "jinxing."]

"He had not been able to hit me, even thought I didn't even know he was there. Up until then, I hadn't even looked for another airplane...and enemy airplane...coming up behind you. After that I did. We had a mirror in the cockpit, but it didn't give much field of view. The best "mirror" was your own eyeballs, as you kept looking left, right, up, behind...It's the guy you don't see that shoots you down."

"There were 16 of us and about 75 of them. Their attacks on us were very well coordinated. They formed themselves into three loops so that there were three guys shooting at us at all times. We tried to stay in formation. We went into a "sissors"—two guys weaving back and forth. The object is to try and suck the attacking plane into a diving turn that brings them across the guns of the other wingman."

"We kept that up and tried to make it out over open sea. The sea belonged to us (UN forces). They didn't follow us out over open water. Probably thought that if we shot down one of their planes that we would capture a Russian pilot."

"Before we reached the water, about 36 F-86s jumped the MIGs and chased them away. I was never so happy to see 86's in my life."

"They didn't actually tell us that they were sending us into a particular area as "bait" for the MIGs, but we strongly suspected that was the case."

"When we would be sent into "MIG Alley," they would tell us that there was "a possibility of intercept by MIGs…but a lot of the time the 86's weren't there!" Stapley remembered.

"The merciless flogging handed the enemy..."

In March, the rail interdiction program remained the major focus of combat operations for the 18th Group. The Wing newspaper, "*The Truckbuster*," reported that "18th fighter pilots play key role in Operation Strangle." On August 18, 1951, the Fifth Air Force kicked off the concentrated interdiction program, code named Operation Strangle, a collective term for tactics to cut the railroads throughout North Korea and to keep them out of commission. Since then, "fighter bombers of the 18th Ftr Bmr

133

Wing, under the protective umbrella of Allied Sabre-Jets, have been carrying this program out twenty-four hours a day denting Red supply routes, knocking out rail lines and causing the enemy its biggest supply problem since the outbreak of the 'police action.' The merciless flogging handed the enemy has achieved the goal for which it was designed," the *Truckbuster* claimed. "With no safe way of transporting troops, ammunition and badly needed food and clothing, the Reds have been forced to retaliate in the air, to give up their previous ground plans, and to place their greatest emphasis on a defensive air War."

"The job of the Fifth Air Force is to make the Communists pay as high rent as possible for their stay in Korea," explained Lt. Gen. Frank F. Everest, CG FAF. "Operation Strangle" has done just that, and "it might just possibly go so far as to 'evict' the Commies," the *Truckbuster* noted.

"conventional aircraft are much superior to jet aircraft..."

In March, the tactics of the Group returned "to the group gaggle principle," Levenson noted in that month's unit report. "We have been hitting, with the entire 5th Air Force, a small section of rails each day. The results have proven very satisfactory. Each pilot of the Group flew close support missions in order to 'keep their hand in.' The close support

Train Under Attack. A Communist train is worked over by a Mustang flown by 2nd Lt. Denis Earp, 2 Squadron SAAF—the "Flying Cheetahs" were attached to the 18th Fighter Bomber Wing. [Eventually, Earp would retire as a Lt. General and Chief of Staff for the South African Air Force.] Gun cameras record actual damage inflicted. 18th Group pilots saw many scenes like this—"right down on the deck."

business is very well liked by all pilots and a welcome change from rail cutting missions."

"No new tactical lessons were learned during the month," the 39th FIS monthly report observed, "though from statements made by ground force officers we learned once again that conventional aircraft are much superior to jet aircraft on close-support type missions. The future appears to have a need for conventional or turbo-prop fighters but as yet there hasn't been any assurance that the future will provide these aircraft."

"...sheer determination to see a job well done..."

"Combat commitments of this organization have been met through sheer determination to see a job well done even in the face of heavy losses of aircraft and a definite shortage of personnel," Lt. Col. Crow noted.

There were too many pilots and not enough enlisted personnel assigned to the 67th. All sections, with the exception of the pilot section, continued to be below authorized strength. The overage of pilots caused individual pilots to feel that they were not being utilized to the fullest extent of their capabilities.

Going to war every day certainly wasn't "business as usual" for the 67th, but the squadron's report for March, 1952 devoted far more attention to the business side of operations than to the operations themselves—there were too many pilots and not enough enlisted personnel.

"As long as the 'Fighting Cocks' remain in Korea, rotation will probably continue to be the largest single factor affecting morale," Crow predicted. "Morale in the enlisted ranks depends a great deal upon the work

Gen. Matthew Ridgeway *is greeted by Lt. Gen. Frank F. Everest, Commanding General of the Fifth Air Force, upon his arrival at an air base somewhere in Korea on April 3, 1952. (NARA)*

load. As long as the men are kept busy with their jobs, they feel that they are important enough to the effort in this theatre to justify their presence in the 67th. To date, the shortage of enlisted personnel causes all men to be kept very busy. Consequently, their morale is very good. Conversely, morale in the Pilot ranks is not good. This section is over manned and missions have come too slowly to the pilots during the last month," Crow reported.

"With the arrival of warm weather, spirits have been zooming!"

Major Stanley Long took over as Executive Officer of the 12th Squadron after Major James M. Todd moved up to Commanding Officer. Long would soon move over and up to become Commander of the 67th Squadron.

The weather was getting better. "With the arrival of warm weather, spirits have been zooming," the 12th Squadron reported in March 1952.

K-10 Officer's Club—"Top 'O the Mark"—*was the place 18th Group pilots went to unwind after a five-day period "on the line" in combat flying from the advanced operating base at K-46, 150 miles further north and much closer to the "bomb line."*

"Charley Tune" area of the K-10 "Top of the Mark" Officers Club *in early 1952 where 18th Group pilots made holes in the floor while singing Ay Ziga Zumba. The officer on the guitar is Lt. A. S. Van der Spuy—"Topper 6" or just "Topper," a pilot with the 2 Squadron SAAF. Behind Topper is 2nd Lt. John W. Yingling. At right rear, 2nd Lt. Archie Connors sings along.*

Several of the Dogpatcher Officer Club paintings such as this one, were hauled all over Korea as the 18th Wing was frequently relocated from one forward base to another.

136

"Interdiction missions against the enemy's transportation system, supply concentrations, troop billets, and artillery positions primarily remain our targets as in preceding months," the 12th reported. "However, we are again taking an active part in close support missions after several months during which we have very few."

"Some experimentation was done in regard to a number of Group gaggles on rail strikes," the report continued. "This concerned mostly the type of formation utilized to and from the target, and the type pass to be used on the target itself. Those gaggles involved a group formation of twenty planes, more or less, and it was a turn around affair. Also, the entire group had a chance to fly a few close support missions for the first time in several months," the 12th explained. "A great deal of valuable experience has been gained through these missions, exceptionally valuable in the case of pilots who have been assigned within the past four months." The targets for CAS missions included "mostly bunkers, gun positions, and troops." Mosquito planes of the T-6 and L-10 type controlled the CAS strikes. [9]

From Toasting to Namedropping to the Brig

The fieldstone fireplace below the painting of the voluptuous girl in the K-10 Officer's Club—"Top 'O the Mark"—was often used for more than simply burning wood to heat the area.

From time to time, usually after some particularly serious "toasting," glasses would be hurled in the general direction of the fireplace where they shattered loudly into O'Club "flak." It was even believed in some circles that as Happy Hour progressed, accuracy might have been "off" somewhat. Generally, the flying glasses hit the fireplace. It was a "tradition" at the Top of the Mark Club at K-10—sort of.

After five or six weeks of combat flying, a Flight was taken "off the line" and sent off for R&R. At the end of March 1952, following a hard month of combat flying, the 67th Squadron's How Flight was sent to Japan for a week of R&R at Johnson AFB at Tachikawa, near Tokyo.

Most of How Flight consisted of relatively new pilots who had survived their first 8-10 missions. They were "combat veterans"…had been "blooded" and were sure that the "peace talks" that had recently begun at Panmunjom would be successful and that they would soon be heading home. Thank goodness, they congratulated themselves, we got over here just in time. A few more weeks and peace would have broken out—and we might have missed the war.

How flight now included 2nd Lt. Archie Connors who had joined them in December after a very short posting to the 40th Fighter-Interceptor Squadron that was attached to the 35th Fighter-Interceptor Wing at Tachikawa Air Base.

Following their arrival in Japan, How Flight headed for the base O-Club to begin the winding down process. After some liquid refreshment at the Tachikawa O-Club, How Flight ran into some its former classmates who were just arriving in theater. "War stories" for the brand new, never been in combat pilots were the order of the evening. Drinks were ordered, then reordered.

Eventually the very relaxed, very happy How Flight pilots were giving and receiving toasts of the "here's to you, here's to us, here's to them" variety. After a particularly vigorous toast, someone remembered the "glasses in the fireplace tradition" at K-10. In moments the air was filled with glasses sailing towards the O'Club fireplace. The crashing and tinkling of the broken glass and the shards flying in all directions brought cheers and laughter. It also brought the now highly irate, non-aviator Captain who managed the club.

Getting more and more agitated and worked up as he dressed them down, he advised them, floridly, that they didn't throw glasses at the fireplace in HIS O'Club. What's more, he began to demand to know the names and

Heading to Japan. *On March 28, 1952 "How Flight," 67th Squadron prepares to leave combat and head out from K-10 to Japan for a much needed R&R. (Bottom, L to R) Assistant Flight Leader 2nd Lt. Wilfred C. ("Flak") Stapley, 2nd Lt. Archie ("Clanky") Connors. (Top Row, L to R) Acting Flight Leader 1st Lt. Shirley B. ("Wash") Tubbs, 2nd Lt. Melvin ("Crash") Souza, Flight Leader 1st Lt. Donald D. ("Lucky") Drage, 2nd Lt. Joel O. ("Jeff") Rives, and 2nd Lt. William E. ("Mutt") McShane. They were about to find out that O-Club "etiquette" in war torn Korea was quite different than O-Club etiquette in Japan. Connors and Souza were killed in action. (Stapley)*

units of those responsible. Some form of punishment or official chastising was just around the corner.

How Flight was incredulous. OK, so some glasses were broken. Tell us the damage and we'll pay for it and get out of here. It wasn't going to be that easy.

The Captain's tirade got worse and worse. He didn't back down until Lt. Connors injected the name of the commanding officer of the squadron to which he had been attached so very briefly a few weeks before. Later, How Flight concluded—with a twinkle in their eyes—that it might even have been possible that the way Connors described things, the Captain could have come to the conclusion that the glass throwing miscreants were attached to the 40th squadron.

The Captain seemed to be backing down as Connors, sensing that the name dropping gambit might just get them out of this broken glasses scrape, laid it on thick and heavy. He was so close to the Colonel, it seemed, that he was very nearly family. Unfortunately for How Flight, as they later found out, the pilots from the 40th Fighter Interceptor Squadron had a bad reputation with the Club Manager Captain. Now he sensed that he had "the goods" on the squadron's commanding officer. He stopped chewing out How Flight and began making mental notes—lots of them.

After the Captain had apparently been suitably cowed by the heavy mention of the Colonel's name, Connors, Stapley and the rest of How Flight got out of the club as quickly as possible. After spending the rest of the night peacefully in the "Transient Barracks," they got up early and dressed for an exciting day on the town-Tokyo. The temporary unpleasantness of the night before was now just a distant memory-to them.

The Captain, meanwhile, had been busy tying a noose, of sorts, around the hapless Colonel's neck. He was out to get those so-and-so troublemakers from the 40th and called the base commanding general to give him a highly detailed account of what the Colonel's guys

(Right) Johnson AFB Officer's Club, near Tokyo. Archie and his fellow How Flight pilots were involved in a glass throwing "misunderstanding" that resulted in his being put in the brig. It was shortly after this photograph was taken that he received a Red Cross telegram informing him of Frankie's tragic accident.

had done. The way he related things raised the General's blood pressure considerably.

The General called the Colonel at "oh dark thirty" in the morning to demand an explanation. The mystified Colonel assured him that none of the names of the glass throwers were from his squadron. When the name "Connors" was mentioned to the Colonel, however, he vaguely remembered that a Second Lieutenant by that name had been in his squadron for a very short period a month or so earlier, and then transferred to the 67th Squadron in Korea. Now the Colonel was steamed. Some troublemaker of a Second Lieutenant had tried to pass himself off as a member of the 40th—after "trashing" the Club.

That explained why, at 0630 in the morning, the residents of the transient barracks were rousted out of their warm cots by a squad of Air Police conducting a bed-to-bed check to find Lieutenants Stapley, Connors and others from How Flight. How Flight, ever the early risers (since they had been thrown out of the O'Club the night before while still relatively sober), were almost out the Main Gate of the air base to find a taxicab that would take them into town-and all the interesting things they would find to do.

Their progress through the gate was arrested, literally, by the arrival of several jeeps using sirens—and full of Air Police, an agitated Colonel and a steamed up General.

The Captain O-Club Manager was also in one of the vehicles. Seeing How Flight about to head through the Main Gate, he stood up and gestured theatrically at Connors: "That's the man!" If it had not really happened, the scene could have been a brainchild of writers for *McHale's Navy* or *No Time for Sergeants*.

The last time How Flight saw Connors that day he was being "escorted" by two burly Air Policemen, one holding each elbow as he was taken into custody. "We didn't stay around to fight for his honor," Stapley laughingly recalled much later.

There was nothing they could do and after all, Connors had brought much of the trouble down on his own head. Periodically, they did make calls back to the base, trying to determine what was going on

Meanwhile, back at the base, Connors finally had a chance to explain the full circumstances to the Colonel and the General. Using all his "reasoning" abilities, Connors finally got the "brass" cooled down and himself released from custody—after he agreed to pay for the glasses. Eventually, he was able to rejoin How Flight later in the day to enjoy Tokyo before heading back into combat.

"...WIFE 7 1/2 MONTHS PREGNANT EXTENSIVE HEAD AND FACE INJURIES SERIOUS CONDITION..."

As Archie was heading off to Japan following five weeks of intensive combat flying, back in the Z.I., Frankie decided that she would drive from her mother's home in Nashville to Jacksonville for a family visit. Family members urged her not to attempt the long, hazardous drive in view of her advanced pregnancy. She insisted that she would be safe. After all, her mother would be with her, and she would be driving their brand new Henry J—what would now be called a "sub-compact." It was a tragic decision.

On a treacherous stretch of highway near Hawkinsville, Georgia, Frankie lost control of the little car, which slammed into a ditch. Without a seat belt, Frankie's face and mouth sustained severe trauma. Extensive plastic surgery would be needed and her life was in danger.

The Hawkinsville, Georgia Chapter of the American Red Cross posted an urgent telegram on April 1st, to its national headquarters:

"MRS. J. M. MCGARRY, MOTHER OF MRS. A. H. CONNORS, JR. REQUESTS EMERGENCY LEAVE SECOND LT. A.H. CONNORS, JR. CARE OFFICERS CLUB JOHNSON AIR BASE JAPAN APO 994 DUE TO WIFE AUTO ACCIDENT IN HAWKINSVILLE GA IN ROUTE TO JACKSONVILLE FLO. DR. W. R. BAKER ATTENDING PHYSICAL TAYLOR MEMORIAL HOSPITAL HAWKINSVILLE GA RECOMMENDS LEAVE. WIFE 7 1/2 MONTHS PREGNANT EXTENSIVE HEAD AND FACE INJURIES SERIOUS CONDITION. DR. ADVISES TIME FOR SVCMN TO ARRIVE DEFINITELY CONCERNED OVER WIFE CONDITION SVCMN PRESENCE NEEDED. REQUEST SVCM BE NOTIFIED. REQUEST LEAVE THIS OFFICE BE NOTIFIED OF DECISION FOR DOCTORS INFORMATION."

Three days later, the 18th Wing Adjutant, Major James Callaway, placed Archie on temporary duty to enable his return to the United States to begin 30 days Emergency Leave and authorized his further transportation to Travis AFB, California.

"Save My Baby"

Before Archie could return to the States, his parents, Arch, Sr. and Eva Connors, drove to Hawkinsville, Georgia to see Frankie and help in any way they could. When they arrived at the hospital, they were stunned by her appearance. So much so, that stern, gruff Arch had to step outside of the hospital room to weep.

Their happy, sassy, beautiful daughter-in-law was barely alive. Her nose was broken, her upper lip was nearly evered and all her front teeth were knocked out. One tooth was eventually found—up in her nose. Black bruises covered her body from her eyes down to her breasts. Massive swelling in her nose had prevented any anesthesia being administered during the childbirth procedure. Frankie had to endure the pain of childbirth on top of the pain of her injuries.

Rescue workers at the scene of the accident recalled that as she drifted in and out of consciousness, she had pleaded with them to "save my baby." The frantic rescuers searched inside and outside the crumpled wreckage—the engine was under the front seat—for an infant before they realized she was pregnant and about to deliver.

The next morning, Arch and Eva had to give Frankie the almost unbearable news—her baby girl did not survive the accident.

The Gruesome Photograph

One of Tracy's Christmas presents in 1951 was his first camera, a Brownie "Hawkeye." It was a small, black plastic single focus camera that used 620 film. He carried it to school to take surprise pictures of usually unwilling and sometimes angry classmates.

On April 3, 1952, several days after Frankie's accident, Woodrow, Miriam, Tracy, David and new daughter, Eva Christine, born the previous November, drove over to Arch and Eva's house for a "prayer meeting." When they arrived, Tracy immediately sensed that there was something else about the meeting he had not been told. Adults would whisper, then, by ones and twos would disappear into the front bedroom off the living room. After a while they would reappear—in tears. At first he was not told the reason. Later, it became clear to him why he had been asked to bring his camera—to a prayer meeting.

Someone asked in a hushed tone if he had brought the camera. When he said yes, he was asked to get it ready and to join them in the bedroom. Apparently, he was the only "photographer" in the family.

Retrieving his camera from the car, he slowly opened the door to the bedroom where he had slept as a guest so many times in earlier, happier times. There, between the two beds, resting on the bed frame was a small wooden box. The top was off and lying to one side. He knew immediately that it was a small coffin.

"Tracy, we want you to take a picture," someone said quietly. Somehow, mechanically, he went about the task. He knew he had to get himself up and over the box, which meant he had to get up onto the bed and to balance there holding the small camera at waist level, shooting down at whatever was inside. In addition, the Hawkeye did not have an attached flash. He would have to have them turn out the lights to give solid darkness. Then he would have to hold the camera with one hand, and the flash with the other. Securing shutter at full open, the flash would be fired and the shutter closed. It was a primitive camera.

Trying not to stare into the coffin, he climbed up onto the bed carefully and into position looking down at the subject. An infant was in the box, all but its tiny, beautiful face covered in fluffy cotton packing. With all the self-control he could muster, he asked that the lights be turned out. He opened the shutter and fired the flash. In that surreal instant, the image burned its way into the film and into his brain of the box full of white cotton cradling a delicate white face—with a single drop of red blood in one nostril.

The room went black, then yellow-white as someone turned the lights back on. He was helped from the bed in a daze. Someone took the camera and rerolled, then removed the film. He never saw the photograph, or was ever told whether it was even developed.

Twelve-year old Tracy Connors *was told to bring his Brownie Hawkeye camera to a "prayer meeting." Ushered into a darkened front bedroom of the Connors' home, he saw a small box resting on the bed frame between two beds. The top was off and lying to one side. He knew immediately that it was a small coffin. "Tracy, we want you to take a picture," someone whispered.*

They named her Sharon Lee Connors, although that information was not included in the brief obituary that appeared in the papers.

In her very brief existence Sharon Lee Connors never drew a breath of her own. Yet, she was another victim of the Korean War as surely as if she had been one of the tens of thousands of Korean children killed during the war itself.

W. M. [Marcy] Mason, President of Mason Lumber Company wrote his friend: "Dear Arch, I was deeply distressed to learn of the accident and the death of your little grand daughter, and I want to offer my sincere sympathy to you and Mrs. Connors."

"You have a fine family and they have all gotten along so well. We cannot understand why things like this have to be, but we just have to accept the inevitable, and I pray that our Heavenly Father will comfort you all in this sad hour."

Emergency Leave

On April 5, 1952, 2nd Lt. Connors was medically certified for return travel to the United States. Two days later, Archie arrived from Korea at Travis AFB, California where he was granted Emergency Leave of thirty days.

Unknown to him at the time, an April 10, 1952 FEAF message had included "spot promotions" to 1st Lieutenant for Lieutenants Archie Connors, Allan Bettis, George Patton, Jack Shepard, Melvin Souza, Wilfred "Budd" Stapley and Donald Trautman, all friends from the 18th Fighter-Bomber Wing. *[Months later, when he was listed as Missing In Action, on April 15, 1953, his temporary promotion was made official and he would rank from 10 April 1952.]*

Services Set Today For Connors Child

Graveside services for the infant daughter of Lt. and Mrs. A. H. Connors Jr. will be held at 1 p.m. today in Riverside Memorial Park. The baby was the granddaughter of Mr. and Mrs. A. H. Connors of 3165 Broadway Ave.

The baby's mother and maternal grandmother, Mrs. Mary McGary of Nashville, Tenn., were injured seriously Monday when their car skidded on a rain-swept highway near Hawkinsville, Ga., and struck an embankment. Both are hospitalized in Hawkinsville.

Lt. Connors is en route here from Tokyo where he has been stationed with the Air Force.

When she could travel, Frankie and Archie arrived at his parent's home where Frankie stayed in seclusion in the front bedroom for weeks. Family members who tried to visit would rarely see Frankie, who was tortured by the events and ashamed of how she looked. She rarely allowed Archie to leave her side. When he visited, Tracy remembered how happy they had all been in that house just a few months before. Now nothing would ever be the same again.

Archie stayed with Frankie for over a month—for the most part he stayed by her side in that front bedroom facing Woodstock Park's Melson Avenue—trying to comfort her and help her heal inside and out.

On April 29th, Archie sent a telegram to the Air Force Director of Military Personnel requesting fifteen days additional emergency leave. He indicated that a "qualifying affidavit for reassignment will be forwarded." Two days later, the Air Force granted a 15-day extension to his emergency leave.

Dr. W. R. Baker provided a letter certifying that "Mrs. A. H. Connors, Jr. of Jacksonville, Florida was under my care from 3-11-52 to 3-31-52 for treatment of injuries received in auto accident 3-11-52. The injuries received were of such nature as to result in facial disfiguration and dental repair. Also, as a result of injuries her 7 1/2 month baby was delivered stillborn. Her injuries required a blood transfusion. It is necessary that she have further surgery done for facial injuries and due to the fact that she has had such a dreadful experience her treatment would be facilitated if it were so that her husband could visit at intervals."

A week later, Archie sent a letter to the Officer Assignment Division at Air Force Headquarters in Washington. "The condition of my wife is such that I would like an assignment in the Z.I. for the next six months. In the accident she was seriously injured and lost the baby. She is under a physician's care, and is on the verge of a nervous breakdown. I did not complete the half tour of overseas duty to qualify for automatic reassignment. My time overseas is as follows: Japan, 10 Nov. 51 to 10 Jan. 52; Korea, 10 Jan. 52 to 5 April 52 and 24 combat missions. Desire jet assignment (S.E. U.S.A.) if possible."

On May 14, 1952, Major Harry J. Morrison, USAF responded to Archie's letter "requesting reassignment in the United States." In fairness to other personnel in similar situations, the Major pointed out, "the Air Force has established criteria for the compassionate return of personnel from overseas. Normally, the foreign service to work of individuals is curtailed only when a serious compassionate problem exists which warrants the officer's early return to the United states. A typical instance would be where critical illness or death has created a problem that can be alleviated only by the officer's presence. Your request is not favorably considered as the circumstances set forth in your letter indicates that the problem is not of sufficient urgent necessity to warrant reassignment. All personnel on active duty, regardless of family responsibilities, are expected to share equitably in manning overseas duty stations. To provide immunity from family separations to individuals of the Department of the Air Force would be prejudicial, since similar consideration cannot be afforded to all." The

Rearming Mustangs of the 67th Squadron at K-46. (Black)

major concluded his letter by authorizing Archie to take an additional 15 days of leave "if you so desire." However, he noted that "leave taken in excess of accrued plus 30 days advance leave is on non-paid basis." By Priority message that day, the Air Force advised Archie's chain of command that he had been granted an additional 15-day extension of leave.

18th Group Combat Operations

Back in Korea, the 18th Group's continuing effort remained the rail interdiction program. Also continued was the tactic of "flying group formations on interdiction missions as initiated in March.."

The FEAF rail interdiction campaign—Operation Saturate—continued with missions "concentrated on two main railroads from Manchuria, the Namsi-dong-Sinanju and the Huichon-Kunu-ri lines. Far East Air Forces rendered the Sinuiju-Sinanju line unserviceable for most of April. In response to rail interdiction efforts, the enemy erected formidable antiaircraft defenses, especially along the Sinanju-Pyongyang line." [10]

The 12th and 67th Fighter-Bomber Squadrons were approximately 16 percent over authorized strength in pilots. Pilots were averaging only nine sorties per month. An administrative request was initiated to halt the flow of new pilots.

The Group lost eight aircraft in April, with four pilots listed as MIA. "All losses were due to small arms fire and automatic weapons, or to unknown causes with ground fire as probable cause. There were no minor casualties," the 18th Group reported. [11]

The Group's target section was busy cataloging photographic reports "on all special rail targets." FAF began assigning targets by code designation on specific sections of rail covering rail complexes in North Korea. The Target Section prepared each target in an individual file "complete with annotated photographs, flak reports and detailed maps. The advance

Maximum Effort. *When intelligence analysts and tactical planners determined that a particular target was important enough to justify a major strike, the 18th Fighter-Bomber Group was tasked to "hit a target with all its available resources— "maximum effort"—Col. Joe Peterburs explained. "The Group would put together a force from all four squadrons, and we would get from 30-50 birds in the air all hitting the same target at the same time." In this photo, Mustangs from all four of the 18th F-B Group squadrons turn up prior to taking off on a maximum effort mission. (Peterburs)*

preparation made it possible to furnish sufficient information for operational planning shortly after receipt of the early warning on the day prior to the mission."

The warmer weather brought problems with tar. As the days warmed up, the tar was "slung on the shock strut by the wheels," then collected grit and dust which wore the packing rings and scratched the polished surface of the strut." This problem was handled locally by manufacturing "strut boots of canvas." By the end of April, about half the Mustangs had strut boots.

Each aircraft now had a "permanent Crew Chief" who followed the airplane back and forth between K-46 and K-10. "The man crews the plane while it is at K-46, then follows it down to K-10 to help work on it when it goes into the hangar," the unit report explained.

The Group reported that morale was 'generally improving." The highest morale detriment was the "crowded quarters at K-46." However, the condition was reported as "corrected" with the construction of sufficient housing "to make comfortable facilities available to all personnel."

Limit: Two Passes At A Target

Operational tactics for the 18th remained "essentially" the same in April. However some "relatively new SOP's devised in Fifth Air Force and the 18th Group" were reported that "directly affected" the squadrons and were "worthy of mention."

"Excessive combat damage" brought about a change in SOP that restricted flight flights to only two passes at a target during close support missions—a "bombing and strafing pass followed by a rocket pass."

Downed pilot capping (Combat Air Patrol operations that provided cover to downed pilots) procedures were also changed "in hopes that the change will cut down the losses suffered on capping missions. The "ever growing intensity and accuracy of enemy flak has taken a heavy toll in aircraft and pilots recently," the 12th reported, "and our tactics have taken a more cautious course as a direct result. The actual capping of a downed pilot must remain to the discretion of the capping flight." However, the flight was being asked to "circle at a safe altitude, keeping an eye on the downed pilot's position and keeping contact with him over the bail-out radio which every pilot must carry." No attacking passes were to be made "unless the capping flight has complete command of the situation." The 12th reported taking part in several successful capping missions in April using "similar tactics."

Group rail cutting missions had become the "rule of the day as a result of a comparatively new policy of the Fifth Air Force which has proven quite effective." A small section of railroad track would be assigned as a target

"How Flight" of the 67th FBS in Spring 1952. *(Left to right) 1st Lt. Wilfred C. "Budd" Stapley, Capt Shirley B. Tubbs (seated, hand on sofa arm), 1st Lt. Donald D. Drage, (unidentified), and 1st Lt. Melvin Souza. Pilot at center rear is currently unidentified. This How Flight photograph was taken during the time when Archie Connors was back in the Z.I. on Emergency Leave.*

Mustangs being repaired at K-46. *The lighter areas pocking the hills behind the mix of 67th and 12th Squadron F-51s are shell holes, Earl Ramsdell noted on this photograph. (Ramsdell)*

and then "bombed all day long until there is virtually nothing to bomb other than the bomb holes already there." The missions were in Group strength and proved "very effective." Railroads that had been out of commission for only a few hours at the most, were not being knocked out for many days. "Our missions have extended much farther north than in the recent past and last an average of about two and a half hours apiece. The intense damage to a relatively small section of track rather than individual cuts over a large section has thwarted the enemy's very efficient repair system," the 12th Squadron noted. [12]

"The morale of the enlisted men rises and falls with the work load..."

"Through sheer determination and the excellent leadership throughout the squadron, the 67th was able to get the most out of the equipment on hand."

In April, 1952 Major Stanley A. Long succeeded Lt. Col. Julian F. Crow as the Commander of the 67th Squadron, which now included 45 officers. During the month, a major influx of enlisted personnel took place. Despite the increase in enlisted strength and a decrease in pilot strength, "neither one as yet, is at a suitable point," Long reported.

The overall qualifications of the reporting replacement personnel were "improving," however the "squadron veterans are still working double time in doing their own job and teaching, and supervising the work of the newer men."

Captain Victor E. Bocquin and Lt. Col. Julian Crow were two of the happiest pilots that month. Both completed 100 missions during April. They were now "Centurians," and would soon be headed home.

Rotation was still the biggest morale factor in any of the units, Long reported. "The morale of the enlisted men rises and falls with the work load. The more recognition for their efforts and achievements the higher the morale." Long also reported that the "maintenance personnel have been shown the pilot's combat film. This gives them a better idea of the good results of their effort." In turn, the pilot's morale was greatly increased when the number of assigned aircraft increased from 10 to 19, as a result of an additional nine aircraft acquired from the 39th Squadron when they left the group.

Communist's Supply Lines Hard Hit

F-51 Mustangs of the 18th Wing continued to direct their firepower toward the North Korean communists in the last two weeks and have marked up new records in the way of rail destruction, *The Truckbuster* reported in April. "Our propeller driven 51's have concentrated their attacks on Red

Repair Crew on the Run. *This dramatic photograph by a low-level reconnaissance flight in Spring 1952, shows Communist rail repair crews scurrying for cover—the circled figures. The striking photo also reveals how the cratered roadbeds were restored to serviceability within a few hours of the damaging cuts. Materials were hauled in on cars. Rail ties, steel rails, sandbags and tools were made available, and manpower was recruited as needed. Three rail lines blend easily into two parallel tracks by a system of simple switches. Section in right foreground shows how the ties were laid, and later wedged by additional ties. White parallel lines at left foreground and extreme background indicated recent repairs to damaged track. Labor crews encircled have one objective at this point—to escape from the overhead aircraft. (NARA)*

rail supply lines and for several days straight blasted the main lines between Chongju and Sinanju. Rail traffic in this area has been virtually paralyzed by the repeated attacks. Dive bombing planes of the 18th and other 5th AF Wings have severed rails in more than 250 separate places and knocked out all rail bridges along the 22-mile stretch of track."

Other Mustangs of the 18th swept up the west coast to strike once again at the Unden Station area. The Communist rail junction was already badly battered from continued bombings, but 18th pilots claimed seven new rail cuts.

Near the end of last month the fighter-bombers were almost daily hampered by extremely poor flying weather and operation was more or less limited to close support work. Heavy anti-aircraft fire was thrown up in front of the low-flying close support fighters across the entire front but the Mustang pilots managed to pound front line enemy positions.

Operation Strangle

Fifth Air Force's "Operation Strangle" was designed to "cut off the main arteries of the enemy's supply and logistical system," the *Truckbuster* reported on April 15, 1952. Strangle, it claimed, had "continued unmolested since its initial mission."

The Mustangs of the 18th's three flying Squadrons had concentrated chiefly on rail interdiction roles in the overall scene, and "have met with continued success." When weather permitted, Mustang pilots had participated in strikes "beginning in the pre-dawn hours and extending into the last light of day."

On a recent mission into Northwest Korea, the Mustangs had hit rail line districts that had been "left alone by UN Air Forces for several weeks. Surprising the enemy, the Mustang jockeys rode in on the target, dropping 500-pound bombs and high velocity rockets that jarred honey-buckets for miles around. Twenty-nine effective cuts were counted, but delayed fusings on other missiles precluded the possibility of other claims. In strafing actions, pilots brought back a log toll of eight KIA, and nine WIAs. On the coastal areas, several large sampans were attacked and one sunk. Four surface vessels sustained heavy battle damage. An interfering gun position was hit hard."

The advent of clearer skies and warmer, longer days held the "unspoken promise that the 18th will continue to bring back large claims of destruction on Communist targets. Fight-bombers attack Red positions all the day long, and night marauders take up the task when the sun has set," the *Truckbuster* explained.

Mustang FF 643 of the 67th Squadron gets refueled at K-10 in 1952. (Krakovsky)

Return to Korea

On May 28, 1952, Archie reported to Camp Stoneman, California for return transportation to his squadron.

At that time, his sister, Lucille was living in Oakland, California and had been keeping in touch with Archie and Frankie by telephone. Late one evening, Lucille received a telephone call—it was Archie telling her that he "was shipping out the next day because his name was at the top of the departure list," Lucille recalled. She and her husband drove to the little town of Pittsburg, California to meet Archie and Frankie for a goodbye dinner. "We had a wonderful time," Lucille remembered, "we went to a nightclub for dancing and drinks. Then, it was finally time to say 'Goodbye.' It was very hard for me, but I kept from bawling for his sake."

Years later she remembered what happened next. "When I kissed Archie Goodbye, a strange thing happened. First, his mouth was cold although it was warm outside. It was as if his life spirit was not in his body—as if there was nothing there! It was almost as if I were kissing a refrigerator. I thought I was crazy. I hated that feeling, and not understanding it, I didn't tell anyone for a long time. Also, I felt guilty for having such a terrible feeling," she recalled.

More ominously, Archie had confided to his mother before leaving Jacksonville, "Mom, I don't think I'm coming back from this one." Eva Connors was speechless, her eldest grandchild, Kathren McCluskey recalled. Such feelings of gloom and despair were not typical for her happy-go-lucky youngest and ever-cheerful, Archie. She kept his parting words to herself for many years, hardly able to talk about such a melancholy conversation, one of the last she would ever have with her beloved son.

In June, 1952, the 67th Squadron was flying its combat missions from Hoengsong, South Korea approximately seven miles North North East of Wonju. It used the forward combat operations base to interdict the enemy's transportation system.

On June 2, all of the 18th Wing's squadrons moved from Chinhae to Hoengsong in two phases. First, all property other than combat cargo was moved. Then combat cargo was moved by air. Both phases were completed on June 2nd.

After a brief refresher at the squadron's gunnery range, Archie was again flying missions—sometimes two a day. He was determined to complete his missions and go home—the sooner the better. He had little time for writing letters and he certainly did not want Frankie to know the extraordinary dangers he was facing as a fighter-bomber pilot in combat.

Meanwhile, Frankie had fully recovered—at least in external appearance—from her injuries, following dental repair and plastic surgery on her mouth. To family members, she seemed as pretty as ever, but the psychological scars were still there.

Eventually, she felt confident enough to seek employment near her new home in California, and sent Archie the following letter:

"No letter again today," Frankie wrote in a June 10th letter full of frustration and pain.

"I'm just ready to quit writing 'til I hear from you. There's never any news and I don't know what you're doing."

"Today Lockheed called to say a Mr. Johns needed a secretary, so I went to see him. He's one of the bosses in production. I have to learn about airplanes, how they're built, cost, etc. and they [will] send me to school. Mr. Johns seems nice but gives me a complex—he's 6'4" and husky. He's invited me out Saturday to swim in his pool—his wife likes swimming, too. So don't think it's a date," she added.

"Heard from both our Moms today. They're fine and both asked about you."

"Mario Lanza is singing "*Be My Love*" and it sure is making me blue."

"Why don't you write me? Maybe I'm trying to make myself believe we're important to each other. I know we aren't as much in love but I still miss you. If I'm kidding myself by staying home just write and tell me. I stayed home once before and it wasn't appreciated and don't want anymore of that."

"Write and let me know, As Ever, Frankie."

"Korea has changed a lot..."

"Dear Mom and Dad: Well, your son is back dealing death and destruction to the Chink Reds," Archie wrote on June 17th in one of his last letters. "Big joke! They put me in a training program and wouldn't let me fly any missions. Just finished yesterday."

"They have changed things around so much that I didn't recognize the place. We don't operate out of two bases anymore. Every thing is up north. They have all new commanding officers here. The base C.O. is straight from the training command. The next thing we know we will be having parades and inspections."

"Most of the fellows I came over with are going home. They have been finishing a lot of the fellows with 75 missions lately to get rid of the surplus pilots."

"Korea has changed a lot too. The hills are all green now. Grass is coming out (so are the mosquitoes). The smell hasn't improved any, if anything it is worse. Whew!! P.U!"

"They even have a chapel here now. They used to hold services in the service club."

"Well, guess I'll close for now. Will try to write at least once a week. Your son, Archie."

"P. S. Tell Jim Cox to spit on the hook. Should get back in the States, if I don't serve a year in Japan, about November or December."

Big Top Secret Deal

Following two weeks of intensive refresher training in combat flying, by June 19th, Archie was again flying combat missions with his squadron. At 1630 that afternoon, he sat down in the ready room at K-46 to write his older brother, Woodrow. He had already flown two missions that day. Having cheated death twice that day, his letter alternated between sophomoric humor and prophetic insights.

"How is the elder son of the clan? Still elder? Oh well, guess my high level of humor is way above your thin head uh, hair that is."

"Now 4:30 p.m. and already have two missions today. What's better than that. The flak on the second wasn't intense, it was unbearable! What a pity it would be for the world to lose my genius at such an early age.

"How is A. H. & Sons? [A. H. Connors & Sons Construction Company.] Still making missions? With this new pay raise…"

His letter of June 19th was interrupted, and then continued on June 20th. He explained: "before I could finish this sentence they came and got me for a big top secret deal. Now I am at K-10 (Chinhae, South Korea), about 170 miles south."

The "big top secret deal" probably referred to planning for raids conducted by the 18th Wing and many other UN fighter squadrons, including VF-74, from June 23rd through June 26th on the North Korean power plants at Suiho, Choshin and Fusen. The first was on the massive hydroelectric plant at Suiho, a fork of the Yalu River. Pyongyang, Chinnampo and much of Manchuria got their electricity from the Suiho plant. The attack was a success.

Another plant at Choshin was hit on June 24th. One of Archie's fellow pilots, Lt. John McAlpine, was killed during the action.

"...I will be making around 5 ½ bills per month," Archie continued the letter a day later. "Guess with the old lady working we should be able to save around $500.00 per. About a year of this and we will be able to make a good down payment on a home. With this new G.I. bill, have been thinking seriously of going back to school and getting a degree."

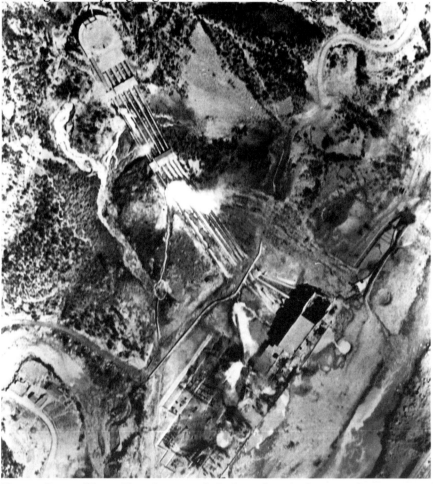

Kyosen Power Plant. *This photograph, looking directly down at what remains of Kyosen Power Plant No.3, discloses heavy structural damage to the plant in July 1952. The penstocks, leading from the reservoir to the power plant, were cut by bomb bursts (note spray from escaping water). At least one direct hit and two near misses were scored on the generator house (near dark shadow), and the control building probably suffered a direct hit and three near misses. Severe damage was done to the transformer yard. (NARA)*

"The Migs are getting worse and worser (sic)," he noted, switching subjects abruptly. "So by the time you hear from me again I may be an ace. They use us as decoys to bring them out where the glory boys in 86's can take a shot. As it now stands we will have them (the 67th would begin the transition into the F-86 in October, 1952) before fall. What could possibly be better than that."

"Well, guess I'll close for now with 72 to go."

"P.S. Tell Jim (Cox) that the fishing over here is limited to suckers. Who won the election and by what majority?"

Last Letters

On June 21st, shortly before the start of the power plant raids, Archie wrote: "Dearest Frankie, Still south but go back tomorrow. They are flying taksan missions now your husband gets shafted as usual." [13]

Archie had had "a long talk with one of the South Afrikans," who gave him "a lot of good advice on marriage…just hope I have sense enough to use it," he said.

"Big dance tonight all the local girls of ill repute will be here and all the brass will make fools of themselves." Sounding more than a little sanctimonious, he continued: "Hon, it is the most disgusting sight that I have ever seen or heard of. Officers you know must be an example."

"They pulled (Melvin) Souza and (Jack) Shepard off report and are sending them to the 8th. They asked for jets so the F.E.A.F. says we have jets here so we won't send you home. The rest of the fellows are getting shafted into this G.C.I deal. Don't tell Polly, if Howard can beat the rap more power to him."

["Howard" was Lt. Howard D. Austin and Polly was his wife. Polly and Frankie were rooming together in Los Angeles while their husbands were in Korea. 1st Lt. Mel Sousa was killed in a flying accident soon after Archie posted this letter.]

"Sure will be glad to get back up to K-46 (Hoengsong) as I should have a lot of mail. Three days since I heard from little fat wife. Love you."

"The mail has been pretty good these last few days, but I had better quit bragging."

"Only need 2:10 for my flight pay and will get about :50 of that tomorrow morning."

"Will close for now hon. Be good and write often. Your (and only yours) husband, Archie."

"P.S. Still hope to finish by September."

It was his last letter.

"Do you think we'll ever lead a normal life..."

"Dearest Archie," Frankie led off in her letter of June 25th. "No letter again today, just hope nothing is wrong."

"Another dull day about [without?] you. All this week has been chilly and smoggy. My sun tan is beginning to fade."

"Sure wish you had told me when (Budd) Stapley was expected in the States. He will have a 30-day leave first, won't he? Come to think of it, nothing has been explained to me."

"Have you heard any more about how much longer you'll be there? They aren't supposed to keep you two winters in Korea—so they say."

"The paper tonight was full of stuff about riots in Tokyo again. Let's don't apply for duty there."

"I'm lonesome but guess you know that. Do you think we'll ever lead a normal life—or be happy if we do? My morale can't help being low. If only you hadn't been so inconsiderate when I had the accident. Hon, I just can't get over things in a week or two and now there's the dullest feeling when I start to think. You killed something in those few weeks and it's hard to get used to. Guess I'll close for now. Be good and write me. All yours, Frankie."

In their last letters to each other neither Frankie nor Archie could bring themselves to close with "love." Her references to "dullest feeling" and "you killed something" strongly indicate their relationship was suffering greatly as a result of his war service that required their long separation. The tragic death of their daughter was never fully resolved.

Frankie always felt some members of Archie's family blamed her for Sharon Lee's death, a tragedy over which she had no control. That was certainly not the case with Archie's parents as future events would prove.

Archie finished a letter to his brother, Woodrow, as he waited in the 67th Squadron's Operations Office for a possible mission on Wednesday, June 25th. It would eventually reach him, but not via the postal service.

Chapter Eight

Rescue Helicopters In Combat

Much closer to the front, Wayne Lear and Bobby Holloway whiled away the rest of that Wednesday morning writing letters and talking to pilots of the L-5 spotter planes that landed from time to time for fuel and to rest the edgy pilots. The small, single engine aircraft were frequent targets for enemy gunners since they helped direct bombing runs and artillery fire.

In their way, they were becoming a part of aviation history.

Rotary-wing aircraft operations conducted to rescue downed airmen, had "its humble beginning in 1944," the 1952 issue of ***The Scrambler*** noted. *The 1952 Scrambler* was the unit history prepared by the Third Air Rescue Squadron, whose motto was "*That Others May Live.*" The title selected for its unit history book— *The Scrambler*—was clearly intended to convey how the squadron often had to operate in the chaotic conditions that existed during the Korean War. The squadron accurately noted that since its establishment in 1944, that it had risen "to a place of prominence as one of the most renowned units of the United States Air Force."

The Third Air Rescue Squadron "has built a past to be proud of for all time," *The Scrambler* continued. "It has seen more actual combat service in any other unit of its kind. Its men wear more decorations for valor and bravery, and have set and broken more records than any other unit in the Air

159

Preparing a casualty for evacuation to a hospital *in a 3rd ARS Squadron H-5. The increased use of helicopters on rescue missions during the Korean War became a significant factor in saving lives. From 1950-1953, men of the 3rd ARS Squadron (later designated a group) earned more than 1,000 personal citations and commendations. By the war's end, ARS crews were credited with the rescue of 9,898 United Nation's personnel; 996 of those represented combat saves.*

Rescue Service. It is a story of work and rework, test and retest, prove and disprove, day in and day out, under all types of conditions."

The Third Air Rescue Squadron was officially established on 15 February 1944 at Gulfport Army Airfield, Gulfport, Mississippi, and was then known as the Third Emergency Rescue Squadron.

"The planning and organization of the squadron was a direct outgrowth of the results of similar organizations operating in the combat theaters during World War II," *The Scrambler* explained. "The British originated the rescue phase through necessity during the first years of the last war, the necessity being the saving of trained aircrew members from the icy waters of the English Channel and returning them to operational status in a minimum of time. The shortage of manpower was of such a critical nature at that time that replacements for trained personnel were unobtainable and, as a result, the air-sea rescue organization was born."

After intensive training at Gulfport and Keesler Field, the squadron was sent overseas. "Men and equipment started the long haul across the country and across the Pacific to the little island of Biak, arriving there in

September 1944. On 17 September 1944, 15 days after they arrived in the combat zone, the squadron was ready for business. During the following months of the war, the squadron participated in the island hopping operations of the Fifth Air Force and moved up through the islands of the Pacific to such places as Noemfoor, Morotai, and Leyte."

Later, in June 1945 the squadron "moved its base of operations to the island of Okinawa, to furnish rescue coverage for the Fifth Air Force's shipping sweeps between Japan and Korea and the China coast installations. When peace came in September of 1945, the squadron landed at Atsugi Air Strip near Yokohama Japan with elements of the Fifth Air Force."

During World War II the third emergency rescue squadron successfully snatched from enemy hands over 220 downed air crewmembers. All the combat operations during the war were not accomplished without casualties however. By 13 October 1944, scarcely more than one month after operations had begun, nine rescue personnel had failed to return from rescue missions.

"Flying over jungle and mountainous terrain, aircrews returned injured personnel to safety within hours," Forrest L. Marion points out in *That Others May Live: USAF Air Rescue in Korea*, "instead of the days or even weeks that a ground party required. Considering that the first practical rotary wing aircraft...had flown only a few years earlier in 1941, the limited accomplishments of helicopters heralded the birth of a new technology with immense potential for military applications, notably, medical evacuation and air crew rescue."

The squadron was reassigned to the Air Rescue Service from the Fifth Air Force in May 1949. While the operating locations of the different flights in Japan remained the same following reassignment, the supervision of the organization now became the responsibility of Headquarters, Air Rescue Service, Washington, DC.

When the Korean War broke out in June 1950, rescue helicopters were soon put to use evacuating wounded United Nations personnel from front-line positions to the rear area hospitals and snatching downed pilots who had crashed or bailed out in enemy territory from enemy hands.

3ARS Korean War Service

Less than five years after World War II ended, the Korean War proved that helicopters from that point on would be indispensable to warfare. Although the technology involved was only a decade old, life-saving medical evacuations and heroic rescue achievements by the air rescue squadron captured worldwide attention. Helicopters proved to be indispensable throughout the Korean War by evacuating thousands of wounded personnel, many of whom would not have survived the torturous land trek over primitive roads to reach even rudimentary medical facilities. While performing its primary mission, the air rescue service helicopters brought back nearly 1,000 United Nations personnel from behind enemy lines. While fulfilling its secondary mission—medical evacuation—it transported over 7000 wounded soldiers during the conflict.

The Third Air Rescue Squadron was one of the first rescue units to use the helicopter in rescue operations, and was the first Air Force squadron to use the helicopter in combat against an armed enemy.

On 10 August 1950, the squadron was again reorganized as the Third Air Rescue Squadron under a new T/O&E [Table of Organization and Equipment], which authorized additional equipment and personnel to assist the squadron in providing adequate rescue coverage and support in the Armed Forces engaged in the Korean War.

Third Air Rescue Squadron helicopters were the only United Nations units having the primary mission of retrieving downed airmen. Other squadrons also provided air rescue support when needed, but not as a primary mission.

When the North Koreans poured into South Korea on June 25, 1950 during a full-scale invasion across the 38th parallel into the Republic of Korea, elements of 3ARS were quickly called on for support. Within hours of the invasion, the squadron was using of cargo planes and helicopters to assist in medical evacuation. By August 5, 1950 the first H-5 helicopter had been used to transport a wounded U.S. Army soldier to an Army hospital. [2]

Thousands more evacuations would take place in the three years of fighting that remain in the Korean War before an armistice would be put into place.

"I'll be back later for another load."

Throughout the Korean War the helicopters of the Third Air Rescue Squadron [redesignated the Third Air Rescue Group [ARG] in November 1952], completed many dramatic rotary wing combat operations. Overcoming many of the shortcomings inherent in a new technology, squadron pilots demonstrated the enormous potential for helicopter operations during combat— especially for rescue and evacuation. Before the Korean War, military helicopters were somewhat of an oddity. After the war helicopters and helicopter operations were indispensable and seen by all as standard equipment.

At the beginning of the Korean War, the concept and doctrine of using helicopters to rescue downed pilots was largely untested. During three years of combat operations in Korea, air rescue service aircraft of all types rescued nearly 1000 UN personnel from behind enemy lines and of these helicopters accounted for approximately 85%.

The Commander of the Third Air Rescue Squadron for most of the Korean War, Lt. Col. Klair E. Back, a native of Whitesburg, Kentucky and a Georgetown College graduate, assumed command in August 1950, and was promoted to full colonel one year later. He had been transferred to Korea after serving as Inspector General at Headquarters, Air Rescue Service in Washington, D.C.

Back remained in command until June 1953, a highly unusual commander's tenure, one that reflected high confidence in his abilities by Fifth Air Force leadership. Back earned the respect of his command by flying combat sorties in four of the seven aircraft types operated by the Third Air Rescue Squadron, including: the SB-17, SA-16, SB-29, and SC-47. During the Korean War the squadron grew significantly in both personnel and aircraft, adding the YH-19 helicopter to its inventory, and successfully field testing the new helicopter under combat conditions in 1951. In early 1952 it brought six more H-19's into its fleet.

Early Helicopter Operations in Korea

In the early stages of the war plan for using the newly arrived H-5's, called for a "strip alert" helicopter for rescue of airmen to fulfill the primary mission. Rescue would also provide 'on call' aircraft to be used by... frontline organizations in evacuation of the most critically wounded..."

To enable prompt rescue of downed fliers, spotter planes (usually T-6 "Texans" and known as "Mosquitoes" based on their radio call sign), maintained radio contact with fighters or bombers operating in the combat area and would relay all reports of distress or damage with bases of operations. When reports were received requesting rescue assistance, the information was immediately relayed to the nearest rescue strip alert helicopter through the Fifth Air Force chain of command.

For helicopters stationed at MASH units, mission calls usually came in via telephone communications. For helicopters standing alert at advanced operating airfields, requests for rescue assistance might come in not only by radio from spotter aircraft, but also from other detachment helicopters returning from missions. Very early in the Korean War a 3ARS Liaison Officer was assigned to the Joint Operations Center at Headquarters, Fifth Air Force in Seoul. Requests for rescue assistance thereafter were coordinated through the Tactical Air Control Center that was located at the JOC and through the JOC rescue coordinator.

By the end of 1950 the Third Air Rescue Squadron expanded the one-officer liaison office into a three-member rescue control center that would be manned at all times. The control center became designated as "Headquarters, 3rd ARS in Korea," and the officer in charge became the Deputy Commander, Third Air Rescue Squadron, responsible for all Korean rescue operations.

On September 4, 1950 an H-5 from the air rescue squadron established a new era in rotary wing aircraft operations when Capt. (later Major) Paul W. Van Boven cross enemy lines to pick up a downed F-51 Mustang pilot.

3ARS, Detachment One

By early 1951, 3 ARS, Detachment One operated from K-16, Seoul's Municipal Airport. It was the Air Rescue Service's most experienced combat unit and now operated 15 helicopters from five sites, all of them very close to the front lines. Four of its "egg beaters" operated from the 8055th MASH located at Uijongbu. Everyday the on-duty helicopter would fly up to the 25th Division command post area near the center of UN lines and stand by for any needed pilot pickups. The other three helicopters stayed at the hospital in case they were needed for medical evacuation.

"During recent months there has been a great increase in the use of helicopters in evacuating ROK wounded," reported Col. Allen D. Smith (Decatur, GA), flight surgeon of the 315th Air Division and Commander of the 801st Medical Air Evacuation Squadron on October 19, 1951.

"Air evacuation by Air Force and Army helicopters," he said, "ties in directly with the frontline airstrip evacuation by C-47 Skytrains carried out by the 315th Air Division, Combat Cargo. Helicopters fly ROK wounded two at a time from the craggiest mountain tops to frontline airstrips where C-47's can land and pick up 25 to 30 wounded at a time for evacuation to major Army hospitals near rear area air bases."

Helicopter evacuation of wounded is particularly important in the areas where the ROK's are fighting, Smith said. "They are fighting in the most mountainous section of Korea, often far from roads, in areas accessible only by mountain trail along the ridge lines. Supplies are either air dropped by Combat Cargo C-119 "Flying Boxcars," or carried up on A-frames on the backs of civilian auxiliaries."

"Before the helicopter came into general use for the ROK's," Col. Smith continued, "wounded could do one of three things. They could crawl to the nearest aid station and stay there until they recovered. They could crawl or drag themselves down. Or, they could jounce down a mountain trail riding the A-frame of a sturdy countryman."

"None of these alternatives was any good," Smith pointed out. "By the time the ROK soldier got to good medical care, he was weak from loss of blood and general collapse due to fatigue, shock and strain."

Air evacuation by helicopter to frontline airstrips, Colonel Smith indicated, was changing medical treatment and evacuation tactics and procedures. "Men are getting to good medical care within hours after being wounded. They will recover much faster, due to the fine teamwork between the helicopter pilots and Combat Cargo's C-47 air evacuation planes and flight nurses."

At that time in the Korean War, the 315th Air Division had already airlifted more than 175,000 wounded.

Pilot Pickup Doctrine

In Korea, the mountainous terrain, primitive roads and extreme seasons made the helicopter an ideal means to transport emergency patients or supplies. However the H-5 had significant operational limitations. For example, operating under instrument conditions was almost impossible. Darkness, heavy rain or hail, icy conditions or high winds also made for highly risky flying conditions in the H-5, that had no armor or armament to protect it from ground fire while on rescue missions. It depended on fighter cover or even friendly ground fire for protection during the time it was most vulnerable, i.e. pickup of downed pilots or wounded personnel.

Pilots normally carried a .45-caliber pistol and medics like Bob Holloway carried and sometimes used M-2 Carbine's. There was no weight allowance for any heavier ordinance.

Fighter cover was used to protect the slow-moving, vulnerable helicopters. After a pilot went down his remaining flight members remained in the area as long as their fuel allowed or until they were relieved by a different rescue combat air patrol with more fuel and ammunition.

A more sophisticated approach was adopted later in the war during which the rescue combat air patrol would be divided into two elements,

one that would keep the downed airman in sight while suppressing enemy ground fire, and a second element that would escort the rescue helicopter into the area and protect it while it was executing the pickup. Often, the helicopter would encounter small arms fire at very close range while making such pickups, and the fighter-bomber escorts were used to make the enemy keep their heads down while the helicopter was most vulnerable. This RESCAP technique would be used to save many American lives two decades later during the Vietnam War.

Living Conditions for Rescue Crews

Living conditions for pilots and crew serving in Korea at the time were Spartan to say the least. Generally squadron personnel stayed in large tents with dirt floors heated by oil burning stoves. It could get so cold during the winter that helicopter crew chiefs would drain half the oil from the helicopter's engine and bring it and the battery into the tent in an effort to keep them from freezing.

Food often consisted of just canned rations including such military standbys as Spam and powdered eggs. Fresh food of any kind was a rarity and even fresh water was sometimes difficult to find. When crews were stationed at mobile Army surgical hospital's, the food and accommodations were considerably better.

ARS3, Det One Operations

One of the new pilots assigned to the squadron's Detachment One in spring 1952 was Captain Wayne Lear, who had just completed advanced training in the H-19. Another new arrival was Airman Bobby Dale Holloway, a Medical Technician from Ruston, Louisiana.

Air Rescue Squadron Three, Detachment One was based at Seoul's K-16. "From there we were able to serve several MASH units operating much closer to the front lines, just south of the 38th Parallel. "Actually, it almost sat on the 38th Parallel," Holloway recalled.

"You normally pulled a tour there of seven days at a stretch, then you would return to K-16 or they might send you up to the island," he said. Cho Do island, off North Korea's west coast remained in UN control throughout the war and was used to stage air rescue and reconnaissance missions.

"We flew into the front lines and brought wounded from there back to the MASH's for more extensive treatment. On some occasions, we flew patients to the 121st evacuation hospital in Seoul. We would also fly patients out to Navy hospital ships that were anchored off the coast, including the USS HOPE," he recalled.

Holloway remembers a helicopter pilot muttering that he hoped that ship was not moving, since he had never landed on a ship before. "Lucky for him the ship was anchored," he said.

Most of the time in the H-5, the patient was in a capsule outside the body of the aircraft. "We could see the head and chest area behind a Plexiglass bubble—like a cocoon. Early in the war they only covered the top half of the patient with the bubble. They quickly went to a full bubble to protect the patient from wind and cold. In the winter time, in particular, you had to have them covered up. It could be bitterly cold over there," he explained.

"We had another version of the H-5 that was configured so that we could fit a stretcher inside the body of the helicopter and not have to leave the patient outside. That version had the hoist on it and we used it to pick people up off the ground," Holloway said.

"If the medic determined that there is something not right with the patient, he told the pilot who then found the first available landing spot to put the bird down. Then the medic got out and checked the patient or administered any needed medical care—whatever had to be done. That didn't happen too often because the patients we transported had had everything that was possible done in order to stabilize them for transport. The doctors and medics that worked at the company and aid station levels were good—really good. They knew their stuff and were very dedicated. They had had a lot of experience," he said.

Once stabilized, "we moved them to where the next level of medical care was waiting. We got 'em in and we got 'em out—in a hurry. I believe that was the 'secret' to the whole thing—speed—time. If you can get someone stabilized and into the hands of a qualified, well-equipped trauma team within the first hour their chances of survival go up dramatically. Even then, we knew that stabilization and movement to well equipped facilities within the first hour was critical to their survival chances. But it was very hard under those circumstances. By the time they were wounded, then initially treated and the helicopter called, then we get there and get out, the minutes and more were ticking by. But we did achieve the speed that was needed because everybody was ready to go," he said.

For example, "say there were four medics at one of the advanced operating bases we had, basically some tents and dry rice paddy very near the front lines. We knew who was 'up,' who had been selected to fly on the next medical evacuation. The duty rotated. No one had to look for you. All they did was holler and you went straight to the helicopter, which itself was ready for almost immediate take-off. Half the time you never knew where you were going until you were in the air," he said.

"After a pilot got to know you—and trusted you—he would hand you the map over his shoulder and say we're going to so-and-so location.

From that point on you—the medic—were the primary navigator to that location," Holloway explained.

"We had one pilot who believed that no one could navigate except him. I didn't ever look forward to flying with him. When he finally admitted that he was lost and I was handed the map, we were sitting out in no-man's land. Matter of fact, we were considerably further north of the center line," he recalled.

All of Holloway's patients were "bad, because they needed a great deal of medical attention as fast as possible."

"You weren't with that person that long. The instant you touched down you were out of the helicopter, threw the bubble open and helped get that patient in and secured. Then jumped back on that helicopter and you're gone—in the air and headed for the MASH or out to the hospital ship. When you were on a evacuation mission, you weren't on the ground any longer than you had to be," he explained.

"We did have one memorable mission, and we didn't have a patient. We got a call to go up to some command post. We finally got there and there was no place to land. So, we kept looking and finally saw an open space out there so we tried to touch down—actually got one wheel on the ground—but there was too much slope. We tried that three times and decided, well, that's not the place to go. So, we flew over to a nearby road to set down. What we didn't see as we touched down was all of their clothes lines and other wires on poles. That rotor took all of them out. Needless to say, the Colonel up there was more than a little upset. Among other things, all of his communications were down. Finally, we got down and shut down the motor. A guy comes running up yelling that we were the luckiest SOB's he had ever seen. How's that, we asked. Well, he explained, breathless, you just made three landings—in a mine field.

It was one of those situations where the man upstairs was looking out for us," Holloway concluded. "We didn't buy the farm—that day."

The H-5

The H-5 "Dragonfly" was originally designated the R-5 (H for Helicopter; R for Rotorcraft). It was designed as a more effective helicopter that would have greater useful load, endurance, speed, and service ceiling than the R-4. The H-5 made its initial flight on August 18, 1943, and seven months later, the AAF ordered 26 for service testing. The first service models were delivered in February 1945.

The H-5 was used for rescue and mercy missions throughout the world, but earned its greatest fame during the Korean War when it was called upon repeatedly to rescue United Nations' pilots shot down behind enemy lines and to evacuate wounded personnel from frontline areas.

When production was concluded in 1951, more than 300 H-5s had been built.

Specifications and Performance:
Main rotor diameter: 48 ft.
Tail rotor diameter: 8 ft. 5 in.
Fuselage Length: 41 ft. 2 in.
Height: 12 ft. 11 in.
Weight: 4,815 lbs. loaded
Armament: None
Engine: Pratt & Whitney R-985 of 450 hp
Maximum speed: 90 mph. Cruising speed: 70 mph.
Range: 280 miles
Service Ceiling: 10,000 ft.

The H-19

The UH-19B was the USAF version of the Sikorsky S-55, an aircraft that was in wide use by U.S. and allied military services in the 1950s and 1960s. "It was the first of the Sikorsky helicopters with enough cabin space and lifting ability to allow satisfactory operation in troop transport or rescue roles," the Air Force Museum points out.

H-19 landing aboard a U.S. Navy transport ship off the Korean coast to pick up a combat wounded patient.

"The engine is mounted in the nose, leaving the main cabin free for passengers or cargo. The prototype was first flown in November 1949, and in 1951 the USAF ordered production model H-19s (redesignated UH-19s in 1962). After receiving 50 H-19As, the USAF acquired 270 H-19Bs with increased engine power. Many were assigned to Air Rescue squadrons as SH-19s (later redesignated HH-19s). For rescue service, a 400 lb. capacity hoist was mounted above the door. The aircraft also could be equipped with an external sling capable of carrying 2,000 lbs. During the Korean War, H-19s were used extensively for rescue and medical evacuation work. Other missions included observation and liaison. The H-19 flew the first helicopter combat airlift missions during the Korean War while serving with the U.S. Marine Corps as the HRS.

Specifications and Performance:
Rotor diameter: 53 ft.
Fuselage Length: 42 ft. 4 in.
Height: 15 ft. 4 in.
Weight: 8,400 lbs. max.
Armament: None
Engine: Wright R-1300-3 of 700 hp.
Cost: $150,000
Maximum speed: 112 mph.
Cruising speed: 92 mph.
Range: 330 miles
Service Ceiling: 15,000 ft.

Chapter Nine

Wayne and Della Lear

As he waited near his H-5 helicopter for a possible mission on Wednesday morning, 25 June, Captain Wayne Lear might have reflected that he had come a long way from the cockpit of a B-29.

Santa Cruz High School in Santa Cruz, California was very proud of Leslie Wayne Lear, President of the 1943 graduating class. When he wasn't heading up the senior class, he was lettering in football, baseball and basketball. Born March 20, 1925, Wayne, as he preferred to be called by friends and family, graduated from Santa Cruz in 1943. Wayne had grown up as a happy, well-adjusted child—loving sports and animals. Like most young men of his age in the middle of World War II, he joined the military.

Wayne entered military service right after completing high school in June 1943. Clearly, the Air Force saw great potential in the handsome young leader and athlete, because following some college training at Cole College in Cedar Rapids, Iowa, he was sent on to complete flight training in both B-17s and B-29s. After completing an accelerated college preparatory program at Cole College, he was returned to Santa Ana Air Base, Santa Ana, California for pre-flight training, then to Ryan Field, California for basic training. For a brief period he was able to see more of his parents—Leslie I. and Leona Mable Lear, who lived on Spurgeon St., Santa Ana. His mother's parents—the Lambs—also lived nearby.

Advance training was completed at Minter Field, California, and then on to Douglas, Arizona for B-17 flight training. After completing B-29 training in Roswell Army Air Field, New Mexico from April 30 until June 3, 1945. He was then ordered to Lincoln, Nebraska, where his new crew was being formed. Once the crew was selected, they were stationed at El Paso, Texas. Even though the war ended in August 1945, Wayne was posted to Japan in December 1945.

The Air Force sent Wayne Lear shuttling around the country for accelerated training, sometimes on airplanes and sometimes on any available trans-

Wayne Lear while he was a student at Santa Cruz High School in Santa Cruz, California.

portation. During one such trip through the mid-West in 1945, he met a pretty, vivacious teenager from St. Paul, Minnesota, but at the time living in Pasadena, Ca.

Della Marie Paddon, was the daughter of John Henry Paddon and Elizabeth Mary Bray. The Paddon's were originally English, although they met in Chicago, Michigan after John's military service as a Canadian in a Scottish Regiment during World War I. Elizabeth had entered the U.S. through Ellis Island. Eventually, they moved to St. Paul, Minnesota, where John was the supervisor for Como Park, and where their daughter Della was born in 1925.

Della Paddon had met brand new 2nd Lt. Wayne Lear

2nd Lt. Wayne Lear shortly after he earned his wings and completed Army Air Force pilot training.

on a train not long before the end of World War II. They both knew almost immediately that they were in love.

Della's parents had moved from Evanston, Illinois to California in January 1943—just when she "was starting my second semester of my senior year at Evanston Township High School. That was a major change for me—missing graduation exercises. However, I did attend a high school in Altadena, California and had my credits sent back to ETHS so that I could get my diploma from that school," Della recalled.

As a "graduation present"—after attending two years of junior college—her parents said she "could go back to Evanston for a couple of weeks to visit friends and relatives there. Keep in mind that World War II was still going on at this time and commercial travel was not easy to obtain. However, on June 16, 1945, I boarded a train headed for Chicago. My parents had been able to obtain an upper berth in a Pullman car for my three day trip."

The train stopped in Pasadena and it was rather late in the afternoon of June 16th, but "what a happy day for me," Della remembered. "If you were fortunate enough to have a berth you had a special seat in the Pullman car. I found my seat partner was a soldier going to a base in Nevada—can't remember anything else about him."

Della Marie Paddon *with her father, John Henry and mother, Elizabeth. (Right) Della had become a beauty by the time she entered junior college. (Holloway)*

"The first night in an upper berth was quite an experience. You had to call for the Porter to get a small ladder for you to get up or down from that berth. It was great but somewhat difficult to change one's clothes that way—use your imagination."

"That next day I walked through other parts of the train to get to the dining car and, of course, looked at various passengers in the other cars that I passed through. Knowing that it was going to be a rather long and boring trip if I just had myself to talk to—keeping in mind that I was truly a very shy person at that time—I thought, well, what the heck, if I see someone interesting, I will just start up a conversation. After all, I would probably never see that person or persons again!!!!!!"

"On my way, back from the dining car, I spotted the most handsome, young, blond, blue-eyed, Second Lieutenant (a pilot by his wings). S-0-0-0-0, I just smiled sweetly and said something like—"do you have far to go on the train?"

"Naturally, that started other questions—where are you from, family, etc. It was great to hear he had been born in Santa Cruz, California, and his family now lived in Santa Ana, he had one sister who was four years younger that he was (he was 20), and that he loved dogs, etc. By the way, I was still only 19 as my birthday was not until July."

"His name was Leslie Wayne Lear and he was on his way to Lincoln, Nebraska, where his B-29 crew was to be formed. He had only recently graduated from flight school. He had wanted to be a fighter pilot but the Air Force felt he was more suited to flying bombers. He was to be a co-pilot and was looking forward to the experience. He was traveling under orders and the Air Force did not supply its men with Pullman accommodations. We talked and talked—it was GREAT. By the way, that was June 17. We had our meals together and I shared some snacks that Mother had packed for me to enjoy on the trip."

"Poor Wayne had no sleeping place except the one seat assigned to him. No, I did not share my upper berth. In my day and age, no one did that sort of thing. I fully realize that is very difficult for the younger generation to believe but it is TRUE."

"By, the 18th of June he presented me with his wings—as a sign that we were engaged. Boy, was that ever thrilling. I had no thoughts of what my parents might think of that arrangement—I was

Della Wears Wings. *In June 1945, Wayne asked Della to wear his pilot's wings. They were engaged.*

just too happy for that. We were trying to figure out how we could see each other during my stay in Chicago."

Since the train did not go through Lincoln, Lear got off in Omaha and arrived at his base on the bus on June 19th. "He wrote his very first letter to me on the same day he arrived at his base and usually wrote one every day thereafter. He was definitely sure that he loved me and would forever."

Lear was not sure how long he would be in Lincoln, Nebraska. He left the train fairly early on the 19th and Della went on to Chicago."

By this time, he had met most of the fellows who would make up his bomber crew. The plane commander was 1st Lt. Vincent Meyer (who gave Della away at their wedding), and his flight engineer was 2nd Lt. Ralph Jones (who was best man at the wedding and his wife was the maid of honor). It was great to hear about these people who later had such important parts in our wedding.

During this time, Della "was able to visit with friends and family in Chicago, Lake Forest, and Evanston. Of course, there were also a few phone calls from Wayne as it looked as thought he could not be able to get pass to come to me so was wondering whether I could change my return ticket to get off in Omaha and spend several days in Lincoln before heading back to Pasadena."

By June 27th, Della recalled that "Wayne had written to his parents telling them he had met the nicest girl on the train and that I lived not too far away from them and we should all meet some Sunday. Bet that was some shock to them—their quiet son—making up his mind so quickly. All this time he also wrote to tell me that he had started to look for rings—that's fast work in my book!"

"We found out that I would be able to change my ticket—getting on in Chicago a couple of days earlier that originally planned and making a couple of days stop-over in Omaha and I would still have my berth for the remainder of the trip."

On July 2, 1945, Della received a telegram from Wayne saying that "everything was OK and he would meet my train in Omaha at 10:40 p.m. and he had made reservations at a hotel for me. Yes, just me—remember this is still the age of no "hanky-panky" before marriage—believe it—it's TRUE."

"Needless to say, we had a marvelous Fourth of July in Lincoln—I was able to stay there until July 8th. Wayne had to report back to the base each night and had some duty to take care of at the base but for the most part we were able to be together to view the sights of Lincoln. I got to meet members of his crew. His 1st pilot was there with his wife and very young baby but they had a CAR and drove us around when gasoline was available—we were well chaperoned," she laughed.

Lt. Leslie Lear, Miss Paddon Married in Texas

White and pastel gladioli decorated the altar of the main chapel at the Biggs Field Army Base, El Paso, Tex., where the marriage of Miss Della-Marie Paddon, daughter of Mr. and Mrs. John H. Paddon of North Euclid Avenue, and Lt. Leslie W. Lear, son of Mr. and Mrs. Leslie I. Lear of Santa Ana, took place on a recent Sunday. The double ring ceremony was read by Chaplain Richard O. Flinn at 1 in the afternoon.

The bride was attended by Mrs. Ralph L. Jones, who served as matron of honor. Lieutenant Lear's best man was Lt. Ralph L. Jones and the bride was escorted to the altar by Lt. Vincent Meyer. Pfc. Mary E. Lindeman played a medley of nuptial music prior to the ceremony, as well as the traditional wedding marches.

The former Miss Paddon chose for her wedding a suit of soft aqua gabardine, with which she wore a matching straw hat and brown accessories. Her corsage was a spray of white orchids. Mrs. Jones was attired in a teal blue suit, with white accessories, and wore a corsage of gardenias.

A wedding breakfast was served at the Officer's Club for the wedding party and friends. Among the guests were Chaplain Flinn, Lieutenant and Mrs. Meyer, Lieutenant and Mrs. Jones, Lt. and Mrs. I. A. Tobin, Lt. Carl Bochek.

Lieutenant and Mrs. Lear are now residing at Pueblo, Colo., where the bridegroom is presently stationed.

Newly married 2nd Lt. Leslie Wayne Lear and Della-Marie Paddon Lear on 26 August 1945 at the Biggs Field Base Chapel in El Paso, Texas.

While the newly minted B-29 co-pilot was en route to combat duties over Japan, he and Della married on 26 August 1945 at the Biggs Field Base Chapel in El Paso, Texas. Many of Wayne's military friends took part in the "double ring ceremony," including Lt. Ralph L. Jones and Lt. Vincent Meyer.

Della was wearing "a suit of soft aqua gabardine, with which she wore a matching straw hat and brown accessories. Her corsage was a spray of white orchids," a newspaper article pointed out." A wedding breakfast was served at the Officer's Club. Soon after the couple left for Pueblo, Colorado "where the bridegroom is presently stationed."

The war ended before Wayne saw combat, however, he was sent to Japan to be part of the U.S. Army of Occupation. The newly weds were separated from the end of December 1945 until the bride arrived in Yokohama on board the *SS Marine Falcon* on Sept. 25, 1946. No wonder that their favorite song was "*Sentimental Journey*." Later, they added "*As Time Goes By*."

Wayne's first duty station in Japan was Fukuoka. Since there was no commissary in Fukuoka, "we had to take all meals at the Officers' Mess or ask for just enough supplies from the kitchen to help out a little at the Japanese house that was our quarters. I recall that one of the mess Sergeants gave me a ten pound sack of salt that I still had part of when I left Japan," Della remembered.

After a few short weeks, the Lear's were sent up to Takarazuka, Honshu. The young couple stayed briefly in the local hotel that had been taken over as a BOQ. Soon, they were assigned to quarters #28—"a very lovely Japanese house," Della recalled, "what a wonderful start for newly weds—home with servants."

Della Paddon Lear with her parents at about the time she she was waiting to catch a boat and join Wayne in Japan.

Living in a recently defeated country was "an experience that was challenging and rewarding," Della remembered. "The war had only ended in August 1945. We wondered about how we would be received. There

Della and Wayne Lear in the garden of their beautiful home in Japan.

was absolutely no fear on my part. For whatever reason, I always felt safe. That might have been due to the customs and upbringing of the Japanese people themselves. Their leaders and their culture demanded respect for authority. Nevertheless, I did feel a little strange at being stared at so often by the young children—forgetting that many of them had never seen a blue eyed blond before. It was a thoroughly delightful and rewarding experience for me. I loved the countryside—the beauty and serenity of the gardens," Della explained.

Once in Japan and assigned to the 89th Bomber Squadron, 38th Bomb Group, Wayne flew the A-26 bomber and served as the Communication Officer at Itami Army Air Base which was situated between Osaka and Kobe. Once again Wayne was involved in athletics enjoying volley ball and as Captain of the team won the tournament.

Della had been able to ship a 1937 Ford automobile over to Japan and when it arrived "we were able to travel around the countryside and see many of the marvelous sights, including Kyoto and Nara. The photograph album rapidly grew as we used it to tell the story of our many adventures in this foreign land."

Della and Wayne Lear in their garden *at Itami AFB, Takarozuka, Japan while he was stationed there in 1947 as part of the Army of Occupation following World War Two. As Captain of the 89th Bomber Squadron volleyball team, Wayne holds the trophy won on 26 March 1948. (Right) Lear flew the A-26.*

On 11 April, 1948, Della and Wayne Lear enjoyed a picnic on the grounds of the Nara Rest Hotel in Japan, with friend 1st Lt. H. M. Hauser. (Della Lear Holloway)

About six months after they arrived in Japan, their love for dogs surfaced and "we acquired a black Cocker puppy that we promptly named "Pepperlee."

Wayne Lear *stands next to a jeep during his tour of duty in Japan. (Holloway)*

Pepperlee. *Della with their pet black Cocker Spaniel pet "Pepperlee."*

The Lears were not allowed to buy any of the local produce—"the Japanese people needed all they could raise for themselves."

The commissary for occupation force personnel was located in Kobe—about a 40 minute drive from where the Lear's lived "Shopping there was some experience—particularly for the new bride—how to put a meal together with so few items that I really knew about. I soon learned to cook with powered milk—but how we did miss fresh milk and ice cream. Canned vegetables became a way of life for a long while. Fresh produce and other foods were finally brought in from the States and we thoroughly enjoyed all we could get," Della explained.

"Meat? Well, that was another story. Strange cuts but I learned to cope with it and enjoyed it all. We had a wonderful life."

There were few other Army Air Force wives there—"only about 5 of us to begin with. We were a well knit family."

One of the families with whom the Lear's were especially close was the Walmsleys—Springer, Flo, and Amy.

Wayne's tour in Japan ended in July 1948 with him now promoted to 1st Lieutenant and headed home with Della. They both experienced "mixed emotions—we were happy to see our families but we were also leaving behind wonderful friends and an assignment that had been delightful. It was now "onward and upward" to March Air Force Base in Riverside, California.

"We came back home by way of a large ship called the *Republic* with wives on one deck and husbands on another deck," Della recalled, "meeting for meals

Wayne's Family. *(Right, l-r) Barbara Lear (Wayne's sister), Mabel Lear (Wayne's mother, Elizabeth Paddon (Della's mother), Pearl Lamb (Wayne's maternal grandmother) and Della Paddon Lear.*

and just walking around to pass time while on our way to the next port—Seattle. Needless to say, Wayne had leave coming to him so we visited with family members and then headed out to visit friends, including the Vincent Meyers family *[Wayne's chief pilot on B-29s]*, who "gave me away. It was great to visit them in their home in Marysville, Missouri."

The Lears were able to ship Pepperlee home to Wayne's parents shortly before they left Japan in July 1948. "Wayne's father picked her up from the port and found he had a rather wild dog on his hands. Perhaps you can imagine what it must have been like for a young dog to spend at least ten days in a wooden kennel—part of the time on the deck of a slow freighter crossing the Pacific Ocean."

Wayne and Della knew they would need transportation when they returned to the Z.I. [Zone of the Interior, i.e. United States], "so we saved our money to buy a car. Yes, cars were once again being produced. Wayne's Dad had a new maroon, Plymouth coupe waiting for us when we arrived in California. Wayne really never liked that car very much but it was adequate."

Seeing that the couple "had no house or furniture, Wayne's father suggested we buy a trailer *[they were not yet called "mobile homes"]* and have it placed permanently at a trailer park that had been designed for the purpose. We did as he suggested but never felt too good about it—it was difficult to make the bed as it was bounded on three sides, and you had to use the park's public facilities. Needless to say, we quickly found ourselves on the look-out for a real home."

They found "a delightful little house under construction in a quiet neighborhood—1961 Dorothy Drive, Riverside, California. It was two bedrooms, one bath, living room and kitchen—heaven to us. We purchased it and furniture—life was GOOD."

March AFB. *Wayne served as the training officer while he was stationed at March Air Force Base in California.*

"Our love for dogs showed up again when were able to secure an AKC boxer puppy we named "Gemzee". We found we had picked a neighborhood that really suited us—friendly, caring people—a cul-de-sac street.

The Leslie Lear's "had lost one of their black cockers and we thought we could fill that void for them by getting a different type of dog. S-o-o-o-o, once again we were purchasing a dog—this time a miniature dachshund that came with the name "Hidee." As it turned out, the senior Lears did not want Hidee "but we sure did. Now we were a family with three dogs—does that tell you something?" Della asked.

Lear's assignment as Training Officer at March Field began in September 1948 and lasted until November 1950. The young couple was saddened by Della's miscarriage in April 1950. "We never intended to be only a family with dogs," Della recalled.

At this point "Wayne began to feel that flying bombers was not the way to make the Air Force his chosen career. An opportunity came along to go to Waco, Texas to learn to fly helicopters and he took advantage of that. He felt helicopters were the planes of the future—both military and civilian.

While they were stationed in Waco, Texas for helicopter training, "Wayne traded the Plymouth for a new black Studebaker car. It was good looking—had overdrive and many extras—including curved windows around the back/trunk area of the car. On the way back to Riverside we were in a sandstorm and the entire front of the car was pitted with sand—Oh my! The first two cars we owned really did not have enough room for traveling; so, before we left Riverside for Mississippi, we purchased a four door Buick sedan—great car. We both liked that one a lot better," Della recalled.

The Air Force "was not doing too much with the helicopters and in November 1950, Wayne was offered an opportunity to go to Electronics School at Kessler Air Base in Biloxi, Mississippi. He felt a career officer should take advantage of schools and accepted the assignment."

However, just five months later, in March 1951, Lt. Lear received orders to Washington, D.C., once again assigned to the Air Rescue Service. "So, it was off to Silver Springs, Maryland for us," Della recalled.

Lear "did not like desk jobs too well and that is what Washington was about most of the time," Della explained. It became difficult to even get "flying time" in at nearby Bolling Air Base, in Anacostia, Maryland.

Lear was promoted to Captain on Sept. 26, 1951.

"It's still sad to recall that Springer was sent to Korea in 1951 and was shot down flying B-26's in North Korea on Sept. 14, 1951," Della recalled. "It was while Wayne was stationed in Washington D.C. that he heard of it at headquarters and we traveled up to New Jersey to be with Flo and children."

Captain Walmsley's Congressional Meal of Honor was later presented to his widow—Flo. It was one of only four such medals awarded to Air Force personnel in the Korean War. [1]

1952 was a busy year for Wayne and Della. On January 23rd, he was ordered to Bridgeport, Connecticut, where he was introduced to the new Sikorsky H-19 helicopter.

A few weeks later he was at Camp Drum, Watertown, New York to test the H-19 during cold weather operations for several more weeks.

"Tomorrow I am to stand alert," Wayne wrote Della on January 31st, "as we have a couple of jumps scheduled and our mission will be to pick up the injured and bring them back to camp or if they are seriously injured, we will fly them directly to the base hospital...They are trying to simulate actual combat conditions as much

Walmsley and Lear. *Wayne and Della were stationed at Bolling AFB on September 14, 1951 with they received word that their friend, Captain Springer Walmsley had been shot down. They immediately drove up to New Jersey to be with Flo Walmsley and the children.*

Lt. Lear became Captain Lear *while he was stationed at Air Rescue Service Headquarters in Washington, D.C. The Promotion Party flyer shows Lear and other promotees kneeling at the statues of their exalted new ranks. The party was held in the Capitol Room of the Bolling AFB Officer's Club.*

Rented Bungalow. *Della and Wayne were proud of their rented bungalow in Silver Springs, MD. Each took a turn with the camera taking pictures of their new car, their dogs and their neighbor's houses.*

as possible so the aid station, evac station, clearing stations and collecting stations are situated near the drop zone. I believe that I will get quite a bit of good experience from this exercise that should help out a lot in my next assignment. I guess that we have one of the most experienced groups of helicopter pilots in the USAF. In addition we have some very good mechanics."

"During the next three days we will run transition training for the co-pilots," he wrote a week later, "and check out as many as possible. As it stands now, 2 co-pilots have been checked out and a third will probably get his check out tomorrow. However, even when the co-pilots are checked out, the pilots that received the factory training will continue to ride with them. Today I had the honor of taking Sir Hubert Wilkins for a short flight in the H-19. Wilkins is an arctic expert, having been the only man to walk across the north and south poles. He is an old fella of about 75, uses a hearing aid and wears a goatee beard, which is completely white in color. We flew him around for about twenty minutes."

"This morning I was on a photo mission," Wayne wrote on February 7th, "we had some cameramen that shot a sequence of movies. They wanted to get pictures of the H-19 departing the base, go to the hospital clearing stations in the drop zone, pick up litter patients and carry them to the assault strip where a C-122 would be unload the patients from the H-19 and load them on the C-122 and then return to the home base."

By May he was at Camp Stoneman, California and preparing to leave for Korea on 6 May 1952 via Japan. After spending a week in Japan at Johnson Air Base, he was assigned to 3ARS, Detachment One based at K-16, Seoul Air Base, Korea.

An H-19 lands on a hospital ship with combat wounded off the Korean coast. (NARA)

Third Air Rescue Squadron H-5's ready for the next mission from an advanced base in March 1952. *(NARA)*

The accommodations were Spartan. Tents and Quonset huts—cold in winter, ovens in summer—served as living quarters. Often they prepared their own meals from dried food, when they could find it. The "shower room" was a tar paper shack, built into a hillside. The water was one temperature—cold.

Lear was assigned as the Training Officer on May 18th. Ironically, after receiving extensive training in the H-19, Lear was himself flying the now obsolete H-5 frequently on missions because the Detachment Commander, Major Emerson E. Heller, did not "trust" the H-19.

"Well, Dear, I have finally arrived at my new home which is Seoul," Wayne wrote Della on May 16, 1952. "We are living in tents which are quite decent as far as tents go. My stuff is spread out all over and I'm having quite a time getting things sorted out. I have no place to put my clothes, etc. when I unpack so will just have to leave my things in the bag till my foot locker arrives or locate a packing crate or something similar. The fellas here are all very pleasant and seem glad to see me, actually we are replacements so they want to treat us pretty good."

U.S. medics gently carry a wounded soldier to a surgical unit tent for emergency treatment after evacuation from the front lines by a Sikorsky H-5 helicopter of the 3rd Air Rescue Squadron somewhere in Korea.

Sikorsky H-5 helicopter of the 3rd Air Rescue Squadron prepares to land at its base in Korea, after picking up wounded GI near the front line. (NARA)

"I'm having an awful hard time trying to get checked out in the H-19," wrote two days later. "The biggest trouble is that the wheels in command don't like the H-19 and in a way are afraid of it. They have a policy here that you have to be operational in the H-5 prior to checking out in the H-19."

"I got to fly the H-5 and as soon as I landed, they had an evac mission in the H-19 so I immediately climbed in as co-pilot," Wayne updated Della on May 19th. After coming back we had another mission which I received credit for, my first one that I flew as pilot. On completion of this one, I was checked out in the H-19. I'm to start my first tour of the element tomorrow; I have an early start in the morning and will be away from home base for 10 days."

"Just a few lines before I hit the sack as we have to be up early (0430) in the morning. [May 20th] We have moved on out to the elements so are now quite busy. I can't say too much of what we are doing or where we are. I have a total of three missions now as I got two more today. I hope I can keep up such a good average."

"Darling, we have quite a food problem while at this particular forward location [an airfield carved from a rice paddy very close to the front lines]. For the most part the food is starchy and heavy. We are completely lacking green vegetables either fresh or canned."

"Well, my day of flying is now complete as we have just returned," he reported on May 21st. "We had quite a trip back as the engine was cutting out, we were making the entire trip over water and we were in a very undesirable section, if you know what I mean. Well, we are back on the ground and everything is under control."

On May 24th, Wayne was "up on a hill that overlooks the surrounding countryside. We still haven't received the proper items with which to fix our airplane. From here there is no indication that a war I going on so close."

As May moved into June, Captain Lear was "given a project of standardizing the H-19 training program. Darling, everyone here flies the airplane differently and some of their procedures are not the best so I'm going to sit down and see what I can do. I want to start on that this evening."

"The young suffer the most…"

"This has been a very busy day for me," Wayne wrote on June 4th. "I have flown more than five hours and I went on my first mission by myself today. Needless to say, the day has gone by very quickly. I stayed at K-16 today but I believe they intend for me to go to the hospital tomorrow. I picked up one patient and took him out to the hospital ship today. The poor fella was really bad off. In fact, it nearly made me sick to see him. He was in shock and his skin was a deep yellowish brown, his head was bandaged and all bloody, his chest had a lot of little holes in it and it was bloody also. They put him in the copter and immediately started to give him oxygen; my medic gave him all the way to the hospital ship. Darling, it is really awful to see things like that. I don't believe the poor fella had much of a chance. If some of the stupid people at home could see some of the misery of war over here and how some people have to suffer, they might wise up. The trouble is only a comparative few suffer doing a war. What makes it worse is that it is the young that suffer the most. The other day when I went out to the hospital ship, we picked up a young kid, maybe 20 but probably less. He had lost his right leg below the knee, was in shock and had kidney poisoning. We

Della Lear *packed this studio photograph with Wayne's baggage when he deployed to Korea in April 1952. (Holloway)*

flew him back here so that he could be air evacuated to a hospital where he could get an artificial kidney. Now, what has that poor fella to look forward to. If he lives, he has become a cripple, for what, do you think that the people back home will think any more of him or pay any special attention or help him out. No, for the most part the darn Americans are so selfish and greedy they can't think of anyone but themselves. When I think of things like this I really get disgusted with people in general. Well, don't mind me, Darling, I guess I'm all worked up this evening."

"This morning I left the home base and flew up to an advance hospital station where we keep an outfit," Wayne wrote on June 5th. "It is very nice here and everything is well set up. They serve the best food that I've had since arriving in Korea. This area is much cleaner than other areas I have been, in fact, I wouldn't mind spending my time right here. Most of the work is medical evacuations from front line positions and carrying patients from various advance hospital units. While up here five of us live in a small tent—we are crowded but comfortable."

On June 6, 1952, Wayne began his daily letter to Della with, "Well, today, Dearest, I got up to where the fighting is going on. In fact, I was looking down the barrels of our big guns, which doesn't give me a particularly healthy feeling. I just took a tour of the front to see what it looked like and to become familiar with the area I'll be working in. What a mess everything is in, in some places where towns were once located all that is now left are a lot of shell holes and piles of rubbish. They have really destroyed

H-5 making a landing on the hospital ship USS Consolation. *(USAFHRA)*

everything. Later on today I took my first front line area evac, I went up near the front and picked up a ROK with head injuries. I didn't have a bit of trouble locating the area or any trouble at all for that matter."

"At present I'm the only one in the tent," he reported on June 7th, "the other boys are over watching an operation. You know I don't go for that sort of thing. To me it is bad enough to see the fellas when we pick them up. When I get a patient that is in bad shape, I just look the other way or get out of the copter and walk away till the boy is in the litter and the top is down. I'm sure that I would get sick if I looked at some of them, in fact, I gag occasionally when they are being loaded in."

"I'm beginning to think I'm too soft hearted for this business.

"Darling, I've had terrible luck with the patients I've picked up," Lear agonized on June 8th, "already four of them have died. That is a poor percentage as I've only picked up about six patients. Honey, I'm beginning to think I'm too soft hearted for this business. Generally, flying you are a long way from seeing so many injured people but now that I'm flying helicopters and making front line evacuations, I see a lot of it and , to me, it is awful. It is certainly a shame to waste life as is being done now and as in all wars. I'm afraid if I had my way at the peace meetings, I'd vote for a truce and get the heck out of here. I just don't understand why the people of the world can't get along together without fighting. To me, there seems to be enough of everything for everyone."

"Darling, I'm really looking for something big to happen about the 25th of June," he noted on June 13th. "I believe that it will either bring peace or an all out war. I certainly hope that it is peace. This darn war has been dragging on for two years now and we are in about the same position as then. Something will have to happen pretty soon, we just can't continue on this basis forever."

"Well, tomorrow [June 17th] is my day to be in the barrel again. I don't know if I explained the situation or not. When I speak of being in the barrel, it means that I will be standing by all day long in the H-5 for any possible emergency. We use the H-19 as a cover ship, which would attempt to rescue the H-5 crew should they go down. We rotate the duties between the pilots at the advance base."

Chapter Ten

Bobby Dale Holloway

    Bobby Dale Holloway led what he considered an almost idyllic boyhood while he was growing up in Ruston, Louisiana, the 18-square mile, 20,000 population parish seat of Lincoln Parish, in north central Louisiana—72 miles east of Shreveport and 32 miles west of Monroe, Louisiana.
    Shortly after the Civil War, during what would be known as the "Era of Reconstruction," the news was quickly spread around the young Lincoln Parish that the Vicksburg, Shreveport and Pacific Railroad would begin to

***Bobby Holloway's parents**, Quida Ferguson Holloway and Ira Virden Holloway. Their home was just outside Ruston, Louisiana. (Holloway).*

run across north Louisiana, linking the "Deep South" with the U.S. west coast. Local resident Robert E. Russ donated 640 acres to the town and the area was eventually known as Ruston (short for Russ town). In 1883 commercial and residential lots were created and sold for $375 a piece. Soon, homes and businesses were under construction.

As the town began to take shape, new churches, businesses, civic organizations and schools were established, the Ruston web site explained. "Cotton farming fueled the economy and in 1900 a second railroad, running north and south, was built through Ruston. This brought even more business and industry to the area and the population continued to provide a foundation for the local economy. By the outbreak of World War I in 1914, Ruston was well established as a center for learning—Louisiana Tech and Grambling State Universities—"a place of civic pride and as an area of economic prosperity throughout the region," as the city's web site proudly points out.

Julia "Ma" Ferguson, Bobby Holloway's maternal grandmother, was liked and respected by her friends and neighbors in Ruston. She was strict but fair. "If she said something, it was clear that she wanted it done, and done now," grandson Bobby recalled. (Holloway)

Ruston continued to grow steadily during the post-war prosperity of the late 1940's.

Holloway's parents, Ira Virden Holloway and Ouida Ferguson Holloway were born in or around Ruston. Their families had been there for years.

His maternal grandmother, Julia, was born in Georgia, but eventually married Bob Ferguson, a farmer who owned a nice piece of property in Dubach, near Ruston. He was also a Deputy U.S. Marshall.

If a visitor had inquired around Dubach about "Julia" Ferguson, the question would have drawn blank stares. But if they had asked about "Ma Ferguson," the response would have been immediate and warm. "No one knew her real name, but everyone knew and loved 'Ma Ferguson,'" Holloway explained.

"If she went to the grocery store, took a basket and put stuff in it, by the time she got up to the register, someone would run up and take the basket away from her, put all the stuff on the counter, repack it when she had paid for it, then would take the basket to the car for her. That was how much she was liked and respected. She was one of those rare people who, if she asked someone on the street to do something, they would do it. After all, it was Ma Ferguson talking and no one argued with her. She was strict, but fair. If she said something, it was clear that she wanted it done, and done now," he recalled.

Ma Ferguson's husband, Bob, died before his namesake grandson, Bob Holloway, was born.

Lula Harrison, Holloway's paternal grandmother, was 4' 11" tall. Her family called her "Mammy," rather than her name or just plain "Grandmother." Her husband, William B. "Will" Holloway, was 6' 2" tall. But when grandmother Holloway asked for something to be done, the only answer was "Yes, dear." "She ruled the roost. The house was hers. If it was outside the house, Will made most of the decisions. But inside, she was in charge. She ruled. That was the way it was," Holloway explained.

Some of Holloway's cousins "were somewhat leery" of Lula and Will's strong-mindedness. "I got along with them fine," Holloway recalled, "I never thought anything about it."

Will Holloway was a farmer who was kept busy tending his 127 acres. "I never knew that he did anything else but farm. That's where I learned to farm. Everybody worked," Holloway continued. "We raised our own vegetables, plus farmed other crops like cotton and raised pigs, horses, cows. There was very little actual money. What little bit of money that came in was from selling some cotton or some other crop. That was the money used to buy staples that could not be raised or bartered with neighbors and relatives. Most of the seed my grandfather raised himself. The best ears of corn were put aside as seed corn. I remember he always had a lot of corn that was ground for corn meal. Once it was ground, then he put it in containers and sealed it. That was what they used for the rest of the year. I don't think there was very much money to buy other things. A dollar then was a dollar—no doubt about it," Holloway explained.

Holloway spent a great deal of time with Lula and Will Holloway. The father and son Holloway homes were only about twenty miles apart.

Ira and Ouida Holloway's property was on two acres, approximately three miles outside the Ruston, Louisiana town limits.

"During the school year I probably spent ninety five percent of my weekends with my grandparents," Holloway remembered. "On Friday afternoon I would catch a different school bus and go over to their house. On Monday morning I would get on the school bus and go back to school. That afternoon, I'd get another school bus that ran close to my parent's home. Basically, I had two homes. We were always back and forth. That was the way things were. My parents never questioned it, they knew that was what I enjoyed and what I wanted," Holloway said.

One reason that young Bob Holloway spent so much time with his Holloway grandparents was because he was responsible for the farm animals, many of them purchased by his Uncle Dalton. His duties involved feeding the animals and seeing that fences and enclosures were in proper order.

Will Holloway had donated land for a small church that was adjacent to the farm. The church held services about once a month and Bob would attend these services with his grandparents. When he was home with his parents, they would all go to a Presbyterian church in Ruston.

Young Bob was not much of a "joiner" at this point in his life, but he was not a "loner" either. He participated in sports while attending high school, and particularly enjoyed baseball and football. He was an outfielder for the baseball team and a linesman on the football team. During summer months he went swimming at the local public pool—when he could tear himself away from the farm—the real center of his world at the time.

Both homes offered many places to hunt, one of Holloway's passions. "I hunted a great deal," he said. Although the family would "take off and go fishing" some weekends.

Holloway "always had hunting dogs—mainly for quail hunting—the wintertime sport," for which he used a twelve-gauge shot gun.

From Forestry to Flying

Bob was attending Louisiana Tech University in 1948, planning to major in Forestry—"where I could support myself and still be outdoors most of the time"—when Ira Holloway died. "It made a big impact on me," Holloway recalled. So much so that eventually, he left college in March 1950 and joined the Air Force.

"The Air Force changed my mind about forestry," Holloway laughed. "They sent me to Lackland AFB for 13 weeks of basic training. I asked for radio school, but didn't get it. Instead, in late June 1950, they sent me to the School of Aviation Medicine at Randolph, AFB." After training as a Air Force Medical Technician, Holloway was sent to Fort Sam Houston for more training as a surgical technician and then on to Kelly Air Force Base to join the Air Evacuation squadron to which he had been assigned. "Most of our patients were from the Korean War," he recalled.

Flying in C-54's configured for medical evacuation, Holloway provided in-flight medical support during long flights back and forth across the United States carrying wounded or sick military personnel. Most of those being transported had been wounded in Korea.

In April 1952, Holloway was transferred to the Third Air Rescue Squadron, located at Johnson Air Force Base, Japan. On April 25, 1952 he departed San Francisco, CA en route to Seoul, Korea via Johnson AFB near Tokyo, Japan. After several days of processing at Johnson, "they put us on a train down to Iwakuni, Japan, where we stayed over night before being flown over to Korea on May 18th. We were Detachment One, 3rd Air Rescue Squadron, based at Seoul City Air Base. "Sixty days from the day I sailed under the Golden Gate Bridge I was shot down—from the Golden Gate to the Gates of Hell," he noted.

From K-16 we were able to serve several MASH units operating much closer to the front lines, just south of the 38th Parallel.

"Our basic mission was getting the wounded out of the front lines, get them to the hospital for treatment, which until that point had been strictly emergency treatment. Our other mission was picking up downed aircrews," he explained.

"Sometimes we would get no missions in a day, or sometimes several," Holloway recalled. "We usually kept three crews ready to respond. We all flew with everyone…got to know what each pilot wanted. We had about ten medics and about an equal number of helicopters. You could be flying with any one of the pilots. We were all on call almost every day," he said.

"Our helicopters were stationed at various locations depending on where it was determined they would be most needed. After four to five days of indoctrination, we began to fly missions."

"The big thing with the H-5 was the ballast. You had to know exactly where to put the ballast…a large can of sand that we moved to different positions within the helicopter. It weighed about 40-50 pounds. It was moved around to help control the center of gravity. You learned very soon where it should be placed to ensure the helicopter was properly balanced. The crewman kept an eye on that can at all times. If it wasn't where it should be, you could lose the whole thing," he said.

Holloway was on his 22nd mission during Mission 1890.

"It took fourteen and a half months to complete the 22nd mission," Holloway noted.

[Holloway spent those intervening months in a prisoner of war camp in North Korea guarded by Chinese soldiers].

Holloway is the only Third Air Rescue Group member to ever be a POW while in Air Rescue.

Chapter Eleven

Mission 1890
The Baited Trap

It was now shortly after noon, and about two miles east of present day Simp'o, North Korea, Ensign Ron Eaton was on the ground, trying to hide from the enemy troops that were all around him. According to the Secret "Report of Incident" prepared by the Third Air Rescue Squadron on 26 June 1952, Eaton's crash site was located at CT 8274, about four miles west of the village of Sinenjung-ni. [1]

Flight line at K-46 in June 1952. *Mission 1890 aircraft are among those parked near the squadron offices of the 67th Fighter-Bomber Squadron, 18th Fighter-Bomber Wing.*

A few minutes earlier, Eaton had radioed that he had been hit by flak, and then abandoned his Corsair. His wingman and other members of the VF-74 flight accompanying him saw him parachute to the ground and then run to take cover in some trees some distance from where he landed. The planes in the air observed numerous enemy troops in the area.

It might have crossed Eaton's mind as he crouched in the underbrush on the side of mountain plateau to wonder why he had not been captured already. Surely they had seen his plane go down and his parachute—didn't they know about where he was hiding?

"Don't you know they saw exactly where he went down," Holloway later noted. "They could have gotten him any time they wanted. I believe it was a set-up, letting him sit out there without capturing him, and letting him be the bait for a rescue attempt. They knew we would send in the helicopter and other airplanes. They just waited for us to show up," he said.

Throughout that Wednesday morning of June 25, 1952, Captain Wayne Lear and Medical Technician Holloway had been on call at an advanced "strip" just behind the bomb line—a "power air strip" at CT 3426 (approximately 20 miles WSW of Kumhwa, SK), a forward operating strip between Old Baldy and Cholwan.

They had flown to the site early that morning from the 8055th MASH. This was only the second time that Holloway had been on call for pilot rescue duty—"pilot pickup" they called it. They were on "stand by" pending a call from the Joint Operations Center in Seoul alerting them for a rescue mission.

Detachment One, 3rd Air Rescue Squadron was stationed at K-16, Seoul City Air Base, about 45 minutes from the bomb line. However, to cut response time to a minimum, its helicopters spent most of the time when assigned pilot pickup duty on standby at the forward strip.

Fifth Air Force Joint Operations Center (JOC) immediately contacted 18th Wing Operations at K-46 (near Hoengson, SK) after it was notified that Eaton was down. Soon after, the on-duty 67th Fighter-Bomber Squadron RESCAP (Rescue Combat Air Patrol) flight was notified and briefed by the 18th Fighter-Bomber Group Operations and Intelligence Duty Officers.

"Filter RESCAP #1" was led by How Flight Commander, Captain Elliot D. Ayer. [2]

Flying as Ayer's wingman was 1st Lt. Archie Connors, who had recently returned to the squadron from a 45-day period of emergency leave.

A radio call was received from Joint Operations Control and relayed to Capt. Lear and Airman Holloway as they waited near their H-5 helicopter—a Navy pilot was down. All the information known to Fifth Air Force was passed along to the pilot and crew. "Everything they knew about the situation and area, they passed along to us," Holloway related.

"One of the Army L-19 spotter plane pilots that was also based there showed us a map of the area. The locations of known anti-aircraft guns were noted on his map with a small black circle or dot. The map in the area in which Eaton was located was almost solid with black dots. The spotter pilot told us that he didn't think we should go in."

Lear called his headquarters to alert them to the spotter pilot's warnings. It was stated squadron policy that helicopter pilots were not to be pressured to attempt rescues under extremely hazardous conditions.

However, Lear was ordered to proceed with the mission—clearly in total contradiction to the squadron's stated policies. Holloway concluded that "headquarters" did not want to "look bad" to a visiting senior officer. The identity of the individual giving the order to proceed with the mission cannot be determined.

"We were told—ordered to go—and we did," Holloway explained succinctly.

Rescue helicopter crews were often called upon to conduct missions into areas that were so dangerous that it was highly likely that the aircraft and crew would be damaged or lost. However, such daring missions were conducted countless times during the war. Although air rescue service policy enabled the rescue pilot to decide for himself whether or not to attempt a pickup, operational realities reported by crew members indicate that at times considerable pressure would be exerted on the crew to conduct the mission regardless of risk.

As noted in *That Others May Live: USAF Air Rescue in Korea*, it was the position in 1992 of retired Brigadier General Kight, former Commander of the Air Rescue Service, that "helicopter pilots were not pressured to attempt rescues under extremely hazardous conditions. More often than not, the pilot decided to proceed with a rescue attempt that the commander would've been reluctant to direct them to do because of the extreme hazard." [3] If so, then the pressure put on Lear to undertake what he and his medical technician were told was virtually a "suicide mission," was in total contradiction to the squadron's stated policies. Lear was not only "pressured" to undertake the mission, he was given a direct order to fly the mission, Holloway reported.

They made a quick take-off in the lumbering H-5 and headed toward the downed pilot at about 50 mph.

Weather conditions in the pickup area were not favorable. The visibility and ceiling were "limited," with winds approaching 45 mph in the pick-up area, approximately 22 miles NNE of Kumhwa, Korea.

"We flew northeast at about 4,000 feet. Flak was popping all around," Holloway said.

The rescue helicopter was given the code sign of "Pedro Tare."

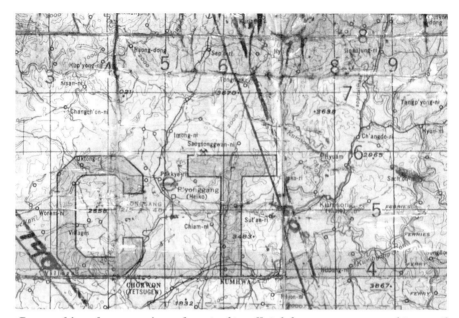

Geographic reference points *often cited in official documents mean nothing until they are correlated with the maps—Pilotage Charts—used by Air Force pilots during the Korean War. All pilots were furnished a folding map printed on varnished cloth/paper carried in the cockpit during missions. The pilots often used a grease pencil to note important information, from call signs to target references. Once the mission was concluded, the now useless information was "scrubbed." Some information was added by the pilots in pencil and not erased—bearings from anywhere in North Korea back to K-46. 1st Lt. Wilfred "Budd" Stapley, a pilot with the 67th Fighter-Bomber Squadron, retained his chart after the war. It was used during the research on this book to identify the locations of Eaton's landing, the helicopter crash, the site of Archie's crash and reported burial location. For example, the reported location of his crash site was CT 905695, approximately 23 miles ENE of P'yonggang (Heiko) or about two miles WNW of Tangp'yong-ni. In 1954, Communist forces reported recovering remains at CT 873711, approximately 1 mile northwest of the reported crash location, CT 905695.*

"Filter RESCAP Special #1, a flight of four F-51s on Mission #1890 was briefed to contact Bromide (a forward TADC) for a steer to the downed pilot, Bromide told the CAP to get further instructions from Dentist (a forward TADC). Dentist instructed the CAP to proceed to Kumhwa to rendezvous with Pedro Tare (Captain Lear and Airman Holloway).

At approximately 1500, the Mustangs of "Filter RESCAP Special #1" located the slow, low helicopter. "Rendezvous was affected between 1500I and 1510I." [4]

["I" or "India" was the time zone for the Korean theater of operations.]

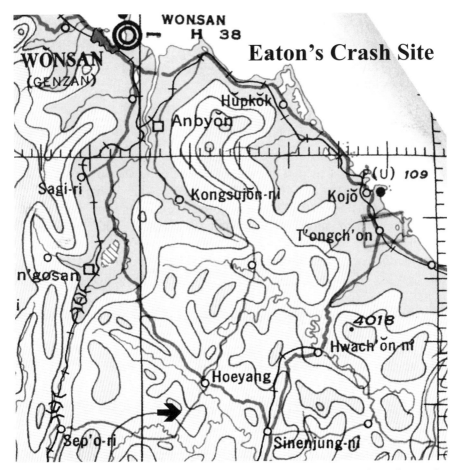

Ensign Ron Eaton *had parachuted from his crippled Corsair about four miles west of the village of Sinenjung-ni (bearing 250 degrees). A nearby mountain was nearly 4,000 feet. A river carved the valley between the rugged peaks. Lear would have to try to rescue the young pilot while dug-in enemy troops with heavy anti-aircraft weapons poured fire down from the surrounding hills on him and the Mustang fighter-bombers.*

"On 25 June 1952 'How' Flight was sent out on a RESCAP Mission number 1890," wrote 1st Lt. John E. Hill in a later report. [5] "We were told to contact Bromide Control for a steer to CT 8274 where we were to CAP. When the flight was half way to the bomb line, Bromide called the leader and said to send Number Three and Four to the target and for Number One and Two to proceed to Chorwon and escort the copter in, and this was done."

Captain Ayer directed his No. 3 and No. 4 Mustang pilots to proceed immediately to Eaton's last known location at CT 8274. Ayer and Connors stayed with "Pedro Tare" to protect the vulnerable helicopter as it approached the pickup point.

"Filter RESCAP joined up with us—they were circling over us because we were so much slower. I know we were in contact with them. It took us about 45 minutes to arrive over the location. They kept directing us into the area," Holloway noted. [6]

First Attempt—Into The Trap

When the two escorting Mustangs and the helicopter arrived in the pickup area, Ayer's second element of How flight Mustangs Nos. 3 and 4, were "orbiting" at 10,000 feet. They were providing "high cover" for "Filter RESCAP Special #2," four additional Mustangs from the 18th that were preparing to suppress any ground fire and flak. The "high cover" fighter-bombers were watchful for any enemy aircraft in the area, but more importantly, trying to spot muzzle flashes from the AA guns and then direct the "low cover" aircraft in successfully attacking the numerous emplacements. [7]

Ayer was not only directing the air covering and fire suppression operation for eight Mustangs, but doing so while his own plane was exposed to significant danger due to his assigning to himself and Connors the most vulnerable, low-level covering position for the helicopter.

Ayer directed a softening up strafing run by four of the Mustangs while he and Connors guarded the helicopter by circling at low altitude.

"The rescue team waited until a covering force of four F-51 fighters had softened up the pickup spot. There were no enemy sighted, but before the rescue helicopter went in one of the fighters buzzed the area a number of times, flying just above ground in an attempt to draw enemy fire (and thereby exposing the enemy positions so the other fighters could attack them). No enemy fire was encountered, so the helicopter started to land." [8]

"We approached the location at about 6,500 feet and immediately they began lobbing anti-aircraft at us. We were in the mountains and it was hard to make out anything below in the maze of rugged hills and valleys," Holloway remembered.

"He's on the tabletop," one of the fighter RESCAP pilots said over the radio. He meant that Eaton was somewhere on a flat topped mountain plateau below the circling aircraft. As Pedro Tare began its descent towards that location, puffs of flak smoke began to erupt in the sky around it.

"When we arrived in the area," Holloway recalled, "the downed pilot signaled us with a survival mirror."

After "Filter RESCAP #2" had strafed the area and drawn no enemy fire, "Pedro Tare" made its first approach to Eaton's position. [9]

"We then proceeded to go in," Holloway said, "to make the hoist pick up. Since he was on the side of a hill, we first attempted to make a running pick up, but with no success."

"We did see that he was on a hillside, not a steep hillside, but enough that trying to hover a helicopter was very delicate. The first time we went in to make a running pickup—maintaining some forward motion with the helicopter, while we lowered the sling "O"-ring and dragged it by him—virtually trolling for the desperate pilot. If the sling was on target the downed pilot could break from cover, grab the sling and put one arm, then the other through the "U"-shaped harness, and be winched aboard the helicopter even as it tried to gain both speed and altitude. The pilot would be dangling in mid-air as the helicopter pulled away from the pick up site," Holloway explained.

Unfortunately, on the first attempt Eaton did not break cover in time to grab the dangling sling.

Eaton was under fire as well, and had been since his parachute descent earlier that afternoon. He was crouching in the brush that covered the mountainside. Before he could catch the sling, he would have to time his break from cover very carefully. If he left his hiding spot too soon, he would have to stand out in the open waiting on the sling to be dangled below the hovering helicopter and dragged toward him. Every second he was without his covering brush, he was a target for enemy small arms fire. If he waited too long to break cover, the sling would be dragged past him and the helicopter would have to go around another time.

Holloway provided directions and vectors as Lear worked the controls feverishly to gain some speed, hold his altitude and make another pass at the hillside that was alive with hostile fire—from small arms to anti-aircraft emplacements, Holloway recounted.

"We went in. We saw his mirror. We knew right where he was," Holloway explained. "We tried to make a running pass. On the slope it was hard to hover, but Capt. Lear wanted to try a running pass. It was not successful because Eaton was not able to grab the yoke."

"Then we got hit—in the nose. The Plexiglas was shattered and the instrument panel that sat in the middle of the cockpit was knocked over at an angle. What hit us was not small arms fire, but serious anti-aircraft rounds," he said. Holloway was cut over the left eye, hands and top of the head. He wiped the blood away to keep the sling in view.

"There was an explosion up in the cockpit. I got cut on the head. I couldn't wear a cap, too much wind, it would not have stayed on. Our earphones were old and wouldn't stay tight. So, we'd pull our collar back and bring the head piece down far enough to where the collar would hold it on. The cut on my head wasn't life threatening, thankfully, and I also had cuts on my hands and face from the shards of plastic and shrapnel that had been thrown around the cockpit."

This was not small arms fire, Holloway explained. "It was too heavy for machine gun fire, it was more like explosions. It was not bullets going through, it was heavy caliber anti-aircraft shells," he recalled.

Meanwhile, the instrument panel was "sitting on an angle, badly damaged—we had no flight instruments from then on," Holloway recalled. "Whatever instruments that had been in that panel were knocked out. Capt. Lear was truly flying by the seat of his pants from then on—both feet and both hands—in a heavily damaged helicopter. We had made a pass and then we got hit."

It was a trap by the Communist forces using Eaton as bait.

Lear in "Pedro Tare" reported to his RESCAP that he was under heavy machine-gun fire and worse, that he had been hit." The situation was deteriorating rapidly.

Second Attempt—Badly Damaged

Lear asked the Mustangs for more strafing attacks to suppress the ground fire. All six Mustangs, including Ayer and Connors, then strafed the ridges where enemy gunners were hidden. The six Mustang CAP made three strafing passes at the ridges before Lear determined to make another rescue attempt. [10]

As Lear circled the heavily damaged helicopter, Holloway provided directions based on Eaton's mirror signals. The flak was much heavier and closer now as the guns zeroed in on the lumbering, awkward helicopter.

As Holloway tried to vector Lear to the location they had last seen the mirror signal, something else caught his eye on the ground. It appeared to be an enemy bunker—probably a communications bunker, he thought, since wires and two antennas stuck up from the emplacement. He could see two Chinese soldiers down in the bunker "moving around."

Quickly reaching for his M-2 Carbine, Holloway "emptied a 30-round clip into the bunker as fast as the fully automatic rifle could fire. I felt like 'you were shooting at me, so I'm going to shoot at you.' After that I didn't see anyone moving around in that bunker." Unknown to him at the time, his return fire with a "machine gun" had been noted by enemy soldiers on the ground. Later, as a POW, Holloway would be forced to answer for his bunker clearing fire suppression efforts.

If a communications bunker was in operation, it further suggests that Lear and Holloway were attempting to extricate Eaton from an area of heavy, dug-in enemy concentrations. Later, after his return, "someone told me that there were an estimated 1,500 troops in the immediate area of Eaton's position," Holloway remembered. "That whole area was solid troops, they told me. I know it seemed as though they were all shooting at us at the same time."

"We were definitely in a 'hot spot'—this was not the place to expect an ice cream social," he recalled.

Lear circled the heavily damaged helicopter until they again spotted the mirror signal. The flak was much heavier and closer now as the guns zeroed in on the lumbering, awkward helicopter.

"Capt. Lear was working that chopper like a man possessed," Holloway reported.

"We then attempted another running pick-up," Holloway continued. "We dropped steadily from about 1,000 feet to less than 500 feet, but I still couldn't make out the pilot's position. Machine guns opened up on us as we came down out of the fire line."

The helicopter was now almost hovering at about 30 feet above the brush.

"Eaton stood up and began jumping up and down—waving us in."

As the helicopter moved over the ectatic pilot, the sling did not quite reach the pilot and the helicopter passed slowly over Eaton.

"As we came out of the second attempt, a shell struck the helicopter below the port "bubble" and exited through the top and up through the rotors, missing them. Somehow, it didn't explode, but it smashed the bubble."

The concussion knocked Holloway out for a short while. He struggled to regain consciousness as Lear yanked the shot-up bird around for another pickup attempt. With many instruments out and the control panel leaning far to one side, Lear nevertheless leaned around to see how Holloway was doing and asked him if he was all right. Holloway shook his head to clear

205

H-5 "Dragonfly" helicopter similar to the one Capt. Wayne Lear was piloting during Mission 1890. A wire rope winch was located on the left side of the aircraft just behind the pilot. Other H-5's had litter carriers mounted outside the fuselage on either side of the aircraft in which to carry sick or wounded personnel.

it and did his best to hear what Lear was saying since the blast had temporarily deafened him.

"As we were coming out of the second attempt we were hit in the left side [Plexiglas] bubble by AA fire. It came in the bottom and exited the top without exploding, showering the interior with shards of plastic and pieces of instrument panel. This was approximately a foot to my left," Holloway said. "The concussion momentarily stunned me. When I came to, I was leaning forward, hanging by my seat belt."

For a moment, Holloway wondered if Lear had survived the blast. Wind was howling around and through the now open nose of the aircraft. Lear had been wounded again, but still maneuvering the aircraft.

"Are you OK," Holloway yelled.

Lear nodded his head in the affirmative as he fought to get the now heavily damaged helicopter under control and back up to about 80 feet.

Third Attempt—Eaton Snagged

Now making his third attempt, Lear changed his approach. Even though coming to a full stop—at a hover—in mid air—required extremely delicate manipulation of the now badly damaged helicopter's controls, and would place him in even more danger from enemy fire, he decided that it would give Eaton a better chance to grab the sling and be hoisted aboard. Trying to keep the damaged helicopter in the air in a hover about 75 feet above the hiding pilot required not only courage, but also extraordinary airmanship.

"We were not moving—absolutely stationary," Holloway recalled.

There was a brief let up in the machine gun and small arms fire "until after we turned around and began to slow into a hover at about 30 feet over the Navy pilot...Capt. Lear somehow hovered the helicopter over the hillside to give Eaton time to get into the hoist sling. Everything was perfect this time" as Holloway leaned out of the helicopter, exposing him to enemy small arms fire, to help maneuver the sling into Eaton's grasp. "He reached out and caught it with both hands" as Holloway motioned frantically for him to get into the sling. As he did so, Holloway continued to lean part way out of the helicopter trying to yell encouragement. As soon as Holloway saw that Eaton had the sling around him, he yelled into the microphone, "I've got him, I've got him. Let's get the hell out of here."

As Holloway operated the hoist that was slowly winching the downed Ensign toward the hovering helicopter, Lear began to climb away from the exposed position, nursing the battered chopper forward, struggling to gain altitude as Eaton was towed through the air, up and away from his brush hideout. Now the dangling Navy pilot and the helicopter were just one big target for any of the countless gunners and ground troops that were shooting at them. They had sprung their trap, but it didn't look as if it was going to be successful. Against all odds, the badly damaged helicopter had finally picked up the pilot and was about to get away. [11]

The hoist started up—dragging Eaton up towards the struggling helicopter.

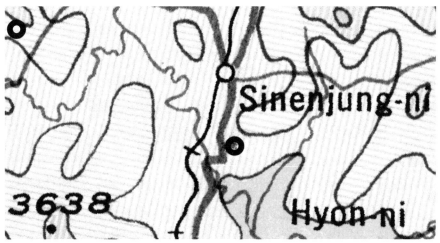

The helicopter crashed at CT 8971, or approximately 175 degrees, 3.5 miles south of Sinenjung-ni. Connors' crash site was reported at CT905695, or 170 degrees, five miles south of Sinenjung-ni. Later, his remains would be reported recovered at CT87.3-71.1, just half a mile to the west of the helicopter crash location. Eaton's pickup point is noted at upper left. The approximate location of the helicopter crash is noted at center.

How Flight clowns for an unknown cameraman in early July 1952. 1st Lt. William E. McShane, Capt. Elliot D. Ayer (Flight Leader), 1st Lt. John E. Hill, 2nd Lt. W. Timmons ("Tim") Urquhart, Capt. Charles T. Hudson and Capt. E. W. Aubuchon (seated). They stand with their Korean "House Boy." 1st Lt. Archie Connors had been killed in action just two weeks before this photograph was taken, only days after returning to the Flight from Emergency Leave. Ayer, who was selected to fly the 45,000th sortie for the 18th Fighter-Bomber Wing about the time this photograph was taken, would be killed in action just two weeks later on July 25, 1952. Connors and Ayer were the last two 67th Squadron pilots killed in action during the Korean War. (Urquhart)

"It seemed like forever, but it was more like a minute," Holloway recalled.

Ignoring his own wounds, Lear demonstrated extraordinary airmanship and determination in maneuvering the now overloaded and heavily damaged helicopter as he tried to keep the badly damaged bird in the air.

Meanwhile, Holloway pulled the grateful Eaton, now without a parachute, through the helicopter door.

"Eaton had just gotten into the helicopter when we were hit the third time. He didn't have time to put on the spare parachute that we carried. The helicopter just seemed to be coming apart," Holloway said.

Two Airmen, One Parachute

"On his third pass Pedro Tare picked up the downed Navy pilot and proceeded southeast to CT 8971*[about five miles ESE of Eaton's original location, approximately four miles WSW of Sinanjung-ni]*. At this time

#1 man [Ayer] of Filter RESCAP Special #1 saw parts flying from Pedro Tare." As "Pedro Tare" began to climb away from the pickup area and to gain speed, escorted by "Filter RESCAP Special #1," Captain Ayer was escorting the helicopter so closely that he reported he was seeing "parts flying from Pedro Tare." [12]

The helicopter had been hit "in the rotor head." Other reports from the RESCAP Mustangs seemed to indicate the tail rotor had been shot off.

"The helicopter was going down in a diving spin (presumed loss of tail rotor)," the Incident Report stated.

"The way it was hit—you know it—you don't wait around. It was more like an explosion. A jolt. I believe we were hit in the rotor head from the jolt and the sound. The helicopter was not spinning, then, but it soon rolled to the right and that's when Eaton and I went out of the aircraft through my door on the left hand side," Holloway said.

They had just seconds to get out the door of the plummeting helicopter.

"Capt. Lear continued to yank on the controls trying to keep it under enough control for us to get out in time," Holloway recalled. Lear was protecting his passengers, trying to control the damaged aircraft long enough for Holloway and Eaton to exit with sufficient altitude for their chutes to open.

"We both went out—at the door I grabbed him and he grabbed me and we went out the door as best we could holding on to each other."

There was no time for Holloway to explain to Eaton that their only chance was to ride the one chute down together. He didn't stop to think that in doing so he would jeopardize his own life. He simply grabbed Eaton and held on. As they fell clear of the spinning helicopter, it was Eaton who reached around to the left side of Holloway's chest and helped Holloway pull the D-ring—together.

"As we cleared the door, we pulled the D-ring. We both pulled the D-ring. They told me later, after I got back, that we cleared the aircraft at 800 feet."

"Face to face—we had hold of each other."

"I never thought about the consequences—I knew he didn't have time to get a parachute on. I had mine on. I hoped we could make it together—on one chute."

The parachute opened moments later. The "snap" was violent and despite the efforts of both men to hang on to each other, it jerked Eaton free from Holloway's grasp. "It was so quick that you had no time to react. There was no time for anything. One instant he was there, then an instant later he was gone."

"Sergeant Holloway bailed out of the helicopter at an altitude of approximately 800 feet. His statements indicate that the emergency occurred so suddenly the Navy pilot had not time to put on a chute and therefore bailed out with Sergeant Holloway. The shoulder strap he was holding broke when the chute opened and the Navy pilot fell almost 800 feet to the ground. Sergeant Holloway's statements further reveal that Captain Lear…bailed out at such a low altitude his chute did not have time to open before hitting the ground." [13]

"The first man left the helicopter from the right side *[Holloway reported the left side]*, and successfully parachuted to the ground. He was seen removing his chute. The other chutes did not open..." [14]

"…I led my element to the downed pilot area and flew top cover at eight thousand feet. When the copter picked up the downed pilot we proceeded to follow him out at this altitude. When he was about five miles south of where he picked up the downed pilot, the copter was seen to be shot down," Hill reported.

"#1 man of FRS #1 saw the helicopter crash at CT 8971. He saw three men leave the helicopter, the first one at approximately 800' altitude, the second at 500', and the third at 300'. The first man left the helicopter from the right side and successfully parachuted to the ground. He was seen removing his chute. The other chutes did not open and the bodies were seen to hit the ground and bounce. #1 man of FRS #1 then made a pass from south to north and observed the chute was not empty. He made two more passes and saw no one around the chute. #1 man reported this to Shirley [combat air controller]. Ten to fifteen minutes later he made a pass and saw eight people, identified as enemy, rolling the chute up. They ran and on his last pass he saw no one. Shirley control then instructed Filter RESCAP #1 flight to return to K-46," the 3ARS Detachment One Incident Report concluded. [15]

*Capt. **Wayne Lear** (left) ignored his wounds and fought to control the plunging helicopter for a few more seconds while his passengers struggled to get out of the fatally damaged aircraft. Medical Technician **Bobby Holloway** (center) shared his parachute with **Ensign Ron Eaton** (right) as they dove out the door of the spinning helicopter.*

Extraordinary Courage and Airmanship

Although he could have refused to go on the highly dangerous rescue mission or aborted the mission at any time from when he came under enemy fire, Wayne Lear refused to give up on the downed pilot, even in the face of strong enemy anti-aircraft defenses in the rescue area. He had piloted a slow, unarmed helicopter in an extraordinarily determined attempt to save a Navy aviator from capture or death at the hands of the enemy. Despite daunting opposition from a heavy concentration of enemy forces using small arms and heavier anti-aircraft weapons, he had maneuvered his helicopter into position over the downed pilot three times under heavy fire before effecting a successful rescue despite heavy damage to his aircraft and being wounded several times. Ignoring his own wounds and overcoming the damage to his helicopter, while displaying extraordinary courage and airmanship, he refused to abandon the rescue mission despite withering enemy fire.

During the third approach to the downed pilot, he elected to hover over the downed airman, an act of daring airmanship in the damaged aircraft, simultaneously exposing himself and his craft to extraordinary danger, but necessary in order to complete the rescue attempt. Finally, he nursed the heavily damaged helicopter back into the air with his wounded medical technician and the rescued Navy pilot following the third—successful—rescue attempt.

When his helicopter was fatally damaged by enemy anti-aircraft fire and beginning a diving spin, Lear, the consummate airman and loving husband, put his own life at great risk as he attempted to maintain control over the stricken craft long enough for his passengers to safely exit the spinning helicopter. When he finally exited the aircraft at approximately 300 feet, there was insufficient altitude for his parachute to open.

Circling over the location of the downed helicopter, approximately 3.5 miles south (approximately 175 degrees) of Sinenjung-ni, Ayer and Connors stayed with the helicopter as its passengers and pilot attempted to bail out. They were themselves in greater danger as they now had to try and determine the fate of the downed airmen. In fact, they flew so close to the helicopter that Ayer *[as Flight Leader he would make radio reports]* was able to report the approximate altitudes at which the pilot and crew left the spinning helicopter and the fact that one parachute had opened. [16]

Enemy fire continued to be intense and accurate.

Risking All To Save A Fellow Airman

The sole survivor from the helicopter, Airman Bobby Holloway landed on a berm that separated two dry rice paddies and he immediately took cover.

In less than two hours, Holloway had played a critical role during a seemingly impossible rescue mission to extract a Naval aviator deep in enemy territory from capture or death. Despite overwhelming opposition from a heavy concentration of enemy forces using small arms and heavy anti-aircraft weapons, Holloway had materially assisted the pilot in maneuvering the helicopter into position over the downed pilot at great personal risk three times before the successful rescue was effected.

When the helicopter was fired on by the enemy, Holloway had returned fire with his Carbine and silenced the immediate danger hazarding the rescue attempt. Wounded on each of the first two rescue attempts, Holloway had disregarded his own wounds and grave personal danger by exposing himself to enemy fire—directing rescue attempts while leaning out of the heavily damaged helicopter.

The third rescue approach, conducted under intense enemy small arms, machine gun and anti-aircraft fire, was successful in retrieving the downed Navy pilot as a direct result of Holloway's bravery by exposing himself to enemy fire and providing his flight recommendations to the pilot.

Later, after Lear and Holloway had successfully retrieved Ron Eaton, the helicopter was fatally damaged by enemy anti-aircraft fire and began a diving spin. Holloway immediately placed his own life at risk—again—by delaying his departure from the spinning helicopter to help his passenger exit the falling aircraft, then grabbing him and holding on as they fell free of the falling aircraft—attempting to allow both of them to ride down on Holloway's parachute—and making these life threatening decisions in just a few seconds.

Tragically, the opening shock ripped Eaton from Holloway's grasp and he fell to his death. However, Holloway demonstrated consummate professionalism as the air crewman who directed three approaches by the helicopter under hostile fire, bravery in personally returning enemy fire threatening his own aircraft, disregarding both his wounds and personal safety while facilitating the actual rescue, and placing his own survival at risk while attempting to save a fellow airman.

The parachute opened so close to the ground that as he swung in shock below the shrouds, Holloway's body completed only one half of a swinging arc before he hit the ground—heavily. Now, he was on the ground, breathless after a rough landing "it swung only half an arc before I hit the ground—hard."

It had only taken a few seconds from the time the helicopter was hit until Holloway was on the ground, in shock and trying to decide what to do next.

"After my landing roll," Holloway recalled, "I immediately got rid of the parachute harness and lay still for a short while. There was still lots of shooting still going on. I couldn't tell where it was directed, but I was not about to get up to see where it was directed," he said.

He didn't see the helicopter again that afternoon.

He told himself, "Don't stand up." Firing was very intense all around him even though the helicopter was now down.

He soon realized why—the fighter bomber escorts—Ayer and Connors—were still over head trying to provide cover and to determine the condition of the men they had seen bail out of the plunging helicopter.

"There were no bullets hitting near me that I could tell—but I wasn't standing up to look, either," Holloway recalled.

Above the "popping" of small arms, machine guns and heavier anti-aircraft cannon now at a crescendo, Holloway heard another sound—the once-heard-never-forgotten snarl of a Merlin engine at full throttle—right overhead. Ayer and Connors had stayed close to the helicopter to provide cover. After the helicopter had crashed, they dropped below 500' and circled the area trying to determine the status of the three helicopter airmen.

"Mayday! Mayday! I'm hit!"

After Holloway was on the ground and out of his chute, he looked up to see one of the RESCAP Mustangs circling "right over where I was"—directly overhead in a tight left bank—a tight circle standing up on his left wing. "He was no more than 150'-200' above me. I could see the pilot looking down, searching for me and the others."

"He was down on the deck covering me, immediately," Holloway recalled. "There was no lapse of time between my hitting the ground and him being overhead. As soon as I was out of the parachute, he was overhead. That was before I crawled in between the rice paddies."

Moments later, as Connors' searched the brush for wreckage and

2nd Lt. William Timmons "Tim" Urquhart, *a native of Houston, Texas, "dreamed of being a fighter pilot just like my older cousins." He entered Aviation Cadet Class 51-G in September 1950 and graduated in October 1951. His entire class of 25 new Lieutenants was assigned to the Air Force "pipeline" to Korea. Three of his classmates were killed at Luke AFB and three more in Korea. Urquhart was added to How Flight late on Wednesday afternoon, 25 June 1952 as they went back to look for Connors and to destroy the helicopter and the downed Mustang.*

213

signs of life, "he came around where I could see him right in front of me, and a puff of smoke came out of the engine," Holloway said.

"Mayday, Mayday, I'm hit," Connors radioed to Ayer and Filter RESCAP pilots. His Mustang began a slow, flat spin to the right from approximately 200-feet. There was not enough altitude to bail out. He dead sticked the plane into a hard belly landing—just seconds after he was hit.

"Once Connors was hit, he tried to right the aircraft, but they really started shooting then—there was a lot of machine gun fire that was going on. The way they were shooting at the Mustang, I would have to say it was machine gun fire that brought him down." The Mustang "rolled over, went right down and I didn't see him after that," Holloway reported.

Lt. Archie Connors

Holloway dared not raise up to try and see the crashing Mustang. Doing so would give away his position and make himself more of a target than he already was.

"Immediately after this happened *[the helicopter crash]*," Hill continued in his report, "Number Two man in our original flight called that he was hit. I observed this pilot *[Connors]* to crash about two thousand feet further south of where the copter went down. [17]

"After Number Two man crashed, the aircraft was still intact and did not burn, but the flight leader [Ayer] made three passes over him but could not determine whether the pilot was alright or not. After this, the Number Four man and I were told to head south to K-46 and land," Hill's report concluded.

Ayer had continued making "passes" over both crash sites—less than a mile apart—subjecting himself to grave danger in the process as he attempted to determine what could be done. He continued to patrol the area at low altitude for over 15 minutes before being ordered to return to base.

"One chute opened successfully and immediately after the copter struck the ground, Lieutenant Connors shouted 'Mayday' and said he had been hit," 1st Lt. William E. McShane, the Number Four man in the Filter RESCAP flight reported.

"I saw his aircraft at approximately 500 feet at exactly the same place the copter had been hit. It appeared to shudder violently and start a diving turn to the right. It seemed to almost stall in flat on a small knoll just a few hundred feet south of the copter wreckage. The aircraft did not explode or burn and major parts of it were still recognizable. The Flight Leader thereafter made several low passes over the area to observe any sign of life either at the copter scene or at the wreckage of the F-51. After observing the empty parachute harness from the copter bailout and several persons apparently enemy, he notified the controller to have a second incoming helicopter to return to friendly territory and the flight returned to the base after being cleared," McShane reported. [18]

"At this same time [the helicopter was crashing] #2 man of FRS #1 was hit and crashed at CT 905695. The #2 man had called "Mayday" twice, but crashed and it appears as no chance of survival," the 3ARS Secret Report of 26 June 1952 stated.

During a harrowing rescue operation that required three approaches by the helicopter before the downed pilot was successfully picked up, Connors had provided highly effective suppression fire while flying "low cover" for the helicopter and protection for his wingman, the Flight Leader. Following the crash of the rescue helicopter with the loss of its three airmen, Holloway reported that Connors had ignored his own personal safety in order to fulfill the rescue mission and to locate the downed airmen. While maneuvering at less than 200' above the downed airmen in an area that for over half an hour had subjected the aircraft to intense and accurate fire, Holloway and McShane saw Connors' aircraft hit by ground fire even as he himself was scanning the ground for survivors.

"He was no more than 150'-200' above me. I could see the pilot looking down, searching for me and the others," Holloway remembered. Moments later Connors was killed when his Mustang crashed within seconds after it had been hit.

Back at K-46, Crew Chief Barry Agovino and his team waited anxiously for "Filter RESCAP Special #1" to return. "Of the four pilots on that mission, I knew and remember Capt. Ayer," he said. "I recall the day we waited for Capt. Ayer and Lt. Connors to return from the mission. We would wait out in the parking area with the crew chiefs whose planes were late for their hoped for return. The wait would sometimes last for hours beyond the time when we knew that the plane must long before have run out of fuel. Somehow we were the last to receive notice that the plane was officially missing or had been seen going in. The feeling of emptiness and helplessness cannot be described."

Later, on August 3, 1952, Lieutenant Hill explained in a letter to Connors' wife, Frankie, that "we were in a flight of four (4) aircraft on a RESCAP Mission to cover the helicopter while it made the pickup. Lieutenant (William) McShane and myself were top cover while Archie and Captain Ayer were bottom cover with another flight that had covered the helicopter while he made a successful pickup, and were escorting him out when Archie was hit. He flew about one mile when we saw his ship crash on the side of a knoll in a flat position. The aircraft did not burn and was intact when Captain Ayer made passes over it, but there was no movement at all in the area of the crash." As soon as he could get refueled and rearmed back at K-46, Ayer was again airborne with How Flight—Hill, and McShane were joined by 2nd Lt. Tim Urquhart. The operations summary called his mission "1 Armed Recce w/4 effective sorties." How Flight headed directly back to CT 905695 where Holloway was hiding as best he could near abandoned rice paddies to avoid capture by enemy soldiers that were walking right by him without stopping—so far.

Helicopter Down, Mustang Down

After his landing roll, Holloway "immediately got rid of the parachute harness and lay still for a short while. I felt for my sidearm, a standard issue service .45-cal. pistol. It was gone. When or how, I had no idea. My survival vest had also been lost during the jump. I couldn't wear the vest and the parachute and operate the hoist. It was just too cumbersome. I had to have freedom of motion and movement enough to work the hoist inside the cramped helicopter. I had taken the vest off and hooked it onto my parachute strap. It was dangling from the strap and had been ripped off during the violent exit with Eaton. Those straps were not very strong. That meant the emergency radio and my sidearm were missing. I would not be able to contact Filter Rescap—or anybody else. I was unarmed and without any way of communicating with the planes that were still circling overhead," Holloway explained.

At that time he regretted losing his .45-caliber pistol as well as his survival vest. Both had been ripped off during the emergency exit of the helicopter, or when the parachute had popped open, or when Eaton was being torn from his grip. However, not having his sidearm probably saved his life three days later.

The covering fighters of Mission 1890 left the area about half an hour after the crash. Holloway could hear them for a while and "then there were no airplanes." How Flight was headed back to K-46 to refuel and rearm. They would also add a new No. Two man to replace Archie. With the dangerous Mustangs no longer a threat, the Chinese soldiers left their shelters and began searching for Holloway. Several of them decided to check out the rice paddies. "They walked within three feet of me lying right up between the rice paddies. All I saw were legs," he recalled.

"The enemy was all around, but I wasn't looking. I was trying to stay hidden from view. I then crawled into the growth between two abandoned rice paddies," he continued. "There was just enough growth to be able to lie down and be concealed. The paddies had not been cultivated in at least a year or so. I was lying in cover, staying hidden while enemy soldiers walked on either side of me—within three or four feet of me—and didn't see me. I believe that one of the reasons they didn't 'see me' was that they could see there were two parachutes on the ground and two bodies. They associated the two parachutes with two bodies. They didn't think of looking for a third."

With the rapid downing of the helicopter, falling bodies, parachute floating down, a Mustang being shot down, perhaps the Chinese lost track of how many airmen were involved. The search of the area following the crashes was also made knowing the much feared Mustangs would probably return—a correct assumption.

Mission 1890 took place on a Wednesday afternoon. Holloway avoided capture until Saturday about noon, after working his way south toward friendly lines.

"Pretty soon the fighter cover departed, and the soldiers started coming out into the open," he continued. "There were at least two soldiers that walked within 5 or 6 feet, on either side of me and did not see me. I had always been taught that a body remaining still was much harder to see. Believe you me, I was very, very still."

"After about an hour—more or less—I wasn't watching my watch—the fighters returned. I heard airplanes in the distance. I sneaked a quick look in the direction of the engine noise. It was the F-51's coming back to look for us." Holloway assumed, correctly, that they had needed fuel and ammunition. Filter Rescap had indeed returned to K-46, quickly refueled and rearmed, and taken off. This time, however, it was newly arrived 2nd Lt. Tim Urquhart who was flying wing for Capt. Ayer.

After making a low level pass over Connors' Mustang, Ayer observed no signs of life or other activity. He then led Filter Rescap in repeated strafings of the area. Their missions were to determine if there were any survivors and their condition if possible, and then make sure the enemy could make no further use of the damaged plane on the ground. [19]

"After making a pass over the site, they climbed out and circled around and made a strafing run. I will say this—four F-51s, with all their .50-cal. machine guns going sure can make the ground vibrate *[each Mustang has six, .50-cal. machine guns and carries a total of 1880 rounds of ammunition]*. All I could see was dirt kicking up all around me. I was lucky because those F-51's were so low that their streams of fire had not converged very much and these double trails of death went by me on either side. They didn't know that I was there. I had lost my radio and could not contact them. I was very lucky in the fact that when they made their strafing run, it was parallel to the position of my body. I was directly between their points of impact, I don't know if they had seen someone on the ground or, if they were attempting to destroy the helicopter," Holloway recalled.

When How Flight arrived over the crash site, they made several low altitude passes over the scene looking for any signs of life. There were none. Following standing orders in such cases, How Flight made a final pass and regrouped in an in-trail formation. One by one they made a firing pass at 363 and the helicopter, now targets that would have no future military use to the enemy. Before that mission was completed, the report would include: "2 artillery positions destroyed, 2 bunkers destroyed, 2 KIA at CT0818; 3 bunkers destroyed, 3 active artillery positions destroyed and 1 secondary explosion at CT819539…"

As far as Fifth Air Force was concerned, Mission 1890 was over.

However, it was not over in the mind of young 2nd Lt. Tim Urquhart, or for the families that would soon begin hearing about its tragic outcome.

It had begun with a young Navy pilot having to bail out of his crippled Corsair fighter in an area that was known for its heavy concentration of enemy positions—especially anti-aircraft batteries. For an hour Eaton's squadron circled overhead, providing air cover. During that period, two of them were hit by AA but were able to land at a nearby airfield, probably K-46. While his squadron circled overhead, the Communist gunners waited, they knew that as long as the downed pilot was signaling his buddies to be rescued, that more aircraft would be coming, probably including a slow-moving helicopter. Their calculated wait became a baited trap for Mission 1890.

If Air Rescue Service policy had been followed, Mission 1890 would not have taken place. Lear was warned by his fellow pilots about the heavy flak, shown a map "almost solid with black dots" representing known AA sites, and advised not to attempt a mission so hazardous that it was almost a suicide mission. When he raised those issues with ARS3, Detachment One, he was nevertheless ordered to undertake the mission—a direct violation of published ARS policy. Was ARS3 Det One aware of the heavy anti-aircraft fire in the area of the downed pilot? Certainly it was known to JOC in Seoul. Two shot-up covering aircraft—Corsairs no less, not a lumbering H-5 helicopter—should have convinced the operators that the situation was untenable.

Had the mission not been undertaken, it is most probable that Eaton would have been captured alive as was Holloway, and spent the remainder of the war as a POW. He, instead of Holloway, would have been returned in September 1953. Holloway would not have been captured. Lear and Connors would not have been killed—on that mission, at least.

Mission 1890, the rescue mission that should never have been flown, was the costliest helicopter rescue mission of the Korean War.

Chapter Twelve

After the Mission, Captivity and Bureaucracy

To The Gates of Hell

Bob Holloway, the 21-year old medical technician had been in Korea for exactly two months. On just his second "pilot pickup" mission, he was now the sole survivor of four airmen, on the ground without a weapon or a radio. He could hardly believe the circumstances that had brought him from Louisiana, into the Air Force, medical training, air evacuation duties for several years, then faster than his mind could grasp, he was hiding in brush between two rice paddies trying not to get shot or captured.

As twilight approached on Wednesday afternoon, Holloway stayed under cover until dark, and then he started moving south. He was only about 13 miles from friendly lines. Movement was extremely difficult—it was night and he "didn't know where any of the enemy positions were located. But I had to get out of there. I knew I couldn't move in the daytime, it was too open." [1]

Finally, he came to a river, but "didn't try to cross then, because the plateau that I was on was probably 100 to 150 feet above the river—a good-sized river—the banks were high and steep, about 150' down to the water. I had to get across that river to head south." Holloway, who did a lot of hunting and fishing in his native Louisiana as a youth, was able to use the sun and stars to "navigate" his way towards friendly lines. He had been given no formal escape and evasion training, only "a few talks on it." The North Star, the experienced outdoorsman and hunter pointed out, "is always in the same position."

As he worked his way down to the river it began to get light. "I found a gully that had been washed out by runoff water. There was some brush and sticks that had piled up and I moved a few of them around and created a hiding place to get into—out of sight." Holloway built himself a camouflaged stick hut in the gully, his home for the next several days.

Back at K-46, that Thursday morning of 26 June 1952, a clerk in the 18th F-B Group Operations Office at K-46 pecked out… "SUBJECT: Daily summary of operations, 18th Fighter-Bomber Group, for 25 June 1952." After noting the sorties and claims of the 12th Squadron, those of the 67th Squadron were summarized: "Five missions: 2 Interdiction w/20 effective sorties; 2 Rescap w/8 effective sorties; 1 Armed Reece w/2 effective sorties. 1 air abort and one ground abort on Interdiction missions. Negative training missions. Claims: 1 bunker destroyed at XC765708. A/C 363 LOST due to ground fire on mission 1890."

No name of the pilot, simply a terse note regarding the side number of the downed Mustang, now just a crumpled "Spam Can" laying on a hillside 25 miles ENE of Kumhwa.

Holloway remained in hiding all day Thursday, coming out that night to scout up and down the river "looking for a place to cross, with no luck. As it was getting light again (Friday morning) I returned to my stick house abode. I remained there during the day, trying to get some sleep."

"...the feeling of loss..."

On Friday, June 27, 1952, as Holloway hid in the bushes near the river waiting for nightfall, Major Stanley A. Long, Commanding Officer of the 67th Squadron drafted a letter to Archie's wife, Frankie Connors.

"It will be difficult to convey to you the feeling of loss prevailing in the Squadron since your husband, First Lieutenant Archibald H. Connors Jr., failed to return from a combat mission. As deep as that feeling may be here, we know that must be exceeded at home, and with that thought in mind, the pilots of the Squadron have asked I conveyed to you their most sincere condolences. I feel that you would like to know the circumstances connected with his missing in action status."

"Your husband was flying No. 2 position in a flight of four aircraft, pre-briefed to fly cover for a helicopter effecting a pickup of a downed pilot. While flying low cover, your husband stated over his radio that his aircraft had been hit. His aircraft was observed in a right turning spiral until it struck the ground. The aircraft did not explode or burn and the major parts of it were still recognizable. The flight leader [Captain Elliot Ayer] made several low passes over the area, but failed to observe any sign of your husband."

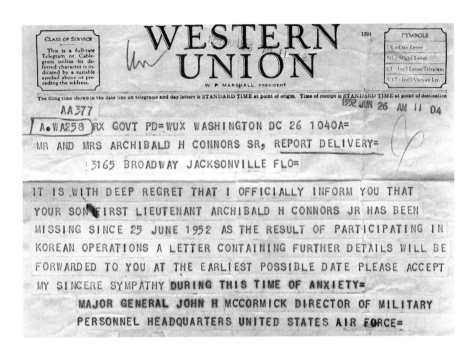

"Lt. Connors was flying his 33rd combat mission when this unfortunate incident occurred. He was outstandingly well qualified as an officer and pilot as evidenced by his devotion to duty and his record of past accomplishments. The report that he is missing in action came to me and his many friends as a great shock, and created a feeling of great loss in the Squadron. Although it is known that no words of mine can ease your anxiety and great sorrow please be assured that the officers and airmen of this command share your deep concern. Should any additional word regarding your husband become available, you will be notified immediately." Five days later he sent the same letter to Archie's parents.

Sentence Prayers

The "with deep regret" telegram arrived at the Connor's home on Thursday, June 26th. Archie's older sister, Julia, was with her mother, Eva, when the messenger arrived. Opening the dreaded envelope with shaking hands, Eva read the contents, then fell back on the sofa moaning, "Oh Lord, and I prayed so hard for his safe return." Her grief nearly broke Julia's heart.

From the day The Telegram arrived for the next three years, every Saturday night, the Connors family joined other relatives and friends in the front room of Eva and Arch Connors' west Jacksonville home for a prayer meeting. The group of relatives was ever changing; not everyone attended every week. However, at least five and as many as fifteen members of the

```
                    WESTERN                   1201
                    UNION (09)
              W. P. MARSHALL, PRESIDENT

..OB015 AA023                              1952 JUN 27 AM 6 22
A.JNA110 PD=JACKSONVILLE FLO 27 800A=
 :MRS A H CONNORS JR=
    1129B EAST CALIFORNIA GLENDALE CALIF:

=DEAR FRANKIE IF YOU'D LIKE TO COME HOME WE WILL BE GLAD TO
HAVE YOU LOVE=
    =MOM DAD AND FAMILY=
```

The day after being notified that their son, Archie, was missing in action, Arch and Eva Connors sent this telegram to their daughter-in-law, Frankie Connors.

growing family would arrive, some for dinner, others just for the prayer service. After a quiet coffee and dessert, everyone would stand and someone would begin "sentence prayers." Around the circle of linked hands the prayers would go, tacitly skipping Arch who joined in the circle but never prayed—except once. [2]

In Washington on that same day, June 27th, Major General John McCormick, Director of Military Personnel for the Air Force signed a similar letter to Frankie, sincerely regretting "that in writing this letter I must confirm the recent message announcing the sad news that your husband, First Lieutenant Archibald H. Connors Jr., has been missing since June 25th 1952, as the result of participating in Korean operations. Our report states that Lieutenant Connors was the pilot of a military aircraft that was one of a flight of four on a combat air patrol mission over Korea. During this mission, your husband radioed that his aircraft was hit. The aircraft was seen to crash into the ground. Since the incident occurred behind enemy lines, no search could be made to determine the fate of your husband. The Department of the Air Force will continue to hold your husband in a missing status until further information becomes available. He has been recorded in the status only because his whereabouts and exact fate are unknown at this time. When additional information is received, you are assured that it will be furnished you without delay."

In Hiding

When it got dark on Friday evening, Holloway "started scouting up the river, but to no avail. That was very touchy because every now and again I would hear someone talking and have to circle around them, trying not to give my position away. I then made my way back to the stick hut."

Lack of water in the brutally hot summer weather was quickly removing any options left to Holloway—he had to get to water. "I just knew I had to get across that river if I was going to make it to friendly lines. I was also getting a little bit thirsty and hungry by Saturday."

"I thought that the only alternative that I had now was to go down a slight wash that led to the river and try to cross. This was near several houses that I could see from across the river. During daylight I had been able to see a trail going up the hill on the other side of the river. I thought that I just had to get over and go up that trail to be able to continue south [towards UN lines only about 13 miles away]. But, that was never to happen. At about 11 o'clock that morning—Saturday—the temperature had gotten so high that it was just too hot to stay in the stick house. I thought, well I can sit up outside and still be below the level of the gully."

When he crawled out and sat up Holloway "was looking directly at two Chinese soldiers. "They were standing on the bank very close to where I was hidden." He hadn't heard them because he had been asleep until just a few minutes before he decided to "get some air."

"I guess if I hadn't lost my pistol when we bailed out I would probably shot both of them, because they had to open the flap on their holsters and unwrap their pistols. They had them wrapped in cloth. I don't know who was the most surprised, me or them."

Had Holloway had his .45 pistol, there is no question in his mind that he would have "shot them dead." Of course, the noise would have brought many more troops to the location and he would almost surely have been killed on the spot. "The classic mistake of the century," is how he describes what would have been his reaction had he been armed. "There were too many people in the area."

"They jabbered at me for a while. I didn't speak Chinese and they didn't speak English…so there you go," he remembered. However, "when

Area where Airman Bobby Holloway was hiding from Wednesday afternoon until Saturday morning. The river that he was trying to cross is shown above at left. Allied lines were only about 17 miles to the south south west of his position.

they start motioning at you with a loaded weapon, you get the idea very quickly what it is they want you to do."

"They did take me near what appeared to be the wreckage of the helicopter. By then, it was covered with brush. They did not let me go near the wreckage. I didn't get a real good look at it, but it looked like a grave—it had a mound over it. And, I only saw one such mound."

"They then took me back to their headquarters or whatever, then started marching me into the mountains. Two of them would take me so far, and then turn me over to someone else. This continued on until I reached an interrogations point," Holloway explained.

When he was captured, Holloway was only about 13 miles behind the lines. He would eventually spend time at several POW camps in North Korea, one of them very close to the Yalu River.

In A Missing Status

On Thursday, 26 June, General McCormick signed out a letter to Della Lear noting that he sincerely regretted "that in writing this letter I must confirm the recent message announcing the sad news that your husband, Captain Leslie W. Lear, has been missing since 25 June 1952, as the result of participating in Korean operations. Our report states that Captain Lear was the pilot of an H-5 helicopter which was hit by enemy gun fire while rescuing a downed pilot of another aircraft. After successfully rescuing the pilot, his aircraft was seen to go into a spin and crash to the ground. Immediately following the crash, three persons were observed leaving the helicopter. Upon return of friendly planes, no persons were observed on the ground near the crashed aircraft."

"The Department of the Air Force," General McCormick advised her "will continue to hold your husband in a missing status until further information becomes available. He has been recorded in this status only because his whereabouts and exact fate are unknown at this time. When additional information is received, you are assured that it will be furnished you without delay."

Your Hour of Anxiety

From aboard the USS Bon Homme Richard (CV 31) on June 30th, VF-74 Commanding Officer CDR Charles D. Fonvielle, Jr., extended "the sincere sympathy of all of Ron's shipmates" to his mother, Elsie Adelia Eaton, in "your hour of anxiety. We all feel our loss deeply, as Ron is well-liked by officers and men alike in all of his official and social contacts. Since August 1951, when he joined our squadron, Ron has been a fine officer and a good friend to us all," Fonvielle noted. [3]

"The flight on which he was brought down was his third attack on the Communist Forces in North Korea. On Monday, 23 June 1952, Ron participated in the coordinated Navy, Air Force, and Marine air attack on the hydroelectric power plants in North Korea. On Tuesday afternoon he was part of a group of aircraft attacking rail lines and bridges along the eastern coast of North Korea near Songjin."

"On Wednesday afternoon, 25 June 1952, Ron was with a large group of planes which were assigned targets near the front lines on the east coast of Korea. We were attacking troop concentrations and truck pools southeast of Wonsan. As we approached the target in an area of intense anti-aircraft fire, Ron radioed that his engine was losing power. He was told to return to the ship and two of his wingmen were detailed to accompany him."

"A few minutes afterward Ron radioed that he was abandoning his plane and the pilots who were accompanying him saw him parachute to the ground and run to take cover in some trees some distance from where his parachute landed. The planes in the air observed numerous enemy troops in the area."

"For about an hour after he landed, his squadron mates machine gunned the surrounding hills and kept the enemy troops from approaching Ron on the ground. Two more of our squadron aircraft were damaged by enemy ground fire while protecting Ron but they were able to remain airborne and land safely at a friendly airfield some distance away. We could see Ron at this time and he was apparently uninjured. Our Navy planes were relieved by some Air Force planes who took over the guarding of Ron while a helicopter was on its way to pick him up. Our planes were low on gas and had to return to the ship."

"On the ship we were notified later that night that the Air Force planes had observed a helicopter to arrive on the scene and pick up Ron in the face of heavy fire from the ground. The helicopter was apparently hit seriously for it crashed a short distance away. The planes in the air saw at least one and possibly more survivors of the three people who were believed to be in the helicopter. These survivors were immediately surrounded by enemy troops and were captured by them.

Commander Charles D. Fonvielle, Jr.,
Commander of Navy Fighter Squadron 74

It is our fervent hope that Ron was one of the survivors and will turn up at some later date in an enemy prisoner-of-war camp. Until that time we have no positive way of knowing if he survived the helicopter crash."

"You may rest assured that Ron was pursuing the occupation which he and all of us love intensely, that of a Naval Aviator, and that he was acting in the interest of all freedom-loving people of the world, supporting the United Nations effort in Korea. You have every reason to be proud of your son and of the part which he has played in this struggle."

"You will be notified officially by the Navy Department of any change in Ron's present status of 'missing in action.' Please feel free to communicate with me for any other information that you may desire. For lack of any further current information on Ron's condition, his personal effects will be inventoried, packed and stowed aboard ship. If we do not hear anything further of Ron's status prior to our return, his effects will be shipped to you. Again please accept my deepest sympathy in this tragedy…"

"...A Storm Was In The Making"

For Dorothy Sharp, learning that Ron Eaton was "missing in action" and there "was a big chance he would never come home—that I would never see him again and our dreams wouldn't be fulfilled"—was a bottomless pit of fear and emptiness. "He had badly injured his ankle in May when he went over the edge of the ship in his plane, and I was concerned that perhaps it wasn't completely healed. He was very anxious to get his missions completed so that he could be rotated home," she recalled. [4]

"Joyce [Eaton, Ron's sister] came to my house that eerie night in June 1952 with

Wilmington Man Missing In Korea

Ronald D. Eaton's Plane Hit in Action June 25

WILMINGTON, July 5 — A resident of this town, fighting as an ensign in the United States navy in Korea is missing in ac-

Ensign Ronald D. Eaton, USN

tion, according to word received from naval headquarters by his parents, Mr. and Mrs. Bernard Eaton of 80 Main street.

Reported as missing following action over Korea on June 25 is Ensign Ronald D. Eaton, a graduate of Wilmington high, who studied at Acadia college, Nova Scotia, for two years before joining the pilot training program. He continued studying for night fighting after becoming an ensign, and was later assigned to the USS Bonhomme Richard, a plane carrier, which left Hawaii but a short time ago for duty in Korea.

According to meagre information received, Ensign Eaton, in his early 20s, was in combat in the Korean theatre of war on June 25 when his plane was hit.

EATON MAY BE PRISONER OF REDS

Ronald Eaton, Ensign USN, of 30 Main Street, who was reported missing in action, in Korea, June 25th, may be a prisoner of the Communist armies, it was learned Monday.

A Wilmington family who is close friends with the Eaton family have received a letter from a buddy of Ronald's, describing the action in which he was shot down.

The letter, from a Lowell man who is in the same outfit as Eaton, says that he had been recommended for the Air Medal, as a result of previous action during the week. It then goes on to describe the action in which his plane was hit.

The plane was hitting enemy targets, and had just delivered a salvo of bombs. Eaton turned around, and was heading back for the carrier when his plane suffered a hit in the engine, disabling it. He was observed to parachute to the ground, in enemy territory.

Shortly after a helicopter attempted to land near where Eaton had landed, in an effort to rescue Eaton. The helicoptper was hit by anti-aircraft fire, and forced to land, but fortunately was able to do so behind the United Nations lines.

A second helicopter then landed, and picked up Eaton, after which it took off, and started to return to the aircraft carrier Bon Homme Richard. After having flown about a mile, this helicopter was hit by anti-aircraft fire, and forced to land behind enemy lines.

At least one person was posiively seen to get out of the helicopter. He was promptly taken prisoner, by enemy forces, the letter said.

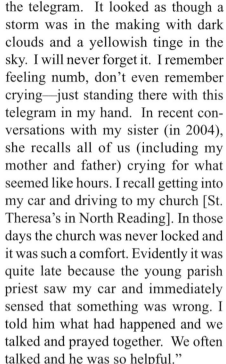

the telegram. It looked as though a storm was in the making with dark clouds and a yellowish tinge in the sky. I will never forget it. I remember feeling numb, don't even remember crying—just standing there with this telegram in my hand. In recent conversations with my sister (in 2004), she recalls all of us (including my mother and father) crying for what seemed like hours. I recall getting into my car and driving to my church [St. Theresa's in North Reading]. In those days the church was never locked and it was such a comfort. Evidently it was quite late because the young parish priest saw my car and immediately sensed that something was wrong. I told him what had happened and we talked and prayed together. We often talked and he was so helpful."

"I remember vividly the day the telegram arrived," Ron's sister Joyce Eaton Dalton recalled. "I was working as a billing clerk at Jordan Marsh [in Boston]. It was very hot, so they sent us home. About half an hour after I arrived home, there was a knock on the door. My mother [Elsie] was sitting at her sewing machine in her bathing suit. She asked me to answer the door. It was a taxi driver with the telegram. My mother said she just knew it was about Ronnie because she had heard on the radio the day before that a plane was shot down and she had a feeling it was Ronnie."

Later, Joyce would often wonder "why was that news brought to us in a telegram? Couldn't they come in person. It seemed very cold," she said.

"When we received the telegram, it said 'Missing in Action.' I told my mother I wanted to postpone my wedding. She told me not to because Ronnie would not want me to. We were married on September 14th as planned."

"How did I feel," Dolly wonders, even today. "How did I cope each day? How did I go to work every day and try to do a good job? Somehow, with the help of family, friends and coworkers, I did go on. I could see the pain in the faces of Ron's family—particularly his parents—it was like the 'light went out' for them. I went to Boston many times with Ron's family to look at pictures of POWs, only to be disappointed each time. I tried to keep my thoughts and attitude positive. However, one part of me hoped Ron had survived the fall and was captured, and another part of me prayed that he died instantly as I didn't want him to suffer. I made many novenas at the mission church in Roxbury, Massachusetts for many years. Several of my coworkers went on Wednesday nights and I joined them," she recalled sadly.

"The people I worked with were very supportive. I became a secretary of a former Commander in the Navy—his assistant had been a gunner in a bomber. They never said very much about my situation, or theirs, but I was very much aware they cared. There were several women in the office, some were my age and others were in the forties. I wondered why so many of them were not married. I found that most had lost their fiancés or husbands in the Korean War or WWII. That's when I realized so many people were walking around carrying the same pain, yet always putting on a happy face."

"In my neighborhood there were a few Korean veterans whose lives were in shambles because of the experiences they had in Korea. One of my coworkers had married a Marine just home from the Korean 'conflict.' He had terrible nightmares and a very difficult time in settling into a job and civilian life, but their love for each other got them through."

Devastated

When Della Lear received the "I regret to inform you…" telegram from the Air Force, she was "devastated and forlorn—was this real—or was this a nightmare?" she asked herself.

The sketchy details offered little in the way of fact to serve as an anchor for hope. She took such comfort as she could with her "faith in Wayne's flying ability," since she "knew he would do everything he could to get home safely." His frequent letters to her after his arrival in Korea "were full of plans for our life when he returned. We both just had too much to live for with a wonderful marriage—we were so much alike in many ways."

Her next thoughts were of Wayne's parents—"surely they had received a similar telegram. I felt I had to get to them as soon as possible to reassure them and give them hope."

Once she had talked to them, she went to her desk and wrote a letter—to Wayne. "I had to let him know I had faith that he would return." She continued to write letters for over a month, then "finally decided it was for the best to discontinue them until I had further word of his whereabouts."

Tidying Up

By July 2, 1952, Air Force headquarters in Washington had received the Casualty Report on Connors and assigned the number Case M-52-327 as the number by which to report "casualty assistance extended to the next of kin." The Commanding Officer of the 2347th Air Force Reserve Training Center in Long Beach, CA was tasked with the responsibility of assisting Frankie Connors.

"I have been appointed Summary Court Officer," 1st Lt. John W. Silvey, wrote Della Lear from Korea on July 3rd, "to properly dispose of the personal effects belonging to your husband, to represent you in settling any debts he may have incurred, and to collect moneys owed to him. Your husband's effects have been carefully packed to preclude damage or pilferage in transit, and were shipped on 2 July 1952, through effects depot facilities to the Effects Quartermaster APO San Francisco…they will be shipped from the depot to you through the Effects Quartermaster (in Kansas City, Missouri). In order that disposition of personal effects will be in accordance with existing state laws," Lt. Silvey continued, "I should like to emphasize that shipment of the property does not in any way vest title in you, but that the property is forwarded so that distribution may be made in accordance with the laws of the state having probate jurisdiction over your husband's estate. Should you think it necessary, your personal attorney or the legal officer of the military installation nearest your home, can assist you in taking proper measures to dispose of this property. Your husband has no debts of which we are aware, and there are no monies to be collected for him," Silvey closed. [5]

Long's Report

On July 4, 1952 Major Long noted as a reason for the report "officer missing in action," and submitted an Officer Effectiveness Report on 1st Lt. Connors, whose duty assignments included operating "a single-engine fighter aircraft to obtain air superiority over enemy. Receives instructions regarding mission, route, formation, altitude, weather conditions and other information; accomplishes mission by offensive action. Flies on strafing, interceptor, patrol, escort, or protective missions." [6]

The terse, condensed report noted that the "officer reported on conformed to the officer's code of conduct to an average degree. His moral standards are above reproach. He had an excellent flying safety record.

*"**Main Street**" for the 18th Fighter-Bomber Wing at K-46. From right to left is the Communications Center and the Operations Offices for the Two Squadron SAAF, the 67th Squadron and the 12th Squadron. (Urquhart)*

He exercises an average degree of judgment in the economical management of personnel and resources under his supervision, commensurate with his responsibilities. Subject officer occupies a T/O&E position of Pilot, Fighter, 1124E 1st Lt."

It was clear from the "boiler plate" phraseology and terseness of the report, that Long was going through the motions of reporting on an officer that he did not know very well and who was almost certainly dead. In fact, Long had assumed command of the 67th Squadron from Lt. Col. Julian Crow during the period when Connors was away from the squadron on emergency leave following Frankie's near-fatal accident. It is doubtful that Long, busily engaged in relocating the 67th from K-10 to K-46 in late May and early June and then planning for major air strikes on North Korea's hydroelectric facilities, had even met Connors more than a few times prior to his last mission.

Perhaps the irony of a reference to an "excellent flying safety record" was lost on Long. Also, Connors had only returned to the squadron a few days prior to his final mission. Nevertheless, Long characterized Connors' management judgment as "average" when, in fact, he had not been able to observe Connors performing any management "collateral duties" prior to June 25th. Why he felt it necessary to "trash" Connors report by damning him with faint praise is unknown. Long ended his Air Force career as a Lieutenant Colonel.

Long also wrote a letter that day to Archie's parents, Arch and Eva Connors, asking them to "accept my deepest sympathy concerning the report that your son, First Lieutenant Archibald H. Connors, Jr., AO 2 221 998, is missing in action. He has been a member of the 67th Fighter Bomber Squadron, 18th Fighter Bomber Wing since January 12, 1952," Long noted.

"I feel that you would like to know the circumstances connected with his missing in action status. Your son was flying number two position in a flight of four aircraft, prebriefed to fly cover for a helicopter effecting a pick up a downed pilot. While flying low cover, your son stated over his radio that his aircraft had been hit. His aircraft was observed in a right turning spiral until it struck the ground. The aircraft did not explode or burn and the major parts of it were still recognizable. The flight leader made several low passes of the area, but failed to observe any sign of your son," Long explained.

"Lieutenant Connors was flying his 33rd combat mission when the unfortunate incident occurred. He was outstandingly well qualified as an officer and pilot as evidenced by his devotion to duty and his record of past accomplishments. The report that he did not return from the mission came to me and his many friends as a real shock, and created a feeling of loss in the organization. Although it is known that no words of mine can ease your anxiety and great sorrow, please be assured that the officers and airmen of this command share your deep concern," Long said and closed the letter by promising them that if any additional word "regarding your son becomes available, we shall notify you immediately."

On July 8, 1952 Frankie Connors received a letter from the Personal Affairs Officer of the 2370th Air Base Squadron. "This office has assumed the responsibility of counseling the dependents of Air Force personnel on personal affairs matters, such as government benefits, insurance, legal matters, etc. Your local Veterans Administration will help you in making out the applications for these benefits. Due to the large area under our jurisdiction it would be impossible to visit each and every Air Force dependent personally. Therefore it would be appreciated if you could, at your convenience, appear at this building for counseling. If it is impossible, or you deem it unnecessary, please notify the section." [7]

After asking her to verify her present address and to notify them of any change or mistake in the address, Captain Hill closed his letter by saying that he would "anticipate hearing from you in the near future."

On 8 July 1952, the Long Beach Air Force squadron recorded the date of its "first contact with next of kin."

"Hard Luck Kid..."

"This is the story of Ensign Ronald D. Eaton, 22, of Wilmington, Mass., the hard luck kid who is listed on his squadron roster as missing in action," a Boston-area newspaper reported soon after Ron's family was notified. They were stunned by the flippancy reflected in the article with the headline, "'Hard Luck Kid' Missing In Korea." [8]

"A Corsair pilot and youngest member of his squadron, Eaton was shot down south of Wonsan, on June 25, 1952, 2nd anniversary of the Korean War. He is either dead or a prisoner of the Communists," the article stated, accurate but without sympathy.

"Eaton's hard luck streak began a month ago, one dark night off Hawaii as the carrier Bon Homme Richard set its course for Korea. Eaton and his plane fell overboard from the flight deck. This almost never happens. But it happened to Eaton. Forty-five minutes later destroyer [sic] had just about given up the search for him when somebody heard his police whistle as he paddled about in the water. They fished him out."

"Eaton arrived in Korean waters in time for the biggest air strike of the war—the raid on the Yalu River power plants. He came through that one all right, but on his third combat mission, a routine attack on ememy [sic] troop concentrations, he got it."

The article relates Eaton's announcement that he had to bail out and his "May Day" distress radio broadcast.

"Because Red troops were shooting at him from below, Eaton did not open his chute until he was about 500 feet from the ground. He made two swings and landed smack between two enemy trenches. But he landed running. He raced 100 yards to the top of a knoll. There he shook hands with himself, prize-fighter style to show he was unhurt," the article continued.

Not only do no other accounts, from official or unofficial sources mention the "prize-fighter" hand shake, it is highly unlikely that the young Ensign would take such action when he was under fire.

"Every time Red soldiers started up the knoll after Eaton, Sargent [LT Jack Sargent, a wingman] and Lt. Com. Franklyn H. Ervin of Danforth, Me., drove them off with their .30-calibre machine guns." Corsairs were armed with .50-caliber machine guns.

"Then something hit Ervin's plane. It was .37-mm cannon. When Ervin made an emergency landing at a nearby airstrip a few minutes later he had 150 holes in his plane. But it was nothing compared to the fact that a shell had hit a 250-pound bomb under his wing and ripped off the fuse. Ervin took one look at the bomb and walked off."

After explaining that Sargent's plane "developed engine trouble" and that he was replaced by LT Edmund O'Callaghan, of Newton Center, Mass., the article noted the arrival of "a rescue helicopter escorted by two Air Force 51's..."

"Whoever that copter pilot was, he was a very brave man," the article noted very correctly. "He took his eggbeater slow moving target, directly through a hail of fire from Red troops and to the knoll where Eaton was dancing and shaking hands with himself."

As Holloway noted, Eaton was hiding in the brush trying to avoid becoming a target until the rescue helicopter could lower its sling and position it very close to him.

"It looked like the hard luck kid had made it. He got in the helicopter and it flailed away. But it had traveled less than two miles [actually about six miles] when enemy fire finally found its mark. With a great whirling of blades the eggbeater came crashing to the ground. Two or three men walked away from the wreckage—Eaton's mates circling overhead couldn't be sure he was one of them, but whoever they were, Red soldiers marched behind them with bayonets at their backs."

The escorting Mustang pilots, following Archie's crash, reported later that men on the ground were rolling up parachutes. No official report mentions any captives or bayonets. The source of this story and the newspaper of origin are unknown. The Eaton family provided a copy from its collection for this book.

"We Just Don't Know…"

Della Lear had been stunned by the news of Wayne's crash and missing in action status. Unlike the other families, however, she had been a service wife for nearly eight years. She knew the system and had friends back in Washington where she and Wayne had been posted prior to his departure for Korea.

She took action and began writing to friends in Washington to see if they could help her learn more about Lear's situation. She knew the Air Force would not tell her everything it knew.

"My dear Della," George E. Halsey wrote on July 14th, "as Jeanne told you in her note, I was on a trip when your letter arrived, and therefore could not transmit an immediate reply. I don't have to tell you how I feel about the entire incident—you know of the high regard I have always had for Wayne. I have monitored very closely all of the information concerning Wayne's incident, and am up to date at this moment concerning everything we know about it. I have also read a copy of the letter you received from Wayne's CO, and checked with the Casualty Office in the Pentagon on the MIA notices you received," he noted. [9]

"Della, I wish that I could put your mind at rest, but we just don't know. I am able to answer some of your questions, and I can give you a frank estimate or judgment of Wayne's probable status. I am unable to answer your questions about his location at that time due to security—I know the exact locations and will let you know them when I can. Remember that security imposed is one way of protecting Wayne as well, so please accept my judgment of its necessity," Halsey said.

"We know positively that one man bailed out successfully from the copter, and that he jumped out its right side. Yes, Della, they do carry chutes for themselves and for the people they pick up, as their operations often involve flights at higher altitudes. The chance of the successful bail-out being Wayne is excellent and most probable—it is SOP for the pilot to go out that side—furthermore, he would be most alert to the need for bail-out and would be the calmer of the occupants. Frankly, my personal opinion is that chances are excellent that this man was Wayne."

"Assuming that this is so, we can only surmise as to Wayne's present status. It is possible that he could evade capture—I personally feel that it is more probable that he is a prisoner of war. I must stress that this is conjecture from very limited information; however, it is also the opinion of some of the boys here in the office who are helicopter returnees from that area."

"Della, any further info that I have is still of a classified nature, and it wouldn't do you any good to know it anyway. If Wayne is an evadee, you certainly wouldn't want to run the risk of compromising the area, and I wouldn't either. We must now just wait, and I don't know how long a wait will be necessary," Halsey cautioned.

"You know that I would not raise your hopes unless I felt there was a good chance of Wayne's survival—I do feel that the chances of this are excellent, and I have formed my opinion from all information known to us at this time. You may be sure that I shall keep my ear to the ground on this incident, and that I will let you know as soon as possible on information that would clarify the big question in all our minds. Regardless of final outcome, you may feel a great pride concerning your husband's achievements, his sense of duty and his courage are beyond reproach by <u>anyone</u>."

"Let us hear from you Della, and tell your folks (yours and Wayne's) hello from the Halseys. I may get out to California in August on a field trip, and I will look all of you up at that time—you might send us your telephone numbers if you will, so that I can locate you when I arrive. I know it's rough not knowing, but this is the best I can do. I have written this letter in the office and have shown it to certain of the boys who knew Wayne—McGovern, Dean, Jeffers, Col. Stevenson—they all join with me in expressing our heartfelt sympathy for you and Wayne' folks in this period of not knowing just exactly what has happened," Halsey closed.

Halsey's note that Wayne, as the pilot would be "most alert to the need to bail-out," was both accurate and significant in light of his decision to delay his exit from the falling aircraft until his passengers had exited.

Saving The Pills

The days and nights were very lonely for Della since she had not gone back to work following her return from their duty in Washington. She visited Wayne's parents in Santa Ana every other weekend and her parents in Pasadena on alternate weekends.

"Sleep became a real problem and lack of it finally forced me to see our family doctor," she recalled. "He gave me sleeping pills which I used several times. However, I finally decided to save them in case Wayne never came home."

Della was considering suicide.

"No," she eventually concluded, "that would not work for me—I am an only child and I just could not do that to my parents. Wayne's parents still had a daughter and grandchild so they were not my concern in that regard."

To keep her sanity, she "finally decided to look for employment and found a temporary legal secretary position in Riverside," where she was living. When that job ended, she applied for employment with the University of California, then establishing a new campus in Riverside. She landed a job as secretary to the Registrar and found "it was very rewarding—just what I needed at a very difficult time in my life."

The Inventories Continue

A little over two weeks after Mission 1890, it seemed clear that Archie Connors, whatever his fate, was not going to return to the 67th Squadron. On July 15, 1952, at K-46 air base near Hoengsong, Korea, 2nd Lt. John A. Zappe, USAF began a very sad duty while he sat on a cot in the How Flight tent—the inventory of Connors' personal effects. [10] The inventory was thorough, starting with "case, brief, black leather, containing 201 file, misc. papers, photos, letters," then moving to "Bag, B-4, brown; Boots, black; Shoes, black dress; Sandals, bath"...then socks, shirts, towels, hair brush, belts, shaving kit, ring case (empty since he was probably wearing the ring), camera, lighter, more shirts, ties, drawers, trousers, and gym trunks. The diligent Lieutenant even noted "supporter, athletic." There was a miniature sword "w/case", a pennant, and a voltage regulator.

Somehow, it is not surprising that the grandson of Civil War veterans on both sides of his family had carried with him to fight a war in Korea—a "cap, gray, Confederate."

The long list concluded with: "socks, cotton khaki; socks, black; laundry bag; Bible."

Archie's mother, Eva May Connors made certain that every one of her children, grand children, and eventually great grandchildren and great-great grandchildren received autographed Bibles from her. Without a doubt, the Bible that Lt. Zappe carefully wrapped and replaced in the trunk for shipment back to the States, was the one Eva had given Lt. Connors before he left to go in the Air Force. Eva Connors died in 1999 at the age of 108. At the time of her death she was the oldest living Gold Star Mother in the United States.

Hearing From The Chaplain

"Dear Mr. and Mrs. Connors," Major Daniel B. Jorgensen, Chaplain of the 18th Fighter-Bomber Wing wrote on July 16, 1952. "On behalf of the men of the 18th Fighter Bomber Wing, I want to express our heart-deep sympathy to you in your hour of anxiety. Your son, First Lieutenant Archibald Haddock Connors, Jr., AO-2221998, of the 67th Fighter Bomber Squadron, was a loyal friend, an able pilot, and a man of conviction. Needless to say, your anxiety is shared by us who served with him."

"As I mentioned to his wife, the news came as an unusual shock to me, for both of us returned here from the United States at the same time. I was called back to Florida on emergency leave, and when I returned by airlift we were on the same Special Orders bringing us here. I knew your son as a splendid young man, and I regret that we did not have the opportunity to know one another better."

"I feel constrained to remind you of the great contribution which your son made to the cause of the United Nations in Korea. He was a member of a distinguished squadron in a wing accomplishing some of the most difficult combat tasks. His numerous combat missions are a testimony to his devotion to duty."

"His fellow officers and airmen join me in this expression of sympathy. We realize the emotional strain which such a report as "Missing in Action" imposes upon the family, and our thoughts go out to you with the prayer that God will give you patience, comfort, and strength. May he speedily bring peace to our troubled world."

"It is regrettable that it takes a time such as this to evoke the first word from a chaplain to the loved ones of those he serves," Base Chaplain Major Conway Lanford wrote to Della on July 23rd. "The news that your husband, Captain Leslie W. Lear, AO 932234, was missing in action stunned our organization. In the month and a half in which he was a member of the 3rd Air Rescue Squadron, his ever present chuckle endeared him to the hearts of all who came in contact with him. The fearless manner in which

Major Daniel B. Jorgensen, *Chaplain of the 18th Fighter Bomber Wing wrote to the Connors' family from the Wing's chapel at K-10. He would soon move with the Wing to K-46.*

he was accomplishing his mission to save another's life is something in which you may be proud. May I command you to your prayers and to your church at this time. Our prayers join with yours for the safe return of your husband and a speedy end to this war. We also are praying for you; that God will comfort you and strengthen you during this period of your anxious waiting," Chaplain Lanford closed. By noting Lear's sense of humor and "ever present chuckle," Chaplain Lanford indicated to Della Lear that he actually knew her husband, unlike Long's more formal letters to Connors' relatives.

45,000th Sortie
Combat Operations Continue

Even as the families affected by Mission 1890 were trying to find out exactly what had happened to their loved ones, for the squadrons of the 18th Wing, the war continued.

During the weeks following June's Mission 1890, the 18th F-B Group "was assigned various types of targets, including rail line bridges, factories, supply areas and ammunition storage areas in the Pyongyang sector, transformer yard and, all across the front lines, personnel and supply targets were

45,000 Missions. On 9 July, Col. **Sheldon S. Brinson** *(far right), new Commander of the 18th Fighter-Bomber Group, congratulated Captain* **Elliot D. Ayer** *(far left), How Flight leader of the 67th Squadron, on completing the 45,000th effective combat sortie of the 18th Fighter-Bomber Group, just six days short of two years of combat flying in the Korean conflict—the greatest number of sorties completed by any combat fighter bomber wing in Korea. Ayer had replaced Lt. Wilfred "Budd" Stapley, who had completed his 100 missions and departed for the Zone of the Interior. As How Flight Leader, it was Ayer who led the Filter RECAP #1, Mission 1890 on June 25th. Two weeks later, on 25 July 1952 he was reported MIA. His remains were never recovered..*

attacked. Close support, interdiction, road recces, and RESCAP missions were still the main types of missions flown during the month." [11]

The "inclement weather with low clouds covering the local area, as well as the combat area," was a major operational issue during July.

"Despite the low cloud cover over and ahead of the bomb line, successful missions were flown against known troop concentrations and supply areas," the Group reported. "The bombing was done by use of MPQ-2 radar sets located in the front line areas. Radar controlled bomb drops are not new innovations but this was the first time extensive use was made of this type of operation. The aircraft were vectored over the target by a radar controller who told the pilot when to release the ordnance. Effective bombing was done with as little as 200 feet error from 11,000 feet altitudes. This type mission can be flown only when base weather is forecast to remain good enough for the flight to return."

Tactics changed in July. The minimum altitude for all action above the bombline was raised to 3,000' above the terrain and it "paid dividends in fewer losses and fewer instances of battle damage to aircraft. The change in pull-out altitude and entry altitude necessitated additional training on the ground-gunnery range. The training paid off in increased effectiveness and less damage to friendly aircraft," the Group reported.

On July 9th, a four-ship flight of the 67th Squadron "returning from a close support mission landed at K-46 airbase. The fourth airplane of the flight completed the 45,000th effective combat sortie of the 18th Fighter-Bomber Wing, six days short of two years of combat flying in the Korean conflict. This number of sorties was the greatest among those completed by any combat fighter bomber wing in Korea." Captain Elliot Ayer, How Flight Leader, was credited with the 45,000th combat sortie.

During 419 combat sorties in July, the 67th claimed destruction of 13 artillery positions, 13 rail bridges, 2 rail cuts, 10 road bridges, 2 box cars, 4 bunkers, 56 mortars, 25 gun positions, 2 machine guns, 7 secondary explosions, 15 self-propelled guns, 1 supply shelter, 4 caves, 2 buildings, 39 villages, 1 factory,

Captain Elliot D. Ayer, How Flight Leader, 67th Fighter-Bomber Squadron, at K-46.

1 truck, 3 transformer yards, 1 (damaged) Ox cart, 1 (damaged) trench (for 720'), and 9 KIA. There was no way to verify the eclectic list of claims, all based on pilot reports. Several studies during the Korean War pointed out the challenges of accurate battle damage assessment when the claims could not be verified as a result of the so-called "fog of war."

On July 25th, a month to the day since the tragic Mission 1890, as darkness was settling over the hills around the Hoengsong Air Base (K-46), Captain Elliot Ayer taxied Mustang tail number 655—"Lovely Lady"—away from the flight line. He then led his four-ship flight of Mustangs—1st Lt. William McShane, 1st Lt. C. J. Gossett, and 1st Lt. Rexford Baldwin—as they took off on a pre-briefed "armed reconnaissance mission against enemy main supply routes in North Korea." [12]

The route that was originally briefed was completely overcast— "under a solid overcast to as low as 3,000 feet"—so Ayer led the flight towards the Wonsan Harbor area where the weather was much clearer. "Shortly after we changed out course," Gossett reported, "the Number Two man saw several trucks." Lt. McShane alerted the rest of the flight to the trucks that were traveling south on the MSR out of Wonsan.

Ayer advised the flight that he and his Number Two man (McShane) would make "one pass only firing rockets and bombs," McShane reported. The Numbers Three (Gossett) and Four (Baldwin) men were to circle over the area to provide "top cover" against possible enemy fighters or to spot anti-aircraft locations.

Ayer radioed that he was "going in" and about 30 seconds later, his wingman did the same. "Captain Ayer began an over head pass to roll out parallel with the road heading North. As he commenced his dive I informed him that his running lights were on and immediately thereafter lost sight of him for a few seconds as he went under a small cloud," McShane said. By then it was about 2000 and "objects were fairly hard to detect," Baldwin later reported. He did "see moderate flack at the time they started their attack and called it in."

Number Three and Four stayed at about 9.000 feet orbiting the area about three miles away from the attack.

Baldwin saw Ayer "fire his rockets at an altitude of about 6,500 feet but did not see his aircraft then or at any time thereafter." Ayer continued with his bomb and rocket pass on the vehicles and was last seen, apparently in no difficulty, as he crossed his wingman's flight path at an altitude of 3,000 feet.

"As I lined up on four trucks in a very shallow bomb run," McShane reported, "I caught a brief glimpse of the leader crossing my flight path at about 3,000 feet at a 10 degree angle some distance ahead and due to this I didn't fire my guns or rockets, but continued on and as I dropped my bombs at about 1,000 feet, several automatic weapons commenced firing from directly ahead and to the left. Their fire appeared very accurate and continued until I had reached approximately 8,000 feet. At this time I called the flight leader at least six times requesting his position, but upon receiving no answer proceeded to join with Number Three and Four and circle the target area."

"Shortly after losing sight of Number One and Two," Gossett reported, "I observed a large quantity of flack in the area in which they were last headed. I observed a large explosion about one or two miles North of where Number Two dropped his bombs. At the time it reminded me of a napalm tank explosion. I do not know whether it was the explosion of the leader's bombs, whether he got a secondary explosion from one of the trucks, or whether it was the leader's airplane," Gossett said.

Subsequently, attempts by the Number Two and Three men to contact the leader by radio for further bombing instructions were unavailing. Two minutes later, the Number Two rejoined the orbiting flight "with no sight of the leader."

They stayed in the area "for about twenty minutes trying to contact the leader with no results."

An explosion was observed at about the time Captain Ayer would have completed his pass on the target at CU 6418, approximately one mile north of Nam Sanyong-ni, North Korea, but whether this was related to the crash of his plane could not be determined, a later incident investigation reported. A twenty minute search of the area by other flight members was hindered by accurate enemy ground fire and restricted visibility caused by approaching darkness, and the reason for the loss of the F-51 or what befell the pilot could not be ascertained.

"After twenty minutes of orbiting with no results, Number Three and Four man dropped their bombs aimed from 10,000 at the MSR and returned to base landing at K-46 at 2040."

Ayer's loss was the last downing of an American F-51 Mustang aircraft in combat from the 18th Fighter-Bomber Wing. A few short months later, the Wing would convert, while still in combat and without "standing down," to the F-86 "Sabrejet."

"Other than the above-mentioned MIA on Captain Ayer, there were no other losses to the squadron this month," the 67th reported to the 18th Wing.

Marguerite's World Ends

As a teenager some years later, Ayer's oldest son, Fred, recorded in his diary, his recollections of the day the Air Force notified his mother that his father was missing in action.

On July 28, 1952, an Air Force Officer knocked on the small suburban door and asked the pretty, dark haired mother of the two boys if she was the wife of Capt. Elliot Dean Ayer.

Nervous with the oldest boy holding her hand and clutching her leg, she answered "Yes."

The pretty southern lady knew already in her heart what the man wanted.

"Mrs. Ayer, I regret to inform you that your husband is missing in action."

The mother, hand shaking, held tightly to the seven year old boy's hand.

Bravely the woman told the officer that she would be OK and the officer left.

Only time and life would reveal that from that moment on, the woman, a good mother, wife and respected Southern lady, would never be "OK" again.

Although the young boy understood something was very wrong, he would not know until many years later that on that day he would stop being a little boy…and for that night, and for the next 30 years, surviving, from one day to the next would be his every day goal."

"Pain that he would accumulate, some deserved, some not, would haunt him day and night, for many years to come," Ayer's recollections recorded.

For Marguerite, it was a crushing blow from which she would never recover.

Marguerite Savage Ayer *and her sons, Boyd and Fred, in a photograph taken in 1952. (Ayer)*

News Trickles In

On August 3, 1952 Lieutenant Hill, a Mission 1890 pilot, explained in a belated letter to Frankie Connors that "we were in a flight of four (4) aircraft on a Rescap Mission to cover the helicopter while it made the pickup. Lieutenant McShane and myself were top cover while Archie and Captain Ayer were bottom cover with another flight that had covered the helicopter while he made a successful pickup, and were escorting him out when Archie was hit. He flew about one mile when we saw his ship crash on the side of a knoll in a flat position. The aircraft did not burn and was intact when Captain Ayer made passes over it, but there was no movement at all in the area of the crash."

"Due to the circumstances I cannot truthfully say one way or the other what chances are of Archie's returning to you. I pray to God that he will. I hope that from my letter you can make up your mind one way or the other to what I am trying to convey to you. I am very sorry that we have to meet under such circumstances. You have my deepest sympathy in your hour of darkness. I hope God sees fit for me to return to my family, I would like to stop by your home while en route to mine," Hill closed.

Beware of Extortion

"Since I last communicated with you," General McCormick wrote to Della Lear on 8 August 1952, "a report has been received from the overseas commander concerning the known events leading to your husband's

Inside the How Flight tent at K-46 in July 1952, 1st Lt. John E. Hill and Capt. Charles T. Hudson await their next mission. It was probably from this desk that Hill wrote his thoughtful letter of condolences to Frankie Connors following Archie's last mission on June 25th. (Urquhart)

missing status. I know that you are anxious to learn as much as possible of what happened to your husband, Captain Leslie W. Lear."

Four days later, McCormick signed out a virtually identical letter to Lt. Connors' parents, changing the name and circumstances slightly as appropriate.

"Our report states that Captain Lear was the pilot of a H-5 helicopter which departed with four F-51's from Hoengsong Airdrome, Korea, 25 June 1552 on a rescue mission. The rescue mission was ordered to rescue a Navy pilot who had been forced down over enemy territory. The flight of F-51's was to render suppression of the enemy while your husband and the medical technician effected the rescue. On the first descent intense enemy fire was encountered. The escort planes readily suppressed them and on their third descent they were successful in rescuing the downed Navy pilot. Even though the helicopter was damaged by enemy fire during this action, your husband skillfully handled the helicopter and directed the craft toward friendly territory. Unfortunately, before being able to reach friendly territory the helicopter was observed by one of the accompanying escort planes to go into a diving spin. Three men were seen to leave the helicopter before it crashed to the ground. However, only one person was seen to successfully parachute to the ground. One of the escort planes flew over and observed only one person walking and removing his parachute. The airplane again passed over the area and observed the parachute empty and the one man had disappeared. Shortly thereafter, another pass was made and eight people, identified as enemies, were rolling up the abandoned parachute and upon the appearance of our aircraft, were seen to run. One last pass was made before our aircraft was ordered away from the vicinity and at this time no one was seen. Since all this took place in enemy occupied territory no organized ground search of the area could be conducted.

"In the event that your husband survived the crash of his plane and was captured, it is possible that you may receive some form of communication from or concerning him. We are requesting that, if you should receive such a communication, you forward the original or a photo static copy of the document and envelope, if any, to this Headquarters. All material we receive will be carefully examined, photo static copies will be made, and the originals will be returned to you immediately thereafter," McCormick continued.

"It is possible that your action may materially assist us in establishing the fate of Captain Lear. Unfortunately, many of these communications are examples of deliberately designed propaganda initiated by the enemy and directed toward influencing the families of those whose fates are uncertain. Although we are vitally interested in receiving everything that is available relating to one of our missing persons, we may be unable to make an official change of status on the basis of such evidence."

"It is very important that you should know that in the past unscrupulous individuals, attempting to turn the grief and anxiety of families to their own use, have been known to extort money by claiming that they have some knowledge of a relative who is reported missing in action. Sometimes they claim that the relative is a prisoner of war and that they are in a position either to get in touch with him or to have him freed from a prison camp in return for a certain sum of money. Experience indicates that such letters may originate in other countries as well as in the United States. If you should receive such a letter or other communication from anyone who claims to be able to assist you for a sum of money, please notify the nearest FBI office before taking any action whatever."

"You are assured that compliance with our request will in no way affect your current rights and benefits as next of kin."

"I want to assure you that if your husband is located or any other information is secured regarding him, a report to that effect will be furnished to you without delay. We will continue to record him as missing in action until such time as his fate is ascertained."

"I join in the hope that there will soon be some definite news of your husband and that it will be favorable. My sympathy continues during this period of waiting," McCormick closed.

Holloway Family notified

The first week in August, General McCormick wrote to Ouida Holloway Preaus, Bobby Holloway's mother. "I know that you are anxious to learn as much as possible of what happened to your son. Our report states that Airman Holloway was the medical technician of an H-5 helicopter which departed with four F-51's from Hoengsong Airdrome, Korea, 25 June 1952 on a rescue mission. The rescue mission was ordered to rescue a Navy pilot to who been forced down over enemy territory. The flight of F-51's was to render suppression of the enemy while your son and the pilot effected the rescue."

"On the first descent intense enemy fire was encountered. The escort planes rarely suppress them and on their third descent they were successful in rescuing the downed Navy pilot. Even though the helicopter was damaged by enemy fire during this action the pilot skillfully handled a helicopter and directed the craft toward a friendly territory."

"Unfortunately, before being able to reach friendly territory the helicopter was observed by one of the accompanying escort planes to go into a diving spin. Three men were seen to leave the helicopter before it crashed to the ground. However, only one person was seen to successfully parachute to the ground. One of the escort planes flew cover and observed only one person walking and removing his parachute."

"The airplane again passed over the area and observed the parachute empty and the one man had disappeared. Shortly thereafter another pass was made and eight people, identified as enemies, rolling up the abandoned parachute and upon the appearance of our aircraft, were seen to run. One last pass was made before our aircraft was ordered away from the vicinity and at this time no one was seen."

"Since all this took place in enemy occupied territory no organized ground search of the area could be conducted I want to assure you that if your son is located or any other information is secured regarding him, a report to that effect will be furnished to you without delay you will continue to record him has missing in action until such time as is fate is ascertained I join in the hope that there will soon be some definite news of your son and that it will be favorable. My sympathy continues during this period of waiting," McCormick closed the letter.

A Medal Arrives

On August 12, 1952, Headquarters 18th Fighter-Bomber Wing "forwarded for necessary action correspondence pertaining to the award of the Air Medal to First Lieutenant Archibald H. Connors, Jr., listed as missing in action."

The award had come too late and it was not for his airmanship and bravery during Mission 1890. It had been awarded to Connors and other pilots that had completed a number of dangerous missions earlier that Spring.

A Friend At Headquarters

"Dear Della," one of Wayne's Air Force colleagues wrote on August 19th from Headquarters Flight Service in Washington, D.C., "I know you have been wondering as to when I would write and give such information as I might be able to find out. Well, at last Hq ARS gave me a clue. I was referred to a Major Halsey last week and then found that he was a very personal friend of Wayne and myself, and further that he had written to you. Major Halsey informed that he had written all he could possibly do without violating security. He did inform me, and I don't know whether he told you, that the exact location of the incident is known at Hq ARS and should the location, at a future date, fall within our forces hands and exposing the location would then not hinder any of the crew's safety he would immediately make such information available to you. Also, Hq ARS is constantly scrutinizing "PW" lists to see if Wayne's name or one of the other two appear. If so, that is one of the three names appear, it is or could be a good indication that all three got out of the helicopter safely and were interned as "PW's." Della, I am extremely sorry that I have nothing further to report but if I should be able to pry something loose I will send it on to you. Grace was shocked at the news and asked me to convey her sympathy to you that she will write in a day or so. Once again I would like to say that we will help in every and any way possible if you will drop us a line. Sincerely, Grity. P.S. Major Halsey called and said he was leaving on a West Coast trip and that he would be seeing you the latter part of August or sometime in the first half of September."

Casualty Assistance

The Long Beach, CA 2370th Air Base Squadron Office of Personal Affairs reported it had received a "casualty notification" on August 18, 1952 and first made contact with Frankie Connors on 20 August 1952.

On that day, Captain Harold Hill queried Frankie to determine her financial situation regarding payment of her husband's insurance premiums, home loan, "or any other loan he might have taken out." He told her that she could "rest assured that all steps possible are being taken to locate your Husband" and that she would be "notified immediately of any information received regarding his status." Captain Hill closed his letter with: "It is recommended that all insurance policies be kept up to date and all premiums promptly paid."

"I have just received your letter concerning my personal affairs and I do need some help," Lutye wrote the Air Force the next day. "Could you advise me as to how I should pay my husband's insurance and anything else that should be kept up? I'm working and think my financial needs are alright...Please notify me if anything else is heard about my husband as soon as possible." [13]

Call For Dental Records

On August 28, 1952 the Air Force Identification Branch forwarded a request to Camp Stoneman, California for "dental information" in the case of Lear, Leslie W. Capt. AO 923 234." It was the beginning of what would become the Individual Deceased Personal File prepared and kept on all U.S. military personnel killed in action. Similar requests were sent other bases where Lear had been stationed, including Itami Air Base in Japan, and Biggs Field, Texas. Headquarters, Air Rescue Service in Washington noted that "there is no record of dental work performed at this station…and there is no information at this station indicating that officer received any medical treatment for fractures, breaks, serious injuries or operations."

Similar letters were posted by the U. S. Army Quartermaster General's Office in Washington on August 28th requesting "all available dental records for all available dental records for military personnel who are missing in action as a result of the Korean conflict. Over the following weeks, Connors' record would reflect the reports of the various commands to which he had been posted as they responded to the request.

Delayed Effects

On 18 September, 1952, Frankie's letter to the Far East Command had been forwarded to the Army Effects Bureau for reply "in connection with the personal effects of your husband."

In fact, it was Department of the Air Force policy, the Liaison Officer, CWO W. L. Mooney, told her "to return the personal effects of our causalities as rapidly as the circumstances permit; however, in view of the unsettled conditions existing in Korea, there will be an understandable delay in the forwarding of this property to the Army Effects Bureau." The effects of personnel listed as missing in action "are not normally returned to the United States until after a 'holding period' of approximately one hundred and twenty days has expired," Mooney explained. "Therefore, unless his casualty status is subsequently changed, the personal effects of your husband may not arrive in the United States for several months."

It would be considerably longer than that before the families would regain custody of the three sets of personal effects.

On November 19, 1952, Frankie Connors noted "this is the second letter I have written in regards to my husband, 1st Lt. A.H. Connors, Jr. AO 2221998, who is missing in action since June 25th. You wrote and asked if I were prepared to pay his insurance, etc. I informed you I was if only you'd tell me where to send it. His belongings have not arrived as yet—would you please help me clear up some of the details? Tell me who to contact in these matters at least. Thank you very much."

On November 26, 1952 Frankie received a letter from the Air Force Liaison Office of the Army Effects Bureau in Kansas City, Missouri advising her that the Agency had "received from overseas certain funds belonging to your husband" asking her to receive the funds "for safekeeping, pending final determination of his status."

In Jacksonville, the Connors family really didn't "celebrate" Christmas that year, it just went through the motions needed to get through the holidays. Trying to cheer them up with some awful doggerel, Archie's older brother, Woodrow rhymed, "Fifty two was awfully blue, but in fifty three Archie we'll see." They prayed he was right.

Life For Holloway As A POW

When Bobby Holloway was first captured, the Chinese soldiers marched him "back into the mountains. There were always two guards. Never one, always at least two. They would march you so far, then some other twosome would take you another distance. When they take you in relays, you start to get tired. They finally got me back into the hills. Next thing I know, I'm looking at a hole in the ground inside of a hill. They motioned me to crawl in there. I finally got into it and found that it was exactly what it looked like, a hole in the ground. You could sit with your legs straight out and your back bent in a sitting position. Or, you could lie on your back with your knees up. That was it. You only came out when they let you out. From time to time they would take you out to interrogate you—try to get you to tell them about our dropping "germ bombs." Of course, I couldn't figure out we were supposed to have dropped any bombs from a little helicopter."

The Chinese guards fed Holloway and did not mistreat him too badly, aside from a "gun butt up side of the head every now and then." He considers himself fortunate to have been captured and held by the Chinese and not the Koreans. "The Chinese were more tolerant. They had more food than the Koreans did."

The interrogator knew that Holloway had been an air crewman on the helicopter. He wanted to know "where we were based...what we were doing...how we operated," Holloway recalled. "I dummied up on them. I didn't know much about helicopter operations, I assured him...hadn't been in Korea too long." One of the interpreters had worked with the British and spoke good English.

"Days didn't mean a lot right then."

"I wasn't going to cooperate with them...I'm just too stubborn. They kept asking me about the 121st Evacuation Hospital."

The interrogator was also persistent in asking Holloway about the "machine gun" on the helicopter. "I didn't know anything about a 'machine gun,' and I told him so. But, I'm sure he was referring to my putting .30-cal. rounds into that commo [communications] bunker," Holloway recalled. During that period they questioned Holloway for over three days about having the "machine gun" on the helicopter.

"That was my M-2 Carbine. They didn't believe me although I kept telling them that I didn't have a machine gun on the helicopter. Well then show it to me, I asked them. 'Oh, we can't do that,' they said. 'Why,' I asked, and so it went," he recalled.

Finally, they moved Holloway "somewhere else for interrogation, but they used a different tactic. They had an old building, perhaps a large Korean house. They would call me in, ask me some questions, then send me back to a room—to wait—to sweat it out for anywhere from 15 minutes to 2-3 hours. You never knew. While you waited, they compared the answers you had previously given them, looking for any changes or inconsistencies. Then they would haul you out, ask you more questions, then send you back to the room—24 hours per day for days on end. They did it with relays of questioners."

"You got to a point where you waited to hear them coming to get you again. It wore you out. That's why you learned very, very quickly. Don't tell them an out and out lie. That's too hard to remember. Twist the truth to where it doesn't mean anything."

On one occasion "somebody was saying something and I said something, I don't even remember what it was, but a guard gave me a good stroke up side of the head with an M-1 Garand—one of our rifles that he had taken or found somehow. That smarted for a while. I can verify," Holloway joked later, "that the butt of an M-1 is hard…that metal butt plate is hard."

They moved Holloway to yet another camp where he was not interrogated so much, and it was the first time in many weeks that he had seen or talked to an American. It was in the mountains, not so much a POW camp, but more like a holding camp. There were Americans and South Korean "prisoners" that Holloway and the other Americans assumed were North Korean spies or moles.

Everything that was said around us the Chinese knew about "real quick. Someone was reporting to them. We learned very quickly to watch what we said and did."

After being in that camp for about week they put us on a truck and took us north in a convoy. The trip, usually at night, took several days. The Chinese were afraid of American fighter bombers. "We did get one F9F attack. We had just passed one convoy when jets appear…then you hear explosions…and the jet engines going…and the guns firing."

"We finally made it to Camp 5 in August 1953, right on the Yalu River."

An Army Lieutenant and I were then transferred to another camp that was called Camp 5B. It was a village. We were in an old school house."

Finding enough food was always a challenge to survival. Holloway and his fellow POW's learned to scrounge and improvise. The way they "cooked the bread," for example.

"The Chinese made up some dough and rolled it out like a log. Then they cut it into sections," Holloway recalled. "I would say, two to three inches square and two inches thick. They had a rack—round—covered with a type of mesh and then placed over a large—maybe forty gallon—pot of boiling water. The hunks of dough are put on the mesh several inches apart. Then perhaps four or five of these racks are stacked up and placed over the boiling water. As the dough on the lower racks is cooked, the racks were rotated from bottom to top. They would keep rotating the dough on the racks until, by their standards, it was cooked. It was still doughy and was not thoroughly cooked."

"But we solved that problem," Holloway recalled. "We built our own oven out of a fifty-five gallon drum. We made a hinge for the lid and added wire racks that we built. We then built a firebox around it that would allow us to bake inside the drum."

"The first time one of the guys made up some home-made biscuits, instead of bread, it was almost a fight to see who was going to get the biggest share of those wonderful biscuits," he recalled.

The basic diet "was rice—every day—although not too much of it. They gave us stalk cabbage—not the cabbage, mind you—just the stalks to cook and put over the rice. It looked somewhat like celery. They didn't have a lot of flavor. Basically, we cooked and ate any kind of food—vegetable or otherwise—that we could get our hands on. Anything to put on the white rice to add flavor and variety. I never saw any brown rice, only white rice," he said.

"We had tea every day, they did give us small amounts of that. You would make up a little bag, put in the tea leaves and throw it into the boiling water. When you figured it was cooked enough you dipped the bag out and squeezed it out, then served the tea."

"Some of the Chinese guards would come in with two little buckets. We would put the cooked food in one and the tea in the other. They would then take them from our compound to the different houses around where they had us confined—where they kept other prisoners. We had the largest compound, but there were other smaller groups of prisoners confined in other buildings nearby. We had guys that had been there since the start of the war and they were not allowed to mix with any other prisoners. There were 32 of us that lived in the one room of an old school house. Then we had one other room with ten others and somewhere around 50-60 other prisoners spread around the valley where we were held. We cooked for our group and for several groups of prisoners that were kept nearby that we never got to see. They would not allow us to meet them or to see them. However, when the guards would march us down the road, the other prisoners would sing to us…talk to us while singing…using the "lyrics" to tell us what they could as we marched by. You had to be creative," Holloway laughed.

"The diet was short on everything, from variety to calories. It would not have been possible to do any heavy work on that diet. The Chinese were raised on that diet, so their bodies were used to that. We were not and it was hard to adjust to that type of diet. We all lost weight, a great deal of weight. When they made us work, it was really hard on us. We didn't have the strength we had to start with. In the summer time we had to build a bunker. They dug out the side of a hill. It was ten or twelve feet deep and perhaps eight feet high. They had us go up into the hills and haul the large logs down to build the walls of the bunker. We dug the bunker into the side of a hill and used the logs to insulate and support the walls. We covered the roof with smaller trees, from one inch to three inches thick. We arranged them much like the sod houses on the prairie with dirt and corn stalks on the roof. It would be where we stored our food in winter," Holloway related.

"The winters were brutal. On one occasion the temperature was 42 degrees—below zero. They told us to fall out for roll call. We went out into the cold and realized that if we stayed out there we would surely freeze to death. So, we filed right back inside the school. They decided not to punish us. I don't know why. There was no body fat left on any of us and we would have frozen."

When Holloway was repatriated in September 1953, he weighed less than 150 pounds.

"There were about 30 of us there in that camp—Army, Marines, Navy and a Canadian. We had mostly officers and NCO's—Army, Navy and Air Force—leaders—they were considered a bad influence on the non-rated guys."

"The primary objective for the Chinese guards was to break down our military chain of command. The first thing they told us was that everyone was the same—there were no more officers or enlisted men. Well, our working term for how we dealt with them was 'we bought the farm,' meaning that we went along with what they said up to a point. We agreed with them to their faces, but of course, were not persuaded in the least by the propaganda. We had our military structure, although the Chinese preached at us not to. Our senior officer was a Major and he was the 'CO.' He had the final say. That was our chain of command. We had our most senior guy in charge, and from there the authorities and responsibilities came on down the line."

"Everybody had a job. There were only two of us who had been medics in the compound. So, we were the ones that looked out for the group, as best we could understanding we had virtually no real medicines or instruments," Holloway explained.

"One Sergeant had bailed out of a B-29 and after he landed, had stepped on a mine. His leg was badly injured. The Chinese called in a "doctor," actually they called him a medicine man (we called him the Witch Doctor.) Every time this guy's leg would start to scab over and heal, the medicine man would come in, yank off the scabs and paint the injury with something, I don't know what is was. We stopped him from going on sick call and the leg finally healed. He walked but with a limp."

"We basically didn't have that much to do...most of our work parties were for things we needed."

"We got quite a few lectures about being respectful to the interpreter. One of them we called the "little interpreter." One day we got about an hour lecture from the Commandant that in the future we would call him 'Comrade Chung.' We listened to the Commandant and from that point on we called him 'Comrade Chung...the Little Interpreter.' In one of the many lectures, the Chinese gave everyone a piece of paper and a pencil so that we could write down any questions we might have regarding their lecture on communism. We used all the paper to play Tic-Tac-Toe and then turned it in at the end of the lecture. That never happened again. Chalk up one for the good guys."

During the entire time Holloway was in prison, only one parcel was allowed to reach the camp.

After his eventual release in September 1953, he devoted a lot of time at first to getting caught up on the news—it was a busy time in world history. He would learn that Marshal Joseph Stalin had died and had been succeeded by G. M. Malenkov. A writer named Ian Fleming had published a novel he called "*Casino Royale*," featuring the exploits of a secret agent, 007, named James Bond. A struggling young editor named Hugh Hefner, published the first issue of a new magazine he called "*Playboy*." A popular musical on Broadway based on Borodin's music for "*Prince Igor*," named "*Kismet*," opened on Broadway. Radio listeners enjoyed popular songs such as "*I Believe*," "*Ebb Tide*," "*Stranger in Paradise*," and "*I Love Paris*." Mount Everest was conquered and Dr. Alfred C. Kinsey published "*Sexual Behavior in the Human Female*," to yet another media frenzy.

Shipments En Route

On January 15, 1953 the Army Effects Agency sent Frankie Connors a check for $347.37 "in connection with funds received here for your husband." It also acknowledged her inquiry of December 27th concerning his personal effects.

"Information has been received from overseas indicating that your husband's effects have been processed for shipment to the United States. The date of arrival is uncertain. Due to difficulties which are often encountered in securing shipping space, distance involved and transportation delays which might occur en route, a period of approximately four months may elapse before Lieutenant Connors' belongings are received here; however, you may be assured that when this property becomes available, I will communicate with you promptly. I would like to extend my sincere sympathy to you in this time of uncertainty," CWO W. L. Mooney said.

Fifty nine pounds of Connors personal effects were finally shipped on March 5, 1953. The box would include bags, billfolds, books, cameras, souvenirs, a bible, insignia, brushes, wash cloths, three pairs of shoes, gloves, headwear, jackets, knives, letters, lighters, papers, a Parkette fountain pen, photographs, ring case (empty), shirts, socks, stationery, t-shirts, towels, trousers, a silk painting (w mailing tube), a B-4 bag and one scarf were examined and packed for shipment.

The miniature sword mentioned in the initial inventory conducted at K-46 of personal effects was not included. The Gray Confederate Cap eventually reappeared—in 2007.

Ayer's Effects

The Army Effects Agency sent Marguerite C. Ayer a notice on March 12, 1953 that it had "received from overseas some personal property belonging to your husband, Captain Elliot D. Ayer." Since its records indicated that he had been reported missing in action, "it is our desire that some close relative receive this property for safekeeping, pending final determination of his status." If she would confirm the address and her willingness to safely keep his property "as gratuitous bailee," Ayer's personal effects would be sent to her. On March 19th, in a large, clear hand, Marguerite Ayer acknowledged the Agency's letter and asked them to send the effects to her. [14]

It was during this period that Marguerite was invited to an awards ceremony at Eglin Air Force Base, not far from her home in Tallahassee. During the ceremony she was presented with the Air Medal, the Distinguished Flying Cross and the Purple Heart on behalf of her husband, Capt. Elliot D. Ayer. "The DFC was awarded to the Captain posthumously for his action in determining the outcome of his wingman and a helicopter pilot they were escorting, who were shot down behind enemy lines because of heavy anti-aircraft fire," the base newspaper reported.

Hope and Heartbreak

On March 5, 1953, the Army Effects Bureau in Kansas City, Missouri, thanked Della Lear for confirming her address "in connection with funds and personal property belonging to your husband, Captain Leslie W. Lear." The letter from CWO W. L. Mooney included several modest checks that had been found with his personal effects. After reminding her that having the personal effects sent to her did not give her actual title to them "pending a final determination of his status," Mooney asked for a receipt "by signing one copy of this letter in the space provided and returning it to this Bureau."

Della signed the receipt for the property she had received, but also noted in the margin of the letter that she had received "one large wooden

(Above) ***A forlorn Marguerite Ayer*** *sits waiting for General Patrick Timberlake, Commander of the Air Proving Ground Command based at Eglin Air Force Base, to present her with her husband's awards, including the Purple Heart, his third Distinguished Flying Cross and a fifth Air Medal. She is already showing the physical effects of the devasting grief that would take her life not many years later. (Ayer)*

box delivered yesterday" (March 23rd) "However," she continued in the margin, "I want to call to your attention the fact that my husband's footlocker has not yet been returned. He flew to Korea. Therefore, his footlocker was transmitted by ship. He had not received delivery of it prior to his 'missing' status. Would you please take the necessary steps to locate the one missing footlocker and forward it to me at 1951 Dorothy Drive in Riverside, California?" She thanked them for their "cooperation in this matter."

Della Lear's note in the margin set off a paperwork "missing footlocker hunt" that would cross the Pacific Ocean several times and take over four months to resolve.

"Thank you for acknowledging receipt of the personal effects belonging to your husband," the Army Effects Bureau wrote to Della Lear on 26 March 1953. "You no doubt realize that when a container such as your husband's footlocker becomes damaged in transit, the contents must be transferred to insure protection and safe delivery. While this Bureau has no definite information such circumstances prevailed in this case, it is a reasonable assumption based on similar cases. However, if you can furnish a list of the specific items contained in the footlocker, tracer action will be initiated in an effort to locate both the footlocker and its contents."

"I personally packed my husband's things for his overseas assignment—footlocker and B-4 bag," Della responded on March 30th. "The items contained in the footlocker were not included with the articles recently sent to me. Because he left in May 1952 the footlocker contained (for the most part) winter clothing. In addition, there were personal papers and various Air Force manuals." She then noted such missing items as flannel pajamas and a lined B-15 jacket (not issued type). "As I mentioned previously, my husband had not received this footlocker prior to his 'missing' status. Could it possibly still be somewhere in Japan?"

On April 7th the Army Effects Agency in Kansas City wrote to the Commander of the Far East Command Personal Effects Depot, indicating it had received some "personal property" belonging to Capt. Leslie W. Lear" and seeking information regarding additional property that was reported missing by Della Lear.

On April 30th, Headquarters, Far East Air Forces invited the attention of the Commanding General, Japan Air Defense Force to several "Inclosures" concerning the disposition of footlocker, personal property of Captain Lear. "Information contained in Inclosure [sic] #2 states that the footlocker was received by the 3rd Air Rescue Squadron on 8 August 1952, and shipped to the Personal Effects Division, 12 August 1952; however, the Personal Effects Division states subject footlocker was never received." FEAF requested a "thorough investigation be conducted to trace the shipment of the footlocker to determine its present location" and to forward it immediately to the Personal Effects Division."

Headquarters, Japan Air Defense Force forwarded a terse memorandum on May 5, 1953 to the Commanding General, 35th Fighter-Interceptor Wing "requesting compliance with instructions" to provide information on the whereabouts of Capt. Lear's personal effects. The Wing then sent a similar memo down the chain of command to the Commander, Third Air Rescue Group for the "necessary action" to be accomplished by 22 May 1953.

On 14 May 1953 Col. Klair Back, Commander of the Third Air Rescue Group (3ARG) advised the Transportation Officer at Johnson Air Base, Japan that "transportation is approved at Government expense for the personal effects of Leslie W. Lear, Captain, USAF MIA."

On 18 May 1953, Headquarters, 3ARG alerted the Commanding General of the 35th Fighter-Interceptor Wing in Japan that "baggage belonging to Captain Leslie W. Lear (MIA) was located in the Commercial Transportation Office, Johnson Air Base." The memorandum promised a "new form 54" and to forward the baggage to 8080th Army Unit.

By 27 May, as a result of probing by the Army Effects Agency in Kansas City, FEAF advised the Personal Effects Division that Lear's personal effects "were located and shipped your depot" by the Third Air Rescue Group.

On June 25th the CP Drew Personal Effects Division Sub Depot reported to the Army Effects Agency in Kansas City that the "personal effects referred to…were forwarded to your Agency in shipment on 25 June

1953"—exactly one year after Mission 1890. The last of Wayne Lear's personal effects were finally headed home, a year after his helicopter was shot down.

However, Della "never gave up hope for Wayne's return. In fact, in the early spring of 1953 I saw a new Buick Special convertible in the dealer's showroom—it was GREEN—Wayne's favorite color—I just had to have it waiting for him when he returned."

Truce Talks Progress

By April 1953, the Connors family had had no further word regarding Archie's fate. On April 3rd, Archie's mother, Eva May Connors wrote to General McCormick to remind him that "since August, 1952 we have not had any communication from the War Department concerning our son, First Lt. Archibald H. Connors, Jr. Naturally our anxiety or concern has not lessened. Would it be possible for us to obtain the names of the pilot of the helicopter who was effecting the pickup of the downed pilot, and the name of the pilot who was be rescued. Also the names of the nearest of kin of both these pilots that we might write each other." [15]

On April 7, 1953, MG McCormick wrote Frankie with information about repatriation plans. Some progress, however halting, was being made at Panmunjom.

"As you probably know, the United Nations is attempting to effect an agreement with the North Korean and Chinese Communists, for the exchange of sick and injured prisoners of war. My purpose in writing to

Della Lear tried hard not to give up hope for Wayne Lear's return. In the spring of 1953, she saw a new Buick Special convertible in the dealer's showroom, green beauty, Wayne's favorite color. She bought it on the spot to have it waiting for him when he returned. Instead, its large trunk would carry Wayne's personal effects from the train depot to their home.

you at this time is to explain the notification procedure the Department of the Air Force will follow should this exchange agreement be affected. The number or identity of prisoners who may be exchanged is unknown. However I do want to assure you that in the event your husband, First Lieutenant Archibald H. Connors, Jr., is among those released by the opposing forces, you will be notified by Telegram immediately of his return and his condition. If your husband is not included among those released, his official Status will remain unchanged. The omission of his name from the list of exchanged prisoners is no indication that he is not being held by the Communists. You may be assured that the United Nations and the government of the United States will continue their efforts to effect an exchange of all prisoners at an early date. You will, of course, be immediately notified if any information is received concerning him. My sincere sympathy is extended to you and a deep concern which I know you must feel for your husband at this time."

An identical letter was sent to Della Lear, changing only the husband's name to Captain Leslie W. Lear.

On April 16, 1953 General McCormick responded to Eva's April 3rd letter and provided the names of Captain Leslie W. Lear, USAF, Ensign Ronald D. Eaton, USNR, and A/1C Bobby D. Holloway. His letter also included the names and addresses of their next of kin. "Your anxiety is understandable, and it is regretted that no additional information has been received since my letter of August 15, 1952. I want to assure you that we are using every available means to ascertain the true status of all our missing personnel and any information which may become known in regard to Lt. Connors will be promptly forwarded to you."

Sitting alone at her west Jacksonville dining room table where she fed her large and growing family, and with the ever present cup of hot tea beside her right hand, Eva Haddock Connors began to write letters to the families of the other pilots of Mission 1890.

"Enclosed is a letter about my son, A. H. Connors, Jr. who was on a rescue mission for your son," Eva wrote to Elsie Eaton. "My son was downed also. If you hear any news about your son will you please advise us, as we think they might all be together in the event they were taken prisoners. Also, another letter gives the names of other pilots and their nearest of kin, if you want that information. Our sympathy and prayers are with you as we know what that sorrow is. Please write if you hear anything," she closed.

"Enclosed are letters concerning my son, A. H. Connors, Jr.," Eva wrote Della Lear, "who was one of the pilots attempting the rescue mission during the accident which also involved your husband. My greatest sympathy and prayers are extended to you as I know only too well what this sorrow is—my son was downed also. Now that some of the prisoners of war are being released, it is our hope that we might hear from some of our boys. If you hear anything, will you please write us? It is our hope that the boys might have survived the crash and are prisoners. The other letter from the war department gives the names of the men involved and the names of the nearest of kin. If you care to write to us, we will be glad to hear from you and hope that all our anxiety will soon be ended, and trust that God will take care of our boys."

On April 15, 1953, General Hoyt S. Vandenberg, Air Force Chief of Staff approved special Orders No. 72. In paragraph 17, Lt. A. H. Connors, Jr. was listed among twenty other Lieutenants whose "USAF-Spot apmt in grade of 1st LT are hereby vac." Archie's new date of rank was listed as 10 April 52.

Archibald "Arch" Connors, Sr. and Eva May Connors *as they appeared during the time that their son, Archibald H. "Archie" Connors, Jr. was missing in action.*

Where Are They?

"Dear Sir," Frankie wrote to the Army Effects Agency on 20 April 1953, "I am writing in reference to your letter of April 16, in which you asked if my husband's belongings had arrived yet. The International Forwarding Company sent me a notice March 23rd stating they had received his effects. Since then I have called them exactly eight times, remained home from work one day when they promised to arrive and by now I'm so mad and upset that I hope you'll handle the rest of it. Today I called again and they were supposed to call back when they located everything but it's past their closing time and they haven't called. Also, two weeks ago they told me to send them the bill of lading and they would deliver it to the lady in the next apartment. No one came out or they would have left a notice of delivery. Please see if you can help me. I've been waiting almost a year for his belongings. Thank you very much for your courtesy and help in the past."

A memo routing slip from the Army Effects Agency indicated that the personal effects of 1st Lt. Archibald H. Connors, Jr. were finally delivered to his wife on 23 April 1953. Just a year before, the contents of the box had been beside his cot in a tent at K-46. At that time, he had been hovering over Frankie's bedside in the front bedroom of his parent's home in Jacksonville for nearly 45 days, trying to help her recover from horrific injuries she had sustained during the automobile crash that killed their unborn daughter, Sharon Lee. Frankie had been traveling to Florida so that Sharon Lee could be born in Jacksonville, her father's hometown. It became her burial site instead.

Operation Little Switch

From April 20 through May 3, 1953, UN and Communist forces were busy, but combat operations were not the primary agenda item. Instead, they were conducting "Operation Little Switch," not a general exchange of POW's, but the exchange of sick and wounded prisoners of the Korean War. The exchange had been agreed to on April 11, during the truce talks at Panmunjom. The breakthrough had begun months before with initiatives at the United Nations and the International Red Cross in Geneva. Later, UN Commander in Chief General Mark W. Clark used an indirect approach to reach North Korean Premier Kim Il Sung and Chinese General Peng Dehuai that eventually brought about the agreement.

During the two week period, the Communist side repatriated 684 UN sick and wounded troops—146 of whom were Americans—while the UN Command (UNC) returned 1,030 Chinese and 5,194 Koreans, together with 446 civilian internees.

Typically, the prisoner exchange was marked by strong disagreement and controversy. Returning Communist prisoners tried to embarrass their former captors by rejecting rations and clothing issued to them. Sensationalistic reports appeared in the Western press alleging that numbers of sick and wounded POWs were still being held by the Communists in spite of the exchange agreements. The polarizing issue that had prolonged the Korean War for two years—that no UN POW would be forcibly repatriated—had not been settled.

Later, there would be speculation that the surprising—to many observers—acceptance of this exchange may have been a result of uncertainty over Soviet policies after the death of Soviet Premier Joseph Stalin.

Will They Come Home, Will We Learn Something About Them?

"It is with deep regret I must advise you," General McCormick wrote to Della Lear on May 1, 1953, "that in the recent exchange of prisoners, no definite information was obtained concerning the welfare of your husband, Captain Leslie W. Lear. In an effort to obtain as much information as possible about the fate of our personnel who have been or may still be held by the enemy, the released prisoners are being questioned. All details regarding individuals with whom they came in personal contact while they were being held by the Communists as well as information they may have received by word-of-mouth is being officially recorded. In this manner and with the constant pressure on the Communists by our peace negotiators, we hope to secure positive facts and the earliest possible release of all prisoners. You will of course be notified immediately any additional information that becomes known concerning your husband."

An identical letter was sent to Frankie Connors on the same date.

We Surely Have A Common Interest

In Dubach, Louisiana, Ouida Preaus, Bob Holloway's mother, who had by then remarried after the death of her husband, Ira, wrote to Della Lear on May 23rd.

"I have wondered so often of those who, like myself, sit and wait. I am very glad you wrote to me. I presume you received the same information concerning your husband and my son as I did. At the time the accident occurred, one of my nephews was in Korea. He talked to some of the boys who saw it happen and he feels that they are P.O.W's. I always grasp at any hope, so maybe I can pass it along to you. Will you please write and tell me something of yourself? We may never see each other, but we surely have a common interest. I am a widow, age 42, and Bobby is my only child. As for Bob, he is 22, weighs when he left here 185, height 5'11", big brown eyes that sparkle and the most engaging smile I ever saw. You can easily see I have no reserve where he is concerned. Please do let me hear from you again while we wait, pray and hope," Ouida Preaus concluded.

Della Lear responded quickly to Bobby's mother and provided the information as requested. "As to details on my husband and myself, I am 27 years old. My husband was 28 this past March. We have been married for about eight years. Ours has been a perfect marriage. I naturally hope it is God's will that my husband will be returned to me so that our happy marriage can continue," Della wrote.

"Your son and my husband are much the same in stature—my husband being just a shade under six feet and weighing around 180 pounds. He has the brightest blue eyes I've ever seen. He is blond but borders on the sandy, redhead side. His hair is curly—if and when he will let it grow and which he seldom does because he prefers it cut very short. As to my husband's personality, well he is just perfect in every way—a very prejudiced wife's opinion. His happy chuckle is infectious. He is always willing to help a friend. He is quiet yet with a great deal of wit. From my knowledge of helicopters and my husband's skill as a pilot, I think there is little or no danger that our loved ones were killed in the helicopter crash. Actually a helicopter is safer than a conventional aircraft. I feel rather certain that our loved ones are prisoners of war," Della concluded.

Of course, Della was unaware of all the circumstances of the helicopter crash. In fact, had Wayne Lear exited the helicopter immediately after the hit on the rotor, his parachute would likely have opened as did Holloway's and he would have been a POW until September 1953. However, he tried to maintain enough control over the diving aircraft to give his passengers time enough to exit, and by doing so, he himself was killed.

Also writing on May 22nd, Dolly Sharp, Ron Eaton's fiancé, wrote to Della Lear. "I have received information that your husband, Captain Leslie W. Lear, was shot down over Wonsan, Korea while on a rescue mission on June 24 [sic], 1952. This information came to me by Mrs. Elsie Eaton of 809 North Main Street, Wilmington, Massachusetts, whose son, Ensign Ronald D. Eaton…means a great deal to me…[and] was the pilot your husband was rescuing. Since that date, Ronald has been listed as missing in action and we have received no further information as to his status. We do know, however, that when the helicopter crashed at least two persons were observed to have left the wreckage and presumably taken prisoner, but yet we have not received official word that he is a POW. If you have received any information concerning your husband or Ronald would you please write to his mother, Mrs. Elsie Eaton, or me as it would be deeply appreciated by his family as well as myself. May I join with you in your prayers and hopes that this separation will soon be at an end. Most sincerely, Dorothy Sharp."

Missing Beyond 12 Months

A 9 June 1953 Memorandum for the Air Force Deputy Chief of Staff for Personnel dealt with whether to continue the "Combat Missing Status Beyond Twelve Months" of Captain Leslie W. Lear and Staff Sergeant Bobby D. Holloway. Eaton's status would be determined by the Department of the Navy, the memo noted. The Memorandum was not shared with the families and was eventually included in the Individual Deceased Personal File maintained by the Department of the Army in Washington.

The Memorandum summarized what the Air Force knew at that time from the various sources to which it had access. That Lear and Holloway "comprised the crew of an H-5 helicopter which, on 25 June 1952, participated in a mission to rescue Ensign Ronald D. Eaton, a Navy pilot, who crashed in enemy territory."

Despite the helicopter being "seriously damaged by enemy fire," it effected a successful pick-up of the downed pilot and proceeded toward friendly territory. "Twenty-five miles northeast of Kumhwa, members of a flight of aircraft furnishing protective escort for the rescue plane observed pieces fly from the plane as it went into an uncontrolled diving spin. Prior to the crash, the three occupants abandoned the helicopter at altitudes varying from 800 to 300 feet. The first individual to bail out emerged from the right side of the plane [sic] and he was seen to land safely and remove his parachute. The other two persons were seen to strike the ground without having used their parachutes. Subsequent low level aerial observation of the area revealed that the enemy quickly gathered at the landing site, but the search failed to disclose evidence which would establish the identity of the individual who successfully parachuted or the fate of the other two persons."

The Memorandum then noted additional information that it had not shared with the families. "An unconfirmed report has been received which appears to relate to this incident and indicates that a pilot was captured on or about 23 June 1952, following the crash of a United Nations helicopter in the location where the subject incident occurred. The report did not mention his name and included no information concerning the fate of the other two individuals. A recent report from the Commander, Far East Air Forces, discloses that no new information has become known during the past year which would clarify the status of these missing persons."

The information of record for the Air Force revealed that "one occupant of the helicopter successfully parachuted form the plane and that in all probability he was the person referred to in the unconfirmed report which was subsequently received. This report failed to reveal the identity of the individual and it is not possible to establish whether the information related to Captain Lear, Sergeant Holloway, or Ensign Eaton. The unsuccessful parachute jump of two of those aboard the plane, whose names are unknown, strongly indicated that they perished. However, the incomplete information available precludes a definite determination as to their identity. Although none of these persons has been reported as a prisoner of war, this is no indication that such is not the case since the North Korean and Chinese Communists have consistently refused to submit complete and authentic information about our personnel who may have been or are now in their custody. Until new information is received establishing the identity of the survivor or other events occur which permit a definite conclusion regarding the fate of the Air Force personnel involved, any change in their status on this date may be premature and beyond the safe calculated risk of error." Lear and Holloway were "continued in a missing status."

Secret Memorandum: Connors May Be Prisoner

On June 12, 1953, a Secret Memorandum was prepared for the Air Force Deputy Chief of Staff for Personnel regarding the "continuance of Combat Missing Status Beyond Twelve Months" for SR&D Case #421, First Lieutenant Archibald H. Connors, Jr., and whether his MIA status "may reasonably be continued after a year's absence, or terminated by a presumptive finding of death."

"On June 25, 1952, Lieutenant Connors was a member of a flight of four F-51 aircraft furnishing protective cover for a helicopter attempting to rescue a Navy pilot downed in North Korea. The initial phase of the mission was accomplished successfully and the F-51's were escorting the rescue helicopter from the area when it was damaged by enemy ground fire and crashed to the ground. At this time, Lieutenant Connors radioed that his plane had been hit. The F-51 started a diving turn to the right from an altitude of approximately 500 feet, appeared to go into a flat stall, and crash landed on a small knoll near Piyang-dong, North Korea. The aircraft did not burn or explode upon impact. The flight leader made several low passes over the crash scene but failed to observe any sign of Lt. Connors."

An Air Intelligence Report, General Ives noted in the classified memorandum, "contains evidence indicating that Lieutenant Connors may be in custody of the enemy. The information was obtained from an enemy soldier captured on June 28, 1952. His report reveals that an aircraft, believed to be an F-51, crashed on June 25, 1952, and that the pilot was captured. The crash is presumed to have occurred in the same general area where a United States Air Force rescue helicopter was also downed. The name of the F-51 pilot was not revealed; however, Far East Air Forces has advised that it is believed the report refers to Lieutenant Connors."

An examination of all available information "compels the conclusion that a reasonable possibility exists for the continued survival of Lt. Connors. This conclusion is supported by the recorded evidence, which discloses that he apparently made a successful crash landing in enemy territory and could have been easily captured. The unconfirmed information contained in an Air Intelligence Report tends to substantiate this conclusion. The absence of a report officially establishing his status as a prisoner of war is no indication that such is not the case since the North Korean and Chinese Communists have consistently refused to submit complete and authentic information about our personnel who may have been or are now in their custody. Until new evidence is produced or other events occur which overcome this possibility, it is reasonable to assume that he may still be alive and that any change in his status on this date may be premature and beyond the safe calculated risk of error."

General Ives then recommended that an official casualty report be issued that would continue Lieutenant Connors in a missing in action status following the expiration of an absence of twelve months.

The Deputy Chief of Staff for Personnel approved the "continuance in a missing status after a 12-months' absence."

In all likelihood, the enemy soldier did have some knowledge of the Mission 1890 crashes, but misidentified Holloway, the sole survivor, as a "pilot."

This memorandum was not shared with the family as it was classified as Secret or Confidential until 1980. However, it was included in Connors' Individual Deceased Personal File, which was obtained in 2000 by the family. Subsequent events would suggest that an Air Force Intelligence Officer had access to this report or the information upon which it was based and shared it with Archie's widow, Frankie. That information would raise what would turn out to be false hopes for his survival, hopes the Connors' family clung to for several years.

On June 26, 1953, both Della and Frankie received similar letters from Major General McCormick expressing his "sincere regret that the fate of your husband…is still uncertain after a year's absence and also to notify you that he is to be continued in a missing in action status for the reasons explained below."

The recording and changing of the status of missing personnel are controlled by public law 490, 77th Congress, as amended, but widely known as the Missing Persons Act. "This section of this law which applies to [the] case requires a full review of all known facts and circumstances when a 12 month period of absence in a missing status is about to expire. It authorizes either a continuance of the Missing Status until new evidence develops for a presumptive finding of death, which ever appears warranted by the available evidence."

"The review just completed concerning your husband," McCormick wrote to Della Lear, "reveals that on 25 June 1952, he was a crew member [pilot] of an H-5 helicopter which participated in a mission to rescue a Navy pilot who crashed in enemy territory. During rescue operations, the helicopter was seriously damaged by enemy machine-gun fire, but effected a successful pick-up of the Navy pilot and proceeded toward friendly territory. Twenty-five miles northeast of Kumhwa, the plane suddenly went into an uncontrolled spin. Prior to its crash, members of a flight of fighter aircraft, furnishing protective escort for this mission, observed the three occupants abandon the helicopter at altitudes varying from 800 to 300 feet. Two were seen to strike the ground without having made use of their parachutes and the other landed safely and disappeared from view. Regrettably, his identity could not be established and the sudden appearance of the enemy in the area prevented further search and rescue efforts. To date, no further information has been received which might clarify the fate of your husband and other two persons involved."

"The review just completed concerning your husband," McCormick wrote to Frankie about Archie, "discloses that on 25 June 1952, he was a member of a flight of four F-51 aircraft furnishing protective cover for a helicopter attempting to rescue a Navy pilot downed in North Korea. The initial phase of the mission was accomplished successfully and the F-51's were escorting the rescue helicopter from the area when it was damaged by enemy ground fire and crashed to the ground. At this time, Lieutenant Connors radioed that his F-51 had been hit. Your husband's plane started a diving turn to the right, appeared to go into a flat stall and crash-landed on a small knoll near Piyang-dong, North Korea. The F-51 did not burn or explode upon impact. The flight leader made several low passes over the crash scene but failed to observe any sign of Lt. Connors. Regrettably, no further information has been received which might clarify his status."

The remainder of the letter was similar for both Lear and Connors.

"The limited information that is available concerning the disappearance of your husband does not justify any change in his status at this time, particularly in view of the continuous refusal of the enemy to conform with international agreements in submitting reports about our personnel known to be deceased or in their custody. Lt. Connors will therefore be continued in a missing in action status until new information is received or other facts develop which will resolve the present uncertainty about his actual fate. Meanwhile, his pay and allowances will continue to be credited to his account and allotments will continue to be paid to authorized allottees. In previous correspondence we expressed our vital interest in securing whatever information becomes known to you about your husband status through other than official channels. I want to again ask your cooperation in notifying this headquarters of any communication you may receive from or concerning Lt. Connors. I realize how disheartening it must be to learn nothing more about your husband after these many months, and hoped with you that his true status may in time be resolved. You will of course be notified of any new information which may become known," McCormick promised them.

Eaton Continued As Missing

The Bureau of Naval Personnel added a file to Ensign Ron Eaton's "Jacket" on June 26, 1953, that concerned his "continuation of missing status." Eaton had been carried in a missing status since he was shot down on 25 June 1952.

"According to a report made by the Commanding Officer of Fighter Squadron 74, dated 30 June 1952, Ensign Eaton was with a large group of planes which were assigned targets near the front lines," the statement by M. S. Reeder, Head of the Casualty Branch noted.

"Upon approaching the target in an area of intense anti-aircraft fire, Ensign Eaton radioed that his engine was losing power, and later radioed that he was abandoning his plane. He was observed to land safely and run for cover in some trees. That night a helicopter arrived and rescued Ensign Eaton but was hit by anti-aircraft fire and crashed. The survivors of the crash were captured by the Communist forces. In view of the fact that Ensign Eaton could have been one of the survivors of the crash who was captured, it is recommended pursuant to the provisions of Public Law 490, 77th Congress as amended, that he be continued as missing in action, possibly captured."

Writing To Former POW's

The Air Force prepared a "Casualty Report" on Connors dated 2 July 1953 that summarized the circumstances surrounding his Missing in Action status and listed three "beneficiaries" based on DD Form 93 dated 20 January 1952, including his wife, Frankie, mother, Eva and father, Arch Connors. "Following a full review of all available information it is held by the Department of the Air Force that this individual is to be continued in a missing-in-action status following the expiration of 12 month's absence."

"We wish to thank you for all previous correspondence and information concerning our son, First Lieutenant A.H. Connors, Jr.," Arch and Eva

Connors wrote the Air Force on July 7, 1953. "It is our desire to write to the recently returned prisoners of war, and if possible, secure further information. Enclosed are mimeographed letters that we would mail, along with pictures of the men involved in this rescue mission. That is, if this meets with your approval and if you will send us a list of the prisoners of war and their mailing addresses. We have a partial list of about 60 men that we clipped from the local newspapers but hope that we may secure a complete list. Please advise. In sincere appreciation, we are, sincerely yours."

Arch and Eva proposed a form letter to General McCormick that they would address to 140 recently returned prisoners of war." *[exchanged during Operation Little Switch]* The letter would include information about Mission 1890 and photos of Lear, Connors and Eaton, explaining that "these men were lost while on a rescue mission, described in the enclosed letters. We would very much appreciate your reading these letters, examining the pictures, and informing us whether you have seen any of these men in a prisoner of war camp, or know anything pertaining to their fate or the outcome of this incident."

The Connors form letter would enclose a self-addressed stamped envelope and expressed their "congratulations on your release—we know how happy your family must be that you once more are with them."

The Air Force answer came three weeks later.

On July 8, 1953, the 2370th Air Base Squadron received a new casualty report on 1st Lt. Connors—"still MIA."

An "Official Statement of Service" was signed by Col. K. E. Thiebaud, USAF on 10 July 1954 for Lt. Connors. The reason for the compilation is not given.

"Archibald Haddock Connors, Junior, 557 83 31, enlisted in the United States Naval Reserve on 26 July 1945 and honorably discharged 12 August 1946. He had active duty from 23 January 1946 to 12 August 1946. He enlisted in the United States Air Force on 26 May 1950, was assigned service number AF 14 353 100, and entered on active duty on 26 May 1950. He was honorably discharged 22 June 1951 to accept a commission. No time was lost under AW 107. He was appointed Second Lieutenant, United States Air Force Reserve, 23 June 1951; accepted 23 June 1951; assigned service number AO 2 221 998; promoted First Lieutenant, temporary (spot), 10 April 1952; promotion as First Lieutenant, temporary (spot), terminated 15 April 1953; promoted First Lieutenant, United States Air Force, 15 April 1953 to rank from 10 April 1952. He has been on continuous active duty as a commissioned officer since 23 June 1951. He has been missing in action since 25 June 1952."

On 8 July 1953 the Army Effects Agency in Kansas City, Kansas sent a message to the Camp Drew Quartermaster Sub Depot, Personal Effects

Division in Japan requesting the "status of Army Effects Agency letter dated 7 April 1953, concerning personal effects of Capt. Leslie W. Lear."

A 17 July message from Camp Drew to the Army Effects Agency in Kansas City, Missouri indicated that Capt. Lear's personal effects had been forwarded "to your agency" in a shipment on 25 June 1953, exactly one year after Mission 1890.

July 18, 1953, the Long Beach Squadron case officer made a personal visit to Frankie and noted the "address of NOK is changed. Sent letter to Washington with correct address."

An Expedite Memo on 27 July 1953 to the Tally in Clerk at the Army Effects Agency in Kansas City regarding Lear's personal effects warned the clerk "since wife has knowledge of the items in the F/L watch the removals." Was pilfering of personal effects such a pervasive problem that an internal warning was necessary?

On August 25, 1953 an Effects Inventory was conducted on Capt. Lear's personal effects and stamped "DAMAGED." The "effects are slightly soiled. Lock is missing on F.L. [foot locker]."

On 27 July the Effects Agency wrote to Della Lear and referred to "previous correspondence" promising to "contact the Far East Command in an endeavor to obtain some information regarding a foot locker belonging to your husband...As a result of this action, we have just received a report stating his locker had been located and presently is en route…assume we should receive the locker within the next sixty to ninety days."

Prisoners And Peace Talks

Sergeant (unknown to him at the time, Holloway had been promoted) Bobby Holloway and other POW's had little idea of how the war was proceeding. Of course, they knew that "peace talks" were underway at the time he was captured. But without news of any kind, there was no way to know how long they might be held. One Chinese guard, "for some reason," Holloway remembered, "I'll never know why, would come around and "tell" me how the peace talks were going. He would say only good or bad meaning this is how the peace talks are going. If there was anyone else around, he would say nothing.

Armistice Signed

On July 27, 1953, thirty seven months after the war had started the United Nations, North Korea and China signed an armistice, which ended the active hostilities but failed to bring about a permanent peace. To date, the Republic of Korea (South) and Democratic Peoples' Republic of Korea (North) have not signed a peace treaty. A total of 33,651 service members died in battle during the Korean War; 27,709 U.S. Army; 4,269 U.S. Marines; 1,198 U.S. Air Force; and 475 U.S. Navy. Some 7,140 service members became prisoners of war.

One of the provisions of the Armistice Agreement included the exchange of military war dead on both sides. In the months that followed after July 1953, members of the U.S. Graves Registration Division in Korea met repeatedly with United Nations and Eighth Army officials to work out the details for how such an exchange might be effected. A draft plan was approved and signed by all the major parties on the Allied side in early July 1954, and was then forwarded to Communist officials. They, in turn, signed the new agreement on July 20, 1953. It included a provision that the exchange of deceased personnel should commence on 1 September 1954 and end no later than 30 October.

From August 5 through December 23, 1953, the opposing sides conducted "Operation Big Switch," the final exchange of prisoners of war by both sides. It too, was characterized by opposing view regarding voluntary repatriation. There were also allegations of brainwashing and torture of UN POWs by the Communists.

During much arguing over the issue of forced repatriation of POWs, Communist negotiators insisted on the return of all captured nationals held by the United Nations Command. This position was adamantly opposed

Truce Headlines. *The headlines scream "Truce Signed," and provide the best reason possible for a celebratory photograph of 18^{tth} Wing armorers at their K-55 base. (L-R) Wilbur Short, Thomas Greene, Merle Keaton and an unidentified Airman. In front, Airman William Ackeridge (right), joins Airman Stanley Bist (left) in their widest grins as they hold the long awaited news. The folded bedroll at left might be a sign someone was ready to head back to the States and home. (Bist)*

by the U.S. and South Korean governments. Some of the other governments that had provided forces to the UN command in Korea argued that the principle of voluntary repatriation should not be permitted to obstruct an early conclusion of hostilities.

Eventually, a UN Neutral Nations Repatriation Commission (NNRC), chaired by India, took responsibility for prisoners that had indicated a desire to remain with their captors. The process included a 90-day period during which the N.N.R.C. maintained custody of the "non-repatriates." The non-returnees were then provided with a series of "explanations" during which they were advised strongly to return to their home nations. Most were not convinced.

For the families of servicemen who had been listed as captured or missing in action, it was a time of both hope and anxiety, excitement and dread. If Ron or Wayne or Archie were alive they would soon be coming home. Hallelujah for answered prayers. The living and the lives that had been on hold for so long could be restarted. The empty feeling in the pit of one's stomach that had become a part of each bleak day, could be filled with the promise of a now brighter future.

But if one or more of them didn't come home—what then?

If one or two of them did come home, but not all—what then for the affected family?

Days were spent with earshot of the radio or one of the still relatively few television sets. At the end of each news broadcast hungry eyes would search the scrolling lists of names for a Lear or Connors or Eaton. When the names were not there the emptiness increasingly became an abyss that grew wider as it divided each family from the present and the fading hope of ever leading a normal life again.

Three Names Provided

In a July 29, 1953 letter, General McCormick answered Arch and Eva Connors' letter of July 7th requesting an address listing of repatriated POWs. He did not provide the names of all the released POW's, only the three Air Force personnel that had been sent home, including: Captain Zach Dean, and Airmen William Hilycord and Robert Weibrandt. "We have no objections to your form letters nor to pictures being forwarded to our repatriated Personnel in your attempt to obtain further information concerning your son, First Lieutenant Archibald H. Connors, Jr. However, occasionally we found that the returnees, when discussing individuals with the next of kin, have related some details not mentioned during the official interrogation is. Since any information you may obtain regarding your son will be of interest to this headquarters, would you be kind enough to advise us. Your cooperation in this matter will be greatly appreciated."

Truce Signed, POW's Treated better

In August 1953, Holloway was finally told he was going home soon. "I knew everything was real good, especially when we began getting better food," he remembered. By then Holloway had lost over 40 pounds.

"They gave us a pig…we were feeding about 30-50 people. We finally butchered and cooked that pig. Boy that little bit of meat tasted so good. You sat there and chewed that meat for 20 minutes before you swallowed it."

"One guy got a small package. The reason I remember that is because it had a small package of coffee in it. We brewed one cup of instant coffee. That's all it would make. I remember everybody got a little sip…until the coffee was down to about half a cup…then we filled the cup up again with hot water…and everybody had a sip…until the cup was half full…then we refilled the cup," Holloway recalled. "We refilled that cup of 'coffee' so many times that finally the water wasn't even colored. Boy that was a GOOD cup of coffee."

"After they finally let us know about the Armistice at 'loll call'…We finally figured out they weren't going to shoot us." Holloway recalled.

Hope We Hear From Our Son Real Soon

"Dear Mrs. Lear," Elsie Eaton began her letter of September 2, 1953, "I'm very sorry to have had so much time lapse since you wrote to me. I do hope we hear from our son and you hear from your husband real soon. We have been praying for the return of our loved ones. It seems as tho things are looking brighter as we read in the paper of the release of Bobby D. Holloway a couple of nights ago. He, you know, was in the same accident our loved ones were in so maybe we will soon have word of some kind. I am enclosing a copy of the letter which was written by Ronnie's Commander to me. I want to thank you for the copies of letters you sent me regarding your husband. It all helps to understand the situation. Have you heard anything about or from your husband? I haven't heard a word from my son." Sincerely yours, Elsie Adela Eaton.

Bernard and Elsie Eaton 1954.

"Your Son Was Released"

Writing to Bobby Holloway's mother, Ouida Preaus on September 2nd, Della Lear was glad to have "noticed in our local papers that your son was released as a POW the night before last. I am thankful that your prayers have been answered. I sincerely hope your son will be with you very soon. I have just one request to make—if your son has any information about my husband (whether good or bad news), I would greatly appreciate his forwarding such information to me. I fully realize that it has probably been an experience that he will want to try to forget as quickly as possible. Yet, if he can help to clear up the facts and circumstances involved in the helicopter crash, I would appreciate hearing any and all details. No doubt he has made a full report to the Government. I really don't think that I have to explain further to you—you well know the anxiety caused by a situation such as this," Della wrote. "My very best wishes to you and your son for a future full of happiness."

The next morning, a telegraph time stamped 0831 arrived for Della from Mrs. Harry Preaus, Sr. "My son, Bobby Holloway, was freed Monday night. Let me hear from you."

"...Not Among Those Repatriated"

On September 4th the Far East Command Personal Effects Depot requested that 3ARS send additional personal effects of Capt. Leslie W. Lear that had been received from the states as "hold baggage" and arrived on 8 August 1952, to the Personal Effects Depot "for consolidation with those already received for Capt. Lear." According to a 3ARS memorandum the late arriving effects were sent along to Far East Command, Personal Effects Depot on 12 August 1952.

Another telegram for Della Lear arrived on September 6th from Major General McCormick. "We have now been advised of the completion of the

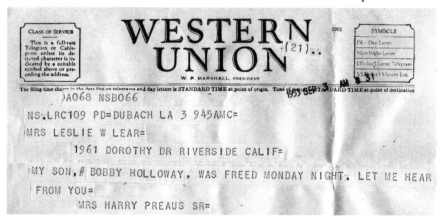

exchange of prisoners under the terms of the truce with the North Korean-Chinese Communists signed 27 July 1953," he wrote.

"I deeply regret that your husband, Captain Leslie W. Lear, was not among those repatriated. You may be sure the personnel released by the Communists are being questioned extensively in an effort to secure any information available concerning your loved one. All data concerning Air Force personnel who were not repatriated will be carefully evaluated by the Department of the Air Force in accordance with the Missing Persons Act. Pending completion of this review and final determination of his status, all pay and allowances will continue as in the past. You will be kept informed of any new developments. My sincere sympathy is again extended to you at this trying time."

"I Feel Sure That He Is Alive"

"Since my husband, 1st Lt. Archibald H. Connors, Jr. was not returned by the Communists," Frankie Connors wrote the Air Force on September 9, 1953, "I feel sure he is still alive and being held yet. A friend of mine told me his name was among those the communists turned over to us at the beginning of the exchange, saying he was in Camp No. 4. Please, if there is anything we can do, let's try. I'm positive he's still alive and there must be some way they will give him up. Thank you for all you've done for my morale so far."

General McCormick telegrammed Della Lear on September 10th and referred to his telegram of the 6th "in the truce signed with the North Korean and Chinese Communists. An agreement was effected whereby they would return all prisoners of war desiring repatriation and submit a list of the names of persons who refuse repatriation, escaped from their custody, or died while in their custody. Unofficial and unverified information indicates that all facts available to the Communists have not been released by them. In an effort to secure additional information, a list of Air Force personnel was submitted to the Communists with an urgent request for an accounting of those persons. The name of your husband, Captain Leslie W. Lear, was included on this list," McCormick assured her. "May I again assure you that you will be kept informed of any new developments."

A week later, on September 16th, McCormick explained to Frankie Connors that "in the truce signed with the North Korean and Chinese Communists, an agreement was effected whereby they would return all prisoners of war desiring repatriation, and submit a list of the names of persons who refuse repatriation, escaped from their custody, or died while in their custody. Unofficial and unverified information indicates that all facts available to the Communists have not been released by them. In an effort to secure additional information, a list of Air Force personnel was submitted to the

Communists with an urgent request for an accounting of those persons. The name of your husband was included on this list. May I again assure you that you will be kept informed of any new developments. I regret that as of this date no further information has been received. However, you are assured that upon receipt of any and all information that may be obtained, you will be immediately notified. My sympathy continues during this trying period of waiting."

Writing To Archie VIA Panmunjom

"Dear Archie," nephew Tracy Connors, wrote on September 13, 1953, "it's me. I'm a senior at Kirby-Smith [Junior High School] now. Christy's almost two now [his sister, born in November, 1951]. MAN have things happened since you were shot down."

Tracy had decided to try and write to his uncle and to send the letter to him via the negotiators at "Tent City," Panmunjom, where some mail was being exchanged for prisoners as they waited to be repatriated. The Connors family still held out hopes that Lt. Connors might yet be among those returned.

"We got word that you were alive Saturday. What a relief to know that. We got word that you had been shot down on the 25th of June, 1952," Tracy pecked out painfully on a manual typewriter, three years before he would actually take a typing class.

The following passage in the letter, returned to its author many months later, is quite factually garbled. However, it represented the misleading or partially true information the family was processing through that period of waiting, clinging to any hope, however faint.

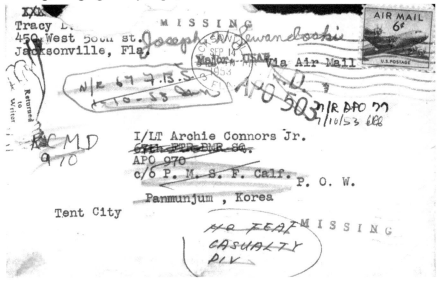

"Then at school one day I met Ensign Glen Moore. He told me about a Navy pilot going down and four Sabers going in after them and keeping the Comies off him for two hours and then you guys going in and bringing a helicopter in with you. You were 80 miles behind the lines and got within 20 miles of our lines before it was hit and then you were hit and said, "May Day, I'm hit" and went down in a slow spiral. You landed on a small knoll. The plane did not disintegrate or burn. The squadron leader made four passes over your plane but you did not get out. That's all we knew until now," Tracy summed up.

"Every Saturday night we went over to grandmother's to have a prayer service and talk. Saturday night we had just started the service when the telephone rang. Grandpa picked up the receiver and started saying, "Praise the Lord, praise the Lord. Thank the Lord." Then out of the side of his mouth he said, 'Archie's alive.' So I knew they would let you go because we knew that you're alive. I've prayed for you every day. Hope you feel better. Your Loving Nephew, Tracy D. Connors, Sr." Then, he added a "P.S. A.H. Sr. has a new car, a blue Plymouth."

He knew Archie would understand that. The night Arch received the call [source unknown] was the only night when, at the end of the sentence prayers, he added "Amen." The family wept quietly.

Incredibly, in the days of a legendary postal service, the letter came back many months later, covered in postmarks. It had made its way through many hands, several of which had stamped "Missing."

"Wonderful News Of Archie"

"Dear Mom and Pop," Frankie Connors wrote on September 12, 1953, "I'm so disappointed in not seeing you. Guess Pop has lots of business so will forgive you."

"Had some wonderful news of Archie. A friend of mine overseas in the Air Force Intelligence looked into Archie's case. He found out the Communists informed the Allies Archie was in Camp #4 as of July 20th-53. There's no reason for them to lie as I can see and the govt. is demanding they account for him. So I'm sure he's alive and that's all I care about. He'll get back eventually and we've waited this long. It's so good to really know he's alive and all those prayers were heard. Just remind Pop that "I told him so." Remember?"

"Ruth and I have been working hard. She's at Lockheed also. My new job is so much more interesting and keeps me on my toes. When Archie comes back my boss wants me to take a leave, in case Archie is stationed around here so I can come back [to work for Lockheed]. Now that I've started working I like it. Maybe Archie won't."

"Write me and tell me all the news. It won't be long now before we will have Archie back. I won't know what to do with a husband again but

I'm sure anxious to find out. Loads of Love, Frankie."

The sad, depressed tone of her last letters to Archie are gone. Her future, like the closing of her chipper, upbeat letter, at last held "loads of love."

Four days later, on September 16th, General McCormick replied to Frankie's letter of September 9th asking for information about her husband. "As stated in my telegram of 10 September, your husband's name has been submitted to the North Korean-Chinese Communists for an accounting. I regret that as of this date no further information has been received. However, you may be assured that upon receipt of any and all information that may be obtained, you will be immediately notified. My sympathy continues during this trying period of waiting," he closed.

Lt. Connors' Name Among PWs Held

Mr. and Mrs. A. H. Connors Sr. of 3165 Broadway Ave. said last night they had received word that the name of their son, 1st Lt. Archibald H. Connors Jr., 26, appears on the list of 944 American prisoners of war still unaccounted for by the Communists in Korea.

The Air Force pilot was reported missing in action in June, 1952. Since that date, no word had been received of him until his wife, living in California, was notified that his name appears on the Pentagon list of prisoners still held by the Reds.

The lieutenant's wife was informed that the Communists had told the U.S. War Department on July 20 that Lt. Connors was in Camp 4, North Korea.

Looking For Names In The News

On July 27, 1953, an armistice was finally signed ending active hostilities in the Korean War. The U.S. had lost 103,284 wounded, and 36,516 killed. Over 4,000 were reported missing in action. Archie Connors was among them.

Not long after that, as prisoners were being exchanged—repatriated—a returning American POW reported that he had seen Lt. Archie Connors as late as July 20, 1953, being held as a prisoner in Camp Four in North Korea. Connors' name appeared on a list of 944 American prisoners unaccounted for by the North Koreans. Hopeful articles appeared in the Jacksonville newspapers. The U.S. government remained silent.

Every evening as the Connors family watched newscaster Douglas Edwards on network television, their eyes were riveted on the names of those American POWs repatriated that day that were slowly scrolled up the screen. Archie's name never appeared.

"The names of nine more Riverside area men, whose fate in the Korean fighting has not been accounted for by the Communists, were released today by the Defense Department," the Riverside Daily Press reported on Saturday, September 12, 1953.

"These men are among 944 missing Americans believed captured in Korea, but never reported by the Communists. Pentagon officials voiced the heartbreaking belief that many of the 944 have died in prison camps. The United Nations command in Korea submitted the names to the Communists Monday at a meeting of the Joint Military Armistice Commission. The U.N. demanded an accounting for each man listed. Officials hope that some of the Americans on the list may still be alive. The Communists say they have returned all U.N. prisoners desiring repatriation. Belief that the missing men were captured by the Communists is based on a compilation of reports by repatriated Americans, Red radio broadcasts and personal letters," the Daily Press noted and listed Captain Leslie W. Lear as among the nine Riverside area men on the list.

"To the wives of three of the four Riverside Air Force officers listed Saturday as presumed prisoners of war not accounted for by the Communists, the news came as the bitterest of disappointments," the Riverside, California Daily Press noted on September 18, 1953. "To the fourth wife, however, it brought the first glimmer of hope that her husband might still be alive."

"Not until last week did Mrs. Della Marie Lear, 1961 Dorothy Drive, learn that her husband, Capt. Leslie W. Lear, might be, or had once been, a prisoner of war. He had been missing in action since June 25, 1952,

Hope Is Renewed For Jax Pilot Lost In Korea

Hope for the life of a Jacksonville Air Force pilot, missing since June 25, 1952, in Korea, was renewed here yesterday when his parents received word he was seen alive as late as July 20 this year in a North Korean prison camp.

The pilot is 1st Lt. Archibald H. Connors Jr., 26, son of Mr. and Mrs. A. H. Connors of 3165 Broadway Ave. His name appeared this week in a Los Angeles newspaper on a list of 944 American prisoners still unaccounted for by the Communists.

Connors' wife, who lives in Glendale, Calif., learned that a returnee had seen her husband in Camp 4, North Korea, in July.

Connors was in a flight of four F-51 Mustang fighter bombers flying cover for a helicopter of the Air Rescue Command. The helicopter was picking up a downed naval flyer, Ens. Ronald D. Eaton of Wilmington, Mass.

The rescue was made but the helicopter and Connors' fighter were knocked down by enemy fire.

Capt. Leslie W. Lear of Riverside, Calif., pilot of the helicopter, was on the same list of unaccounted for prisoners released by the Pentagon last week.

However, the medical technician on the helicopter, Bobby D. Holloway of Dubach, La., has been released by the Communists and is due back in the U. S. Holloway's mother telegraphed the news of her son's release to the local family and informed them Holloway would write to them shortly.

The Defense Department still lists Connors as officially missing in action.

when his helicopter was shot down during a rescue mission. Like the other wives, Mrs. Lear had never heard any direct word from her husband since he was reported missing. The others, however, had all had previous notification from the Defense Department that their husbands might be in Communist custody. "I think it's always best to hope," Mrs. Lear said. "That's what keeps a person going."

Captain Lear "participated in many air rescue missions around Riverside from 1948 to 1950," the Daily Press noted.

Another of the wives quoted in the Daily Press article, Mrs. Irma Austin, wife of Major Arthur M. Austin, missing since April 27, 1951 was "pessimistic" over the news. "I just can't go through another disappointment," she said.

On September 3rd, The Army Effects Agency wrote Della Lear, confirming that it had "received additional property belonging to your husband, Captain Leslie W. Lear," advised her that she did not have title "pending final determination of his status," and requested a receipt for the foot locker."

Ham Sandwich Welcome Home

After being released in early September 1953, now Staff Sergeant Holloway "sailed under the Golden Gate Bridge on the afternoon of 20 September 1953. The Air Force wanted to fly all the Air Force prisoners back. But the Army was in charge and they sent all of us back by transport. Every military person that was on that ship was given a job to do—from cleaning to cooking—except the former POWs. They wouldn't let us do anything. But with two weeks at sea and nothing to occupy your time, it got rather boring. You started looking for something to do. You just can't take standing around."

When Holloway arrived in San Francisco, and was about to leave the ship, "a Major and a Lt. Col. from Hamilton AFB talked to me…they were from Air Rescue... they caught me as I came off the ship…interviewed me," he recalled.

After the interview, someone finally asked if anyone was hungry. The food on board the ship wasn't bad, but most of the returning POW's wanted steak." However, what Holloway "really wanted was a ham and cheese sandwich."

"At lunch they said what do you want for lunch when we reached this very nice restaurant on Lombard Street. We sat down…the waiter asked for my order. 'I want a ham and cheese sandwich,' I told the waiter. The Colonel added, 'this gentleman has just returned from Korea where he was a POW for over a year.' Now I have had many sandwiches," Holloway recalled, "but never one quite like this one."

"You would never have believed that sandwich unless you had seen it. It must have been a foot high…crammed with ham and cheese and lettuce and tomato in alternating layers."

"The bread was toasted, then a layer of ham and a layer of cheese, lettuce, ham and cheese, tomato, ham and cheese, lettuce, ham and cheese, etc. It was so thick you couldn't just bite off a piece; you had to work at it slowly. That was probably the best sandwich I have ever had."

Holloway ate "the who-o-o-o-le, thing."

When the waiter brought the bills, "he did so with a flourish—like he was dealing cards. 'Here's yours, and yours, and yours…and yours,' he said looking at me…'is on the house…compliments of the chef,'" Holloway laughed. The ham and cheese sandwich was Bob Holloway's Welcome Home.

The Visit with Della

After more interviews the Air Rescue Service representatives took Holloway to a hotel and told him they would pick him up the next morning and to get the processing finished and get him "on the way home."

When the former POW's were getting on the bus, had Holloway stepped up into the bus "my Mom would have seen me. As it was, I didn't get that far, so she missed me at the dock."

That night he received a telephone call from his Mother—"somehow she had contacted someone, who finally found out where I was at the time. I don't know who. We got together that night and made plans to leave as soon as I finished processing, which didn't take too long."

What Holloway did not know at the time "was that my Mother had planned to stop in Riverside and visit with Mrs. Lear. I tried in vain to talk her out of this, but to no avail. I just did not want to face her at that time. What could I say? Right about then I would have rather faced a constipated grizzly with a sore tooth."

Mrs. Preaus "was adamant, so we went to Riverside, where we met a gracious Lady, who looked at me and said, 'Please take that footlocker out of the car and take it inside,'" Holloway recalled.

"Being there was a very hard thing to do," he said. "How do you tell someone you just met that a loved one isn't coming back? Someone you decided you liked, even though she was ordering you around!"

The Arrivals

It was a pleasant fall day in Riverside, California, when Della Lear received word that her husband's personal effects had finally arrived at the Riverside, California railroad depot. It had taken her over a year to get them back from Korea. She asked for some time off from her administrative position at the University of California Campus (just being opened in Riverside) to pick up the footlocker.

At the station she got some help from a porter in getting the footlocker into the truck of her green Buick and headed home, her mind in turmoil thinking about what was in the trunk and what it represented. These were the same personal items that she had packed herself so many months ago, that Wayne had used for the brief six weeks he was in Korea before Mission 1890, and then were inventoried and packed by someone else when he didn't return. In a daze, she drove back home, turned into her driveway and parked. Just a she was wondering how she was going to get the heavy foot locker out of the trunk, a strange car pulled up to the curb with two men and a woman inside.

"I did not have any advance warning that Bob, his mother and stepfather would be arriving at my front door that very afternoon," she later explained. "In fact, I had just driven in my driveway when their car drove up. I realized who they must be and my heart just about stopped beating—very mixed emotions. Here was someone from my husband's crash who might still give me some hope—information that might lead to another prisoner—Wayne."

Understandably, Della was "so shook-up" that she doesn't recall "whether or not I was as friendly and polite as I should have been. I just recall saying to Bob—'Wayne's footlocker is in the trunk of my car—will you please take it out for me?' I do recall that I finally found my manners and we were seated in my living room for a friendly chat. However, I could sense a strained manner in Bob—almost as though he did not want to recall the entire incident. I wondered whether or not I should push for more details or wait until he had longer to come to terms with all that had gone on in prison camp. It was a most difficult time for me. Needless to say, I wanted any and all information that I could get."

Della Lear had no way of knowing that for Sergeant Holloway, the visit with her was the hardest thing he had had to do since he had started the fateful mission nearly a year and half earlier.

"I believe that if anyone had said something about 'we shouldn't be doing this,' we would have turned the car around and been gone. I just dreaded—dreaded—talking to her," he recalled.

"Did you think that I was going to ask 'why you and not Wayne,'" Della asked Bobby during an interview many years later.

"I don't know," he said, "not knowing someone…I admit I was kinda high strung right about then—I was strung pretty tight."

"Fortunately, I could see that," Della answered. "I felt that I shouldn't ask him too many questions, but I'm sure that I did ask him a great many questions. I just had to know for my own peace of mind. I now regret that there was not more of an attempt to get Wayne's family involved in meeting with Bobby. It was just so emotional and overwhelming at the time. They didn't live that far away. We lived in Riverside, they lived in Santa Anna. But I could see the agitated way Bob was at the time. I didn't think he could go through it again. And, I so appreciated his willingness to talk to me. Perhaps we can do this at a later date, I thought, but it was never done. As a result the Lear family became alienated," she said.

All too soon, Bob Holloway and his mother, explained that they had "to be on their way and would not even spend the night in Riverside before heading for Ruston, Louisiana—many miles away."

Now that Bob was in town and in her living room, Della was hoping for a longer visit.

"I felt we all needed time to digest the information and ask questions. I particularly wanted Bob to visit with Wayne's parents. He absolutely refused to do this," she recalled.

Della hoped that Bob would change his mind and she gently encouraged him to stay over for a day or so, and to visit with Wayne's parents. "At the time, I hoped that he would change his mind," she said.

In coming years, Della's relationship with Wayne's family would be strained. When Della did not somehow force Bob to meet with them, they blamed Della.

"This was the start to my later having problems with Wayne's parents—they never really forgave me for not forcing the issue with Bob. At that time, I was trying desperately trying to think of all the individuals' feelings," she explained.

Returning to Shreveport

"After leaving Riverside," Holloway recalled, "the trip was uneventful, except, when we left El Paso, Texas, I drove straight through to Shreveport, Louisiana, with stops only for food and gas. That was quite a drive."

All returned Korean War POW's were considered "patients," and as such, had been assigned to a hospital.

Based on what he heard through the grape vine of all the returning Air Force POW's, three did not get the hospital of their choice—"I was one of the three."

Holloway had requested the hospital at Barksdale AFB. Instead, he was assigned to a hospital in Hot Springs, Arkansas.

"When I checked in there, at the end of my travel time, they told me that they would get me a bed on one of the wards and in three or four days get one of the doctors to give me a physical. I told them that just was not acceptable. My mom and a friend were with me and that I would like to start my convalescent leave. No one seemed to want to listen, so I asked the Deputy Commander of the hospital if he had a phone I could use. He wanted to know who I needed to talk to and I told him I needed to talk to the Commanding General of the Air Rescue Service, in Washington, D.C."

"That seemed to turn things around and I got my physical that evening," Holloway recalled with a smile.

After a hasty OSI [Office of Special Investigations] interview in Little Rock, Holloway was released on 30 days leave after which he was assigned to the Air Rescue Unit at Ellington, AFB.

A Visit With The Holloways

It was many days before Della's emotions settled down somewhat from the Holloway visit and the strangely disturbing fact that Wayne's personal effects were sitting in a trunk that was just around the corner from her room.

About two weeks later, Della's telephone rang. It was Ouida Preaus, Bob's mother, pleading for Della to come to Ruston, Louisiana.

"Bob was having nightmares about the whole thing and she felt that I could help. I still really don't know why she felt that way—unless Bob had said or done something that caused her to think I could be the key that would unlock his bad memories and put them to rest. I never had the courage to ask her 'why,'" Della recalled.

With mixed feelings, Della "made the necessary arrangements" to travel to Louisiana. However, there were no direct flights to Monroe, so Bob told her "he could pick me up at the Dallas airport—nothing flew directly into Monroe—just Shreveport."

Not realizing the distances involved, Della chose to fly into Dallas, Texas, a direct flight, rather than one that would require a transfer to Shreveport.

"Bob knew the time of my arrival and assured me he would be there." However, when she arrived—on schedule—Bob was not there. After waiting two hours, Della called his home to find out the reason for the delay. Mrs. Preaus, explained to Della that "Bob had gone to a rodeo in another town and had evidently lost tract of time."

"This did not set too well" with Della, who was "really upset by this and really hurt."

Della began making arrangements for her return flight and found one that left in a few hours. She settled in to wait for her plane back to California.

Bob finally arrived—four hours late. He was very apologetic.

"His only excuse was that he was so interested in the rodeo that he last track of time. Just where did that put me in the whole scheme of things?" Della asked herself.

An even more difficult visit was ahead for her during a five-day stay in Ruston.

"During that time Bob and his mother insisted that all members of Bob's large family be visited because every one was so delighted to have Bob home safely."

Della could understand their joy, but inside she "was really suffering—wasn't anyone going to say how sorry they were that my husband was not coming home! Were they afraid to say anything?"

"The whole family just took to her," Bob related. "They could have done without me," he joked, "but they loved Della."

"I must have made a good impression," Della remembered, "because they decided that I wasn't a 'damned Yankee'," she laughed many years later.

Caught up in their own elation that their Bob was back among them having survived a tragic crash followed by over a year of brutal captivity, the Holloway family didn't realize how much it hurt Della that they didn't ask about her loss and were "showing great joy during my sorrow! How I kept my tears in check, I will never know. By that time, I was just numb. I was so happy to be on the plane home to California," she recalled.

On the way back to California, with time to think about the whirlwind visit, Della realized, as "strange as it may seem, I felt that Bob's feelings towards me were definitely romantic."

In fact, he had already asked her during one of their lengthy conversations during the visit, "you won't consider marrying me—would you?"

Della was flattered, but nonplussed.

"Boy, I was not sure how to answer that—I had such a perfect marriage with Wayne. I was not sure I was able or ready to enter into marriage with another person."

By this time, Della knew that Wayne was not going to return. The various official documents she had reviewed, the reports from the squadron that formed the basis for the Air Force's official determination of death, and Bob's own painful recollection of what had happened that Wednesday afternoon a year and a half before were convincing in the sad conclusion that Wayne had died when he jumped from the spinning helicopter too late for his parachute to open. Delaying his own bail out to help save his passengers had cost him his own life.

Clearly, Della was a widow—but still a vibrant young woman with a future that was surely going in a new direction. But what choice should she make? She was 27 years old, with a good job working for the University of California and a home of her own.

"Should I consider marriage at this time or wait until my feelings were really settled?" she asked herself.

Bob was persistent, and urged her to make another trip to Ruston.

The Proposal

It wasn't long before Della heard from the family once more. They asked her to come back in December. It was during that visit that Bob finally asked Della to marry him—sort of.

"You wouldn't want to marry me, would you?" he asked her again at one point.

"It was the most negative proposal I've ever had in my life," she joked many years later.

At the time she told the nervous suitor, "I'll think about it."

"And she never lets me forget it, either," he joked later.

"We never even got to set the wedding date. His Mom decided that Bob had to be married by a certain, good Baptist minister. The only time he had on his schedule at the time was on the afternoon of December 25, 1953—Christmas afternoon.

Bobby Marries Della. *On the afternoon of Christmas Day 1953, SSgt. Bobby Holloway and Della Paddon Lear were married by the pastor of the First Baptist Church of Farmerville, Louisiana.*

And, thanks to the Air Force, the Holloway's didn't have to pay for their honeymoon. S/Sgt. Holloway had received orders to report to Washington, D.C. for additional duty. General DuBose had some publicity in mind for Holloway as the only Air Rescue Service survivor to return from MIA status.

"I want to see that man," DuBose had told his staff.

"And, they got me up there pronto," Holloway recalled.

It was a first for Bobby Holloway. For Della, it was a return to her "old stomping grounds," since she and Wayne had been stationed there right after World War Two.

Before They Gave Up Hope

"In the early years before [the Ayer family] they gave up "Official" hope, that the handsome father would be found," Fred Ayer recorded in his diary, "the boy [him] would sit up with the mother and listen to Armed Forces Radio as the announcer read out the names of former prisoners of war being exchanged and released at the Panmunjom 'Freedom Bridge.'"

Always the radio started with the 'A's' and the mother and the little boy would sit through the 'Z's.' Never hearing the name they both so desperately needed to hear.

In the beginning, during the first year the woman would just cry and by the second year, the crying would be accompanied by a few drinks.

The little boy with the younger brother asleep in the next room would hold and comfort his mother. He never cried aloud, although he hurt badly from the pain that his mother was feeling.

He constantly told her that the father nicknamed "Honey," would come home. After a while the mother would drift off to sleep, the cigarette that she never used to smoke was taken from her hand and snuffed out by the little boy.

He had grown to dislike his Mom smoking, as he again cleaned up the glass ashtrays.

She would awake for a moment and tell him to go to bed, that she would take care of the increasingly untidy home that at one time she used to keep so neat. The little boy knew that he would have to clean up again and make toast for his brother for breakfast.

At night the young boy cried himself to sleep and would pray that his father would come home and take care of the woman who was changing and was not like the mother he used to have. The father would never come home and the young boy who could not be a little boy any more would have his earliest lessons in pain and surviving.

After four long years, the father was officially declared dead. The young boy had seen the mother stop caring about everything around her, heavy drinking numbed her pain and her caring.

Money had come from the government and been squandered almost as fast as it came. 'Close relatives' 'borrowed' money that was never returned to the weak woman.

Some, later would flinch when the subject was brought up, later most would say 'but look what I've done for you' as the Southern lady withered away.

The young boy cooked now mostly for himself and his brother. Often they ate toast twice a day. New clothes and jeans were rare. Most Christmases were meager at best with the mother often drunk and angry. The boy, Dean, rarely knowing why. Christmas and special occasions lost their specialness. Those kind of days would remain that way too many "special" times too often.

A blinding hardness inside but along that hardness was a survival instinct that he would constantly learn to hone like a razor. Trial and error disappointment, frustration, fear of constantly being let down, all this would mould Dean into something he would regret many times over.

Soon, the mother began disappearing and the loving grandparents cared for Dean and his brother. The grandmother would become the only person in the boy's life he could trust and love. The wise old woman with the long, beautiful auburn hair would be a light for the embittered boy to hold on to in later years.

Her influence would, in the end, be dominant in his life.

Any kind of trust would be based on his haunting memories of the soft spoken 'Tish,' know to him then and forever as 'Momma.'

Sometimes, when the tired mother would return, the two boys would go with her and live for while. Sometime, with a strange man they didn't know. The young brother, too young to know and sheltered as much as possible from the "situations," by the older brother, was often happy to see the mother. The older boy, Dean, became harder inside, knowing that the family and live that he searched for was not going to come with the mother and that saying "I care," meant going away—again.'

Mistrust of women was born for the boy and would hinder his [Fred Ayer's] search for 'the family' for many years to come.

Final Determinations In Process

On December 4th, 1953, Major General McCormick advised Della that "your husband, Captain Leslie W. Lear, is still recorded in a missing status. We are now engaged in reviewing all available information relating to his with the purpose of making a final determination of his status. You will be notified immediately when action is completed. May I extend my sincere sympathy," he concluded.

On December 21st, General McCormick again wrote Della "in reply to your recent letter," assuring her that "the anxiety you are experiencing because your husband's missing status is still unresolved is most understandable and I am extremely sorry that no information has been received concerning him which would resolve his ultimate fate. As you were advised in my telegram of 3 December, we are now engaged in reviewing all available information relating to Captain Lear and others, with the purpose making a final determination. This includes statements secured by interrogation and re-interrogation of repatriates as well as data gleaned from intelligence sources. Every effort to obtain additional information from the Communists since the signing of the truce agreement has thus far produced no positive results. However, we are continuing our attempts to get any known information they possess relative to the status of our missing personnel. Regrettably, in many instances, our efforts may be unavailing and in the absence of further information, we will be required by law to make a presumptive finding of death. We do not know when this review will be completed but you may be assured that you will be notified immediately should such action be taken concerning your loved one."

By this time, Della had accepted Bob's proposal of marriage. However, setting a date for their wedding was soon complicated because "Bob got orders to report to Washington D.C. for further debriefing."

Bob and his mother wanted the couple to be married by their longtime minister, but he could only do it on Christmas day. Some of Bob's immediate family "thought it would be an ideal thing to go to Washington as part of the honeymoon," Della recalled. "I'm not sure I really had time or made the effort to express any of my feelings on the subject," Della said, "I was just going 'with the flow.'

As it turned out, it was just Bob and Della that made the long trip from Ruston, Louisiana to Washington, D.C. following their marriage on Christmas Day 1953.

Typically, Della's thoughts turned to others that were caught up in the aftermath of Mission 1890.

"Looking back," Della said recently, "I can see that I just added to the difficult time for the Lears. They just were not ready to face the fact that Wayne was dead and I can understand that from the point of having become a parent myself. Still, I was too young to really understand them as I felt I had some living to do yet and I did not want to do that alone. I still feel it would have been so much easier on all of us if Bob had gone to them earlier."

Wayne's sister, Barbara, worked to bring the family together. Finally, several years after Della and Bob were married, a meeting was finally arranged. "It did clear the air somewhat—they finally invited us into their home for a short visit. Strange to say, that after Wayne's mother passed away, his father did not wait long to marry a longtime family friend. Life can be odd—times change and people change!" Della noted.

Presumptive Findings Of Death
Body Not Recovered

On February 26, 1954, BG John S. Hardy, Acting Director of Military Personnel for the Air Force, signed a Memorandum recommending that fifty-five Air Force personnel that had been continued in a missing in action status at the expiration of their initial 12 months' period of absence, be terminated "by a presumptive finding of death." The official date of death for them from then on would be 28 February 1954. The names on the list included senior officers and noncoms. The aircraft they had flown included B-26s, B-29s, F-84s, B-25s, F-86s, and F-51s—two of them, one shot down in April and one in June, 1952.

A legal Presumptive Finding of Death—Body not Recovered (BNR) was entered on 25 January 1954 for Captain Leslie W. Lear.

The Navy's Bureau of Naval Personnel (BUPERS), Personal Affairs Division signed out a "Determination of Death" letter on 28 January 1954. "Pursuant to the provisions of Public Law 490, 77th Congress, as amended, and pursuant to a letter, dated 16 July 1951, signed by the Secretary of the Navy, the Director, Personal Affairs Division of the Bureau of Naval Personnel, this 28th day of January 1954 determines Ensign Ronald Dow Eaton, 543824, USNR, to be dead. The above-named officer was reported missing in action as of 25 June 1952. The date of death is hereby fixed at 25 June 1952. Information conclusively establishing the death of Ensign Ronald Dow Eaton, and constituting an official report of his death was received by the Director, Personal Affairs Division…on 28 January 1954."

"Ensign Eaton was participating in an attack on the east coast of Korea when he radioed that his engine was losing power," the statement attached to the Determination letter explained. "He was ordered to return to his ship and two of his wingmen were detailed to accompany him back. A few minutes later Ensign Eaton radioed that he was abandoning his plane. The pilots who were accompanying him back saw him parachute to the ground and run to take cover in some trees. Numerous enemy troops were observed to be in the area. Later that night an Air Force helicopter arrived on the scene and rescued him but the helicopter was hit by enemy ground fire and crashed. No further information was received concerning Ensign Eaton until Operation "Big Switch," at which time a statement was made by a repatriated prisoner of war, S/Sgt. Bobby D. Holloway, USAF in which he reported that he and another pilot were sent out to rescue Ensign Eaton who was downed behind enemy lines. The helicopter was hit and Holloway was ordered to bail out. There was no parachute for Ensign Eaton so he was told to cling to Holloway but a strap broke and he plunged to his death. He further reported that the pilot of the helicopter was also killed. It is deemed that Ensign Eaton met his death when the strap broke and he fell to the ground. The evidence conclusively establishes his death on 25 June 1952." [16]

"Guess This Is Foolish To Ask"

In February 1954, Arch and Eva Connors wrote another letter to the Air Force Director of Military Personnel, this time more pointed in requesting action and information.

"Again we thank you for previous information concerning our son, First Lieutenant Archibald H. Connors, Jr., to make this short and to the point, we want more information. Friends from California forwarded a clipping stating that our son was one of the 944 POWs unaccounted for to be held by the Communists. What information has the government received concerning our son? If he is a POW, where did they get the information? Did some of the released POWs say they saw him in one of the POW camps? Or was his name given over the Communist radio as one of the captured fliers? I'm sure you understand our anxiety so we won't apologize for asking so many questions. If it is at all possible, please tell us all you can what is the government going to do about the fliers still held as POWs? Guess this is foolish to ask, but we can't help it."

"No Reasonable Possibility Exists For His Continued Survival"

On March 1, 1954, McCormick notified Frankie Connors "with deep regret" that the missing status for her husband had been terminated.

"As explained to you upon completion of our previous review, your husband was participating in Korean operations when he became missing and regrettably he has not been seen or heard from since that time. The review just completed was initiated after the cessation of Korean hostilities. It reveals that your husband's name was included on the list presented to the Communists for an accounting, but no report concerning him has been forthcoming. Furthermore no supplemental information has been received through interrogation and re-interrogation of former prisoners of war, or from any other officials or an official source which would establish his ultimate fate."

"Consideration of these facts compels the conclusion that no reasonable possibility exists for his continued survival. Consequently, it has become necessary under the provisions of the "Missing Persons Act to terminate his Missing Status by a presumptive finding of death, the presumed date being recorded as 28 February 1954. This is not considered to be the actual or probable date of death, but it is established in accordance with the cited law for the purpose of terminating pay and settling accounts. An official report of the change in his status has been issued by the Department of the Air Force. We realize how distressing it must be to receive so little information about his fate. While we can offer no assurance of further particulars, I do want to assure you that determination of his Missing Status will not affect our efforts to obtain more complete details. You may be certain that you will be notified immediately if additional information is received concerning his death or the recovery of his remains. Within a short time a Personal Affairs Officer from an Air Force installation will communicate with you. This officer is prepared to assist you in obtaining any government benefits allowable as the result of the death of your husband and will help in any other way that he can. I am extremely sorry that this message does not lighten the grief in your home please accept my deepest sympathy in your bereavement." The exact letter was sent to Archie's parents in Jacksonville.

The next day, March 2nd, McCormick again wrote to Archie's parents in Jacksonville.

"You have no doubt received my letter of 1 March advising you of the termination of your son's Missing Status. However, in view of your anxiety, I believe this letter will answer some of your questions. Under the terms of the truce agreement, the opposing forces consented to give a complete account of all persons who had ever been in their custody or about whose fate they had knowledge and who were not returned in the prisoner exchanges, or otherwise reported. This was to include all those who died subsequent to capture or had escaped from custody. Many United Nations personnel remained unaccounted for after these exchanges and, from this number, a list was prepared for submission to the Communists. In many cases, we already had received information from the repatriates which established that these persons had died while in captivity but had not been so reported by the Communists. In other cases the repatriates informed us that they had been told by their captors or other prisoners, who later died, that certain persons were known to have perished in the crash of their planes. Others were included because, while no information was available about them, members of their crews were repatriated or were reported as believed to be in the custody of the enemy. This latter group was included in the hope of securing information about their ultimate fate. In several instances upon interrogation of the repatriated crew members, we learned that the emergency of the crash was so severe and so sudden that no other persons were believed to have been able to survive. Newspapers, periodicals and other news media have carried stories concerning this vital issue and have given that wide publicity. Some of them have strongly implied that all persons on this list are known to be alive and in the custody of the Communists in various regions behind the Iron curtain. False hope, thus fostered, has caused additional anguish to the families of these individuals. It is expected that a certain amount of publicity may continue along these lines."

The Disputed Insurance Claim

The official change in Connors status from MIA to KIA with a presumptive finding of death, brought with it the determination of who would receive his Serviceman's Group Life Insurance policy of $10,000.

Shortly after he reported to the 67th Squadron, 18th Fighter-Bomber Wing, Connors had executed an updated Record of Emergency Data. On 20 January 1952 he clearly named Lutye Frances Connors, wife, to receive "100% of his pay "in the event that I am listed as missing." Only in the event that he was not survived by a spouse or eligible child would payment be made to the dependent relative shown below—Eva Connors. For some reason, that DD Form 93 was not in his records at the time—although it is now a part of his jacket—and its absence would create major heartburn for everyone concerned.

On March 9, 1954 the 2370th Air Base Squadron received the "MIA to Death report" and made "an appointment for a visit—17 March 1954 in afternoon."

On March 16th, Captain Jenkins reported a "phone call from NOK. She had just been notified by her mother-in-law [Eva Connors] that the insurance is in her name. Letter sent to Dir Mil Pers for AF Form 381 and AF Form 93 to aid widow with insurance claim." The missing DD 93 that Connors signed on 20 January 1952 clearing making Frankie his NOK was beginning to cause serious mischief for all concerned.

The next day, the local Air Force Casualty Assistance Officer visited with Frankie "and explained all death benefits. Insurance is going to mother-in-law." During the visit, a call was placed to Eva and Arch Connors in Jacksonville, Florida. "Talked to in-laws on phone and explained how come that they had been listed as beneficiary on the VA records. Possibility that NOK will still get insurance as parents feel that it should go to her."

Air Force records during spring, 1954 contain numerous memos and references to Archie's "disputed insurance claim." Officials at many levels in the chain of command were trying to sort out who Archie had wanted to be the beneficiary of his government life insurance policy: his parents or his new wife. Requests for the latest copy of his DD Form 93, Record of Emergency Data and AF Form 381, Air Force Personal Affairs Statement were urgently submitted to the Director of Military Personnel. A search of his records found a "duplicate copy of VA Form 9-350, Application for National Service Life Insurance, dated 2 June 1950," indicating "principal beneficiary as Mrs. Eva May Connors, and contingent, Mr. Archibald H. Connors. A change may have been executed subsequent to that date, however, a copy of the official VA form was not included in the Master Personnel Record."

In April, the Personal Affairs Officer for the Long Beach, CA Air Force Reserve Training Center notified Frankie that the "DD Form 93 that he made out does not give the information on the beneficiaries." She suggested that Frankie "screen his personal papers very thoroughly for a later copy" of the vital VA or Air Force form.

An internal Air Force memo outlined the problem: "The National Service Life Insurance in this case is going to the parents of the deceased rather than to the wife. This officer had indicated to his wife on several occasions that she was beneficiary on this insurance policy. Information under Beneficiary on the Casualty Report also indicated that she probably is beneficiary."

On March 24, Captain Jenkins sent Frankie a "postcard telling her of PX hours."

In March, 1954, Frankie asked the Air Force for her husband's military awards. The Air Force noted a slight delay "before these awards are furnished" to assemble his records.

On March 17th, the 2347th Air Force Reserve Training Center requested help from the Air Force Personnel Services Division in Washington in obtaining "a photo static copy of the latest DD Form 93, Record of Emergency Data and AF Form 381. Air Force Personal Affairs Statement on subject officer in order that we may assist Mrs. Connors with a disputed insurance claim." The DD Form 93 was furnished, but the California command was advised that entries on Form 381 had no bearing in designating or changing insurance beneficiaries and was used for general information purposes only.

On April 1, 1954, Captain Jenkins sent off a request for Awards and Decorations.

"As Time Lessens The Poignancy Of Your Grief"

On April 7, 1954, Frankie received a letter from Air Force chief of staff, General Nathan F. Twining.

"We of the Air Force share your sorrow and the loss of your husband, first Lt. Archibald H. Connors, Jr. The fact that you so long hoped and prayed for his safe return has, I know, made this loss particularly difficult for you to bear. I trust, however, that as time lessens the poignancy of your grief, you will find comfort and pride in remembering that your husband gave his life in the service of this country and for the principles of freedom. Lieutenant Connors death has deeply saddened all who knew him for he was an outstanding officer and a truly fine person. My heartfelt sympathy is extended to you and other members of the family," Twining concluded.

The Air Force Reserve Training Center in Long Beach, California was the official liaison command for Frankie's contact with the Air Force regarding Archie's effects and benefits. On April 2, 1954 it forwarded a requested to the St. Louis Records Administration Center for a Statement of Military Service on the late Lt. Connors, including prior service with the United States Navy "to aid this headquarters in rendering casualty assistance to next of kin."

On April 15, 1954, Archie's oldest brother, Woodrow, wrote to President Eisenhower urging him to have Secretary of State John Foster Dulles put more pressure on the North Koreans at the Geneva Conference then being held. "I think I now speak for all the friends and relatives of these boys, when I say that any small reassurance you could give us would be appreciated," he wrote. Washington was preoccupied with the Army-McCarthy hearings which began on April 22nd.

"Dear Mr. President," Archie's brother, Woodrow Connors wrote on April 15, 1954. "I am a brother of one of the flyers now held by the Communists in North Korea and as such I am vitally concerned as to their future. The cartoon that I am enclosing represents my understanding of the situation over there. Is this a true picture or is something being done to bring these boys home? I am also sending these cartoons to news commentators and other public officials. I hope at the Geneva Conference Mr. Dulles requests release of U.N. prisoners now held. I think I now speak for all the friends and relatives of these boys, when I say that any small reassurance you could give us frm time to time would be appreciated."

"He still intended to give the insurance to his mother…"

It must have been difficult for 1st Lt. Florence Hess, the Personal Affairs Officer for the Air Force Reserve Training Center in Long Beach to have to write a letter on 12 April 1954 to Frankie, advising her that they had received a reply from the Director of Military Personnel. However, it was not good news in resolving the disputed insurance money.

"The latest change of beneficiary that they have listed for the NSLI Insurance is 2 June 1950. Were you married as of that date or not? If so, it would appear that he still intended to give the insurance to his mother. I would suggest that you screen his personal papers very thoroughly for a later copy of VA Form 9-350, or for a copy of AF Form 381," Lt. Hess advised. "In the meantime," Hess continued, "you can tell his folks that his personal affairs statement, AF Form 381, was not in his master file in Washington, D.C., and has apparently become lost. If you are unable to locate either of these documents, just for information, you might write to the Veteran's Administration and ask what the date is on the VA Form 9-350, "Designation of Beneficiary…" under which they are settling the claims."

The Deputy Chief of Staff for Personnel, Lt. Gen. Emmett O'Donnell, Jr., sent Frankie a letter on April 17, 1954, explaining that "throughout the years the armed forces have tendered awards in honor of their fallen countrymen. The Secretary of the Air Force has requested me to transmit to you the Purple Heart which has been awarded posthumously to your husband, First Lieutenant Archibald H. Connors, Jr., who sacrificed his life in defense of his country. This medal is of slight intrinsic value but is rich with the tradition for which Americans fight and so gallantly give their lives. General Washington, whose profile adorns the metal, symbolizes our efforts in behalf of freedom loving people throughout the world. In addition, I am forwarding to you the accolade, awarded by the president, which is our nation's highest token of appreciation. Nothing the Air Force can do or say will in any sense repair the loss of your loved one. He has gone in honor and in the company of his compatriots. Let me, in conveying to you the country's deep sympathy, also express my gratitude for his valor and devotion."

An internal "memo for the record" on the letter noted: "Korean Casualty (KIA). Ltr transmits to NOK PH and Accolade. These awards are given to NOK of all military personnel who are KIA or die as a result of wounds inflicted by the enemy."

"It is noted that Lieutenant Connors performed service with the United States Navy during World War II," the Air Force Personnel Management Division wrote to Frankie on June 18, 1954, telling her how to order the awards. "It is our sincere hope that these mementos of your husband's service to his country may bring some measure of comfort to you."

Recovery and Return of Remains

Colonel Carlberg wrote to Arch and Eva Connors on April 29, 1954 to "advise you regarding the possible recovery of his remains for return to the United States." The Connors family was stunned by the unexpected news.

"The truce agreement reached with the Communist forces provides for certain activities in connection with the recovery of remains of our honored dead from Communist-held territory. It also provides that the specific procedures and time lime for the recovery operation shall be determined by the Military Armistice Commission. Until the necessary arrangements for the operation have been completed, we will not know when recovery and return of remains can be initiated. I appreciate the anxiety you are experiencing, and regret that no information other than that which has now been furnished you is available at this time. You may be sure, however, that we will notify you immediately when further information becomes available."

On May 15, 1954 the Wilkins Air Force Depot in Shelby, Ohio shipped to the Commander, 2370th Air Base Squadron in Long Beach, California "Air Medal, complete, with container…Purple Heart, complete, with container…" engraved with Archie's name and marked for presentation to Frankie.

Eva As Beneficiary

In May 1954, Eva Haddock Connors received a Serviceman's Group Life Insurance check for $10,000 from the government. She had filed for it in April 1954. "As noted on Thirty Day Status Report, serviceman's records were not in order at time of this death, therefore insurance went to mother rather than widow," an Air Force Memorandum for the Record succinctly recorded.

A later report on the "Status of Casualty Assistance Rendered Mrs. Lutye Frances Connors," noted that "the National Service Life Insurance in this case is going to the parents of the deceased rather than to the wife. This officer had indicated to his wife on several occasions that she was beneficiary on this insurance policy. Information under Beneficiary on the Casualty Reports also indicates that she probably is beneficiary. In entirely too many instances, the National Service Life Insurance is going to some other person than the one that the serviceman had intended or thought was the beneficiary. Most of these disputed insurance claims can be traced back to the serviceman not being informed, or some clerk along the line not completing the paper work involved in change of beneficiary for the NSLI Insurance…This misunderstanding regarding the NSLI Insurance has made for ill will among families with whom this headquarters has come in contact. The person who the serviceman had actually intended to be beneficiary on his insurance often says, 'It is the fault of the Air Force for not telling my husband (or whoever the individual might be) the right thing to do and for not filling out the papers.' This is a very serious problem which should be corrected if at all possible."

Eva's receipt of Archie's life insurance had been preceded by a whirlwind of paperwork for the Air Force. Archie had only had government insurance. The SGLI payment was the only lump sum of any consequence that Frankie would receive. Archie's apparent oversight in changing his beneficiary and next of kin had required the Air Force to issue the check to his mother. Frankie questioned the payment through the local Air Force liaison office in Long Beach, California and was queried as to "the dates on which you filed for benefits and the dates that they were received."

Arch and Eva Connors on the back steps of their west Jacksonville, Florida home.

Arch and Eva held the check for a few weeks while the Air Force combed its records to find the last known Record of Emergency Data. At least the Air Force had sent a check to someone in the family. However, if the Air Force determined that Frankie was the intended beneficiary, what would the process then become? Return the check and the Air Force cut a new one? Until the Air Force made a final decision, they held on to the money. Much earlier they had assured Frankie and the Air Force Liaison Officer during a telephone conversation that if it turned out that they were the legal beneficiaries, they still intended to give the money to Frankie. However, Frankie had her doubts and said so to friends. There were times that she let herself believe that Arch and Eva would simply keep the money, as they had every legal right to do. That never entered their minds.

On the September 2nd questionnaire, Frankie noted that she had not applied for a Commissary or PX card, nor requested vocational or educational assistance.

On May 18, 1954 the Wilkins Air Force Depot in Shelby, Ohio shipped two items to the 2370th Air Base Squadron in Long Beach, CA. "Air Medal, complete, with container. Purple Heart, complete, with container." The directions on the requisition included: "engrave Air Medal and Purple Heart as follows: 'Archibald H. Connors, Jr.'"

On August 7, 1954, Captain Jenkins log noted that "NOK received awards and decorations at parade," including: the Purple Heart, Air Medal, United National Service Medal, Korean Service Medal (two Bronze service stars), National Defense Service Medal and the "Pilot" Aviation Badge." She was also "entitled to receive a Gold Star Lapel Button to be worn in your husband's honor. This lapel button, engraved with your initials, will be included with the awards."

There was to be no personal award for his part in Mission 1890. Later, the mention of a Distinguished Flying Cross in Archie's obituary was either incorrect or premature. An award application prepared and mentioned to Frankie by some 18th Wing staff officer might have been lost or disapproved. In any event, the DFC or even another Air Medal was never approved for his heroic role in Mission 1890.

"We are still waiting to hear more…"

"I am the mother of Captain Leslie W. Lear," Wayne's mother, Mabel, explained in a letter to Bernard and Elsie Eaton in her letter of August 6, 1954, "who rescued your son Ensign Ronald Eaton June 25, 1952 and then was later shot down over enemy territory. I know that you folks have suffered greatly, like us, and many more families that have waited for information regarding their loved ones. Our son's status was terminated January 29, 1954 with a determination of death set at June 25, 1952. Yet we go in hopes that this is not true, as long as there are men who were held back by the Communists, there is a chance that our sons might be alive yet and will return some day. We don't feel that there is proof that our son was killed. Of course, I don't know how you feel, or the information that you received concerning your son. If you have time to write us information that you were told regarding your son. Was his missing status closed? We also received a

Mabel Lear in happier times.

letter from the Mortuary Branch, May 5, 1954 telling us under the Truce Agreement that they would be allowed to go into Communist-held territory to recover the remains of our dead. We are still waiting to hear more from them concerning this operation. We know that our son's body would be close to the helicopter if he didn't survive the crash. Sergeant Holloway said he saw one grave close to the helicopter after he was captured, three days after the crash. Sergeant Holloway was the medic on the helicopter. He was taken prisoner and came through the exchange September 1953. He said he knew nothing to help us in the way of information. We would like to hear from you if you have the time to write us," she concluded and mailed her letter from 13551 Sandhurst Place, Santa Ana, California.

Awards And A Parade

On August 7th, Frankie received the "awards and decorations at parade," the Casualty Assistance Officer noted for the record.

"Dear Folks," Frankie wrote on August 30, 1954, "Glad to hear from you—was afraid someone was sick."

"Thanks for Archie's picture. It looks just like him."

"I went to Long Beach and they presented Archie's medals to me. He received the Purple Heart, Bronze Star *[there is no mention of the Bronze Star Award in his record]*, and the Air Medal. I'll send you the write up in the paper. In the same paper, I read where McCarthy was raising a rumpus about the men who are still missing and declared "presumed dead." They talk but don't do anything."

"I'm trying to get Mom to stay out here but she can't decide. She's so lonesome and I feel so sorry for her but she's so darned independent."

"I'm real unhappy about the *[James]* Cox's bad luck. They're both such nice people. Is she taking treatments for her nose?

"The old laundry is chugging right along and I'm trying to chug right along with it. Tell Pop he shouldn't expect the place to buy new machines in just 2 ½ months. We're going to try using the old ones until we have expensive repairs, then buy new ones. Maybe we can hold out until we have enough backing to pay everything out of company funds."

"Must close—write me soon and give everyone my love. Loads of Love, Frankie."

On September 2, 1954, Frankie returned a form to the Air Force Personal Affairs Office in Long Beach, CA indicating the status of various benefits to which she was entitled as a military widow. She had received the Government Life Insurance benefit in May, but had not applied for the commissary and PX cards to which she was entitled. She had received all of her husband's personal effects.

Frankie had used Archie's insurance money to open a self-service laundry in Glendale, California.

Wearing Archie's Things

Eva gave Archie's athletic gear to her oldest grandson, Tracy. Pulling on the shoulder pads and then the blue and gray jersey, Tracy used Archie's old high school football uniform—"37"—to play "football" with his brother and other neighborhood kids in their North Shore yard on the corner of Vermillion and 58th Streets. The pads were still much too big, but he'd get them on, grab the ball and go plowing through the mass of kids oblivious to their attempts to tackle him. After all, he had on real pads, Archie's pads, and their "hits" didn't hurt.

He remembered feeling especially strong for another reason—Archie—his granite hard uncle—had actually worn these in a real game. Maybe it was the adrenaline, but when he wore that uniform he was unstoppable. He would plough through the "line" of neighborhood kids, suited in his uncle's football "armor." Number 37 was once again unstoppable. In time, with repeated washings, the royal blue faded to robin's egg blue. The gold numbers wasted away to pale yellow. Finally, a violent yank by a would-be tackler took an arm off the jersey. It was time to hang up Number 37.

In several short years, Tracy out grew the pads, which now lay unusable in the rear of his closet. One morning in a shocking self-revelation, he realized that he was now bigger and taller than Archie had been. Archie's track shoes, now Tracy's, would not fit on his growing feet. He would have to hang up Archie's "spikes," as well.

When Tracy visited at his grandparents, he would sit in Archie's old bedroom and go through those things that had been left behind. After he was declared MIA, Archie's mother kept his room much it was when he was alive for over 15 years. Tracy would try on Archie's Air Force officer's cap and wear it while looking into the mirror over the bureau. At first it was far too large, then almost overnight it seemed, it was too small for his head.

Archie had left a pipe in his drawer. Although he rarely smoked a pipe, it still had crusts of half-burned tobacco in the bowl. Tracy would stand there in front of the bureau, looking into the mirror at himself "puffing" away on Archie's pipe. Yes, he did look distinguished, he admitted to himself. The old tobacco left a slightly sour taste in his mouth, but it was something of Archie's.

Operation Glory

The repatriation of the remains of United Nations servicemen killed in during the Korean War was given a name—Korean Communications Zone (KCOMZ) Operations Plan 14-54. Mindful of public relations, some decision-maker soon renamed it "Operation GLORY."

Initial implementation was begun on 22 July 1954. First, a railhead and reception area had to be constructed at which to receive the remains. United States Engineers furnished by the United Nations Command, Military Armistice Commission Support Group, constructed the railhead and reception area near Munsan-ni, Korea. The UN Command also provided a battalion from the 1st Signal Unit to establish signal communications. Meanwhile, the Army Transportation Corps made plans for the evacuation, by rail, of all deceased military personnel on the UN side. The Quartermaster Corps issued all necessary supplies and materials. And the KCOMZ Quartermaster Graves Registration Division proceeded to disinter all the remains of deceased former enemy military personnel interred in South Korea.

In the weeks prior to the actual exchange of military remains, the Quartermaster Graves Registration Committee held three additional meetings with the Communist side to discuss the approximate number of deceased involved, examine the signatures of officers who sign receipts for the remains, and to decide how both sides would proceed from the railheads to the reception areas within the demilitarized zone. The meetings also reviewed policies regarding the means of identification, use of vehicles in the proscribed areas, and ground rules for photographers and news correspondents.

By August 30, 1954, the disinterment of all former enemy deceased military personnel was completed, and all of those remains had been delivered and stored at "Glory Railhead." At 0930 on September 1st, the Chief of KCOMZ Graves Registration Division met his North Korean counterpart at the reception area within the demilitarized zone, and received the first 200 remains of deceased UN military personnel. By 1300 hours these remains had been evacuated to "Glory Railhead," where a solemn ceremony was held attended by senior officials from the United Nations Command, U.S. Far East Command, Military Armistice Commission, and representatives from the Republic of Korea Army. A religious ceremony was conducted by chaplains of the Catholic, Protestant, and Jewish faiths.

Over the next three weeks, the exchange of remains between the United Nations in South Korea, and the Communists in North Korea, continued daily, except Sundays. On September 21st however, North Korean representatives turned over 123 remains, and advised UN graves registration officials that there were no more to be delivered. The United Nations group continued delivering its remains of former enemy personnel until 11 October. A tally in mid-October indicated that 4,023 UN deceased personnel had been received from the North Koreans, and that 13,528 had been delivered to them.

The last formal meeting between the two sides on the matter of remains, was held on October 11th, with both sides agreeing to continue searching in remote areas. If additional remains were discovered, they would be returned prior to the end of the month, if possible. The UN Chief of the Graves Registration Committee further advised the North Koreans that the exchange facilities would be left standing for as long as was felt necessary.

Additional remains were returned by the North Koreans in October and November, eventually bringing the total number of United Nations deceased military personnel turned over by the North Koreans during Operation GLORY to 4,167.

Once the repatriated remains were turned over to United Nations personnel at the Glory railhead, they were shipped to Moji Port, Japan—two shipments each week. By the middle of October 1954, 4,101 remains were on hand in the mausoleum at Jono. A final shipment was received on 10 December 1954.

Even though the turnover of remains portion of Operation GLORY had officially ended, AGRS personnel continued processing unidentified remains from Moji Port for more than a year—until the mission was completed. By February 29, 1956, all Graves Registration personnel at Kokura, Japan, had been reassigned, property disposed of, and the buildings and grounds turned back to the post engineer. Another significant chapter in the history-making field of U. S. Army Quartermaster Mortuary Affairs had been concluded.

From January 1951 to March 1956, the AGRS Group at Kokura, Japan, had processed over 32,000 war casualties of the Korean Conflict, plus more than 300 deaths occurring in Japan.

Dental Records Requested

"I regret that I must communicate with you at this time concerning your son, First Lieutenant Archibald H. Connors, Jr.," wrote Col. L. F. Carlberg on October 4, 1954 from Air Force Headquarters in Washington.

"I would like to advise you that the Department of the Air Force is continually making every effort to resolve all casualties of the Korean conflict and that most of our heroic dead have been identified and returned to their next of kin for final burial. We still have a small number of remains in our custody which have not yet been identified, primarily because the records of some of our casualties lack identifying information as to any dental treatments received and/or bone fractures by our military personnel prior to their entry into service."

"Since your son is one of our unresolved casualties," Carlberg continued, "we should like to have a complete record of any of his physical and dental characteristics which may have been recorded by your family dentist or doctor prior to his entry into the service. This information should include dental treatments such as extractions, fillings, bridge work, dentures and peculiarities of the teeth, as well as physical treatments for injuries to the bones or the body which may have resulted in fracture. Any available X-rays of bones and teeth will also be of great assistance. These X-rays will be returned, if so desired, after our records have been annotated to reflect the information. If you prefer, you may forward the name and address of your family dentist and/or doctor, and we will contact him directly for his information."

"Any of the information you or your family doctor or dentist may be able to furnish will be forwarded to our laboratories in Camp Kokura, Japan. There, under the direction of professional anthropologists and identification specialists, all remains and available identification data are systematically and scientifically examined to insure conclusive identification," he concluded.

On October 8, 1954, Eva Connors sent a handwritten letter addressed simply to the Department of the Air Force: "Gentlemen, Archibald H. Connors, Jr., had no dental work or broken bones by which he could be identified. Write his wife...she could tell you if he had any dental work done since going into service. Thank you so much for writing," she closed.

Lear Trophy for Best Helicopter Crew

In November 1955, the Third Air Rescue Group created the "Lear Trophy" to be awarded to the "best helicopter crew." "In looking for an award to be given the best helicopter crew the name of Captain Lear and the memory of his outstanding service in the helicopter made the choice of a trophy name instantaneous and unanimous," Col. Tracy J. Petersen, 3ARG Commander explained to Della Lear in a subsequent letter. The Group had the trophy made in Tokyo and would make a formal presentation in February after a challenging selection process for the "helicopter crew showing the greatest proficiency during the meet."

On February 24, 1954, Della received a letter from Col. Tracy Petersen advising her that the 36th Air Rescue Squadron had turned in the best record during the competitive meet held in Ashiya, Japan. The 36th ARS had bested the other squadrons in all categories that included: simulated mission; instrument and emergency procedures; water pickup procedures, aerial delivery; auto-rotations; maximum performance take off; slow, steep approaches and H-19 examinations.

"I hope this information on our Lear Trophy will give you a better idea of its origin and its meaning to our mission," Petersen explained. "Captain Lear's actions were in the highest traditions of the Air Rescue Service, so we are most proud to have this continuing reminder of his service as a Third Air Rescue Group Trophy."

Sergeant Sees Combat Become Movie

After his repatriation in September 1953, Staff Sergeant Bobby Holloway had been assigned to the 47th Air Rescue Squadron at Ellington AFB, Texas. In March 1954, Holloway had reenlisted in the Air Force and asked to be assigned to March AFB, California.

By early 1955 Holloway was on duty at March Air Force Base in California serving with the 42nd Rescue Squadron. Meanwhile, United Artists had begun production of a movie adapted loosely around Holloway's experiences in the Korean War. The new film would be called *"Battle Taxi"* and would star Sterling Hayden in the leading role.

Following his release in September 1953, Holloway had been ordered to Washington. The Air Rescue Service was proud of his status as the only member of ARS to survive a rescue mission crash and imprisonment and began to require his participation in radio and television appearances that highlighted his Korean War experiences. During a meeting with Hollywood producer Ivan Tors, the idea for *Battle Taxi* was born.

"Essentially, the screenplay depicts the combat work of the Air Rescue helicopters during the Korean War," the *Riverside Daily News* reported on January 28, 1955.

"Since Sgt. Holloway flew in the war as an Aero-Medic on H-5 and H-19 "choppers" with the 3rd Air Rescue Squadron, he was able to add a great deal of insight to the subject that helped the producers in firming up basic ideas for the picture." March Air Force Base provided helicopters for filming and Holloway was the technical advisor although the producers had "brought with them" a Captain from "Air Rescue Headquarters," who received the film credits.

Later, when Holloway was asked if he thought the film was "an authentic account of the action in Korea," he responded that "it is a very

Following his release as a POW, SSgt. Bobby Holloway was summoned to Washington to tell his story to the media. The Air Force also arranged a meeting with Hollywood producer, Ivan Tors. Two years later, Tors and Producer Art Arthur released a movie—Battle Taxi—set during the height of the Korean War. It was clear that Tor's meeting with SSgt. Bobby Holloway gave him the basic story and insights he needed to bring Battle Taxi to the screen.

good film, and I thought it was as accurate as it possibly could be under the circumstances."

Holloway was invited to a special showing of the film in Hollywood. Ironically, "he almost missed the preview because he was on a helicopter rescue mission to Santa Rosa Island where he helped evacuate a patient suffering from an appendicitis attack. He made it though, and was in Los Angeles in time to see the first showing."

Los Angeles Times* TUESDAY, JAN. 25, 1955—Part I 11

Air Medic Tells Capture by Reds in Korea Fight

Rescued Pilot Killed in Bail-out When Helicopter Was Shot Down, Sergeant Relates

A young aero medic who was a prisoner of the Chinese Reds for 13 months told yesterday of the dramatic moments that preceded his capture and gave some details of his imprisonment.

Staff Sgt. Bobby D. Holloway, crew member on an air rescue helicopter in the Korean war, parachuted 800 feet after the copter was hit by ground fire and sought vainly to carry a fighter pilot to earth with him—a pilot without a parachute.

Sgt. Holloway, now attached to the 42nd Air Rescue Squadron, March Air Force Base, told his story yesterday at a press preview of the United Artists film "Battle Taxi," a story of helicopter rescues in combat.

Decked Up Pilot

"It happened on my 21st mission," he said. "The chopper (helicopter) pilot and I had just picked up a fighter pilot who had parachuted behind the Red lines.

"As we gained altitude after the pickup our ship was struck three times by ground fire and went out of control.

"I had a chute, of course, but the man we'd rescued had already used his and had none. There was nothing else to do but grab each other, jump and pray we'd make it.

"We only had four or five seconds—not enough time for him to interlace his arms and hands in the chute straps. We tumbled out and I pulled the clear. The opening shock tore him away from me . . ."

The young, dark-eyed Louisianan evaded capture for three days, living without food and water, but eventually he was captured by two Chinese Red infantrymen.

"I lost my 45 in the bail-out," he said, "or I probably would be dead now. If I had it I might have shot one or both of them, but there were hundreds of others all around me . . ."

Got 'Fair' Treatment

Holloway described his treatment by the Reds as "fair" with only a few incidents wherein he was "bumped around a bit."

The sergeant, who was recovered in Operation Big Switch, estimated he and the helicopter pilots with whom he rode saved between 35 and 40 fliers, rescuing them from behind the enemy lines or in combat.

TELLS THRILLER — Staff Sgt. Bobby D. Holloway tells of dramatic 'chute leap and capture by Reds during Korean fighting.

While Holloway was stationed at March, he was awarded an Air Medal "for meritorious achievement while participating in aerial flight in Korea as a member of the Far East Air Forces." The citation noted that "despite the hazards of marginal weather conditions, aerial interception, and intense anti-aircraft artillery fire, his exceptional marksmanship in combat operations against the enemy contributed immeasurably to the successful execution of the United Nations mission."

305

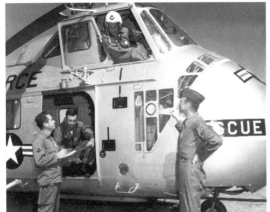

"Just another day at the office," *for Staff Sergeant Holloway during the period he served with the 42nd Air Rescue Service following his release as a Korean War POW. Here he pre-flights an H-19 helicopter, then demonstrates the winch rescue system.*

Holloway certainly deserved the medal for the 21 missions he successfully completed prior to June 25, 1952. However, it seems clear that the citation for this particular Air Medal was not written for Holloway but was generic for aviators in general, referring to his marksmanship. His extraordinary bravery under fire and contributions to the initial success of Mission 1890 were not mentioned in this award. In fact, he has never been

Major General Archie J. Old, Jr. Commander, 15th Air Force pins the Air Medal on Staff Sergeant Bobby D. Holloway in 1955 "for meritorious achievement while participating in aerial flight in Korea as a member of the Far East Air Forces." The March Air Force Base newspaper explained that "despite the hazards of marginal weather conditons, aerial interception, and intense anti-aircraft artillery fire, his exceptional marksmanship in combat operations against the enemy contributed immesasurably to the successful execution of the United Nations' mission. The technical skill, personal courage, and selfless devotion to duty which he displayed reflected the highest credit upon himself, his organization, and the United States Air Force." Holloway was serving with the 42nd Air Rescue Service.

recognized by the Air Force for this mission, his wounds in combat during that mission or even for his Prisoner of War service.

Remains Recovered—But Whose?

The tag on the container didn't reveal much about the contents, reading simply "EVAC. #17153, SHMT. #___, P.List #20, UNK., 38°35'03"—127°42'18", NONE." [17]

Ellis R. Kerley, a physical anthropologist with the 8204th Army Unit mortuary unpacked the simple container on April 27, 1955, and began a methodical inventory of the sad contents. An incomplete set of human remains—bones, many of them shattered, 19 teeth, remnants of clothing, including a U.S. Air Force vest insignia, military-style leather shoes size 7EEE, some fragments of an airplane, including a radio receiver—BG 453-B made by Western Electric—"one piece of metal with a nomenclature plate, badly damaged." Virtually all of the ribs were broken and the right leg was broken in two places. The skull was shattered.

Of the nineteen teeth that remained, five were chipped or broken. The location—front right, upper and lower jaw area—of the missing or damaged teeth indicated severe trauma to the face. The estimated height of the former serviceman was 5' 7" 3/8" based on the bones from a "Caucasoid" of between 23-26 years of age. The nasal bones were missing, and sections of both the maxilla and mandible were "fractured and missing."

Kerley had access to the basic information kept on file regarding the circumstances and physical characteristics of all Korean War personnel missing in action and not accounting for during the exchange of prisoners that had taken place in 1953. He soon narrowed the possibilities down to a few Air Force pilots, and then to one whose reported crash site was very close to that reported as the recovery site by those providing the box. Comparing the last known dental record of 1st Lt. Archibald H. Connors, Jr. of 12 January 1952 completed upon his arrival at K-10 (Chinhae, SK), Kerley identified four identical teeth from the remains that matched the records. The height of the deceased Caucasoid serviceman was 5'7" and his age was noted as "24 yrs. 10 mos. 29 days."

Keisaburo Nakayama, a laboratory chemical technician assigned to the Laboratory of Hygienic and Forensic Chemistry, Medical Department, Tokyo University examined the nomenclature plate carefully. There wasn't much to analyze. The small plate was riveted to a badly crumpled fragment of sheet metal that looked as if it had been ripped from its original piece of equipment like a piece of paper.

Kerley had another idea. Not satisfied with just a comparison of the fragmentary remains with dental and personnel records, Kerley reached for the telephone to call the 6025th Flying Training Squadron at Tsuiki Air

Force Base. He requested information "as to whether or not Radio Receiver BG 453-B is applicable to F-51 D type aircraft." Lt. Dale Goller called him back the same day with the confirmation that the radio receiver found with the remains was installed on the F-51D fighter-bomber.

Headquarters, American Graves Registration Service Group, 8204th Army Unit issued Special Orders Number 44 on 26 May 1955 that appointed a Board of Review to review and act upon all cases pertaining to the identity of remains referred by the headquarters to the board. Ten officers were appointed to the board with any three of them able to constitute a quorum for a decision.

On July 7, 1955, Captain Jenkins noted that he had contacted "NOK, she stated she received FEC, approximately October, 54. Case can be closed." Lt. Connors' personal effects had finally made it home, but would he?

A Name For Evac N-17153

DD Form 551 was the Department of Defense "Report of Interment."

On 26 September 1955, 8204th AU CIU Case #30,891 was transcribed onto a DD 551 for 1st Lt. Archibald H. Connors, Jr.

No identification tags were received with the remains, it noted and explained that they had been "received under Passenger List #20, Supplemental Shipment #2, Evac N-17153, Enemy Tr #52 as UNKNOWN." No personal effects were included with the remains that had been recovered from an "isolated burial" at 38°35'03"N, 127°42'18"E in North Korea. The remains were stored in the 8204th Mausoleum and a General Memorial service had been conducted by Chaplain Durward O. Deaver.

On 27 September, 1955, a Board of Officers appointed by Headquarters, American Graves Registration Service Group, 8204th Army Unit, convened at 0800. The board was being asked to determine the identification of "EVAC N-17153 (Isolated)."

A subsequent report filed on October 4th, listed the identifying factors the board would consider to reason its determination.

Evac N-17153 was "recovered by Communist Forces and transferred to U.N. Forces under Operation "Glory."

The recovery site in North Korea is indicated as 38 degrees 35 minutes 03 second North Latitude and 127 degrees 42 minutes 18 seconds West Longitude, "transposed to read grid coordinates CT 87.3-71.1, Map Sheet 6729IV."

The report cited letters and witness statements establishing that Lt. Connors of the 67th Fighter-Bomber Squadron was the pilot of an F-51D type aircraft (SN 44-74363A), on 25 June 1952 "which was hit by enemy ground-fire and crashed at coordinates CT 905695 (MS 6729-IV)."

The association of Evac N-17153 "with Lt. Connors is based on comparison of physical and dental characteristics."

One Nomenclature Plate from a BG-453-B type Radio Receiver was "found with remains. This type of Radio Receiver is applicable to F-51D aircraft," the report noted.

The cause of death for N-17153 was "indicated as air crash. Laboratory processing of remains reveals extensive shattering."

The Board—Lt. Col. Mark J. Gill, Maj. Alexander Capasso and 1st Lt. Clinton Diefenderfer—concluded its report by noting that the "records of all U.S. unresolved casualties for North Korea were considered. It is therefore determined, through comparison of dental and physical characteristics and/or other pertinent information of record, that 1st Lt. Archibald H. Connors, Jr., AO 2 221 998, is the only casualty who can be conclusively associated with Evac N-17153."

"The Air Force desires to furnish you information concerning the remains of your son, First Lieutenant Archibald H. Connors, Jr., "Colonel L. F. Carlberg wrote to Arch and Eva Connors on October 21, 1955.

"The Far East Commander has just advised me that remains returned to us during the recent mutual exchange have been identified as those of your son. This exchange was the result of negotiations between the United National Military Armistice Commission and the Communists regarding the recovery of United Nations personnel interred in Communist-held territory."

"All remains received in the exchange were removed to our mortuary at Camp Kokura, Japan. At the mortuary, professional anthropologists and identification specialists examined the remains to verify or establish identities. Identification of your son's remains was verified through favorable comparison of physical characteristics and information available in his records. His remains have been prepared for return to the United States. I am unable at this time to tell you when they will be returned; however this information will be furnished you as soon as available." The Air Force would ask Frankie for "disposition instructions."

"It is realized that there is nothing that can be said or done to lessen the suffering you have endured since the loss of your loved one. I can only say that I hope you may find lasting consolation in the knowledge that your son served his country well."

Planning For A Funeral

The family began to make plans for Archie's funeral. The Saturday evening prayer meetings were discontinued. They had prayed that their

Archie would come home. The Air Force was telling them that he was, at last, coming home.

On November 1, 1955 the Air Force issued "an official death report" stating that First Lieutenant Archibald H. Connors, Jr., AO 2 221 998, "was killed (Battle) on 25 June 1952, as the result of an aircraft accident while participating in Korean operations."

McCormick's memorandum provided a final summary of the information available to the Air Force about 1st Lt. Connors "who was reported missing in action on 25 June 1952. He was the pilot of an F-51 aircraft which was hit by enemy ground fire while furnishing aerial protective cover for a helicopter rescue of a Navy pilot. The F-51 went into a diving turn to the right from an altitude of approximately 500 feet, appeared to go into a flat stall, and crash landed on a small knoll near Piyang-dong, North Korea, at grid reference CT-905695. The pilot was not seen to parachute and the aircraft did not burn or explode upon impact. When twelve months in a missing in action status were about to expire, his case was reviewed under the provisions of Section 5, public law 490, March 7, 1942, as amended, and he was continued in a missing in action status. After the cessation of hostilities and completion of the exchange of prisoners, his case was again reviewed in February 1954, and a finding of death was issued based upon available information. In the absence of recovery of remains and a specific date of death, his presumed date of death was recorded as February 28, 1954."

This memorandum indicated that on October 21, 1955, "information was received from the Mortuary and Graves Registration Service, Directorate of Supply and Services, DCS/M, which revealed that identification of remains unknown Evac N-17153, transferred to the United Nations Forces under Operation "Glory," has been established as those of First Lieutenant Archibald H. Connors, Jr., AO 2 221 998. Communist forces report the recovery site of these remains as CT 873711, which is approximately 1 mile northwest of the reported crash location, CT 905695. Identification of remains was based upon favorable comparison of physical and dental characteristics with those of Lt. Connors. The cause of death is indicated as resulting from an air crash since laboratory processing of remains revealed extensive shattering. These facts conclusively establish that Lieutenant Connors died as a result of the aircraft accident on June 25, 1952, the day he became missing in action."

The crash scene location is approximately 23 miles ENE of P'yonggang (Heiko) or about two miles WNW of Tangp'yong-ni.

A letter was forwarded on November 1, 1955, from Major General R. J. Reeves, Air Force Director of Military Personnel to Frankie Connors, informing her that "a change has been made in the records of your husband,

First Lieutenant Archibald H. Connors, Jr." Since your husband's remains have been recovered, available evidence is now considered sufficient to establish that Lieutenant Connors died as the result of the crash of this aircraft on June 25, 1952, the date he was reported missing in action. Therefore, Department of the Air Force official records have been amended to show his death occurred on that date. The amended date of death will in no way affect the previous action taken in the settlement of your husband's accounts. Again may I extend my sincere sympathy."

A footnote on the file copy noted that a similar letter was sent to Archie's parents as well as a "to the wife."

The Casualty Report issued by Order of the Secretary of the Air Force on November 2, 1955 listed 1st Lt. A. H. Connors, Jr. as "Killed in Action" on 25 June 1952. A "finding of death has been issued previously under Section 5, Public Law 490, 7 March 1942 as amended, showing presumed date of death as 28 February 1954. This Report of Casualty is based on information received since that date is issued in accordance with Section 9, of said Act, and its effect on prior payment and settlements is as presented and Section 9. Remains have been recovered and identified. In line of duty—not misconduct."

Disposition Instructions

The final administrative nuances had been completed. The 25-month Air Force career of 1st Lieutenant Archie Connors was finally over. His "case" was closed—almost.

On November 14, 1955, Col. L. F. Carlberg, Chief of the Administrative Support and Services Division of the Air Force Deputy Chief of Staff, forwarded a Memorandum outlining the "Disposition Instructions" in the case of 1st Lt. Archibald H. Connors, Jr., "for necessary action." The memorandum provided such information as next of kin, the "consignee" of the remains, Hardage and Sons Funeral Home in Jacksonville, and the fact that final burial location was a private cemetery—Riverside Memorial Gardens in west Jacksonville. Arch and Eva had bought a number of plots there in the mid-Forties and various family members had done so, as well. That part of the cemetery would eventually be the burial site for the majority of the Connors family, starting with Arch's mother, Julia Victoria Connors in 1945. In 1952, the family had buried Archie's still-born daughter, Sharon Lee there. Now, her father would join her next to the plot that would eventually be Eva's.

On November 18, 1955, Frankie received a letter from the Chief of the Casualty Branch of the Directorate of Military Personnel, Lt. Col. Richard A. Steele. "The authenticated casualty report pertaining to your husband,

First Lieutenants Archibald H. Connors, Jr., are afforded for your use where evidence of the official date of his death may be required."

Archie's Remains Return To Jacksonville

In late November 1955, nephew Tracy was a sophomore in high school. His grandfather, Arch Connors was stricken with his first heart attack. While in the hospital, a nurse attempted to deliver a telegram. Sensing bad news, Woodrow, who was visiting his father at the time, intercepted the message which alerted the family to the fact that the Air Force had, somehow, obtained Archie's remains.

Woodrow insisted that any further communications be directed to him. On December 6, 1955, he and Frankie received a telegram from the Air Force that provided details on the arrival of Archie's remains in Jacksonville on December 10th.

The remains of 1st Lt. Archibald H. Connors, Jr. would depart New York on Friday 9 December via the Atlantic Coast Line's Train #1 and arrive in Jacksonville the next morning at 0700, escorted by 1st Lt. Theodore Essinger.

Early the next morning, Woodrow and Tracy rode together down to Jacksonville's Railway Express Terminal. Joined by Woodrow's brother Gerald, they watched with infinite sadness as the Atlantic Coast Line Train #1 slowly entered the station. Soon, the baggage car opened to reveal a flag draped coffin, escorted by a young Lieutenant Ted Essinger. Archie was home.

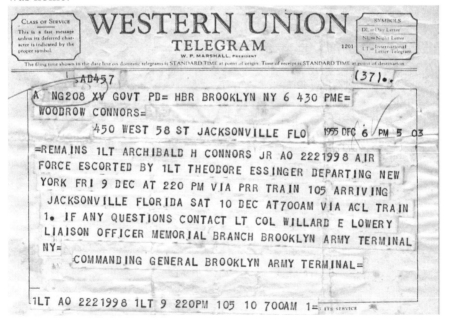

After overseeing placement of the casket in the waiting hearse, they departed for their homes. In his nervousness while getting back into the brand new Buick Special, Tracy bumped the radio knob with his knee. It broke off. He waited for Woodrow's irritation at the broken knob. But nothing was said, he just drove them home. It was not a day for anger. It was simply too sad for words. Nothing much was said on the way home. But they both doubted whether it was really Archie in the coffin.

The Air Force noted in his records how it obtained his remains through an exchange but it did not use the term "Operation Glory." That information was obtained when the family reviewed his records under the Freedom of Information Act decades later. When the sealed coffin was opened, the remains were incomplete, including the skull, as incomplete as the family's ability to come to closure on its doubts as to what had really happened to this great guy.

Nonrecoverability

The Memorial Division of the Army's Office of the Quartermaster General in Washington convened a Board of Officers on January 16, 1956 to review "all relevant data pertaining to unresolved casualties of the late Korean Conflict, and, after considering the pertinent factors involved...duly approved Findings of Nonrecoverability of Remains in the case of Lear, Leslie Wayne, Captain, AO 932 234, USAF."

After noting that American Graves Registration personnel had concluded "thorough and systematic search and recovery operations in all of South Korea," the board noted as far as those casualties that

LT. A. H. CONNORS JR.

Rites Scheduled For War Victim

Funeral services for Lt. A. H. Connors Jr., Jacksonvile airman was killed in action in Korea in June 1952, will be held at 2:30 p.m. Wednesday in the Woodstock Park Baptist Church. The Rev. O. E. Boals, pastor, will officiate.

Pallbearers will be Fred Harrelson, Paul Pace, George Davis, Richard Moffet, Charlie Jackson and James Cox. Burial will be in Riverside Memorail Park under the direction of Hardage and Sons Funeral Home, 517 Park St.

Lt. Connors was awarded the Distinguished Flying Cross, Air Medal and Purple Heart posthumosuly. Surviving are his widow, Mrs. Luyte Connors, of Glendale, Calif.; his parents, Mr. and Mrs. A. H. Connors, Jacksonville; two brothers, Woodrow Connors and Gerald Connors, Jacksonville; and four sisters, Mrs. Mary Hagan and Mrs. Florence Spink, Jacksonville; Mrs. Lucille Strecker, of Lewiston, Idaho, and Mrs. Julia Cathey, of Pullman, Wash.

Funeral Tomorrow. *In this strange black and white polaroid photograph that still has the original pull tab attached, the image captures deep but mixed, feelings. Eva wrote on the back of the photo that, "This was made one day before Archie's funeral. The one sitting beside Frankie is Essie Strickland--one of Aunt Mary's girls." Over three years of uncertainty, of keeping hope alive that Archie might yet come home, of prayers and grieving were ending. Archie had come home, not to rebuild his life, but to be buried. Eva, sitting at left foreground, could not muster a "smile for the camera" pose, nor could Lucille standing behind her mother. The others smile wanly as best they can, including (l-r): Mary Elizabeth (behind Frank Coles), Frankie Connors, Essie Strickland and Julia Connors Coles.*

had died in North Korea were concerned "specific information is lacking as to the number, identity or circumstances surrounding their disappearance." Shortly after the Korean Armistice was signed in July 1953, both sides permitted search and recovery operations in the Demilitarized Zone for 45 days. While some remains were recovered, no further searches had been permitted.

"In September 1954, the United Nations Military Armistice Commission and the Communists concluded negotiations regarding the recovery of those deceased servicemen who were interred in territory under the control of the opposing forces. As a result of these negotiations, disinterments were accomplished by the occupant of the territory and a mutual exchange of remains *[Operation Glory]* was subsequently effected. The agreement did not permit either side to enter the territory of the opposing side to conduct search and recovery operations. Although the Communists turned over approximately 4,000 United Nations deceased personnel, it is now known that not all of the United States servicemen actually interred in North Korea were returned. All United States remains recovered by Graves Registration units or received from the Communists during the exchange of remains in 1954 were removed to laboratories in Kokura, Japan, where they were scientifically processed by identification specialists and physical anthropologists. Despite the most exhaustive efforts," the Memorandum continued, "identification of a number of these remains could not be established."

In view of the completion of search and recovery activities in accessible territory, the inaccessibility of both the Demilitarized Zone and North Korea, and the inability to associate a remains in our custody at this time with the decedent, "it is concluded that his remains are nonrecoverable."

A similar letter was prepared and sent to the Eaton family regarding Ensign Ron Eaton.

Markers For Graves

On May 4, 1956 Frankie Connors wrote the Air Force "in regard to my husband's marker which has not been delivered yet....His remains were shipped to Jacksonville, Florida and buried in December, 1955. Would you please check and notify me as soon as possible why the delay? Thank you."

On May 17, 1956 the Director of Military Personnel for the Air Force acknowledged receiving a letter from Frankie "regarding the delay in the delivery of a marker for the grave of your husband." The Office of the Quartermaster General, Department of the Army, assured the Air Force that the bronze marker was shipped to the Riverside Memorial Park Cemetery in Jacksonville, Florida. Frankie was told she could contact the Superintendent of the cemetery to determine whether or not the marker had arrived.

The Memorial Division sent a memorandum on 12 April 1957 to the Navy Bureau of Naval Personnel, then located in the Navy Annex across the street from Arlington National Cemetery in Northern Virginia asking that the Navy "advise the place of death and disposition of remains for the late Ronald Dow Eaton." The memo further requested that the Navy "furnish a complete record of decorations authorized to be inscribed on a marker for this veteran, specifying the Air Medal and the Purple Heart."

The Navy replied on 6 May 1957 that Ensign Eaton "was missing in action on 25 June 1952 (26 miles south southeast of Wongan) North Korea. There is no record of the recovery of remains. Death was officially confirmed 28 January 1954."

On May 20, 1957, the Memorial Division responded to Bernard Eaton's request for a "government bronze marker to be placed in Wildwood Cemetery in memory of your son, the late Ensign Ronald Dow Eaton."

The Eaton family wished to erect a memorial marker for Ron whether or not his remains were physically returned. The answer they received to their request saddened them.

"There has been no authority delegated whereby a Government marker may be furnished for placement in a private cemetery, as a memorial, when the remains of the veteran are not interred therein," Carl T. Noll explained. He did advise them that "plans have been formulated for memorializing those who died overseas during the Korean Conflict and whose remains have not been recovered. The names of these heroic dead will be inscribed on a memorial in the National Memorial Cemetery of the Pacific, which is located in Honolulu, Territory of Hawaii."

If the Eatons wanted to see a memorial to their son in the United States, they would have to pay for it themselves—and they did. Soon thereafter a large granite stone was erected in memory of Ronald Dow Eaton on the corner of the Main Street house in which he had grown up. An American flag and a POW/MIA flag were hoisted on the flag pole behind the memorial. They fly there to this day, a proud family's reminder of the sacrifice made by their son and brother.

On May 30, 1958, a symbolic Unknown representing the unidentified dead of the Korean Conflict was brought to Arlington National Cemetery and entombed with solemn ceremonies near the Unknown Soldier of World War I. The Quartermaster General, Major General Andrew T. McNamara, served as Chairman and Coordinator for the Unknown Project, and oversaw the process from beginning to end, and faithfully executed the nation's bidding.

"The supreme sacrifice...will long be remembered by a grateful nation."

On July 28, 1960, Archie's widow, Frankie, received a letter from Major General A. P. Clark, USAF, Director of Military Personnel.

"I am writing you concerning your husband," he wrote, "whose name was included in the list of American military personnel for whom the United States government has been attempting to secure an accounting from the North Korean and Chinese Communist. As you recall, shortly after the official exchange of prisoners of war had been completed in the fall of 1953, the United Nations command handed the Communists a list of missing personnel including the names of United States servicemen and about whose fate we had reason to believe the Communist should have some knowledge. Because the Communist response to numerous requests for an accounting was unsatisfactory, and because additional information subsequently available to us produced a definite evidence of death in many cases, the list was eventually reduced to 452. The records show that the remains of your husband were subsequently recovered and returned to the

United States for interment in accordance with the wishes of his next of kin. Therefore, his name is being deleted from the list of those for whom we're still demanding an accounting. It is the policy of the Department of Defense to keep the families informed of any action being taken in revising the list of names presented to the Communist for an accounting. For this reason, I want you to be the first to know of this action. The supreme sacrifice your husband made will long be remembered by a grateful nation."

It would be the last official letter the family would receive concerning 1st Lt. Archibald H. Connors, Jr.

Epilogue

18th Fighter-Bomber Wing

Brigadier General Turner C. "TeeCee" Rogers, 18th Wing Commander in 1951-1952, noted in a message to the Wing when it concluded a year of combat in 1951, "that in the years to come the 18th Wing will be a cherished memory in the hearts of the Korean people—such as the memories that I know all we Americans will keep of those hard-fighting 'Zulu Warriors,' of the 2nd South African Air Force Squadron."

There were many reasons, he explained that the 18th Wing was "The Best Damn Fighter Wing in the World."

The assessment of the Wing's Korean War combat operations, the focus of research for ***Truckbusters From Dogpatch,*** [18] confirmed that what this unit had accomplished during its Korean War service should rank it alongside other legendary military units of the United States Armed Forces.

Futrell [19] reports that FEAF units flew a total of 720,980 combat sorties, of which 181,659 were cargo missions, clearly beyond the capabilities of the F-51 Mustang. Subtracting the cargo missions from the total leaves 539,321 combat sorties. Reviews of unit histories from the 18th Wing, Group and component squadrons conservatively indicated a total of 62,162 sorties for 18th Wing units from July 1950-July 1953. Unit data document that 18th Wing squadrons flew in excess of 10 percent (11.5 percent) of all FEAF combat sorties for counter-air, interdiction, close support, reconnaissance, air control and training missions. Moreover, during 37 months of air combat, the 18th Fighter-Bomber Wing not only had to transition from two different types of aircraft—jet to piston, piston to jet—without standing down from operations, but went on to fly more combat missions than any other unit of the Korean War. It remains based outside the United States to this day with one of the proudest records of any U.S. military unit.

Third Air Rescue Squadron/Group

From June 1950 until the end of hostilities in July 1953, 3ARS rescued almost 10,000 UN personnel, almost 1,000 of them from behind enemy lines, and over 200 from the water. For numerous commendable and heroic rescues, the 3rd ARS/ARG earned three Distinguished Unit Citations.

Arch Connors

Archie's father died in June 1959, at the age of 73, suddenly, in a one-horse town in Colorado en route to see his first great-grandchild. Arch and Eva were about to leave their motel in Kit Carson, Colorado, to go out for breakfast when he collapsed and died in Eva's arms. It was a terrible emotional shock as Eva had never been so alone in her whole life. Numb with grief, she waited at the motel for her brothers to fly out and drive her home. Family members were comforted by the fact that he died doing what he loved best—traveling. At the time of his death he was still running his own construction company, A. H. Connors & Son. Arch was buried in Riverside Memorial Gardens in Jacksonville. One space was left between his and Archie's grave for Eva.

After their father's death, Woodrow and Gerry created Connors Construction Company, which they operated until Woodrow's retirement in 1978.

Eva May Haddock Connors

Archie's mother lived to be nearly 109, and kept her own home—the same home that Archie and his siblings grew up in—until she was 101. After Arch's death, her children wondered how she would survive as she had never driven a car or handled finances on her own. However, she had met tragedy before, her daughter Lucille explained, and her deep-rooted faith and optimism always brought her through it.

Even after the Department of Defense had returned what it had determined to be Archie's remains, the family had its doubts. The information later found in his Individual Deceased Personal File regarding how the remains were determined to be his, was not shared with the family.

During this period Eva told family members that Archie came to her in a dream. "Archie, honey, are you alive?" she asked his spirit.

"Mama," he replied softly, "how could I be after all I went through."

From that time on she sadly accepted the fact that he perished in Mission 1890. It was only in 2002, however, that the details of his final moments were described by the only survivor of that Mission, MSGT Bobby Holloway.

For the next forty years Eva would become the rock that anchored her family. She was an inspiration to everyone. At the age of 70, she realized her lifelong dream of taking piano lessons. After becoming an accomplished pianist, she took up the organ. At one point, she had both a piano and an organ in her living room. She practiced until she could play every song in the Baptist hymnal. Her long, lonely nights were comforted by singing the old songs. Until the end of her life, she said, "I sing myself to sleep." Her life centered around her constantly growing family of grand children, great- and great-great grandchildren.

Eva spent a lot of time in her garden as the years moved by, as her granddaughter Kathryn Coles McCluskey recalls on a web site she and her family created at *www.ourgrandmother.com. [The web site remains on-line and available.]* The house was circled with azaleas, and in front of them she had a border of colorful caladiums and Impatiens plants. People admired her flowers and she gave away many cuttings. One morning she went out to get the newspaper, and all of the caladiums were gone! Apparently someone had stolen them during the night by the light of the street light.

No one who took a tour of her yard could ever forget her rose garden. She alternated roses with gardenia bushes and the fragrance was pure magic.

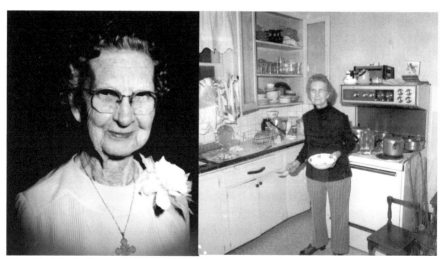

Eva Haddock Connors in a portrait that captures her warmest and inner beauty and a snap shot of her in her "office," the old fashioned kitchen in the home where she kept her own house until she was 101 years old. She would not let her sons, Woodrow and Gerald remodel the kitchen although they urged her to let them do so many times.

She also had pear trees, a fig tree, and three huge pecan trees. She harvested bushels and bushels of nuts in the fall, fighting the squirrels for them, and spent all winter shelling them. Over the years she sent countless packages of shelled pecans to friends and loved ones throughout the country, along with her famous sweet potato pie.

And she continued the trips out West that she and Arch had loved. Every year, she would jump on a Greyhound and make the rounds of all her children and grandchildren in the West who had made the mistake of moving away from Jacksonville. Eventually there were many great-grandchildren to visit, and everyone she visited found a generous check on their dining room table to cover the cost of her "keep." If the grandchild she visited had young children of her own, Eva always ironed a basketful of toddler's clothes before she left.

Her cooking legend continued to grow. At church dinners, her cakes were never put out with all the others, because the ladies who worked in the kitchen kept her cake back for their own enjoyment. Her last big holiday dinner at her home was in 1988, when, at the age of 97, she fed 33 people and two send-outs. After that her children rebelled and said she could no longer do all that work.

Her birthday parties became huge family reunions attended by hordes of friends from the neighborhood, from far-flung places, and even from Washington, D.C. *[Jacksonville's beloved Congressman Charles E. Bennett occasionally showed up]*. Her love of people was evident at these events—Eva's friends were lifelong and totally devoted.

By now she had traveled by auto, train, bus, ship or jet to every one of the 50 states, to Canada, Europe, South America, the Caribbean, and the Middle East. Her favorite trips were two excursions to Israel. On her last trip there she was 99.

While in Egypt, she wanted to ride a camel, so she approached the camel driver and asked him how much. He replied that there was no charge to get up on the camel. So he made the camel kneel down and helped her climb up into the saddle. After plodding around for a while she decided she had had enough and asked him to get the camel to lie down again. "Oh," he said, "that will cost you $7.50." She ended up having to pay to get off the camel, but she got more than $7.50 worth of fun out of telling the story to everyone about how the camel driver got the best of her!

On her 100th birthday, she was featured in the Florida Times-Union and when the reporter showed up at her house to interview her, she baked cookies for him. The day after the article appeared, she got a call from her first cousin, Elizabeth, whom she had not heard from in 50 years. "Eva," she exclaimed, "I thought you were dead!" Her cousin was 102. They arranged to meet and reminisce about old times. When the reporter got wind of it, he came to their reunion and eavesdropped enough to write a second article.

The Times-Union published several articles on her and her life. In February 1999, feature story writer Bob Phelps enjoyed a good time with Eva and her family at her birthday party, then wrote "At 108, grandma's going strong." (http://www.jacksonville.com/tu-online/stories/021599/met_2b1108th.html)

Eva Connors died in September 1999 and was buried between her husband, Arch, and Archie.

Frankie Connors

Archie's wife began a blighted life that would eventually include three other husbands. However, she remained close to her former mother-in-law, Eva, throughout her life. She and Eva traveled frequently throughout the United States and overseas.

Frankie died in June, 2001 in Jacksonville. Her ashes were divided between the Pacific Ocean and Archie's grave and that of their still born daughter, Sharon Lee, buried at Archie's feet when his remains were returned in 1955.

During her final illness, as she drifted in and out of consciousness, Frankie insisted that a particular cardboard box be destroyed. In fact, it was, briefly, put into a garbage can before a family member retrieved it to ensure that some review was given the contents prior to disposal. Eventually, the box was given to the author. It contained numerous personal letters, many of which are included in this work, photographs and a great deal of Archie's personal effects from his youth and military years. Had it not been for an alert, prudent family member, this important personal history would have been lost. The letter that Archie had completed to his brother, Woodrow, but not posted before Mission 1890, was among the letters in the box. Woodrow finally read the letter over fifty years after it was written to him.

When family members gathered at Archie's grave to add Frankie's ashes to the site, W. Bruce Connors, Jr., pointing at the date on the headstone, told his mother, Suzanne Catto, "Look at the date." It was June 25th, exactly 49 years after Archie's death.

Several years after Frankie's death, a Pacifica, California real estate agent contacted Suzanne H. Catto, a family member who had helped Frankie greatly during her final illness. The agent said he wanted to return to the family a cardboard box that had been found in Frankie's home after it had been sold. When the author was given the contents of the box by Suzanne Catto, he found Archie's 67th Squadron "year book," photographs, the flag that had covered his coffin, citations for two of his personal awards—and a crumpled, flattened cap, grey Confederate—Archie's Rebel cap was finally home.

1st Lt. Archibald Haddock "Archie" Connors, Jr.

The remains returned in "Evac N-17153" and identified as Archie Connors, were buried in Jacksonville's Riverside Memorial Cemetery in the silver-toned coffin the Air Force provided. The tiny wooden coffin with his daughter, Sharon Lee inside was buried at his feet. His mother, Eva, lies beside him. The family's memories, and the inevitable pain they bring with them, cannot be buried. With bittersweet persistence they come back to them in dreams, and in flash backs triggered by a phrase, a smell—or a nuggie. His participation in Mission 1890 was recognized by the award of a Purple Heart for having been killed. The newspaper article announcing his funeral arrangements mentioned the award of a Distinguished Flying Cross, the same award that was awarded Capt. Elliot Ayer. However, no such award or citation was found in his effects. On Thanksgiving or on one of their birthdays, Tracy bakes a batch of Eva's ginger snaps and places one on each of their stones. Each succeeding generation of the Connors family has taken pride in his bravery and devotion to duty.

Mission 1890 was not over for former 2nd Lt. William Timmons "Tim" Urquhart for many decades. "For over 50 years I lived with the thoughts of what I believed was a terrible wrong committed during the "Fog of War" by a young fighter pilot in 'How Flight,' 67th Fighter-Bomber Squadron during the summer of 1952," he recalled over fifty years later.

"We were briefed about a mission to destroy one of our downed aircraft. I thought our target was to be a Navy F4U. I remember spotting a silver aircraft on the ground and followed my flight leader in making several firing passes until we finished and went home. Navy aircraft were painted dark blue and USAF aircraft were painted silver. Our fellow pilot, Archie Connors, had crash-landed his F-51 Mustang earlier in the day during Mission 1890. I didn't know for fifty years whether or not he was in the aircraft we shot up. Also, I thought we had gotten the wrong aircraft—silver instead of blue."

It was only when Urquhart was contacted during the research for this book did he finally realize that in all probablity Archie Connors' body had been removed from the cockpit by enemy troops soon after the crash. In any event, later information would make it clear that he died almost immediately from the trauma of the crash itself. The "true story" meant a great deal to Urquhart who could now put his conscience at ease. The information "brought closure to many loose ends. I am eternally grateful," he said.

Captain Elliot D. Ayer

The How Flight leader of Mission 1890 was killed exactly four weeks after that mission. His remains were never recovered. He was awarded a Distinguished Flying Cross for his actions during Mission 1890.

Marguerite Savage Ayer

Ayer's widow, Marguerite, devastated by his loss, eventually succumbed to alcoholism and died at age 42. His son, Fred, serving in Vietnam in an elite Army unit, was awarded the Silver Star and two Purple Hearts before being medically discharged. He completed a distinguished career with the State of Florida.

Dorothy "Dolly" Sharp Clements

Ron Eaton's girl friend and intended wife, finally married over seven years after Ron Eaton's death. After many years of marriage and several children, her husband asked for a divorce saying that he could not live up to or with Eaton's "ghost."

Dolly recalls that it "was the people in my life—family, friends, co-workers—and my faith in God that brought me through. And, by the way," she added, "it's still working for me! I feel that because I had the faith and the courage to go on, I was blessed with a wonderful family."

"As for the war in Iraq, it pains me to know that so many mothers, fathers, wives, husbands and children are suffering the loss of their loved ones. If more politicians suffered the same losses, I doubt if they would be so quick to pull the trigger."

Ensign Ronald D. Eaton

The brave young Ensign's remains have yet to be recovered from North Korea. He was awarded the Air Medal for his participation in the successful missions against Communist hydro-electric facilities on 23-24 June 1952. His family erected an impressive monument to his sacrifice on Main Street in Wilmington, Massachusetts. The American flag and the POW/MIA flag fly every day behind the monument. All of Ron's siblings are alive at the time this work was printed. They miss him still and the life they would have shared with him and his family.

Elsie Adelia Anderson Eaton

Ron Eaton's mother suffered a stroke and was blind when she died September 7, 1981. She was 78.

Bernard H. N. Eaton

Ron's father suffered a stroke in 1985. He died in January 1992, just three months shy of his 94th birthday.

Joyce Eaton Dalton and **Verlie Eaton Quinan** (right), Ron Eaton's sisters, with President George W. Bush at the White House in May 2007. The Eaton Family remains committed to having their brother's remains located and returned for reburial near his home in Wilmington, MA. During a recent briefing conducted by Defense Department representatives, they were assured that the location of Eaton's remains (and those of Captain Wayne Lear) is well documented and that recovery efforts will be made when approved by North Korea.

Leslie and Mabel Lear

At the time of Wayne Lear's birth, his parents, Les and Mabel Lear were living in Santa Cruz, California. Les Lear worked in a local butcher shop and Mabel was a "stay at home Mom," recalled Della Lear Holloway. Shortly after their daughter, Barbara, was born, Mabel was involved in a serious automobile accident that later lead to lingering health problems. However, the Lears were a close knit and happy family—including Mabel's parents—Edward and Pearl Lamb. In the Forties, Les Lear went to Alaska to work on the newly started pipe line. He would retain fond memories of those years even thought the work kept him away from his much loved family. Les was an excellent carpenter and built one of their homes in Southern California, himself. The loss of their only son, Wayne, was a terrific blow—a child can never be replaced. By this time their daughter had three children and these were a joy to the Lears. Mabel Lear died about fifteen years after Wayne was killed. Her loss was hard for Les to bear. He later remarried a family friend—known from their days in Santa Cruz. Les Lear died in the late 1980's.

Captain Wayne Lear

The extraordinarily brave and relentlessly determined pilot never received any commendation for his unsurpassed airmanship, relentless drive to effect the rescue of Ensign Eaton, or his loyalty to his passengers in delaying his own exit from the crashing helicopter to ensure they had a chance—a loyalty that cost him his own life. His remains and those of Ron Eaton are still in North Korea.

At the author's request, U.S. Senator Bob Graham raised the matter of appropriate awards for Lear, Holloway and Connors with the Air Force in November 2003. The Air Force responded with a list of "documents needed to process a decoration recommendation," including: an original or reconstructed narrative of the action being recommended...signed by the recommending official" and a chain of command endorsement, plus other stipulations. These documents, where applicable, had been provided in the original package.

A number of formerly classified documents are available and clearly attest to the facts of the mission and would support a very high level award for personal bravery. Of course, the chain of command for Mission 1890 has not existed for decades. The former Commander of ARS Three, Detachment One, Major (later Lt. Col.) Emerson Heller was killed in 1969. The Air Force has moved on, so to speak, and has shown no interest in officially recognizing Capt. Lear's extraordinary airmanship and sacrifice.

The official Air Force "biography" of Capt. Lear is included below and provides officially prepared and authorized assessments of the events that took place during Mission 1890. It was reviewed and approved as recently as June 26, 2002 and includes a summarized account of Mission 1890 that offers in harrowing

Captain Wayne Lear's extraordinary airmanship, bravery and self-sacrifice went far above and beyond the "call of duty." His citation, had the Air Force ever bothered to create one for his role in Mission 1890, would have read "By exceptional skill, devotion to duty and courage, Captain Lear has brought great credit upon himself and the United States Air Force." Even that would have been a major understatement.

detail what the Air Force knows about the mission from its own sources and documents.

"The surviving fighter pilots witnessed Captain Lear, who had remained in his seat, trying to keep the helicopter stable enough for the airman and the Navy pilot to jump. Capt. Lear jumped from the helicopter at an altitude of about 300 feet, too low for his chute to deploy properly."

Is not Lear's action, coming at the conclusion of over half an hour of extraordinary airmanship and courage in pressing three rescue approaches under fire—during which he was wounded—even more heroic than one of our brave soldiers throwing themselves on a grenade? A recent Medal of Honor conferred for bravery in Iraq, was awarded for just such an action.

Lear's heroic actions were consistently brave and resourceful—not measured in seconds, but during a lengthy mission during which he was personally flying the aircraft, much of the time while wounded and exhausted after fighting to keep the damaged helicopter in the air. At the conclusion of one of the most heroic helicopter rescues of any era, Lear could have bailed out immediately after the aircraft was hit. If he had, there would have been altitude enough for his own parachute to open. To do so, however, he would have to abandon his airman and his rescued pilot to their own fates. Instead, he fulfilled a higher standard of loyalty and stayed at his post until those for whom he was responsible were clear of the falling aircraft. Clearly, his actions and sacrifice rank among the most compelling in our military history. Equally as clearly, the Air Force should have recognized his airmanship, bravery and devotion to duty with a personal award.

Perhaps if the Air Force consulted its own records and accounts regarding Capt. Lear it would convince them that a tragic injustice has been done to Capt. Lear and his family by "the system," first by not preparing personal award recommendations at the time of the action and later, by brushing off a U.S. Senator who attempted to intervene on behalf of the family to have the case reviewed.

"During the summer of 1952," the Air Force biography on Capt. Lear begins, "the Fifth Air Force concentrated so much effort against the communist's resupply network of railroads and rail yards that the pilots had a new theme song—"We've Been Working on the Railroad." The Fifth Air Force was using everything they had, from fighters to heavy bombers, and were flying missions day and night against enemy targets. In response, the communists were concentrating their air defense systems around these targets and succeeded in shooting down a large number of American planes. As in any war, the planes could be readily replaced, but not so the trained and experienced pilots. That is why the Air Rescue crews were so critical; they rescued many downed pilots. They were also a boon to the morale of every pilot. Pilots performed better when they felt that, thanks to the

Air Rescue crews, they had some chance of getting back to friendly hands should their plane be shot down behind enemy lines. Of course, there was a great deal of danger involved in a rescue mission, and most of the danger fell on the Air Rescue crew. The majority of times the Air Rescue pilots had to fly their slow and cumbersome helicopters into enemy territory coming under enemy fire. With only some air cover and their own side arms for protection, the Air Rescue crews had to land, pick-up the downed pilot (commonly injured and in need of assistance), lift off, and fly "home" while evading enemy ground fire. It was a very tough but critical job, and only the bravest could handle it."

"It was during just such a rescue mission that Captain Lear was lost. He and his crewman, an Air Force Airman 1st Class [Bobby Holloway], were dispatched to rescue a Navy pilot who had been shot down over enemy territory. Operating with the code name 'Pedro Tare', the rescue team waited until a covering force of four F-51 fighters had softened up the pick-up spot. There were no enemy sighted, but before the rescue helicopter went in one of the fighters buzzed the area a number of times, flying just above ground level in an attempt to draw enemy fire (and thereby exposing the enemy positions so the other fighters could attack them). No enemy fire was encountered, so the helicopter started to land. Just then, hidden enemy positions opened fire on the  helicopter with heavy machine gun fire. Captain Lear pulled back and the fighters then made three strafing runs on the enemy positions, after which Captain Lear made a second attempt, but with the same results as the first. After the fighters had again strafed the suspected enemy positions, Captain Lear made a third attempt and succeeded in recovering the downed Navy pilot [Ensign Ron Eaton]."

"Captain Lear's helicopter and its air cover were on the way south when they ran into heavy enemy anti-aircraft fire. Within moments, the helicopter and one of the F-51s were shot down. The F-51 crashed before its pilot could get out, but the three men in the helicopter jumped before it crashed. The enlisted airman jumped with a parachute, and the Navy pilot (who didn't have one) jumped with him. The airman, who landed safely, reported that the Navy pilot was to hang on to his legs and ride down with him but that the pilot had lost his grip and fell to his death. The surviving fighter pilots witnessed Captain Lear, who had remained in his seat, trying to keep the helicopter stable enough for the airman and the Navy pilot to jump. Capt. Lear jumped from the helicopter at an altitude of about 300 feet, too low for his chute to deploy properly. The enlisted airman, who was captured and released from an enemy POW camp at the end of the war, upon his repatriation reported that he was the sole survivor of the crash."

"In an effort to achieve a full accounting of missing U.S. servicemen, DPMO has negotiated with the government of North Korea for access to crash sites, battlefields, and prison camp cemeteries. Excavations in northeast North Korea, 1996 through 2000, have resulted in the recovery and repatriation of remains of over 100 U.S. servicemen and that effort is continuing. The North Koreans have authorized limited access to their main military museum and national library in Pyongyang for POW/MIS-related research, but the U.S. researchers have not located any information on Captain Lear during archival research visits in 1997, 1998, and 1999. We continue to actively seek information about the loss of Captain Lear and we will forward new discoveries to family members through the U.S. Air Force Casualty Office."

The Lear Trophy.

Established during the Korean War as the first Air Force award recognizing the best Air Force helicopter squadron, the the original Lear Trophy may be stored in some Air Force closet somewhere, but its current whereabouts are unknown. Meanwhile, the Air Force has "moved on" to award another trophy named for someone else.

Della Paddon Lear married **Bobby Dale Holloway** on Christmas Day 1953 and on that day in 2003 celebrated their Fiftieth Wedding Anniversary.

Regarding his time as a Prisoner of War, Bobby Holloway points out that "you learn about yourself. You really realize what you can do—how much you can do—and how much you can take. It is amazing what the human body can withstand. What your dear old brain can put up with and keep going. It's a hard lesson—really and truly—it was a school of hard knocks, things you learn on the spot as it's happening. You learn what you can endure," he explained.

"It costs to do anything," he continued. "The loss of even one life is priceless when you really get down to it. I'm looking at things from the stand point that you have to stop Communism and similar totalitarian governments—it's not good for the world—for the people. I saw how they had to live—the Korean families—stopping Communism—was worth it. Would I do it again, and if I were back in the military, I probably would. That's your duty—if you can't do your duty—then you better get out," he said.

Master Sergeant (Retired) Bobby D. Holloway and Della-Marie Lear Holloway are very active in their community. Della is a much valued volunteer for her church. Bobby is heavily involved in Shriner philanthropy support, especially medical facilities and services for children.

Tragic events such as Mission 1890 reshape the future for the families involved, Della pointed out, "how their characters are shaped and what they do with their lives."

"Perhaps it was my strong faith in God and a wonderful strong upbringing that lead me on a very different path than that taken by some of the other wives and sweethearts of those on Mission 1890. Don't get the wrong idea—it was very difficult for me to part with Wayne and the marvelous years we had together. I had to ask myself many questions: what would he have wanted me to do? How would my decisions effect others—family and friends? Could I make my life count for something other than continued sadness?"

"If one has faith in God, it is true that when one door closes another one opens," Della said. "With faith you will find that God will not put you through anymore than you can handle. I look back and know that God has had a marvelous path for me to follow. I have been truly blessed. I have had two wonderful marriages—each different yet wonderful."

"Bob and I have had marvelous trips—seen fantastic places. When the children were young, I had a five-year plan in which they would see all of the United States—their capitols, battlefields, national parks, etc. We traveled by car and camped in tents plus using motels. Trips to Canada and Alaska opened up new worlds to the children with the grandeur of the Rockies. Of course, we did have to fly to Hawaii—visited three of the islands—what gorgeous vegetation."

"After the children left home, we took trips abroad—New Zealand by bus, (after a very long air flight); did all of the British Isles (England,

Wales, Ireland and Scotland) by bus; Spain, Morocco, and Portugal also by bus. There have been cruises through the Panama Canal to various Islands, Cruises to all of the Scandinavian countries, etc."

"Probably best of all is that we have a wonderful son, daughter, daughter-in-law, and three very wonderful grandsons—Ryan Blake Holloway, 16; Wesley Tod Holloway, 13; and Brent Patrick Holloway, 10. There is nothing better than seeing your young ones grow into marvelous adults. Yes, we have been truly blessed—over and over again."

"You will find enclosed copies of letters I received from Mrs. A. H. Connors—the mother of Lt. Connors," Della wrote the author in October 2002. "She was kind enough to send copies of the information she had received from the Government. My big concern is that none of these brave men received any real recognition for their valiant attempt to save another person's life. Of course, a great deal of this was caused by the lack of consideration on the part of the commanding officers at that time. I know the one who was in charge of Air Rescue was not one to take the necessary time to do the paper work. Is there any way we can correct this now? I will be very happy to do anything that is in my power to do so."

Lt. Col. Emerson E. Heller

The 3ARS Commander at the time of Mission 1890, was killed in a plane crash April 25, 1969 in Thailand's Quang Tri Province. Heller was the aircraft commander on a mission the day before he was to have departed for the U.S. to retire. Disregarding the technical manual that specified when thunderstorms were within five miles of the airfield, takeoffs and landings would not be attempted, Heller decided to take off in severe weather. The plane  was forced down, caught fire and exploded killing him and the wing flying safety officer.

As the Commander of the Third Air Rescue Squadron, Detachment One in June 1952, Major Heller, should have prepared and processed award nominations for both Lear and Holloway, but inexplicably did not—perhaps because he was no longer in command of 3ARS, Detachment One by July 1953.

There was certainly enough information about the mission upon which to base recommendations for personal awards. From the moment the remaining 67th Squadron F-51's returned to K-46 there was a great deal of information and agreement as to the events and the heroism involved that was available from the participants who conveyed the information to the Intelligence Officers, who in turn, incorporated the facts into a classified incident report that was available to anyone with the clearances to read it—it went all the way to Washington in short order.

Major Heller prepared a boiler plate letter to Della Lear on June 28, 1952. It was obvious that he didn't know Wayne Lear personally, he referred to him several times in the letter as "Leslie." However, the circumstances he relates in the letter, even highly condensed and watered down, are clearly worthy of official commendation. "I feel you should know of the heroic attempt he made to rescue a Navy pilot from the hands of the enemy," Heller began. "As he descended, the enemy tried to repel him..." Heller continued. "Your husband very gallantly returned to the area and retrieved the downed pilot. Leslie's helicopter was damaged by enemy fire during this action but he calmly and skillfully continued towards friendly territory. However, a short distance from his goal the helicopter could no longer sustain flight and all of the occupants bailed out."

"I can assure you," he concluded, "that Leslie's fellow pilots join me in feeling a deep loss, and that we are inspired by his outstanding devotion to duty," Heller concluded. Of course, Heller never mentioned, much less explained, why Lear had been ordered to undertake Mission 1890 in the first place in direct violation of Squadron policy.

Had Mission 1890 not been flown, Eaton most probably would have been captured and spent the remainder of the war as a POW—but he would almost certainly have returned, as did Holloway. Instead, Lear, Eaton and Connors were killed. The most probable outcome had Mission 1890 not been flown was that no one would have been killed and one would have been a POW for the duration of the war. All of them would have had the opportunity to continue their lives. Lear would have continued his Air Force career. Eaton and Connors would have returned to school and entered a profession.

Why Heller, or his successor in command of Detachment One, failed to prepare appropriate personal award recommendations after the tragic mission was completed and to serve as an advocate for such well-deserved personal recognition for Lear and Holloway is unknown—but it represents an egregious dereliction of duty. It was certainly not an oversight.

There is ample evidence in the squadron's history that personal awards were being prepared for rescue pilots and crew members. For example, in April 1952 the squadron conferred 38 Air Medals, 2 DFC's, 2 Soldier Medals and a Purple Heart. In June, the squadron conferred 4 DFC's, 2 Commendation Ribbons and 33 Air Medals. In July, 3rd ARS received approval to award 50 Air Medals, 3 DFC's (including one for Major Heller), and 1 Silver Star. Five DFC's were actually awarded that month. In September, 66 Air Medals were awarded, in addition to a Silver Star, Bronze Star, and a DFC. Why personal awards for Lear and Holloway were not prepared is not known, but remains a constant emptiness to the families involved to this day.

Although an award nomination for Lt. Connors was (apparently) not sent forward by the 18th Fighter-Bomber Wing, Capt. Elliot Ayer, the Mission 1890 Flight Leader, was awarded the Distinguished Flying Cross for that mission. There is also the strong possibility that a similar award was processed for Connors, as noted in his obituary, but for some reason not finalized.

The decision to send Lear and Holloway out on what was essentially a suicide mission resulted in the Korean War's deadliest helicopter rescue mission. Was the 3rd Air Rescue Squadron afraid to draw attention to the decisions that brought about this horrific loss? The effect of this decision to not prepare or pursue personal awards for these two extraordinarily brave and dedicated airmen ensured that their airmanship, devotion to duty, and ultimate sacrifice was known only to their families. In fact, the complete "story" only emerged during the research and fact finding for this book.

The astonishing injustice done to Capt. Wayne Lear and the other members of Mission 1890 continues to this day. Their valor and sacrifice in the defense of Freedom and to save another American serviceman inspired this book and should indeed "long be remembered by a grateful nation."

Notes

**Chapter One
Beating To Quarters**

1 Specific references to operations conducted by USS Bon Homme Richard, its officers and men, were taken from the ship's Action Report to Chief of Naval Operations (generally known as the "deck log"), 21 June-27 June 1952, 1 July 1952, passim. These records are now maintained by the National Archives and Records Administration, Adelphi, Maryland.

2 Vice Admiral Joseph J. "Jocko" Clark, was the last commander of the Navy's 7th Fleet during the Korean War. The first native American to graduate from Annapolis and of Cherokee descendent, he devised a plan calling for air strikes that concentrated his fleet's efforts on destroying enemy weapons and supplies behind enemy lines. The "Cherokee Strikes" served as a much-needed morale boost for American frontline troops.

3 Although the ship carried 1,295,000 gallons of "heavy fuel," it could easily burn over 83,000 gallons of that in a single day of high speed operations. Every three or four days it would rendezvous with an "oiler" to replenish its NSFO—Navy Standard Fuel Oil. Such evolutions usually included underway replenishment events with other replenishment group ships to replace expended munitions, aviation gas, food and other supplies as they arrived in the area and were brought out to the ships on station.

**Chapter Two
Truckbusters At Dogpatch**

1 Air Force units throughout the Korean War prepared and filed with their commands a classified monthly unit history report. Information that references the unit report or unit history report was taken from the appropriate report for that period. For June 1952, the basic document, Monthly Historical Report, 18th Fighter-Bomber Wing, June, 1952, is maintained at the U.S. Air Force Historical Research Agency (USAFHRA), Maxwell AFB, AL. The "Truckbusters From Dogpatch"—their nickname—were already well past their 40,000th

combat mission of the war. They had been ordered into combat just days after the invasion began. Some years later, the official Air Force history would credit close air support for turning the tide of the Korean War even before the Inchon Landing. The 18th was one of the first U.S. military units to be called into action following the North Korean invasion of the South and was certainly a major factor in turning the tide of the war prior to Inchon. It would continue combat operations until the Armistice was finally signed in July 1953, by which time it would have flown more air combat missions that any other military unit in the Korean War.

2 If any United Nations pilot was shot down anywhere in North Korea, the duty fighter-bomber flight would be alerted by the Joint Operations Control office in Seoul for immediate take-off. The Mustangs would relieve the downed pilot's own flight, which would be orbiting overhead to provide as much protection as possible while the rescue helicopter was on the way—a process that might take a while since the helicopter's over the ground speed was less than 75 miles an hour. Prior to the downed pilot's own flight having to abandon him to be captured or killed by enemy ground forces, the RESCAP would arrive overhead with full tanks of fuel, six HVARs (High Velocity Aerial Rocket) apiece and 1,880 rounds of .50-cal. machine gun ammunition aboard each F-51. In addition to rockets and machine gun ammunition, a RESCAP flight was fitted with extra drop tanks to enable it to remain near or over a crash site for extended periods—protecting the search and rescue forces during recovery operations. The Mustangs could circle for hours over the site, if necessary, and then be available to provide close air support to suppress enemy fire while the helicopter—slow and vulnerable—went in to pick up the downed pilot.

3 Originally designated the P-51 for pursuit, prior to the Korean War it had been redesignated the F-51 for "fighter." It had also been modified to enable it to carry bombs, rockets and napalm. The Mustang is a single-place, low-wing built by North American Aviation. The 12-cylinder Merlin engine developed over 1,400 hp on takeoff.

Chapter Three
That Others May Live

1 Back, Klare. Third Air Rescue Squadron cruisebook "Scramble" unit Korean War photographic history, 1952, Introduction.

2 Marion, Forrest L. "The Grand Experiment: Detachment F's Helicopter Combat Operations in Korea, 1950-1053. " Air Power History (Summer 1993), passim p. 38-51.

3 In November 1952, the 3rd Air Rescue Squadron designation was changed to 3rd Air Rescue Group. Its component "flights" were redesignated as squadrons attached to the group.

4 Air Force historian Forrest L. Marion is unaware of any operational rescue boat drop from a B-29 during the Korean War. The capability was there, as noted by General Spivey, but apparently was not used.

5 Back, Klare. "Mission of the Air Rescue Service." 3rd ARS Unit History, January 1952. USAFHRA.

6 The H-5 "Dragonfly" was originally designated the R-5 (H for Helicopter; R for Rotorcraft), and was designed during WWII to provide a helicopter that had greater useful load, endurance, speed, and service ceiling than the R-4. The first XR-5 made its initial flight on August 18, 1943. The first Dragonfly was delivered in February 1945. More than 300 H-5s had been built by the time production was halted in 1951. In production since 1945 and designed as a general utility helicopter, the "Dragonfly" was already obsolete. It could lift only 1,250 pounds, but when it was fully fueled, that number dropped to two passengers and the pilot. Most medical helicopter sorties in Korea were flown with a pilot and a medical specialist. If more than one patient was transported, it meant that the plane was flown beyond its maximum weight. The center of gravity was also a problem. Every H-5 carried a bag of sand or a jerry can that weighed about 60 pounds and could be shifted around as needed to restore the "CG." The main rotor of the H-5 extended 48 feet and the tail rotor diameter was nearly 8 and a half feet. The bubble-nosed fuselage was over 41 feet long and the aircraft weighed 4,815 pounds fully loaded. It had no armament of its own. However, crew members often carried side arms and small caliber weapons.

7 Monthly Historical Report, 3ARS, January, 1952. USAFHRA.

8 Monthly Historical Report, 3ARS, January, 1952. USAFHRA.

Chapter Four
Crippled Corsair

1 USS Bon Homme Richard (CV 31) Action Report to Chief of Naval Operations (deck log), 25 June 1952. NARA, Adelphi, Maryland.

2 Field, James A., Jr. History of United States Naval Operations: Korea. Naval Historical Center, Washington, DC.

3 Clipping has no attribution or other information regarding source or date.

Chapter Five
Ron Eaton's Story—"The Hardluck Kid"

1 Not long after the Civil War, Horace Caswell had built the house for himself and his bride, Emma Marshall. Emma's mother, a widow, operated a nearby boarding house before and during the Civil War in which the men lived who worked as bakers in the Bond Cracker bakeries nearby.
In those days, Silver Lake was known as Sandy Pond. It was a quiet and beautiful place. There were still ice houses across the pond owned by the Union Ice Company of Boston. The superintendent of the Ice Company, John Wilde, lived nearby. Each winter ice was harvested and stored, and in the summer it was sent to Boston by freight car, to be sold. It was a thriving business.
After he retired, Caswell built an ice cream parlor on Main Street near his home. When the street cars would bring the summer crowds out from the city to enjoy Silver Lake, Horace would be there to greet them, with homemade ice cream to help them enjoy the lazy summer day at the lake.
Horace Caswell died in 1917, and his son, Bertram Caswell, M.D., took over the house. Dr. Caswell did not open up a practice in his house although it was ideally situated as a medical office. Instead, he commuted most days from Wilmington into Boston where he worked for the Metropolitan Life Insurance Company. For many years he was known and remembered for his "long, low car" and his driving. "He was one of the most steady plodders the writer has even known," a local reporter noted in an unsigned, undated article, "and he drove his car the same way."

The Eatons moved into the Caswell House in about 1945. The large, roomy house was perfect for the growing Eaton family.

2 USS Bon Homme Richard (CV 31) Action Report to Chief of Naval Operations (deck log), 28 May 1952. NARA, Adelphi, Maryland.

3 "Dogging the watch" is the shipboard practice of breaking the 1600-2000 watch into equal periods called the "first dog watch" and the "second dog watch" to give the watchstanders an opportunity to enjoy the evening meal either before or after assuming the watch. The practice also provided nine watches in a 24-hour period, ensuring that daily watchstanders would not have to stand the same watch every day, but instead would stand the bridge watch next on the rotation the next day. For example, a watch team of Officer of the Deck, Junior Officer of the Deck and Junior Officer of the Watch would typically stand a midwatch one day--0001-0400--then the morning watch--0400-0800--the following day.

4 After a day of flight operations on an aircraft carrier, it was not uncommon for the flight deck officer to "respot the deck"—moving the planes into a new arrangement depending what flight operations were planned for the evening or for the next day. Pilots were required to be in the aircraft during the respotting process. Engines were started prior to taxiing the aircraft to another location on the small, sometimes pitching flight deck. Because the ship was in a combat zone, the ship was in a condition known as "darken ship." No lights were showing "top side." The only lights available for the flight deck crews and pilots were the pale wands—flashlights with colored plastic tips—used to signal the pilots which way to maneuver the aircraft. The planes were required to taxi perilously close to the deck edge with only a thin pipe and a piece of netting between the flight deck and tossing sea some 45 feet below. The pipe and netting were there to help prevent members of the flight deck crew from falling overboard. They were not designed to hold an airplane. Apparently, in the dark and perhaps with some help from the angling of the deck during the turn to starboard, Ensign Ron Eaton's Corsair was taxied off the edge of the Bon Homme Richard's flight deck.

5 USS Bon Homme Richard (CV 31) Action Report to Chief of Naval Operations (deck log), 28 May 1952. NARA, Adelphi, Maryland. p. 1.

6 USS Bon Homme Richard (CV 31) Action Report to Chief of Naval

Operations, 21 June-27 June 1952. 1 July 1952. NARA, Adelphi, Maryland. p. 4.

7 USS Bon Homme Richard (CV 31) Action Report to Chief of Naval Operations, 21 June-27 June 1952. 1 July 1952. NARA, Adelphi, Maryland. p. 4.

8 VF-74 Unit History 1 January 1952-30 June 1952 of 28 July 1952, Part II, page 1.

9 VF-74 Unit History 1 January 1952-30 June 1952 of 28 July 1952, Part II, page 5.

Chapter Six
Elliot Dean Ayer, Mission 1890 Flight Leader

1 Service record information was excerpted from the Individual Deceased Personal File for Captain Elliot D. Ayer, USAF, U.S. Army Human Resources Command, Alexandria, VA.

Chapter Seven
Archie Connors, Mission 1890 Number Two Man

1 Service record information was excerpted from the Individual Deceased Personal File for 1st Lt. Archibald Haddock Connors, Jr., USAF, U.S. Army Human Resources Command, Alexandria, VA.

2 Wilfred "Budd" Stapley was Archie's roommate during his pilot training at Craig AFB and later they flew combat missions together as members of How Flight of the 67th Fighter Bomber Squadron.

3 The official designation of the Mustang by then was "F-51." However, the "F" "was not widely used by the pilots," Lt. Col. John Caldwell explained. "It was P-51, or "Spam Can" affectionately."

4 Personal interviews with Wilfred "Budd" Stapley were conducted during 2003. Stapley served as a Flight Leader in the 67th Fighter-Bomber Squadron and received the Distinguished Flying Cross among other service awards.

5 USAFHRA. Monthly Historical Report, 67th Fighter-Bomber Squadron, January, 1952.

6 Personal interviews with William Timmons "Tim" Urquhart were conducted during 2003.

7 USAFHRA. Monthly Historical Report, 18th Fighter-Bomber Group, February 1952, p. 7.

8 USAFHRA. Monthly Historical Report, 18th Fighter-Bomber Wing, February 1952. p. 3.

9 USAFHRA. Monthly Historical Report, 12th Fighter-Bomber Squadron, March 1952. p. 2.

10 On Feb. 25, 1952, FAF director of intelligence strongly recommended the implementation of "Operation Saturate," an around-the-clock concentration of available railway-interdiction effort against short segments of railway track, including Kunu-ri to Huichon, Sunchon to Samdong-ni, Sinanju to Namsi-dong and Pyongyang to Namchonjom. Operation Saturate was put into effect on March 3rd. Attacks were sustained throughout April and May. Soon after the operation began, flak batteries had been put into place along nearly all rail lines. Losses of tactical aircraft were high.

11 USAFHRA. Monthly Historical Report, 18th Fighter-Bomber Group Group, April 1952. p. 1.

12 USAFHRA. Monthly Historical Report, 12th Fighter-Bomber Squadron, April 1952. p. 2.

13 "Taksan is Japanese for large or many," Will Stapley explained years later. "Apparently they were getting lots of missions up north (K-46) and Archie was sitting down south (K-10) upset that he wasn't getting in on the action." Like all the pilots, he wanted to fly as many missions as possible and get back home.

Chapter Eight
Rescue Helicopters in Combat

1 Marion, Forrest L. That Others May Live: USAF Air Rescue in Korea. Air Force History and Museums Program. 2004. p. 1.

2 At that time the only helicopter in use in Korea was the Sikorsky S-51 that

the Air Force designated the H-5. It had been produced since 1946 and was designed as a general utility helicopter seating just four people. It only had an operating weight of 1250 pounds, and when fully fueled could only hold two passengers in addition to the pilot. Because the typical H-5 crew included a pilot and a medic, only one passenger could be picked up at a time. There were occasions, however, when experienced pilots in desperate situations flew with more passengers, but it was highly risky.

The center of gravity was a big problem and required that a 5-gallon can of sand or oil weighing approximately 60 pounds be carried in the bird at all times. With just the pilot and medical board, the can was carried up front. When a third or perhaps fourth person was brought aboard the craft, the can had to be carried by the crewmen to the tail compartment.

The H-5 cruised at about 60 knots and had a maximum elevation for takeoff or landing in the mountains of about 4,000 feet above sea level. Its maximum range was about 150 miles.

The Sikorsky S-55, which was designated the H-19 by the Air Force, was first flown in 1949. At the beginning of 1951, FEAF had requested the Air Force Chief of Staff to replace the H-5's with H-19's. In March 1951, one YH-19 arrived in Korea to began its tactical evaluation under actual combat conditions. By September 1951 a second H-19 had arrived and from that point on H-19's would continue to arrive in theater. However, the detachment would continue to operate both types of helicopters for the remainder of the war despite the limitations of the H-5, limitations that would doom at least one of its flight crews.

The H-19 was a great improvement over the H-5 in range, speed, altitude, and armor protection of important components. The H-19 carried one or two pilots and up to 10 passengers, or a medical technician and eight litters. The H-19 was also equipped with the instrumentation needed for instrument flying although most rescue helicopter operations remain daytime missions.

3 Interviews with Master Sergeant (Retired) Bobby D. Holloway, U.S. Army Reserve were conducted in person and via e-mail from 2002-2007. Holloway eventually transferred from the Air Force and completed his military career in the U.S. Army Reserve Force.

Chapter Nine
Wayne and Della Lear

1 Captain Lear's personal history was compiled from letters, materials and

photographs provided by Della Paddon Lear Holloway from 2002-2007.

2 Captain John Springer Walmsley, Jr., a flying instructor during World War II in the United States and Japan, was posted to Korea in June 1951 to the 8th Squadron, 3rd Bomb Group. He completed twenty-five combat missions flying the A-26 bomber. On September 14, 1951, during a night attack mission, Capt. Walmsley disabled an enemy supply train and kept attacking until he ran out of ammunition. He then called for other friendly aircraft in the area to complete destruction of the target. Using the searchlight mounted on his aircraft, he guided another B-26 aircraft to the target area, meanwhile constantly exposing himself to enemy fire—he twice aligned himself with the target, his searchlight illuminating the area, in a determined effort to give the attacking aircraft full visibility. As the friendly aircraft prepared for another attack, Captain Walmsley descended into the valley in a low level run over the target with searchlight blazing, exposing himself to vicious enemy antiaircraft fire. He refused to employ evasive tactics and pressed forward straight through an intense barrage, thus insuring complete destruction of the enemy's vitally needed war cargo. While he courageously pressed his attack Captain Walmsley's plane was hit and crashed into the surrounding mountains, exploding upon impact.

Chapter Ten
Bobby Dale Holloway

1 Interviews with Master Sergeant (Retired) Bobby D. Holloway were conducted in person and via e-mail from 2002-2007.

2 Master Sergeant Holloway's personal history was compiled from letters, materials and photographs provided by him during interviews and correspondence from 2002-2007.

Chapter Eleven
Ambush of Mission 1890

1 Third Air Rescue Squadron. Report of Incident, 26 June 1952, filed on unit letterhead by Major Emerson E. Heller, Commander. Classified as SECRET on 2 July 1952 and later declassified.

2 The radio call sign "Filter" applied to all 18th Fighter-Bomber Wing aircraft during air operations. For example, a flight leader for a mission

composed of How Flight aircraft might call Mellow Control using: "Mellow Control, this is Filter How."

3 Marion, Forrest L. That Others May Live: USAF Air Rescue in Korea. Air Force History and Museums Program. 2004.

4 Ibid, Report of Incident.

5 Hill, John. Witness Statement, Mission 1890. Included in Individual Personal Deceased File of 1st Lt. A. H. Connors, Jr., USAF.

6 Master Sergeant (Retired) Bobby D. Holloway personal interview. Conducted in person and via e-mail from 2002-2007.

7 Ibid, Report of Incident.

8 Lear, Captain Leslie, CILHI/REFNO # FSC 548-A. Circumstances of Loss.

9 Ibid, Report of Incident.

10 Ibid, Report of Incident.

11 Later information confirmed that Lear did get away from Eaton's crash site. In 2005, the Individual Deceased Personal Records for Lear, Eaton, Connors and Ayer were obtained through the Freedom of Information Act. When the coordinates cited in these official documents were compared, it was clear that the location of Eaton's crash site was at least five miles from the location cited for the helicopter crash. After picking Eaton up, Lear had headed southeast down the river valley, dodging and weaving the damaged helicopter as best he could trying to avoid the hail of anti-aircraft fire coming up from the nearby hills.

12 Ibid, Report of Incident.

13 AFPMP-12-E-3/RT 42755 of 19 January 1954 ICO Lear, Leslie W. AO 932234 Determination Case #191 included in Lear's IDPR. The broken strap referred to in the Report of Death was not the parachute strap, but a strap on the survival vest Airman Holloway had reattached below his waist. He was unable to wear a parachute and a vest and still have enough mobility to operate the helicopter hoist. The vest included a survival radio that he could have used to communicate with the escort

fighters, but it was lost, along with his service revolver. He would land in enemy territory, defenseless and unable to communicate with the fighter aircraft circling overhead.

14 Ibid, Report of Incident.

15 Ibid, Report of Incident.

16 Ibid, Report of Incident.

17 Ibid, Hill statement. The location reported for Connors crash site was about 1.5 miles southeast of the helicopter crash, or five miles, 170 degrees from Sinenjung-ni. Hill's estimation differed slightly from the reported crash site, but later information would lead to a strong possibility that Hill's estimate was very close to the mark.

18 McShane, William. Witness Statement, Mission 1890. Included in Individual Personal Deceased File of 1st Lt. A. H. Connors, Jr., USAF.

19 Urquhard, William Timmons. Author interview.

Glossary

(-)
Minus

.50 Caliber guns
The F-51D carried six free-firing .50 caliber machine guns, three in each wing. The guns were manually charged (loaded) on the ground, and fired simultaneously when the pilot pressed the trigger switch on the front of the control stick ("joy stick") grip. The maximum ammunition capacity was 400 rounds for each of the inboard guns, and 270 rounds for the center and outboard guns—a total ammunition load of 1880 rounds. Typically, the guns were aligned to converge at range of from 250-300 yards.

38th Parallel
The 38th degree of north latitude as it bisects the Korean Peninsula became the arbitrary demarcation line between North and South Korea from 1945 to 1948 and the border between the Republic of Korea and the Democratic People's Republic of Korea from 1948 to 1950.

Aeromedical Battlefield Evacuation
One of the major innovations of the Korean War was the use of helicopters for evacuating the wounded from the battlefield.

Air Medal
First authorized in World War II, the Air Medal was awarded during the Korean War in the name of the President of the United States, recognizing single acts of merit or heroism for aerial flight. Also awarded at times during the Korean War for a given number of combat flights.

Airfields
During the Korean War, the U.N. Far East Air Force (FEAF) used some 15 air bases in Japan to support combat operations in Korea. In Korea itself, the Air Force either improved or constructed some 55 airfields. These air bases were all numbered and some became better known by their number than by their name. The more important of these airfields included: K-1 Pusan West; K-2 Taegu; K-3 Pohang; K-5 Taejon; K-6 Pyongtaek;

K-8 Kunsan; K-9 Pusan East ; K-10 Chinhae; K-13 Suwon; K-14 Kimpo; K-16 Seoul; K-40 Cheju-do Island; K-46 Hoengsong; K-47 Chunchon; K-55 Osan.

Albatross

SA-16; amphibious rescue aircraft. See Cho-do.

AOCP

Aircraft Out of Commission for Parts. "The landing strip at K-10 is dirt and problems were immediately encountered. Large rocks on the runway were sucked into the propeller during run-ups, resulting in damage to numerous propellers and only extraordinary supply action kept such aircraft from becoming AOCP." [1]

Armed Reconnaissance

"Formation to the target area will be battle formation flown at an altitude of 7,000 feet or at an altitude practical to avoid known anti-aircraft guns, small arm s fire and overcasts," 18th Fighter-Bomber Group Standardized Procedures for Combat Operations explained. "The Flight Leader should be on the deck, flying at an indicated air speed of at least 300 mph. He should pull up occasionally (above 3,000') in order to orient himself and to regain his low level air speed. The leaders' wing man should fly up with No's. 3 and 4, who should be flying at least 4,500' above the terrain. These three aircraft will fly a spread formation, weaving for mutual protection as well as flak evasion. The element leader will advise the flight leader of known flak positions, towns, villages, railroads, etc., that the Flight Leader cannot see. When a worthy target is found, the flight leader will determine whether to utilize two or four aircraft in the attack. In either instance, spacing between aircraft should be such that the most difficult target is presented to ground fire. This is usually accomplished with four aircraft in the form of a Clover Leaf Pattern with one aircraft always in a firing position. With two aircraft in the attack, the wing man should make his pass at least 45 degrees off from the axis of the leader's attack. At the completion of the last pass, the Flight Leader will so inform the flight. Aircraft on the deck will be constantly turning to present a difficult target for enemy ground fire. Do not "Stooge" at low air speed, straight and level, or in one small area. Make a few turns then move down on a road a few miles farther over this area, then move to another road. Don't follow one road from town to town, if you do, the enemy will be waiting for you with everything they have. Find targets for you napalm early so you'll have a more responsive aircraft. It is almost impossible to see small arms fire unless you see the flash or the person shooting, so assume that you are being fire at continuously and make yourself hard to hit. Fire your guns until you reach your tracer ammunition, the rest of your 1.50 caliber ammunition is a reserve to fight you home if you are jumped. After you have completed your reconnaissance and have expended your ordnance, climb to a safe altitude and proceed Home. Use tactical formation from the target area to your home base. Don't go to sleep going Home! Keep looking around."

Armistice Agreement

Agreement between the United Nations Command and the military forces of the North Korean People's Army and the Chinese Communist Forces (CCF) that went into effect July 27, 1953.

ARS

Air Rescue Squadron/Service

Augur in

Pilot slang for crash. "Heard that two of my classmates augured in..."

B-26

Douglas "Invader": twin-engine light bomber (USA)

B-29

Boeing "Superfortress": four-engine bomber (USA)

Bailout

The process of exiting the aircraft while it is airborne. Pilots were advised to "slow the airplane to the lowest speed that is reasonably safe—150 mph. The lower the speed at which you bail out, the less risk there is. But don't slow the airplane dangerously near the stalling point, particularly if you have no power. Lower the seat, duck your head, and jettison the canopy. Disconnect your headset and oxygen hose, and release the safety belt and shoulder harness. Pull yourself up onto the seat so that you're in a crouching position with your feet in the seat. Dive with head down toward the trailing edge of the right wing, unless a fire or some other condition makes it advisable to go out the left side." **Bedcheck Charley**

Enemy aircraft, nicknamed "Bedcheck Charlies," used to harass Allied positions. Two types of antique aircraft were most often used, including: Soviet-built Yakovlev YAK-18 training planes; and Polikarpov PO-2 wood and fabric biplanes, both with a cruising speed of about 100 knots. Even ground personnel were not immune to the perceived threat of enemy air attack, particularly at K-16 where "Bed Check Charlie," a small, two-place, enemy bi-plane made regular appearances. Hedgehopping down the valleys and hilly countryside to avoid air search radar, "Charlie" would arrive in the early morning hours, "dropping hand grenades, mortar shells, and strafing the area with a hand held sub-machine gun. No damage was inflicted by this 'bogie' other than a few barked shins, skinned elbows, caused when personnel stumbled over tent ropes enroute to their fox holes," the 39th FIS reported.

Belly landing

A forced landing with wheels up. "Forced landings with wheels down should be made only when you're absolutely certain that such a procedures will be safe." See Ditching.

BIG SWITCH

Name for the main POW exchange that followed the signing of the Korean Armistice agreement July 27, 1953. Operation Big Switch was conducted from August 5 through December 23, 1953. It was the final exchange of prsoners of war by both sides. [3]

Bird baths

Airman slang for taking a "bath" from one's helmet. "Bathed out of our **helmets, "bird baths."**

BIRD DOG

Search And Rescue. Also referred to light observation type aircraft.

Birddog

See L-19.

BNR

Body not recovered.

Bogeys

Unidentified aircraft or attacking aircraft, e.g. "Bogeys at six o'clock level."

Bomb line

The designated line, 1,000 yards beyond which was considered enemy territory. Beyond the bomb line combat operations were conducted were only under the positive control of a Mosquito or FAC. "Accordingly the bomb (battle) line was withdrawn from the boundary (Manchurian-Korean) perimeter and the "chop line" as a line of "no combat" demarcation was abandoned." [5]

Bombs

Removable bomb racks on the F-51D were designed to hold 100-, 250-, or 500-pound bombs. 1000-pound bombs could be carried "to accomplish particular missions, but the extra weight is undesirable and restricts the airplane to straight and level flight." If bombs were not installed, "chemical smoke tanks" (napalm) or droppable fuel tanks could be carried.

Bronze Star Medal

First authorized in World War II, the Bronze Star Medal was awarded in the name of the President of the United States for heroic or meritorious achievement or service in connection with military operations against an armed enemy not involving participation in aerial flight. Awards, denoted by a metallic V device worn on the medal ribbon, were made for heroism performed under circumstances of a lesser degree than those required for award of the Silver Star.

Buy the farm/bought the farm

Pilot slang for killed or died.

Campaigns

The Korean War consisted of 10 campaigns, including: UN Defensive—June 27-Sept. 15, 1950; UN Offensive—Sept. 16-Nov. 2, 1950; CCF Intervention—Nov. 3, 1950-Jan. 24, 1951; First UN counteroffensive—Jan. 25-April 21, 1951; CCF Spring Offensive—April 22-July 8, 1951; UN Summer-Fall Offensive—July 9-Nov. 27, 1951; Second Korean Winter—Nov. 28, 1951-April 30, 1952; Korea Summer-Fall 1952—May 1-Nov. 30, 1952; Third Korean Winter—Dec. 1, 1952-April 30, 1953; Korea Summer-Fall—May 1-July 27, 1953.

CAP

Combat Air Patrol, or "CAP," is an aircraft patrol stationed over an objective area, a force to be protected, or in an air defense area whose mission is to intercept and destroy hostile aircraft before they can reach their targets.

Capped

Provided combat air patrol for, e.g. "The procedures of capping a downed pilot were also changed in hopes that the change will cut down the losses suffered on capping missions."

Casualties

A broad term encompassing those killed or wounded in action, those who later died of their wounds, those missing in action and those taken as prisoners of war.

CCF

Chinese Communist Forces

CCT

Combat Crew Training

Ceiling

Height above ground or water lowest layer of clouds below 20,000 feet that covers more than half of the sky. An aircraft's service ceiling is the density altitude at which its maximum rate of climb is no greater than 100 feet per minute. Its absolute ceiling is the highest altitude at which the aircraft can maintain level flight.

Chairman, Joint Chiefs of Staff

Senior officer of the U.S. armed services. A statutory adviser to the National Security Council, he presides over the Joint Chiefs of Staff consisting of the chiefs of staff from the Army and Air Force and the Chief of Naval Operations. Unlike during the Korean War, today the Joint Chiefs of Staff also includes the Marine Corps Commandant.

Chinese Communist Forces (CCF)

Elements of the Chinese People's Liberation Army moved into Korea Oct. 4, 1950.

Chodo

Island about one third up the West coast of North Korea controlled by U.N. forces. Air surveillance and air rescue personnel based there saved many lives. Facilities included a tactical air-direction center with limited capabilities, but helpful in providing local air-control and warning services in that area of Korea. When fighter-bombers or Sabres ventured into Northwest Korea, an SA-16 would be deployed from Seoul to orbit north of Cho-do. If a fighter pilot ran into trouble he "Maydayed" and tried to reach a pre-determined orbit-rescue point off the west coast. His own flight would provide RESCAP until the Albatross arrived. See Bingo. By December 1951 a detachment of H-5 helicopters were stationed at Cho-do for rescue alert. In February 1952, more capable H-19 helicopters were stationed on Cho-do.

CHOKE

A main supply route interdiction plan used by FAF during which last light fighter-bombers attacked selected road bridges. Shortly after dark fighter-bombers, usually B-26's would attack vehicles stalled behind the blow-out bridges.

Chopline

The FEAF CHOPLINE or line of "no combat" demarcation was instituted on 15 October 1950, which limited the air operations to actions 20 miles south of the Manchurian border from longitude 12 degrees to the west coast. This was equally divided into three areas, Recce Areas I, II, and III. See Bombline.

CINCFE

Commander-in-Chief, Far East

CINCPAC

Commander in Chief, Pacific

CINCPACFLT

Commander-in-Chief, Pacific Fleet

CINCUNC

Commander-in-Chief, United Nations Command

Clanky

Air Force fighter pilot slang for combat fatigue. Also "flak happy."

Clark, Mark Wayne

General Clark replaced Gen. Matthew B. Ridgway as commander in chief, Far East Command and commander in chief, United Nations Command.

Clearance

Authorization from air traffic control to proceed as requested or instructed. Used for ground and air maneuvering, e.g. "cleared for take-off."

Close Air Support

One of the three "classic" missions of tactical airpower, including air superiority and interdiction. CAS was the most complex of these three missions "since it involved an intimate cooperation of ground and air forces and an intricate system of communications." [7] Close air support involves the use of fighter, fighter-bomber and, in exceptional cases, bomber aircraft to strike enemy targets just in front of the battle lines. "Upon reaching the target designated by the TACP, the flight leader should observe the terrain and other conditions in order to establish the best axis and method of attack," 18th Fighter-Bomber Group Standardized Procedures for Combat Operations explained. "The objective is to deliver maximum firepower to enemy positions while absorbing a minimum of return fire from them. To accomplish this, the method of deploying aircraft to attack at different angles and altitudes has been proven highly successful. These aircraft, evenly spaced will provide almost continuous fire on enemy positions, while in the target area. After completing a bomb, rocket, or firing run, evasive action should be taken by a series of sharp turns, or a change in direction, or by hitting the deck. Aircraft making rocket-firing and gunnery runs at a high angle present a more difficult target for ground gun crews and at the same time provide a more effective concentration of fire against ground personnel and equipment. This type of attack is best utilized under good weather conditions, however, it is difficult to adapt to low ceiling conditions. [8]

CO
Commanding Officer
CofS
Chief of Staff
Comd
Command
Comdr
Commander
COMINT
Communications intelligence (now known as SIGINT, i.e., signals intelligence)
Comm
Communication
Company
In the U.S. Army and Marine Corps a company is the basic organizational unit.
COMSEVENTHFLT
Commander, Seventh Fleet
CONUS
Continental United States. See ZI.
CP
Command post

CRS

Course, the intended direction of flight in the horizontal plane expressed in degrees of the compass.

Deadstick

Descent and landing with engine(s) shut down and propeller(s) stopped.

Demilitarized Zone (DMZ)

Created by the 1953 Korean Armistice agreement, the DMZ consists of a buffer zone two kilometers on either side of a military demarcation line that follows the general location of the front lines at the close of the war.

Det

Detachment

DF

Radio Direction Finding.

Dinghy

Inflatable, one-man rescue raft. "…Then up onto the wing, where the erk awaits you with your dinghy. This thing must save your life when you fall into cold water with sharks, and also serves as a cushion to sit on, since all parachutes are of the back type. This 'Cushion' is about a soft as sack full of broken bricks. A brief skirmish between you and the erk and the dinghy, and then you can climb into the cockpit." [10]

Distinguished Flying Cross

Awarded in the name of the President of the United States for heroism or extraordinary achievement while participating in aerial flight.

Distinguished Service Cross

America's second highest award for bravery.

Ditching

A forced landing (see belly landing) in water. "Never attempt to ditch the F-51 except as a last resort. Fighter planes are not designed to float on water, and the F-51 has an even greater tendency to dive because of the airscoop underneath. It will go down in 1 ½ to 2 seconds."

Dive Bombing

"Dive bomb runs must originate from an altitude so that the aircraft can be aligned with the target long enough to make an accurate release of bombs and still recover from the dive and break away without entering the area of bomb blast. This entry altitude is usually above five thousands feet and varies with the steepness of the dive. The aircraft should be trimmed for the dive as soon as possible after entering bomb run in order to make a more effective alignment on the target. The point of release depends on the steepness of the dive. The greater the angle of dive, the less correction will be necessary for the bombs' trajectory. The high angle dive bomb run is the most effective means of pinpointing a target. In breaking away from the target after the bomb release, it is recommended that the break be made down and away from the target to the deck, taking evasive action." [11] See Skip Bombing and Glide Bombing.

Division

Basic combined arms organization for waging war. Normally commanded by a major general. During the Korean War it typically consisted of three regiments of infantry; a four-battalion division artillery (three battalions with 105-mm howitzers, one with 155-mm howitzers); an anti-aircraft artillery battalion; a tank battalion; a reconnaissance company; an engineer battalion; a medical battalion; and supporting medical, ordnance, quartermaster and signal companies.

Dog Patch Century Flight

Pilots assigned to the 18th Fighter Bomber Wing who successfully completed 100 combat missions.

DOW

Died of wounds

DPRK

Democratic People's Republic of Korea

DR

Dead (deduced) reckoning. Plotting position by calculating the effects of speed, course, time and wind against last known position (fix).

Drop-tank

Gasoline tank, externally hung.

DTG

Distance To Go; Date Time Group (message address component)

ECM

Electronic Countermeasures

Eighth U.S. Army

The major U.S. Army headquarters in Japan when the Korean War began. **Element**

A "two ship" unit of a "four ship" aircraft flight (see).

EUSA

Eighth U.S. Army

EUSAK

Eighth United States Army in Korea, title created on July 13th at Taegu City, SK by LTC Walton H. Walker upon assuming command of all American ground forces in Korea. The new command absorbed the Army personnel of USAFIK, ADCOM and KMAG, all of which were discontinued.

F/S

Fire Support

F2H

McDonnell "Banshee": single-engine jet fighter (USA)

F3D
Douglas "Skyknight": single-engine jet fighter (USA)
F4U
Vought "Corsair": single-engine fighter (USA)
F-51D
North American "Mustang": single-engine fighter (USA). The Mustang was built by North American Aviation and was a single-place, low-wing monoplane powered by a Packard-built Rolls Royce engine. Originally designed primarily as a fighter airplane, it was later equipped to carry bombs, rockets and chemical tanks (napalm). The aircraft was equipped with six .50-caliber machine guns as standard equipment.
F-80
Lockheed "Shooting Star": single-engine jet fighter (USA)
F-86
North American "Sabre": single-engine jet fighter (USA)
F9F
Grumman "Panther": single-engine jet fighter (USA)
FA
Field Artillery; Final Approach
FAC
Forward Air Controller
FAF
Fifth Air Force
FAFIK
Fifth Air Force in Korea
Far East Air Forces (FEAF)
Activated at Brisbane, Australia, June 15, 1944, the Far East Air Force fought its way across the Pacific during World War II. When the Korean War began, it was part of the postwar occupation of Japan, with headquarters in Tokyo.
Far East Command
Shortly after the Korean War began, Far East Command was given operational command of the Republic of Korea (ROK) armed forces by ROK President Syngman Rhee. Soon after, the FECOM was designated as the U.N. Command (UNC), which gave it authority over Allied personnel as well.
FBG
Fighter Bomber Group
FBS
Fighter Bomber Squadron
FBW
Fighter Bomber Wing

FEAF
Far East Air Forces (U.S.)
FEAMCOM
Far East Materiel Command
FEC
Far East Command
FIG
Fighter Interceptor Group
Final(s)
Final approach. The part of a landing sequence or airport circuit procedure in which the aircraft has made its final turn and is inbound to the active runway. Downwind is the segment of the circuit paralleling the runway and flown on a reciprocal heading. Base leg is the crosswind segment bringing the aircraft from the downwind leg to final approach. The leg before downwind is called the Crosswind leg.
FIS
Fighter Interceptor Squadron
FIW
Fighter Interceptor Wing
Flak Happy
Air Force pilot slang for combat fatigue. Also "clanky."
FLAK
Flieger Abwehr Kanonen, German anti-aircraft guns. Term carried over into subsequent wars and referred to ground fire coming from anti-aircraft guns as opposed to "pot shots" or ground fire from small arms. Flak was encountered "in increased intensity in the P'yongyang and Kangdong areas. This included 20-mm and 40-mm automatic weapons fire, "as well as small arms fire." One pilot, Captain Elzeard Deschamps, is presumed "missing in action" due to enemy anti-aircraft fire encountered over Kangdong airdrome." [13]

Flak traps
Ambush areas devised by Communist gunners to lure UN pilots into traps—heavy concentrations of anti-aircraft guns. Traps include open parachutes hanging on trees, dummy troops made of straw, cables strung across valleys, and strings of lights at measured intervals along mountainsides that looked like a convoy. By July 1951 the Reds had 275 antiaircraft artillery guns and 600 automatic weapons emplaced in Korea. "Pyongyang was defended by 48 guns and more than 100 automatic weapons, making it one of the worst 'flak traps' in Korea." [14]

Flight
A group of aircraft operating together. A "four-ship flight" consisted of four aircraft organized in two "elements." Two-, four-, and eight-aircraft

Mustang flights were used during combat situations throughout the war. The majority of all flights consisted of four-aircraft flights where "two aircraft [an "element"] were designated to furnish top (aerial) cover during armed reconnaissance flights or during strafing passes against enemy personnel, materiel and rolling stock."

FLT
Flight

Fluid four
A flight formation of four aircraft spaced generally in fingertip formation. The two element leaders applying the firepower, while the wingmen covered the rear.

Flying Boxcar
C-119, twin engine, transport aircraft

Flying Cheetahs
Nickname for the 2 Squadron, South African Air Force operationally attached to the 18th Fighter-Bomber Wing.

Formations
   Element: two aircraft.
   Flight: two elements.
   Section: two flights.
   Squadron: two or more sections.
   Group: two or more squadrons.
   Trail formation: aircraft following single file approximately two ship lengths distance and "stacked down" approximately 15 feet below the one ahead.
   Close trail formation: each aircraft "stacked down" about 15' below 2/3s behind the one ahead and above. Propeller will be midway between scoop and tail section.
   Echelon formation: aircraft flying "line abreast" approximately 3' apart and below and with the wing of each succeeding aircraft about 2/3's behind the nose of adjacent aircraft.
   Finger formation: visually approximating the positions of the right four fingers held closely together. "Middle finger" in front, the other "fingers" to the left (one aircraft) and right (two aircraft) flying 3' apart and below each other. "Wings overlapping approximately 3 feet laterally, stack down one ship height, and echelon depth that is necessary to keep #2 wing directly opposite star insignia on lead aircraft."
   Battle or tactical formation: a "finger formation"—wingtip of #2 aircraft will be directly opposite star insignia of lead aircraft—space laterally will be that necessary for wingman to accomplish a 180 degree turn into element lead and pull out 180 degrees to the line of flight of element leader. The horizontal separation of the battle or tactical formation is

extended to one "turning diameter" between each aircraft.

Frag Order

The daily Wing operations orders generally directed the Fighter-Bomber Group to perform missions as directed by daily Fifth Air Force Operations orders. The Fighter Group published as a daily operations order the "fragment" which concerned the Squadrons. Thus, the Group orders were known as "frag orders."

Frozen Chosin

Korea in the winter.

G/S

Groundspeed. The speed an aircraft makes over the ground, a product of its airspeed and wind speed. Also, Glide Slope.

G-2

Intelligence section of divisional or higher staff

G-3

Operations and training section of divisional or higher staff

Gaggle

Pilot slang for a "loose formation of attacking aircraft." Also, referred to a 16-ship formation—four flights, one from each 18th squadron—a "gaggle" or "wing gaggle."

Gang

River in the Korean language.

GCI

Ground Controlled Intercept

GEN

General

GHQ

General Headquarters

GLO

Ground Liaison Officer

Globemaster

C-124; four engine strategic transport aircraft introduced into USAF service during the Korean War. Also known as an "aluminum overcast."

GMT

Greenwich Mean Time

GO

General Orders

Golf balls

Pilot slang for "flak" or anti-aircraft fire. "There was a hell of a firefight going on down there," Capt. Jack Hawley, of Bridgeport, Mich., said, "and they weren't all firing at each other. Some of them were firing at us. Golf balls were going by us from all angles. I think that's when rigor mortis of my trigger finger set in."

Goony bird
See C-47/R4D.
Ground pounders
Pilot slang for non-rated (not aviators), staff officers.
Group
In the Air Force, two-four squadron combat organization, normally commanded by a colonel, in the U.S. Army a group is a command structure controlling several battalion sized elements and is subordinate to a brigade.
GS
General Staff
GS
Glideslope—the vertical guidance component of an instrument landing system that establishes a safe glide path (usually three degrees) to a runway. Also Ground Speed.
Gun camera
The F-51D could be equipped with a gun camera mounted in the leading edge of the left wing. The camera was loaded and adjusted from the left wheel well. A small door covered the camera when the landing gear was down. A three-position switch on the front switch panel controlled guns and camera. With the switch flicked up to GUNS, CAMERA & SIGHT, the guns fired and the camera operated with the pilot pressed the trigger on the stick. If the switch were pushed down to CAMERA & SIGHT, the pilots could take photographs without firing the guns. Both guns and camera were heated electrically to enable their operation even at high altitude.
Gunnery
The common error in air-to-ground gunnery "is allowing the burst of fire to travel from the first point of fire, through the target and beyond. The most destructive fire is that which is held on the desired target for the length of the time actual firing is accomplished. There are occasions when a dispersed fire is desired, however, most targets are stationary and by "walking" your rounds through your target only a small percentage of them are effective. Here again a steep angle of attack is desired, with the subsequent break-away for evasive action. Depending on the nature of the target, the number of passes will be made to be most effective, that is if it is a heavily defended area a second pass should not be made whereas close support attacks can be pressed." [15]
H-19
Helicopter
H-5
Helicopter
Hammer mission
Name given by 18th Fighter Bomber Group to missions in which group

Mustangs were teamed with 67th Tactical Reconnaissance Wing aircraft to attack "specific enemy artillery positions, supply and troop areas" following the completion of the primary mission in late 1951—rail interdiction.

Hangar flying

Pilot slang for anecdotal experience passed along pilot-to-pilot. "The combination of pilots new to jet aircraft but with a great deal of combat experience and pilots with jet training but no combat experience proved very good," the 67th reported. "By exchanging knowledge and much 'hangar flying', a very effective team developed as the squadron combat record proves," the 67th reported in March 1953.

Hdg

Heading. The direction in which an aircraft's nose points in flight in the horizontal plane, expressed in compass degrees.

HE

High explosive

Heartbreak Ridge

Named by news correspondents covering the action, "Heartbreak Ridge" was an extension of Bloody Ridge three miles to the south and was located in the eastern sector of the Eighth U.S. Army defensive line in the Punchbowl area.

HEAT

High explosive, antitank

HF

High Frequency

Hit and run

Due to the "vastly increased amount of flak utilized by the enemy," it was becoming "common practice" to use the tactic of "hit-and-run"—"striking those targets closely protected by the enemy no more than twice per mission. It is believed this effects a valuable saving in equipment and personnel while still accomplishing the assigned mission." [16]

Hit the deck

Slang term meaning to either fall onto the ground, or if flying an airplane, to fly as close to the ground as possible (without touching).

Hq

Headquarters

Hunter-Killer Plan

A roadblock plan developed in September 1952 during which the "hunter" crew reconnoitered an assigned roadblock area and determined the best location to establish a roadblock with bombs or other ordnance. After making the roadblock, a "killer" would arrive later to attack backed up vehicles. The locate-block-wait-attack process could be repeated as long as results were obtained.

HVAR

High Velocity Aircraft Rocket. USAF fighter-bombers used the HVAR to knock out Communist tanks, trains, and bunkers. Two types of aircraft rockets were employed in Korea, the 5.0" HVAR and the 6.5" ATAR (anti-tank aircraft rocket).

I&R

Intelligence & Reconnaissance

IAS

Indicated Air Speed

ID

Infantry Division

IFF

Identification Friend or Foe, electronic identification system.

IFR

Instrument flight rules prescribed for the operation of aircraft in instrument meteorological conditions (i.e. "bad weather.") Also, In-Flight Refueling.

INBD

Inbound

Inchon Invasion

The X Corps amphibious invasion at Inchon on Korea's western coast Sept. 15, 1950, ranks as one of the boldest military maneuvers in history.

Inf

Infantry

Infiltration

Enemy soldiers posing as refugees (wearing traditional Korean white robes over their uniforms) easily blended in with the millions of South Koreans who had fled their home to avoid the war. Once behind friendly lines, these infiltrators regrouped and attacked Allied positions from the rear.

INST

Instrument

Instr

Instruction

INTC

Intercept

Intel

Intelligence

Interdiction

Generic term used by the Air Force meaning any air action that prevents, or delays, or destroys enemy movements of men, equipment and supplies to the zone of a ground battle.

Interrog

Interrogation

INTSUM
Intelligence Summary
IP
Instructor Pilot; Interception Point.
Iron Triangle
The so-called Iron Triangle of the Korean War was a triangularly shaped area of relatively flat terrain about 30 miles north of the 38th Parallel in the mountains of east-central North Korea.
JADF
Japan Air Defense Force
JAG
Judge Advocate General
JCS
Joint Chiefs of Staff
JOC Alert Missions
When on JOC alert, the "pilots stood by in Squadron Operations awaiting word from Combat Operations that they were to scramble. Fifteen minutes was allowed to obtain the 'flims' [19] (which gave controllers, coordinates, time on target and mission number) and the authentication sheets, to brief, and to get airborne. As soon as the four or eight aircraft committed were landed from a mission, the same number was expected to be ready to go again. There was normally at least an hour or so between each 'scramble.' However, because the missions were rotated among the three Squadrons, forty minutes was allowed normally between receipt of the mission information at combat operations and the time on target, since the front was 18 minutes away at the closest point and 25 at the furthest," the 12th reported. [20]
JOC
Joint Operations Center. "The physical make-up of the center included an Air Force combat operations section and an Army air-ground operations section." [21] The Tactical Air Control Center (TACC), was designed to operate in close association with the JOC and serve as the focal point for aircraft control and warning activities of the tactical air force.
Joto
Slang meaning "OK." "This afternoon the mobile UHF repair team came and fixed up our radios for us. They took until after dark, but everything is joto now," noted Lt. Ken Barber near the Yalu River on 14 November 1950.
Josephine
Radio code word meaning "low on," as in "Josephine ammo" or "Josephine fuel."
JP-1
Jet fuel (refined kerosene). Produced in various "grades," e.g. JP-3

(Navy) or JP-4 (F-86F).
JTF
Joint Task Force
K
K-site, Korean Airbase
K-1
Pusan West
K-2
Taegu
K-3
Pohang
K-5
Taejon
K-6
Pyongtaek
K-8
Kunsan
K-9
Pusan East
K-10
Chinhae, approximately 3 miles southeast of Chinhae, Korea.
K-13
Suwon
K-14
Kimpo
K-16
Seoul
K-40
Cheju-do Island
K-46

Approximately 7 mi. NNE of Wonju—127 degrees 57 minutes 30 seconds longitude west, 38 degrees 26 minutes 30 seconds North. The 18th Group used the K-46 air strip as a forward combat operations base located approximately five miles southeast of Hoensong, Korea.

K-47
Chunchon
K-55
Osan.-ni, approximately 12 miles southeast of Suwon, Korea.
Kaesong

A city in western Korea just south of the 38th Parallel, Kaesong was the ancient capital of Korea. It was the first city to fall to the North Koreans June 25, 1950.

KHz
Kilohertz, the frequency of a radio carrier wave measured in thousands of cycles per second. 1 kHz = 1,000 Hertz.
KIA
Killed in Action
KMAG
Korean Military Advisory Group (Army). See EUSAK.
KPA
Korean People's Army
KT
Knots
L-19
 A light two seat observation and liaison monoplane aircraft. Combat roles for the L-19 included artillery spotting, scouting and reconnaissance. 23
LITTLE SWITCH
Operation Little Switch, April 20–May 3, 1953, was the initial exchange of sick and wounded prisoners of the Korean War that was agreed to during the truce talks at Panmunjom on April 11, 1953. The Communist side repatriated 684 U.N. sick and wounded troops, while the UNC turned over 1,030 Chinese and 5,194 Koreans. The exchange was marked by demonstrations by the prisoners designed to embarrass UN forces by throwing away food and clothing that had been issued to them.
LON
Longitude
Loran
Low-frequency radio long-range navigation system; measures time difference between reception of synchronized signals transmitted from ground transmitters.
Mach number
Ratio of true airspeed to the speed of sound. Mach 1 is the speed of sound at sea level, ISA, approximately 1,100 feet per second or 760 mph.
Mae West
Air crew life vest for use in a ditching or over water bailout. (Note the correct spelling - it was named for the movie actress) "...Then over all that goes the 'Mae West,' which, when inflated, makes the origin of the name quite obvious. The item was designed to save the wearer from drowning, but not from freezing." *Truckbuster*, September 30, 1952.
MAG
Magnetic
MAINT
Maintenance

MAN
Manual
MASH
Mobile Army Surgical Hospitals
MATS
Military Air Transport Service
Maximum Effort
A strike by a large number of planes on a single target. When intelligence analysts and tactical planners determined that a particular target was important enough to justify a major strike, a squadron or more likely a group, would be tasked to "hit a target with all its available resources— "maximum effort"—Col. Joe Peterburs explained. "The Group would put together a force from all four squadrons and we would get from 30-50 birds in the air all hitting the same target at the same time."
Mayday
International radio distress call (from the French, *m'aidez* or "help me."). It signifies imminent danger to life requiring immediate assistance. Pilots were advised to "transmit 'Mayday' three times, followed by the call sign of your plane three times," followed by detailed information regarding estimated position, time, course, speed, altitude, intentions, etc.
Medal of Honor
The highest American military award for battlefield bravery.
Mellow Control
On July 20, 1950 control of tactical support aircraft was assumed at Taegu by the FAF-Eighth Army JOC. Its radio control station at Taegu was given the call sign of "Mellow." Fighter aircraft were directed to the front by Mellow Control (Tactical Air Control Center) and Mosquito Mellow. When they arrived in the operating area, airborne Mosquitoes FACs directed them to specific targets.
MIA
Missing in Action
MIG Alley
The area between the Chongchon and Yalu Rivers in northwestern Korea—roughly bordered by Sinuiju/Antung, Changju , Huichon and Sinanju—where Communist air forces were numerically superior.
MIG-15
Mikoyan "Fagot": single-engine jet fighter (Soviet)
Milk run
Easy mission or assignment.
Million dollar wound
A wound serious enough to get you sent home, but from which one would recover with no permanent disabilities. "One man was shot through

the fat of his leg--the million dollar wound, another broke his leg, one had his helmet creased by a bullet." (Lt. Ken Barber's Korean War diary)

Mission assignment

"Normally, all mission assignments will be extracted form the Fifth Air Force Operations Order for the day by A-3 [Operations Officer] of the 18th Fighter bomber Wing, who will coordinate the assignment with S3 section of the Group. Breakdown of commitments will be accomplished by Group Operations and distributed to each squadron in sufficient time to accomplish the assigned mission. Flight Scheduling for each mission will be at the discretion of the individual Squadron Commanders, however, care should be exercised to insure equitable distribution of missions to pilots in his organization." [24]

MLR

Main Line of Resistance or the location of the main battle lines or front lines.

Mosquito Mellow

Air borne forward air control aircraft, whose crew included U.S. Army personnel, relayed information to aircraft and could divert air strikes for greater efficiency. See Mellow Control.

Mosquito

A Fifth Air Force (FAF) fragmentary operations order issued on July 15, 1950 assigned airborne controllers radio call signs as "Mosquito Able," Mosquito Baker," and "Mosquito How." The catchy call signs soon became the unofficial nickname for the "Mosquito squadron." Soon, pilots were calling airborne controllers and their planes "Mosquitoes." By August 1, 1950, the 614th Tactical Control Squadron (Airborne) was created and assigned to the FAF at Taegu. Almost immediately, the Eighth Army began to assigned officers and NCOs to the "mosquito" squadron as observers to ride in the back seat of the T-6s patrolling the lines and controlling air strikes. Because the T-6s often flew far below the "radio horizon," the 614th kept another plane orbiting at a much greater altitude—"Mosquito Mellow"—that relayed messages of the airborne controllers into the TACC. Mosquitos were seldom permitted to penetrate more than several miles into or over enemy territory.

Msg
Message
MSgt
Master Sergeant
MSR
Main Supply Route
MSTS
Military Sea Transportation Service

Mustang
(Navy) Officer raised from the enlisted ranks.
(Air Force) Name of the F-51 Mustang fighter plane, a single engine, propeller driven aircraft, primarily used for fighter-bomber missions during the Korean War.
N
North
N/A
Not Applicable
Naktong Perimeter, Battle of
Also known as the "Pusan Perimeter," the Naktong Perimeter battle was the name given to Eighth U.S. Army's initial defense of the Republic of Korea.
Napalm
An acronym derived from naphtehnic and palmitic acids whose salts are used in its manufacture. NAPALM is a jellied gasoline used in flame-throwers, fougasses and aerial bombs. Napalm was used in two forms, the 110-gallon drop tank with one or two igniters and the AN/M-76 gasoline jel bomb using an AN/M-103 nose fuse and an AN/M-101-A2 tail fuse. Normal loading for napalm was two tanks or bombs per fighter-bomber aircraft. "Napalm destroyed or neutralized more T-34 tanks than all other airborne weapons combined," according to FAF operational analyses.
NAV
Navigation
NAVAID
Navigational Aid
NAVFE
U.S. Naval Forces, Far East
NCO
Non-commissioned officer
NKA
North Korean Army
NKAF
North Korean Air Force
NKPA
North Korean People's Army
NM
Nautical Mile
NOTAM
Notices to Airmen, issued by aviation authorities to inform pilots of new or changed aeronautical facilities, services, procedures or hazards, temporary or permanent.

Oak Leaf Cluster
A metallic oak leaf cluster is worn on the ribbon of a medal to denote subsequent awards of the same decoration in the Army and Air Force.
OB
Order of Battle
OPAREA
Operating Area
Operation Glory
The Armistice Agreement signed in Panamunjom in June 1953 included a provision agreeing to the exchange of military war dead on both sides. On July 20, 1954, it was agreed that the exchange of deceased personnel should formally commence on 1 September 1954 and end no later than 30 October, if possible. Implementation of Korean Communications Zone (KCOMZ) Op Plan 14-54 – better known as "Operation GLORY" – was put into effect on 22 July 1954. On August 30, 1954, the disinterment of all enemy deceased military personnel was completed, and all remains delivered and stored at "Glory Railhead," near Munsan-Ni, Korea. The exchange of deceased military personnel between the United Nations in South Korea, and the Communists in North Korea, continued daily, except Sundays, until September 21, 1954. A final tally indicated that 4,023 UN deceased personnel had been received from the North Koreans, and that 13,528 had been delivered to them. [27]
OPLR
Outpost Line of Resistance, a series of strong points in advance of the MLR (main line of resistance).
OPPLAN
Operational/operations Plan
OSAF
Office of the Secretary of the Air Force
OTC
Officer in Tactical Command
Paengnyong-do
A small island on Korea's west coast south of Cho-do (See) on which a lightweight air search and control radar was operated.
Papasan
Term used to designate the male head of a Korean family. To be a "real" papasan. the titleholder had to wear a very high black stovepipe hat.
Ping pong
Pilot slang for Pyongyang, capitol of North Korea.
Piss Call Charlie
A lone North Korean bomber "who would fly over the base [K-9] at about the same time each night, just before midnight, and drop a bomb somewhere on or near the airfield."

PLA
People's Liberation Army
Plat
Platoon
PLM
Production Line Maintenance System.
POE
Port of Embarkation
POL
Petroleum, oil, and lubricants
Police Action
President Harry S. Truman used this phrase to describe the U.S. intervention in Korea.
POS
Position
Post-holing
When "post-holing roads with 500-lb GP bombs it was found that a dive angle of 30 degrees with an air speed of 300 mph and release points of 800 feet produced the best results. For destruction of tunnels, skip bomb tactics were used." [30]
POW
Prisoner of War
Prang
Pilot slang for crash or badly damaged. "I had three other guys let the torque get the best of them and prang on take off," Colonel Joe Peterburs, former training officer for the 18th Fighter-Bomber Wing and the 12th Squadron in 1952. In September 1951, the Truckbuster ran a photograph of Capt. Alonzo Wagner, 39th FIS, standing behind a "practically non-existent elevator...ribs and little else." Wagner said he thought the fighter "acted a little funny" when he came in for a landing. "It's a good thing I didn't realize how badly pranged that elevator was or I'd probably have bailed out."
Pre-briefed Targets
"Targets that are of such a nature as to warrant assignment of a specific mission before take off are pre-briefed targets and generally include bridges, rail and road cuts, flak batteries, marshalling yards, etc. The armament load will be determined by the particular type of mission, which in turn will have a direct bearing on the type of tactics employed. Upon completion of the assigned mission, the flight will return to base, providing all armament has been expended. If the flight has not expended all armament and has sufficient fuel, they will perform an armed reconnaissance of the area en route to the base." [31]
PSP
Pierced Steel Plank, used to create temporary runways.

Pusan

Located in southeastern Korea near the delta of the Naktong River, Pusan was and is South Korea's second largest city.

PW

Prisoner of War

Pyongyang

Capital of North Korea.

R&R

Rest and Recuperation or "rape and rampage" as it was sometimes known. Selected by their units, participants were flown to Japan on Air Force transports for five days temporary duty in Japan. On arrival they were paid, issued uniforms, fed and provided with a billet in a Special Services hotel or on one of the many military bases in Japan. Then they were left alone to "rest and recuperate." **R&R**

Rearming and Refueling ramp. An R&R Operation meant "a situation whereby a sufficient number of personnel and equipment are sent to a forward strip to refuel and to rearm the tactical planes and to brief and debrief the pilots. The aircraft operate from the strip during the day but return to home base over night," an 18th Fighter-Bomber Wing directive explained.

Rated Officer

Air Force officer having earned his wings as a pilot.

RB-26

Douglas "Invader": twin-engine reconnaissance plane (USA)

RCC

Rescue Control Center

RDF

Radio Direction Finding. A name first used for what became Radar

Recce areas

Reconnaissance areas or sectors.

Recey

See Armed reconnaissance. The 67th reported, "due to difficulties encountered in seeking camouflaged targets while carrying external tanks on low altitude reconnaissance missions, Squadron Operations gained the prerogative to recey without tanks on routes within 260 miles of the base."

Recon

Reconnaissance

Reconnaissance

Process of seeking out of information about enemy positions and dispositions.

RESCAP

Rescue Combat Air Patrol. An aircraft patrol stationed over a combat search and rescue objective areawhose mission is to intercept and destroy hostile aircraft. Its primary mission is to protect the search and rescue task forces during recovery operations.

RF
Radio Frequency

Rockets
The F-51D could carry ten 5-inch rockets, five under each wing. A safety-wired latch keep the rocket from slipping forward and falling off. When the rocket was ignited, its forward thrust shears the safety wife, allowing it to shoot forward from the launchers. Rocket control switches were located on the front switch panel. Pressing the button on top of the control stick fired the rockets. Rockets could be fired one at a time or "in train," a salvo of all ten rockets released within about one second.

ROK
Republic of Korea

ROKAF
Republic of Korea Air Force

ROKN
Republic of Korea Navy

RON
Remain Over Night

RT
Radio telephony or voice communications, as opposed to WT, wireless telegraphy. Also styled RTF.

S-1
Adjutant

S-2
Intelligence Officer

S-3
Operations and Training Officer

S-4
Supply Officer

SAAF
South African Air Force

Sabre or Sabrejet
F-86; jet powered fighter interceptor aircraft

SAR
Special Action Report; Search and Rescue

Sariwo
A city in central North Korea that was one of the apexes of the "Iron Triangle", known for its heavy and accurate flak batteries. Many American jet and prop planes were shot down in this area.

SATURATE
On Feb. 25, 1952, FAF director of intelligence strongly recommended

the implementation of "Operation Saturate," an around-the-clock concentration of available railway-interdiction effort against short segments of railway track, including Kunu-ri to Huichon, Sunchon to Samdong-ni, Sinanju to Namsi-dong and Pyongyang to Namchonjom. Operation Saturate was put into effect on March 3rd. Attacks were sustained throughout April and May. Soon after the operation began, flak batteries had been put into place along nearly all rail lines. Losses of tactical aircraft were high.

SCAP

Supreme Commander for the Allied Powers, i.e. General McArthur. Mustangs from the 18th Fighter Bomber Group were called on to provide air cover for McArthur's plane when he visited "the front."

SCATTER

Korean War screening plan for the repatriation of prisoners of war.

Scosh

Slang for "little bit," as in "It got a scosh cold last night. It must have been 20 degrees below zero because it's been 5 degrees below all day today." (Lt. Ken Barber's diary of 14 November 1950 written about 50 miles south of the Yalu River in North Korea.)

SCR-300

"Walkie-Talkie" radio.

Scramble

Immediate take-off order to pilots standing by for prompt take-off and combat operations. "…We alternated on strip alert with the 67th Fighter Bomber Squadron between the morning and evening alert by were not 'scrambled.'" See JOC Alert Missions and Strip Alert.

Scroung/scrounger

Slang term used to describe an individual with the ability to obtain supplies, parts or materiel outside of normal supply channels that were often unable to deliver the critical items.

Scud layer

Low clouds.

Seoul City Sue

The North Korean Axis Sally or Tokyo Rose.

Shirley Control

Allied fliers checked in with "Shirley Control" when leaving friendly territory and when reentering. "Shirley Control could also redirect your mission when you were up North," explained Budd Stapley.

Sitrep

Situation Report

Sitting duck mission

"It was a sitting duck mission—that is, we go up there and take whatever targets are given us. And that's just what those boats turned out to be: sitting ducks." Captain Richard D. Kimball, *Truckbuster*, September 30,

1952. "In sitting duck missions, aircraft were assigned to the Naval Forces near Chodo Island to attack shore defenses around the Chinnamipo Estuary," the 12th Squadron reported in 1953. The Group was also called on in January 1953 to fly sorties for "sitting duck" missions. "On these missions, a flight of four aircraft was dispatched to Chodo Island where they contacted the Naval forces stationed there. They were then directed, usually by the Fire Control Section of one of the destroyers, into attacks on observed shore batteries or activities across the straits from Chodo Island."

Skip bombing

Skip bombing and glide bombing are "adaptations of dive-bombing and require more technique that does dive-bombing, the 18th Fighter-Bomber Group Standardized Procedures for Combat Operations explained. "The bomb in both instances is released from a lower altitude and should incorporate a delayed fuse. In glide bomb runs, allowance must be made for a bigger arc in bomb trajectory than was true of dive-bombing. Skip bomb runs are made from low altitudes with the aiming point in front of the target. A hit can be scored by either skipping the bomb into the target or by driving the bomb directly into the target. As was the case in other bomb runs, accomplish evasive maneuvers at all times except while on the alignment run prior to bomb release." See Post-holing.

Slot

Number Four position in the echelon formation was known as "the slot."

SOB

Souls on board, the number of persons on board an aircraft. Also POB.

Socked-in

Colloquialism referring to an airport closed to air traffic by bad weather; also, similarly "clamped."

SOP

Standard operating procedure.

Sortie

One trip by one plane. From June 27, 1950 to July 27, 1953, U.N. aircraft flew more than 1,040,708 close support, counter-air, interdiction, cargo and miscellaneous sorties in support of the U.N. military operations in Korea.

Spam

A spicy canned ham product packaged in a 12-ounce can produced by the Hormel Company since 1937. A overnight success, Spam, as it was called following a naming contest, grabbed 18 percent of its market. Over five billion cans have been sold.

Spam-can

Pilot's term for the F-51 Mustang. "Ten pilots of this organization climbed into the old familiar 'Spam-can' and the mission was completed successfully."

Split Operation

A situation whereby the tactical effort in whole or in part is made at a forward base, while the administration, base supply and field maintenance is conduted at a rear installation. The 18th Wing operated from K-46, a base closer to the front lines by 150 miles, although for much of the war its headquarters were at K-10, near Pusan.

Spot Promotions

Temporary promotions to the next highest rank. Used as a morale boosting policy, especially for junior officers/pilots.

Staging Operation

"A situation similar to refueling and rearming (see) except that aircraft are staged at the forward strip but rotated to their home base for inspection and heavy maintenance."

Stars and Stripes

Stars and Stripes was the official military newspaper of the Far East.

Stooge

Pilot slang for "loiter" or linger unnecessarily long in a specific area. "Do not "Stooge" at low air speed, straight and level, or in one small area. "Make a few turns then move down on a road a few miles farther over this area, then move to another road."

STRANGLE

Korean War (1951-1952) air operations plan to disrupt North Korean logistics through interdiction bombing. The FEAF Rail Interdiction Program—"Operation Strangle"—was conducted in Korea from the summer of 1951 to early 1952. Its official objective was to interfere with and disrupt the enemy's lines of communications to such an extent that he will be unable to contain a determined offensive by friendly forces or be unable to mount a sustained major offensive himself." [36] The name "Strangle" was "devised to glamorize the task for the benefit of ground officers who had never been charmed by "interdiction." [37] FAF set out to exploit all means of interdiction, including: bridge attacks, tunnel attcks, cratered roadbeds, delayed action bombs. Initally, Operation Strangle was a success in slowing and catching retreating Communist troops. Eventually, the flexibility of the Communist logistic system enabled the damage to be repaired or circumvented to a great extent.

Strip alert

"The squadron was also called on to perform 'strip alert'—four or eight aircraft parked at the end of the take off runway in readiness for immediate take-off."

T/O
Tables of Organization
T/O&E
Table of Organization and Equipment, i.e. the mix of equipment and supplies that had been determined was required for a unit/squadron to perform its missions.
TACC
Tactical Air Control Center. See Mellow Control.
TACP
Tactical Air Control Parties, provided ground control of close air support in concert with airborne T-6 aircraft "Mosquitos." Each TACP consisted of an experienced pilot officer, who served as a forward air controller (FAC), and the airmen needed to operate and maintain the party's vehicular-mounted communications equipment. Troops on the ground could communicate directly with airborne forward air controllers via the SCR-300 "walkie-talkie" if necessary. Combat squadrons were required to supply pilots for temporary duty with the TACPs.
TADC
Tactical Air Direction Center
Tadpoles
Tactical Air-Direction Posts.
TARCAP
Tactical Air Reconnaissance Combat Air Patrol
TAS
True airspeed, corrected for altitude and outside air temperature, as opposed to IAS, or indicated air speed.
Task Force
A term widely used during the Korean War. It was used by the Army to identify an ad hoc organization composed of a variety of units temporarily assembled under a single designated commander to accomplish a specific mission. For the Navy, "task force," and "task group" were subdivisions of the fleet.
TBD
To Be Determined
TF
Task Force (Navy)
TG
Task Group (Navy)
TGT
Target
Three-in-one mission
Pilot slang meaning three missions during one sortie. The F-51s provided a fighter escort for the parachute drops—paradrops—at Sukchon

and Sunchon, where the 187th Regimental Combat Team was being landed to cut off retreating North Korean troops. They then provided an escort home for General MacArthur's C-54, from which he had been observing the operation. They left the C-54 over the MLR, and then dove down to provide close air support for ROK forces near Wonsan, and finished up the day, after rearming and refueling, by providing a fighter escort for B-26s of the 3rd Bomb Wing.

Thunderjet
F-84; jet powered fighter and fighter-bomber aircraft.

Tiger Squadron
Colloquial name for 12th FBS because it sported the familiar shark's teeth nose art.

Tip Tanks
External aircraft fuel tanks mounted near the tips of the wings used to significantly extend combat range and "loiter time."

to (do)
Province, used in combined form, as Kangwoon-do for Kangwon Province, or Chungch'ong-pukto for North Ch'ungch'ong Province. There are eight mainland provinces and one island province in the Republic of Korea. *Do*, or *to* also means island, as in Cheju-do.

top cover
Pilot slang for one or more aircraft positioned above attacking aircraft to deal with any attacks by enemy aircraft and to help pinpoint anti-aircraft positions on the ground. The "standard two-ship reconnaissance flights were continued with excellent results. This system calls for one aircraft to fly at 100 to 350 foot altitudes, depending on terrains, while the second aircraft remained at 500 to 1,000 foot altitudes to provide top cover." [38]

Tornado
RB-45, the first jet reconnaissance aircraft in the USAF.

Track
Actual flight path of an aircraft over the ground.

Train formation
As a means of providing improved mutual cover, Sabre wings adopted a "train" type of squadron formation consisting of six flights, each of four aircraft. A refinement of the jet stream, the flights flew the usual 'fluid-four' formation, but remained in a loose trail formation, each flight following another within an easy supporting distance of about one mile. [39]

TRS
Tactical Reconnaissance Squadron

Truckbusters
Nickname for the 18th Fighter-Bomber Wing. Also, *Truckbuster* was the name for the bi-monthly newspaper published by the 18th Fighter-Bomber Wing during the Korean War.

UFN
Until further notice.
UN
United Nations. When the Korean War broke out in June 1950, the U.N. was a relatively new organization.
UNC
United Nations Command
UNCOK
United Nations Commission on Korea
UNCURK
United Nations Commission for the Unification and Rehabilitation of Korea
Unguibus Et Rostro
With talons and beak—was approved as the motto for the 18th Group on 21 Feb 1931 and for the 18th Wing on 17 Apr 1953 just prior to Korean Armistice.
URC-4
Emergency radio "used by airmen forced down behind the enemy lines."
USA
U.S. Army; United States of America
USAFIK
U.S. Army Forces in Korea
USMC
U.S. Marine Corps
USSR
Union of Soviet Socialist Republics
V
Velocity
V/
Vice
VA
Navy attack squadron
VF
Navy fighter squadron
VFR
Visual Flight Rules, outline procedures for operating aircraft in visual meteorological conditions (VMC), generally defined as five miles visibility or more and 1,000 feet vertical and one nautical mile horizontal clearance from cloud.
VHF
Very high frequency; 30-300 MHz band, used for most civil air-to-

ground communication. The F-51 was equipped with a VHF transmitter and receiver. The VHF antenna mast extended vertically above the fuselage aft of the cockpit. The VHF radio included a control box with five push buttons—an OFF switch and A, B, C, and D switches by which four different crystal-controlled frequencies could be selected. Pilots could transmit and receive on only one channel at a time.

Vis
Visibility.

VLF
Very low frequency; in the 3-30 kHz band.

VMF
Marine Fighter Squadron

VP
Navy Patrol Squadron

VT
Variable Time (radar-controlled) proximity fuse.

WESPAC
Western Pacific

WIA
Wounded in Action.

Wigwam
Pilot slang for Waegwan, South Korea.

Windmill
Slang for helicopter, e.g. "...shortly thereafter the "windmill" (helicopter) arrived and the downed pilot was safely removed to Kimpo, AB.

WINDR
Wind Direction

Wing
A major organizational element of the Air Force, Navy and Marine Corps.

Wonsan
A port city and rail center on Korea's eastern coast about 110 air miles north of the 38th Parallel at Korea's narrow waist.

Wx
Weather.

X-C
Cross Country

XMIT
Transmit

Yak-18
Yakovlev: single-engine trainer (Soviet)

Yak-9

Yakovlev "Frank": single-engine fighter (Soviet)

Yalu River

The 491-mile long Yalu River flows from Mount Paektu in central North Korea westward to the Yellow Sea.

Yellow Sea

The Yellow Sea lies between mainland China and the Korean Peninsula and forms the west border of Korea.

Yo-yo maneuvers

Developed shortly after Mustangs were introduced into the Korean conflict. "Instead of two or more ships going in to search or attack a target simultaneously, we'd keep one ship high—above 2000 feet, just high enough to stay out of much small arms (rifle and machine gun) range—while the other went down onto the deck. Then, if the enemy fired on the attacking plane, the top-cover could usually spot the muzzle blasts and be able to dive in to attack, while the first attacker would pull up to fly "shotgun," continuing the one up, one down coverage for as long as there were targets in the area." (Lt. Col. Duane Biteman).

Yo-Yo

All attacks pressed by enemy jet type fighters "were made from altitude and a "yo-yo" pattern (i.e. Dive and Zoom) would be established. With the conventional type aircraft an enemy peculiarity was revealed. Whether pressing an attack and/or fleeing from an attack, these fighters (Yak-9 type) would turn with great maneuverability and/or snap-roll, sometimes 3 or 4 snap-rolls, followed by a split "S". [40] Maneuver reintroduced in June 1951 by Communist MIG pilots in which 20 or more of them would establish orbits over UN air formations, then "preferably from up-sun and usually in elements of two, the MIG's dived downward and attacked United Nations aircraft from high astern,; and, finally, the elements zoomed back up into the pool of orbiting MIG's overhead." [41]

Z

Zulu (Greenwich Mean Time)

Zone of the Interior (ZI)

During the Korean War, the military term Zone of the Interior or ZI was used in official documents to designate the continental United States.

Index

Numbered Organizations

2 Squadron South African Air Force 12, 15, 78, 123, 135
3rd Air Rescue Squadron 23, 26, 28, 32, 37, 159, 160, 162, 197
3rd Air Rescue Squadron/Group 319
3rd Air Rescue Squadron, Detachment One 32
12th Fighter-Bomber Squadron 12, 125, 136, 239
18th Fighter-Bomber Group 12, 15, 43, 122, 146, 147, 220, 237
18th Fighter-Bomber Wing 12, 14, 41, 121, 133, 238, 318
35th Fighter-Interceptor Wing 121, 138
39th Fighter-Interceptor Squadron 78, 123
40th Fighter-Interceptor Squadron 121, 138
42nd Rescue Squadron 307
67th Fighter-Bomber Squadron 12, 14, 15, 17, 20, 43, 78, 121, 123, 138, 146
89th Bomber Squadron 179
2347th Air Force Reserve Training Center 233
315th Air Division 166
6147th Tactical Control Group 38, 41
6l47th Tactical Control Group 40
801st Medical Air Evacuation Squadron 165
8055th Mobile Army Surgical Hospital   23, 34, 165, 198
8204th Army Unit 308

A

Acadia University 47-48, 52
Air Group Seven 63
Air Rescue Service 183, 279
Akridge, Dr. Garth 93
Albatross 29
Almond, MG Edward M. 102
American Graves Registration Service Group 309
Army Effects Bureau 251
Aubuchon, 1st Lt. E. W. 18, 208
Ayer, Capt. Elliot D. 15, 18, 21, 74, 201, 208, 211. 237-241, 324
Ayer, Frederick Ayer 241, 285
Ayer, Marguerite S. Ayer 75, 241, 253, 254, 285

B

Back, Col. Klair E. 24-25, 27, 163, 256
Barkus, Lt. Gen. Glenn 262
Rexford Baldwin 239
Battle Taxi 304
Bedevilers 63
Sheldon S. Brinson 237

C

Cambridge, Massachusetts 59
Camp Drum, Watertown, New York 184
Camp Stoneman, California 119
Capp, Al Capp 124-127
Carmody, Linda Carmody 323
Carrier Air Group 7 63
Cathey, Julia C. 221, 315
Cho-do Island 33, 129
Clark, VADM J.J. 5
Clark, Gen. Mark W. 26
Cole College 172
Connally AFB, Texas 100
Connors, Arch and Eva Connors 87, 90, 258
Connors, Sr. Archibald Haddock 79, 81, 87, 90, 96-98, 109, 222, 296, 319
Connors, Jr. 1st Lt. Archibald Haddock "Archie" 14, 16, 79, 81, 89, 100, 104, 128, 138, 139, 140, 211, 313
Connors, Eva Haddock 79, 83, 86, 89, 103, 222, 257, 258, 267, 289, 296, 319
Connors, Frances "Frankie" Lutye Simpson 14, 16, 95, 107, 109, 115, 120, 141, 144, 273, 276, 323
Connors, Sr., Gerald 87
Connors, John David 88, 101, 142
Connors, Lucille 87, 152, 315
Connors, Sharon Lee 144
Connors, Captain Tracy D.   81, 88, 95, 100, 109, 142-143, 274-275, 299
Connors, Woodrow D. 81, 109, 293
Craig AFB 110, 112
Cranston, Robert 15, 17, 130
Crosson, Col. Gerald J. 37
Crow, Lt. Col. Julian F. Crow 20, 123, 131, 135, 137, 149

D

Dalton, Joyce Eaton 40, 57, 69, 227, 228
Dogpatch 18, 121, 128
Drage, 1st Lt. Donald D. ("Lucky") 139, 149

E

Earp, Lt. Gen. Denis, SAAF 134
Eaton, Bernard H. N. 44-45, 271-272, 324
Eaton, Elsie Adelia 58, 224, 258, 271, 325
Eaton, Ens. Ronald D. 3, 9, 38, 45, 58, 61, 68, 70, 197, 206, 227, 212, 266, 288, 325
Eglin Air Force Base 254
Ephesus Baptist Church 85
Evanston, Illinois 173
Everest, LGen Frank F. 135-136

F

F4U-4 Corsair 10, 63
F-9F "Pantherjet" 40
F-51 Mustang 12, 107
F-86 "Sabre" 133
Far East Air Forces 113
Ferguson, Bob 193
Ferguson, Julia 193
Fiesta of Five Flags 55
Fifth Air Force 5, 35, 38, 41, 131, 136, 147, 201
Fighting Cocks 20, 123
Flying Cheetahs 135
Fonvielle, Jr., CDR Charles D. 4, 65, 68, 224, 225
Frag Order 19, 20

G

Gossett, 1st Lt. C. J. 22, 239
Graham, Senator Bob 325
Gulfport Army Airfield 160

H

H-5 29, 32, 170
H-19 33
Haddock, Joseph 83
Haddock, Mary Jane 84-86
Haddock, Rufus Goldwire 82-85
Halsey, Maj. George E. 233
Harrison, Lula 194
Haydon, Sterling 304
Heller, Lt. Col. Emerson E. 31-34, 35, 187, 331

Hildegarde 83
Hill, 1st Lt. John 15, 18, 201, 211, 215, 242
Holloway, MSgt Bobby Dale 23, 24, 36, 167, 192, 206, 219, 248, 252, 269, 278, 284, 304, 305, 329
Holloway, Della L. See Lear, Della Paddon
Holloway, Ira Virden 192, 193
Holloway, Ouida Ferguson 192, 244, 261, 272
Holloway, Will 194
Horton Academy 48
How Flight 18, 138, 148
Hudson, 1st Lt. Charles T. 18, 208, 242
Hulse, Flight Lieutenant, Graham 108
HVAR 40

I

Inchon Amphibious landing 102
Iron Triangle 39
Itami Army Air Base 179

J

Jacksonville, Florida 58, 80
Jacksonville Junior College/Jacksonville University 91-94
Johnson AFB 196, 138
Joint Operations Center 164
Jorgensen, Maj. Daniel B. 236

K

K-10 121, 137
K-16 23, 164
K-46 12, 125, 128, 131, 197
Kessler Air Base 183
Kight, BGen Richard 35, 199
Kim II Sung 269
Kings Ferry, 82-83
Armistice Signed 279
Kyosen #4 Hydro-Electric Power plant 73, 155

L

L-5 29
Lear, Barbara 181
Lear, Della Paddon 172, 173, 189, 256, 284, 287, 329
Lear, Leslie I. 172, 325
Lear, Mabel 181, 297, 325
Lear Trophy 303
Lear, Capt. Leslie Wayne 23, 24, 29, 36, 39, 167, 172, 177, 180, 206, 326

Lee, Robert E. Senior High School 8, 91
Lenhart, Maj. Warren T. 43
Leven, Col. Seymour 131
Long, Major Stanley A. 15, 20, 21, 79, 136, 149, 220, 229-230
Louisiana Tech University 195
Low, Col. Curtis 125
Luke AFB, Arizona 115, 116

M

MacArthur, Gen. of the Armies Douglas 101, 112, 113, 102
March Air Force Base 183, 311
Marion, Dr. Forrest 161
Mason, W. M. (Marcy) 144
McAlpine, 1st Lt. John 155
McCluskey, Kathryn Coles 81, 153, 320
McCormick, MGen John 221, 243
McShane, 1st Lt. William E. 15, 18, 139, 208, 214, 239
Meyer, Vincent Meyer 175
MIG-Alley 133
Military Air Transportation Service 31
Mission 1890 36, 74
Morris, Miriam 88
Mosquitoes 164
Mustang 106

N

NAAS Oceana, Virginia 63
NAS Atlantic City, New Jersey 63
NAS Corpus Christi, Texas 57
NAS Norfolk, Virginia 161
NAS Pensacola, Florida 51, 56
NAS Quonset Point, Rhode Island 63
NAS San Diego, California 65
NAS Wildwood, New Jersey 63
Nassau County 83
Norfolk, Virginia 57

O

O'Donnell, LGen Emmett 294
Old, MGen Archie 307
Operation GLORY 300
Operation Little Switch 267
Operation Saturate 146

Operation Strangle 132, 134, 151

P

Pyongyang 30
Paddon, Della Marie 173 (Also see Lear, Della Marie)
Paddon, Elizabeth 181
Paddon, John Henry 173
Paengnyong-do 32
Partridge, LGen Earle E. 30
Patton, 1st Lt. George V. 114, 129
Peterburs, Col. Joseph 147
Pilot Pickup 34
Pusan Perimeter 26, 30

Q

Quonset Point, Rhode Island 58

R

Ramsdell, Earl 149
Rescue Combat Air Patrol (RESCAP) 15, 17, 166
Ridgway, Gen. Matthew B. 112, 113, 135
Riverside, California 182
Rives, 1st Lt. Joel O. Rives 139
Robert E. Lee High School 91
Rogers, Bgen Turner C. "TeeCee" 318
Roswell Army Air Field, New Mexico 172
Ruston, Louisiana 192

S

SA-16 29
Santa Ana Air Base 172
Santa Cruz, California 172
SB-17 29
SC-47 29
Serviceman's Group Life Insurance 291
Sharp, Dorothy "Dolly" 6, 59, 60, 226, 262, 324
Shepard, Col. Jack 144, 156
Silver Lake 45
Silvey, 1st. Lt. John W. 229
Simp'o, North Korea 200
Smith, MGen Joseph T. 31
SNB 58
Soucek, RAdm Apollo 5
Souze, 1st Lt. Melvin 139, 149
Spivey, BGen. Delmar T. 26

St. Marys River 83
Stapley, 1st Lt. Wilfred C. "Budd" 18, 103, 106, 108, 114, 116-117, 128, 130, 138, 144, 149
Stars and Stripes 39
Stratemeyer, Gen. George E. 34
Sunchon 30
Svore, LTC Ferdinand L. 32, 35

T

T-6 "Mosquito" 38
Task Force 77 5, 71
The Scrambler 158
Third Air Rescue Squadron 195
Top 'O the Mark 138
Tors, Ivan 304
Truckbuster 134, 150
Truman, President Harry 112, 113
Tubbs, 1st. Lt. Shirley B. 139
Twining, Gen. Nathan F. 293
Typhoon Dinah 6

U

U.S. Graves Registration Division 300
UH-19B 171
UN Neutral Nations Repatriation Commission 270
United Nations Security Council 101
Urquhart, 1st Lt. William "Tim" 14, 18, 22, 28, 122, 208, 213, 216, 323
USS Bon Homme Richard (CV/A 31) 3, 42, 63, 65, 70-73, 224
USS Boxer 5
USS Charette (DD 581) 92
USS Conner (DD 582) 92
USS Consolation 190
USS Epperson (DD 719) 66
USS Franklin D. Roosevelt (CVA 42) 63
USS Helena 5
USS Juneau 5
USS Leyte (CV 32) 64, 65
USS Mt. McKinley (AGC 7) 102
USS Philip (DD 498) 66
USS Philippine Sea (CVA 47) 5, 63
USS Princeton 5

V

Van Fleet, LGen. James A. 113
Vandenberg, Gen. Hoyt S. 259

VF-74 4, 62-65

W

Walmsley, Capt. Springer 181, 184
Watson, CAPT Paul W. 6, 8
Wehland, Joseph Wehland 323
Whiting Airfield 53

Acknowledgements

18th Fighter Wing Association
Lt. Col. Timothy O. Austin, USAF (Ret.)
Frederick B. Ayer
Lt. Col. Kenneth H. Barber, USAF (Ret.)
Lt. Col. Duane "Bud" Biteman, USAF (Ret.)
Ginny Brinkley
J. William Brinkley
Lt. Col. John Caldwell, USAF (Ret.)
Suzanne Harper Catto
Dorothy Sharp Clements
Faith R. Connors
J. David Connors
Joyce Hannon Connors
W. Bruce Connors
CAPT C. Todd Creekman, USN (Ret.)
Lt. Col. Julian Crow, USAF (Ret.)
Joyce Eaton Dalton
Robert F. Dorr
Eaton Family
CAPT L. Tyke Furey, USN (Ret.)
Dale J. Gordon
Col. Baylor Haynes, USAF (Ret.)
Dr. Martin Heesacker
CDR Jeffrey A. Henson, JAG, USN (Ret.)
Karen C. Henson
MSGT Bobby D. Holloway, USAR (Ret.)
Della Lear Holloway
Dr. Michael Horseman, M.D.
CAPT Seth Hudak, USCG (Ret.)
Dr. Frances B. Kinne
Dr. Forest L. Marion
Col. Edward J. Mason, USAF (Ret.)
Dean McCarns
Miriam C. McCarns
Kathryn C. McCluskey
CAPT James A. Noone, USN (Ret.)
Col. Robert P. Pasqualicchio, USAF (Ret.)
Col. Joseph A. Peterburs, USAF (Ret.)
Col. James C. Peek, USAF (Ret.)
CAPT William R. McKown, USN (Ret.)

CAPT William Pokorny, USN (Ret.)
Lucille Connors Ritchie
Col. Ralph H. Saltsman, Jr., USAF (Ret.)
Col. Richard H. Schiebel, USAF (Ret.)
Col. Charles E. Schreffler, USAF (Ret.)
Col. Jack E. Shepard, USAF (Ret.)
Wilfred "Budd" Stapley
CDR Richard Thompson, USN (Ret.)
Ernest Wakehouse
Col. Darrel Whitcomb, USAF (Ret.)
U.S. Air Force Historical Research Agency
U.S. National Archives and Records Administration
U.S. Navy Historical Center
U.S. Navy Historical Foundation
William Timons Urquhart

Photographic Credits

Acadia University
Frederick Ayer
Elbert Black
Suzanne Harper Catto
William J. "Sandy" Colton
Connors' Family Collection
Dorothy Sharp Clements
Robert Cranston
Joyce Eaton Dalton
Eaton Family Collection
Bobby Dale Holloway
Dr. Vern Holmes
Della Marie Lear Holloway
Joseph Krakovsky
Ione R. Lenhart
Col. Edward Mason, USAF (Ret.)
Col. Bill Myers, USAF (Ret.)
National Archives and Records Administration (NARA)
Col. Joseph Peterburs, USAF (Ret.)
Roy Pylant
Earl Ramsdell
Col. Jack Shepard, USAF (Ret.)
Wilfred "Budd" Stapley
U.S. Air Force Historical Research Agency (AFHRA)
U. S. Navy History Museum
William Timmons Urquhart

About Baited Trap

There is so much of oneself that becomes invested in an effort such as this book, a story that in many respects I have been living a part of since I remember wrestling as a boy with my uncle, Archie, in my grandparent's living room. His loss on 25 June 1952 was devastating to the family, and to me personally. It was as if I had lost my older brother. In fact, he was closer in age to me, his nephew, than he was to my father, his older brother.

As you review *Baited Trap*, I know that we share a deep appreciation for the air rescue mission and those who fulfill it, then and now. I also know that when you finish the book, you will have an even greater appreciation for those pioneers of the air rescue service, such as Captain Wayne Lear and Master Sergeant Bobby Holloway--who flew daunting missions in rickety aircraft and created the new air rescue doctrine out of whole cloth.

I thought that I should explain some of the "back story" of *Baited Trap*, events, objectives and how the story unwinds, of what happened that Wednesday afternoon on June 25, 1952—and afterwards.

Because I grew up with Archie, I knew he was special—witty, mischievous, a leader and risk taker. He was exciting to be around.

As I learned more about Wayne Lear and Ron Eaton, I was also impressed by their character, drive, professionalism and deep down "goodness," if you will. The same is true of other principals in the story including Bobby Holloway and Elliot Ayer.

The more I learned about them, the more that I wanted you to know about them.

Baited Trap, the Ambush of Mission 1890 is, as the title notes, an incredible story of airmanship, bravery and dedication. It is even more the life story of the three airmen who were killed on that mission.

I wanted you to know as much as possible about them—as well as what they did. Knowing them as you will, I knew that you would appreciate the rich and promising lives these young men had before them and that they put on line when they served their country in "defense of Freedom," as it is called. And, once you knew Wayne and Ron and Archie, I felt certain that you would miss them almost as much as we who knew them in real life still do. I hoped that your sharing their loss would illustrate through the "human drama," the real price of "defending Freedom," including the bleak aftermath facing the devastated families they left behind—the "what might have beens" and the costs of lost opportunities represented by lives that were ended many decades too soon.

You will find a great deal of imagery in Mission 1890—photographs, cartoons and memorabilia.

The Bowker's Book Wire reviewer pointed out the ways in which I used this technique in *Truckbusters From Dogpatch*: "With more than 1,000 black-and-white photographs and an engaging page layout somewhere between magazine and scrapbook, *Truckbusters from Dogpatch* is a rich historical document, entertaining read, and ode to the dedication, professionalism, creative problem-solving, and sacrifice of more than 3,500 of the Air Force's finest."

Baited Trap includes not only photographs, of which there are hundreds, but also images that represent and illustrate important aspects of their lives--a letter of acceptance, a dog tag, a sports medal. I believe images help the reader share the look and feel and impact of the world lived by those we are attempting to bring back to life.

Having lived the *Baited Trap* story in many ways, I knew the impact that Archie's loss had on our family. I did not know or appreciate the extent of similar losses to the other families involved. I do now...and so will you.

Most military histories focus on the mission, or perhaps those who flew it, as well.

I have also tried to accomplish these worthy objectives in *Baited Trap*, because the mission and the units behind those who flew them truly made history. For the Third Air Rescue Squadron (3ARS), the 18th Fighter-Bomber Wing and the USAF, Mission 1890 was over on 25 June 1952. For the families, however, it will never be over. The "story" of Mission 1890 continues to this day. Long after the shooting on that North Korean plateau had ended, the families were caught up in the agonies and bleaknesses of the "missing in action, presumed alive" world—an empty life of hanging on to any shred of information, parsing every word of every sentence of every turgid letter from the "Bureau of Personnel," writing letters of hope to other family members and trying to sound up beat and positive, even when all reasonable hope was a distant glimmer at the end of a bleak tunnel of dread.

Baited Trap includes many letters to the families and from the officials dealing with status, personal effects and human remains. These letters constituted both a thread of hope and a bleak tunnel of dread for the families in the years following 1952. Some of the information included verges on repetitious. Some official information is erroneous. It is recounted in the book as it happened because that is how the "story" unfolded for the families—watching the mail box and dreading the telegrams, glued to the television news in the hope that a repatriated POW's name might be familiar, or miracle of miracles, the one name above all you would want to see is there. That roller coaster of uncertainty, doubt and endless unanswered questions faced each of the families involved and is also part of the story.

Slowly, as one set of hopes died, others would begin to grow, as *Baited Trap* recounts. Lives, however battered and broken, could be put back together. All of them tried—Della, Frankie, Dolly and Marguerite—not all were successful. The eventual toll for Mission 1890 was much greater than the three servicemen, as it turned out. That too, is part of the story.

If a message emerges from the true stories recounted in *Baited Trap* it might be something like this...

When it is necessary to send the fine young men and women of America's military into harm's way to defend Freedom, remember that for some, perhaps the bravest and the best, the price will be their lives, their futures.

The real price will be the "cost of lost opportunity," the "what might have beens," for them and for many of their family and those they left behind to try and rebuild shattered lives.

The price for the servicemen and women will be their lives and it will be paid at the time they are killed in action.

The price for the families and loved ones is unknowable and endless. It continues from the day of the "I regret to inform you" telegram or notification until the last member of that family dies who knew and loved them. It continues for our country by its not benefiting from the lifetime of contributions to our society made by these outstanding individuals whose lives ended so prematurely.

To America's leaders: be cautious with the futures of our young men and women, and the families from which they came. Because they are our beloved sons and daughters, husbands and wives, we know they will fulfill the mission to the best of their ability when we send them. Just make sure the mission is worthy of their sacrifice...and make sure their sacrifices are truly "long remembered by a grateful nation."

Thank you also for your personal investment in this incredible story. Once you have read *Baited Trap*, I hope you will agree with the Air Force general whose last letter to one of the widows created by that heroic mission assured her that her husband's sacrifice would "long be remembered by a grateful Nation." This book is to ensure that our Nation does long remember, with gratitude, Wayne and Archie and Ron, and all the other servicemen and women whose defense of Freedom has cost them their lives.

Tracy Connors
Gainesville, Florida
Summer 2007

Perspective
Air Rescue in the Korean War Era

Many share my belief that senior leadership throughout the USAF chain of command has been inadequate at best and derelict at worst in the recognition and application of rotary wing capabilities and potential. The shortcomings became obvious in the Korean War and have continued to this day. USAF helicopter utilization remains limited by target fixation on other options and lack of knowledge, interest and imagination.

In the great Missouri Waltz that followed the inauguration of Harry S Truman and the cessation of hostilities of the Second World War, the most powerful armed forces ever known on planet earth were disbanded with little if any thought to current or future threats.

We were as a nation experiencing ineptness and even disregard of the facts as evidenced by the attempts of the new Secretary of Defense Louis Johnson as he cut military budgets to the bone and failed miserably to recognize the current and future threats to our country's security.

In the new and greatly reduced Department of the Air Force, the political musical chairs were arranged so that the bomber and secondly the fighter generals received the dollar allocations, and even more significantly, the choice of fast track personnel. The support commands got what amounted to second or third priority in money, equipment and personnel.

Resources for recognizing and developing new concepts or equipment were extremely limited. This situation was compounded by the inadequacy of leadership in the support commands and the overwhelming prestige of the bomber and fighter generals.

The Air Rescue Service and helicopter development were among the significant victims of this failure to recognize the present or anticipate the future. One consequence was that few senior officers were qualified to recognize the potential of rotary wing aircraft. For years, the helicopter and its operational capabilities wallowed in the forgotten mudpits of ignorance.

A few, relatively junior officers recognized the potential promised by the versatile helicopter and volunteered to become qualified to operate the frequently ridiculed machine. More by accident than by design the actions of these pioneer helicopter crews—pilots, medics and sometimes maintenance personnel, began to get the attention of some senior officers, especially when they accomplished near impossible feats of airmanship during dangerous, risky rescue operations.

Still, the rule of too little, too late was to apply. Bureaucratic fumbling was to limit the number of front-line rescue helicopters allocated to Korea. To make matters worse, only the operators in the field understood the capabilities of their equipment. As the war progressed, the newer model H-19B was retained in the USA while the worn out and significantly less efficient H-5 and H-19A aircraft were allocated to Korea.

The lack of helicopter experience or even knowledge in Japan's 3rd Air Rescue Group and Korea's 5th Air Force resulted in confusion and inadequate application of capabilities. Despite this fiasco, no pilot to my knowledge ever failed to attempt a rescue within range of his helicopter. The Medics responded with the same bravery that was to make them a legend in Vietnam. It is significant also that helicopter flight crews frequently went unnoticed and deserved decorations were neither recommended nor awarded.

In summary, the junior officers, flight crews and ground support personnel did an outstanding job in Korea despite an overall lack of support at all levels above the squadron.

Lt. Col. John Caldwell, USAF (Ret) is a veteran of 28 years of active service including four tours in Pacific areas. He is a command pilot who has checked out in fighters, bombers, transport and eight types and models of helicopters. Col. Caldwell is credited with three behind the lines rescues in Korea. He has served as a staff officer in a variety of assignments, including nuclear tests and satellite recovery. He is the first USAF Officer to serve in tactical command of two USAF Navy ships. He is active in the 18th Fighter Wing Association, the USAF Helicopter Pilot's Association, and Jolly Greens, as well as a number of other Veteran's organizations.

About the Author

Tracy D. Connors attended Jacksonville University, and earned Bachelor and Master of Arts degrees from the University of Florida and the University of Rhode Island, respectively. His management and military career includes over 40 years total experience in a variety of responsible positions in business, government and philanthropic organizations.

Captain Connors' military career began when he enlisted at age 17 as an Airman Recruit in the Naval Air Reserve, followed by training as an Aircrewman and Hospital Corpsman. It concluded in Washington many years later where he served on the staff of the Secretary of the Navy as the senior military officer of the LIFELines Initiative. In between was sea duty on several ships, Surface Warfare Officer qualifications, duty on numerous senior flag staffs, and several tours of duty on the staff of the Chief of Naval Operations with duties in public affairs and project management.

His civilian career includes senior management positions with private and public sector organizations, including serving as Chief of Staff for Congressman Charles E. Bennett and as Director of Satellite Learning Services for the U.S. Chamber of Commerce in Washington.

His personal military awards include the Legion of Merit, the Defense Meritorious Service Medal, the Meritorious Service Medal (six awards), the Navy Commendation Medal (two awards) and the Navy Achievement Medal.

In addition to *Mission 1890*, his other publications include:

· *Truckbusters From Dogpatch: The Combat Diary of the 18th Fighter-Bomber Wing in the Korean War, 1950-1953*, BelleAire Press, 2006

· *Nonprofit Handbook: Management* (Third Edition + Annual Supplements), John Wiley & Sons, 1990-2001

· *Flavors of the Fjords*, Co-authored with Faith R. Connors, BelleAire Press, 1996

Periodical publications in national news media and trade press, include: *U.S. Naval Institute Proceedings* Magazine, *All Hands* Magazine, *Surface Warfare* Magazine, *Direction*, Navy News, Navy Wire Service, *International Defense Images*, *Public Affairs Communicator*, *National Productivity Review* and *Sea History* Magazine.

Captain Connors lives in Gainesville, Florida with his wife, Faith, also a writer (*Flavors of the Fjords* and *Love, Midgie*).